THE WOMEN AND THE CRISIS

Women of the North in the Civil War

By the same author:

Light in the Sky

Blaze of Glory

Clown of the Gods

Scalpel

THE WOMEN AND
THE CRISIS

Women of the North in the Civil War

BY AGATHA YOUNG

McDOWELL, OBOLENSKY, NEW YORK

This book is for
my friend and publisher
Bob Haas

ACKNOWLEDGMENTS

One of the pleasures associated with the finishing of a book is the acknowledgment of a debt of gratitude to those who have helped the project on its way. Sometimes friendship is a legacy of the work, and so to Matilda Spence Rowland and Faith Waterman, both partners in this undertaking, it is gratifying to acknowledge both aid and affection. There are sometimes patient listeners, on whom one leans for advice, and among them have been Robert Binger, Vincent Sheean, David McDowell and Harrison Smith. Many libraries have furnished aid, the chief among them being the New York Public Library, especially the Department of American History and the Berg Collection, and the New York Academy of Medicine, including the Rare Book Room. This undertaking would have been difficult indeed without the wisdom and helpfulness of their staffs. Historical societies and their libraries, too numerous to specify, have searched for and found countless pieces of information, and those which have responded most frequently to requests for help are the Illinois State Historical Library, the Massachusetts Historical Society, the New York Historical Society, the Concord (Massachusetts) Committee on Archives and Records, and the Park Historian, Gettysburg National Military Park. To all these people and institutions go my heartfelt thanks.

CONTENTS

———————————★———————————

Introduction	•	WOMEN ON THE THRESHOLD OF WAR	3
I	•	THE IMPENDING CRISIS	26
II	•	THE DRUMS BEGIN TO BEAT	39
III	•	THROUGH THE STREETS OF A CITY	48
IV	•	FEAR IN WASHINGTON	58
V	•	THE WOMEN MOBILIZE	66
VI	•	A HUNDRED CIRCLING CAMPS	82
VII	•	THE TOWN NOBODY LOVED	89
VIII	•	THE ARMY MOVES	105
IX	•	FIRST BULL RUN	117
X	•	AFTERMATH	127
XI	•	WOMEN OF THE WEST	139
XII	•	BLOODY SHILOH	157
XIII	•	LADIES OF THE TRANSPORT SERVICE	173
XIV	•	THE WAR MOVES NORTH	190
XV	•	REBELS IN THE CORN	206
XVI	•	BURNSIDE'S BLUNDER	218
XVII	•	THE PERILS OF A REAL PAULINE	233
XVIII	•	UNCLE SAM'S WEB-FEET	245

XIX   •   WOMEN OF VICKSBURG   259

XX   •   WHERE THE GRAPES OF WRATH ARE STORED   270

XXI   •   THE LAST FULL MEASURE   284

XXII •   THE LASH AND THE SWORD   296

XXIII •   THE BRAVE AND THE FAIR   306

XXIV •   NORTHERN FLAGS IN SOUTHERN BREEZES   315

XXV   •   WITH CHARITY FOR ALL   325

XXVI •   THE END CAME SWIFTLY   340

XXVII •   THEIR LEGACY   349

Bibliography   353

Biographical Notes   365

Index   385

THE WOMEN AND THE CRISIS

Women of the North in the Civil War

INTRODUCTION

WOMEN ON THE THRESHOLD
OF WAR

————————————————★————————————————

> *From women's eyes this doctrine I derive:*
> *They sparkle still the right Promethean fire;*
> *They are the books, the arts, the academes,*
> *That show, contain, and nourish all the world.*
> —William Shakespeare

THE CIVIL WAR WAS, in reality, a revolution in that it was a continuation of the ancient fight for liberty and resulted in the emancipation of an oppressed part of the population. There were, however, revolutionary results of the Civil War, less conspicuous than the freeing of the slaves, and one of the more important was the greater freedom of women. The betterment of the status of women was not a goal of the war, any more than the freeing of the slaves was at the start a goal, except for the vocal few in the Abolitionist movement. It came about because during the Civil War the old restrictions and conventions relating to women's activities were lifted, as a matter of expediency, to meet the unusual demands of the war.

A similar lifting of various sorts of restraints on civilians in general occurs in any war large enough to require their participation. It is never intended that the suspension of the old order be anything but temporary. It is always more or less assumed by everyone that peace will bring a return to the status quo, as it was assumed during the Civil War that at the end of the emergency women would quietly return to their

former place in society. But those who have benefited by the opportunities of war do not readily relinquish their gains when war is at an end.

The nature of the freedom which women found they possessed when men marched away to war was the opportunity to work—outside the home and for a cause. Since no nation-full of women had ever before recognized the existence of such an opportunity, there were no preconceived ideas about such work, no rules, no patterns. They were free to create (in the purest sense of the word) their own standards for their work and to a large extent they were free to define its scope.

Their accomplishment in a material sense was enormous. If it had gone no further than their success in turning out vast quantities of supplies and raising large sums of money, it would be notable, but there is another aspect of the women's work which outshines these achievements. Florence Nightingale's lamp had illuminated for a shocked world the inhumanity of the tradition of war which relegated the wounded soldier to the category of expended matériel. It remained for the women of America, and more especially, for the women of the North, to take the actual steps which permanently abolished that tradition. When their work was done, it was so well and thoroughly done that it was never again possible for the government of a major power to fight a war without accepting full responsibility for the care and rehabilitation of the wounded. Their achievement was a milestone in human progress.

If there is one reason more cogent than another why the women succeeded, aside from the drive of their determination, it is because they organized. And this also was new. They organized at once, almost before the guns at Sumter were silenced. They formed themselves into societies, then into a national network of societies under the aegis of the Sanitary Commission. Their work had the double purpose of supplementing the work of government when government failed to care for its soldiers and of bringing pressure on government to correct its failures and shortcomings.

From the beginning the women's work was imbued with a warmth toward the soldiers, a loving solicitude which illuminated their whole story. Hundreds of women made themselves substitute mothers for the boys who were wounded and dying. Many gave the full four and a half years—some gave their lives—in the cause of humanity. And if their loving kindness did not move mountains (the point is arguable) it did move generals, politicians, public opinion and the hearts of men.

Most of the women, laboring in mud and blood, breathing an atmosphere of disease and suppurating wounds, never thought of themselves

as heroines. As individuals they had faults and weaknesses, and most of them are the more appealing for that reason. About some of these women little is known. Others have come down to us with personalities undimmed by time. Their path was rough and there were stumblings and failures along the way. Time passed before the women understood that benevolence could not be limited by township or state, or even confined to one side of the two warring factions. More time passed and the war ended before it was fully realized that in humanitarian work there is no place to build a barrier, but when that realization came, the banner of the International Red Cross was unfurled.

When the drums began to beat, the women erupted into instantaneous, violent, though highly disciplined activity and with a unanimity which caused Dr. Bellows of the Sanitary Commission to speak of it as an uprising. This was without precedent in history. The women assumed duties which involved not a few in danger and required them to set aside convention. They faced horrors for months, years, at a stretch. They did it coolly and on their own initiative.

The women who accomplished these things certainly were not the bloodless females of Victorian tradition. Obviously they had more stamina, ability and knowledge than anyone suspected. And because their lives had been circumscribed and sheltered, there was no place in which these traits could develop but the home.

The mid-Victorian home was in many respects an excellent culture medium for character, and a reflection of the ideals and longings of the women. Feminine taste dominated the house and leaned so far toward the romantic and fanciful that it suggests a desire on woman's part to escape reality into a world she had created in imagination. We speak of these as "solid" homes, and in a sense they were, but their outward aspects were the stuff that dreams are made of.

In New England, the lovely old four-square houses were being hidden by verandas and piazzas, foreign words which are themselves indicative of restlessness. Regional tastes differed, but not the desire for a richer world. New York was launched on the brownstone era, clapboard castles rose above the trees along the Hudson, Pennsylvania disguised the gray stone houses with jig-saw fancies and Chicago wore its cupolas with a difference.

Men cooperated enthusiastically in the perpetration of these artistic crimes, not only by paying for them but by designing them. Even Bronson Alcott, who forced plain living and high thinking on his family to the point of hardship, admired the architecturally intricate and became

an indefatigable builder of gazebos. In the nearby woods he collected sticks for them with the most serious attention to shape, and while Emerson was in Europe he built one on his front lawn as a surprise. It must have been a surprise indeed.

Indoors women had an even freer hand. Fine old tables disappeared under throws with fringe which touched the floor, fireplace mantels were draped in lambrequins which were beaded, appliqued and feather-stitched until the foundation material had all but vanished. At least two, and sometimes three sets of curtains hung at the windows, usually surmounted by a pressed brass cornice from which hung another lambrequin. These rooms had "ladies' " chairs and "gentlemen's" chairs, both liberally studded with buttons—the difference being that the ladies' chairs had low sides that the huge skirts might sweep unimpeded over them. Carpets were laid on straw which had to be renewed once a year and which gave out a soft and eerie rustling whenever trod upon. From a boss in the center of the room hung an ornate gaselier, lit with a long pole which had a notch in one end for turning the key, and a wax "spill" with a lever for pushing it forward as it was consumed. The gas made a steady, faint hissing sound and, as it was never entirely consumed, a closed room slowly filled with its odor.

The rooms were large and the wallpapers bold. Mrs. Southworth, the famous lady novelist, who never left the reader in doubt about details, describes one of these wallpapers and, whether imagined or not, she obviously thought it a work of art:

"The scene represented the martyrdom at the moment when life was offered the young saint as she stood upon the scaffold, on condition of her recantation. She stood in the centre of the scaffold, arrayed in a scant white tunic, her white and slender limbs exposed, her hands clasped upon her bosom, and her fine blue eyes raised to heaven, her golden locks rolling to her waist; behind her, leaning on his axe, whose end rested on the block, stood the executioner; on her left hand stood the group of imperial officers, with their offer of mercy; on her right knelt her aged father, with his gray locks streaming in the wind, his face upturned to hers in the agony of supplication, holding towards her a babe of a few days old—her babe, of which she had been delivered in prison—appealing to her by the venerableness of his own gray hairs, the innocence of its infancy, and the helplessness of both, to avoid death, to recant her faith, and to live for them; but the eyes of the saint never fell from their high glance, the look alike above the terror, the bribe, and the love below her."[1]

This, bear in mind, is *wallpaper* she is describing.

The hard work necessary to maintain these homes must have had a direct bearing on the apparent unconcern with which women undertook great labors during the war. They were accustomed to it. Even the cleaning of such rooms was a fearsome undertaking. The carpets were swept vigorously and the loost dirt gathered in a dust pan. This left the air a haze of dust and it was necessary to go away while it settled and return later to finish. In spring the carpet was taken up, carried outdoors and attacked with wire or wicker carpet beaters. Fresh straw was put down and the carpet relaid. The wallpaper was cleaned with chunks of fresh-baked bread and the fireplace sealed for the summer.

The heart of the house was the kitchen and the focal point of the kitchen a giant wood-burning range. These cook stoves were, Mrs. Stowe remarked, "infinite in their caprices." They had to be polished with blacking, and large indeed was the house which did not echo to the slamming of the iron lids. They heated the kitchen to a temperature nearly equal to that inside the oven and many houses had a "summer kitchen," which was in reality an airy shed containing a smaller stove for hot weather use.

The kitchen sink was made of soapstone and there might be a cold water faucet or a pump which drew water from a cistern under the house. The kitchen floors were wood, often unpainted, in which case they absorbed every spot of grease which fell on them and had to be scoured with river sand. If the house were heated by a furnace, and quite a few of them were, the pipes carried the heat only to the first floor, leaving the bedroom floor in a state of glacial discomfort. Fredrika Bremer, accustomed to the cozy porcelain stoves of Sweden, suffered a good deal from this arrangement and complained about it with insistence in her travel journals.

The cellars of city houses were dank and dark with every corner festooned in cobwebs—a favorite bandage for a cut finger. In the region of the Great Lakes big houses had an ice room below stairs, a chamber lined with huge blocks of sawed ice packed in sawdust. Here game and wild fowl were hung. Here too were stored the wild pigeon packed in barrels of salt. Farmhouse cellars were pleasant places with their smell of clean earth and their double doors opening to the outer air. Apples and pears were stored on lath racks; there were sacks of potatoes, shelves of preserves (which Fredrika Bremer complained usually turned out to be peaches) and a keg or two of cider hardening in the corner.

These were the homes of the well-to-do and the much-traveled Bremer found them "in many respects the ideal of a home. . . . Everything can

be found there which can make existence fresh and comfortable and agreeable, from the bathroom to the little garden." But she was surprised, and perhaps shocked, that so many New England women who were obviously ladies, did their own housework.

The New England lady's attitude toward work might well confuse someone not prepared to regard work as a philosophical concept, to be observed as a symbolic rite by those to whom it was not a dire necessity. Lucretia Mott, leader in the woman's movement, entertaining twenty-four guests for dinner (among them William Lloyd Garrison), washed the silver and fine china herself. She did it at the dinner table in a small cedar tub, while keeping up the conversation with her guests, passing each piece to Susan B. Anthony to be dried.² This symbolic dish-washing was the outward sign of spiritual grace. These were ladies of the same school as those who let a delicate china cup slip out of their fingers because a guest, who must not be allowed to feel embarrassed, had had the misfortune to break one, and the same who refrained from any trace of a smile when, at a tea party, John Brown's widow poured her tea in a saucer to drink it.

Farm life, whether in a sod hut on the prairie or in a gray fieldstone house on the grain lands of Pennsylvania, represented degrees in the scale of hardship. A frozen pump was a minor annoyance and something not to bother the men about. A sick child and no doctor within reach was a tragedy of every day. The work of running the farm house and the city mansion alike was arduous—and it was women's work. Doing it conditioned them for the harder work of the battle fields and hospitals.

To a degree we know nothing about today, the men of the family were dependent on women. Their food, clothing, health, general comfort and, to some extent, their religion and morals, were in the women's care. The home was a matriarchy and the boys who went from these homes to war were mothers' boys. Fresh from the big farm houses of New England, New York State and the Middle West, these boys sat around their camp fires and a hundred or more young voices sang,

> Just before the battle, mother,
> I am thinking most of you.

Hers surpassed every other relationship. In one collection of war songs, mother is mentioned in thirty-one percent of the songs, and wife and sweetheart both yield place to her. The women did all that was possible to preserve the ties with home in the camps and hospitals and the

homesick boys of the volunteer army, which was by-and-large a young army, accepted their efforts gratefully. They called the older women nurses "mother" and all of the nurses, whether young or old, considered motherliness their first duty. On the beam of the reading room of the great Benton Barracks Hospital at Mound City were inscribed the words, "Mother, Home, Heaven." They expressed the ideal which permeated the war.

If the mother ideal was the common denominator of the homes of the North, it was almost the only one, for the women represented the whole scale of social and economic background. The same was true of culture in general, and there were no generally accepted standards of education. The daughters of a wealthy family might be taught little more than reading, writing, rudimentary arithmetic, embroidery and enough music to sing or play pretty little airs to entertain company. Farm families banded together to employ a teacher, quite often a woman, and some of these schools were supported by the communities. There were few schools for higher education, the leading one being Oberlin, which had opened a "Female Wing" as early as 1837. This venture prospered and before the war, contracts were let for a "Ladies Hall." There was a wood and water room on every floor, with a dumb-waiter for carrying the firewood up and the ashes down. Water was piped and there was a sink into which slops were thrown.

Wesleyan Female College, which had little in common with a modern college, was opened in 1839, Elmira College in 1855, and there were a few others. Antioch allowed women to enroll, but they led a life of no such comfort as those at Oberlin, for they had not only to carry wood up two or three flights, but to saw it into stove-length pieces as well. Fredrika Bremer thought these educational opportunities far superior to those in Europe.

Technical schools were, in the main, closed to women. There were two art schools where they might study, one in Boston and one in Philadelphia. There were no training schools for nurses and the one opened by Florence Nightingale at St. Thomas' Hospital in London in 1860 with 15 student nurses aroused much interest here. There were a few women who used the title "doctor," but they were little more than midwives who had been taught by other midwives with perhaps a smattering of training from some practicing physician. No medical school would accept a woman as a student until Elizabeth Blackwell broke down the barriers at the Geneva, New York, Medical School in 1849.

Most of the women who took education seriously planned to become

teachers, and Mrs. Bremer thought that the young women of New England must have a special aptitude for that profession, for she found them everywhere, from southern plantations to the log school houses of the Far West. A teacher's pay was seldom enough to live on unless her board and lodging were given her. Salaries ranged from about six hundred to a thousand dollars a year, which was less than a man received for the same work.

Few other non-industrial careers were open to women, but dressmaking, millinery and writing. More women than ever before were picking up their pens, and with the sharp steel points some of them were entrenching themselves permanently in our literature. Others, whose books sold in the hundreds of thousands, are forgotten now, though it is precisely these forgotten books which best reflect their period. In some ways writing was an ideal profession for a woman in the Fifties and Sixties when many means of earning money were closed to her. Writing was "genteel," it could be done at home and, for the lucky ones, the financial rewards were high. Consequently the middle of the century saw a flood of fiction by lady writers.

Out of the twenty-seven novels which rose to the rank of best seller[3] from 1850 through 1860, twelve were written by women—a far higher percentage of best sellers by women writers than the lists of recent years have shown. These twelve books were written by ten women: two of them, George Eliot and Dinah Maria Mulock, were English; one, Augusta Evans, belonged to the South, the remainder came largely from various parts of New England. The list contains *Uncle Tom's Cabin* by Harriet Beecher Stowe, which is the best selling novel of all time.

This was the day of the long novel and some of them ran to three volumes. They cost about an average of a dollar and a half a volume, but there were paper-backed copies which could be bought for a few cents, and some novels, printed in newspaper format, were sold by newsboys on the streets. They were read from drawing room to farmhouse kitchen with, it appears, almost equal enthusiasm. Most of the successful women writers not only wrote long books, but wrote a great many of them. Mary Jane Holmes, for example, wrote a book a year for upward of thirty years and made herself an income in the neighborhood of sixty thousand dollars a year. The well-loved Mrs. E. D. E. N. Southworth, who in her early days went through as many hardships as one of her own heroines, was the author of some ninety novels.

Because these books were concerned in one way or another with home life, they have come to be known as the "Domestic" novels. They form

a distinct school of literature, though their literary quality is not high. The characterization is seldom good, the plots are repetitive and contrived, the style is often imitative and they are packed with coincidence beyond the limits of credibility. They irritated Hawthorne exceedingly. "America," he said, "is now given over to a d——d mob of scribbling women, and I should have no chance of success while the public taste is occupied with their trash—and should be ashamed of myself if I did succeed. What is the mystery of these innumerable editions of the *Lamplighter,* and other books neither better nor worse?—worse they could not be, and better they need not be, when they sell by the 100,000."[4]

But if these novels created false artistic standards, they served another purpose admirably. They were a dream world, remote from reality, and in them women found, not a reflection of life, but a materialization of their inmost and sometimes subconscious longings. And therein lies both the secret of their extraordinary popularity and a clue to the nature of the women themselves.

They were written to a pattern which fitted the needs of an entire generation, involving a number of variations on a central theme which remained comparatively constant. The chief character of the book must be a young woman with whom the reader could identify herself or a child with whom she could sympathize. The setting was the pure fabric of daydreams, a romantic castle, a rich city house, a rose-girt cottage, with a slum or a hovel of the worst sort put in to point the contrast.

The important part of the pattern, however, and also that which makes these novels so revealing, is the structure of the plot. The story takes the heroine through incredible vicissitudes to a happy ending, and rare indeed is the book which does not have one, but before the heroine fades into the rose-and-pearl mist, there is a scene in which she triumphs, and her triumph is the whole crux of the matter. According to pattern, the object of her triumph must be some man who has done her wrong—a lover who deserts her, a guardian who has stolen her fortune, a father, brother, husband who has been the cause of all the suffering. Over him does she triumph, her victory having been won by the moral qualities of her nature.

Sometimes a change is rung by making the heroine a child and on page one this child, usually a girl, must be orphaned, ill-treated, cold and hungry. Perhaps she is found by the reader standing in the snow, gazing through the window at a rich, fire-lit group of people who, in the end, turn out to be her own family. Those who have caused her suffering are brought low, her fortune is restored or the father who was thought dead

returns from a dissolute life on foreign shores to be led in the path of righteousness by her sweet nobility of character.

Even the minor conventions of the pattern point up the central theme of female triumph over male. Deathbed scenes are sprinkled liberally through these novels, for one of the functions of this school of fiction is to provide an outlet for unshed tears. It is usually a young and beautiful woman who dies, or rather fades gently away, from some disease without symptoms, for these deaths are without pain. If it is a man who dies, however, the pattern requires that he must do so in such agonizing torture as to suggest that the women readers found no little satisfaction in his suffering.

These are novels for women, about women, and men figure in them to as slight an extent as the triumph-theme will permit. The formula of feminine triumph would seem to suggest a generation of women readers who harbor consciously, or just below the conscious level, a resentment against the dominance of the male. And how the masculine wrong-doer of fiction is made to grovel! The heroine's goodness, patient endurance and piety overwhelm him. Then, when her virtues have reduced him to an emotional pulp, leaving him only just able to gasp out his remorse, she forgives him.

"Oh Mildred," he groaned: "I have not deserved this—your goodness crushes me!"

"You will deserve it," she answered. ". . . I do believe it is never too late for the most distorted soul to be set aright."[5]

She forgives him wholly, fluently, and in detail, not neglecting such embellishments as eyes cast toward heaven, tears, and the roseate flush tingeing alabaster cheek. After a few pages of this sort of thing, he recovers sufficiently to ask her if he dare hope and she seals her forgiveness by confessing that she loves him. These novels are intensely, mawkishly sentimental—but this was a period when "feelings" were a virtue in life and an essential in art. The amount of sensitivity a character in fiction possessed was the measure of worth. Sentimentality was not a pose of the lady scribblers. Neither was it confined to fiction. It was an attitude toward life, wholly sincere, albeit in these days before the war already on the wane.

The fiction of the Fifties betrays the women readers as restive, resentful of men, aware of their own vitality and dissatisfied by the limitations which their way of life put on their powers. When suddenly the Civil War altered the aspect of their lives, they lost not one moment of time in moving into their new and larger world.

Women had already begun to make a place for themselves in industry, especially in the textile mills of New England. The start of the industrial revolution did not cause the extreme hardship here that it brought to England, and in the beginning the owners of the New England mills were comparatively humanitarian in their relations with their women employees. The girls lived and ate on the premises, and the employers, anxious that so radical an innovation as women in factories should receive the sanction of public opinion, kept a strict supervision over the behavior and morals of the girls.

These ladies of the loom could never be described as meek, though for the most part they submitted to the paternalism of their employers with reasonably good grace. There were flare-ups of resentment against the bosses, however, usually about working conditions, and in 1836 the girls of Lowell went on strike. It was called a "turn-out" and was intended to protest a wage cut imposed by the owners to offset a decline in business. The women lost and were forced to return to their machines, but they had staged the first strike of working women in history, six years before the right to strike was legalized by a decision in a Massachusetts court.[6]

During the Forties and Fifties the mill owners felt severely the effects of sharp business recessions and the rising cost of living. They attempted to meet these economic threats by lowering wages and increasing the output of work, and, to counter the dissatisfaction caused by such a policy, their paternalism grew more severe. The position of the women workers had seriously deteriorated. The mill owners, anxious to keep alive the popular impression that these mills were an industrial utopia, sponsored poets to write about the beauties of mill life:

> Oh, sing me a song of the Factory girl!
> So merry and glad and free!
> The bloom on her cheeks, of health how it speaks.
> Oh, happy a creature is she![7]

Visitors from foreign lands, who would be likely to publish diaries of their observations in America were invited to the mills, entertained, and shown the establishment in the best possible light, and by this means the mill owners were able to secure an amount of publicity which would be envied by a modern public relations counsel. Dickens was one of these distinguished visitors to Lowell. Anthony Trollope proclaimed these mills to be a "philanthropical manufacturing college." Fredrika Bremer, watched with delight the "procession of operatives, two and two, in

shawls, bonnets and green veils, as they went to their dinner" and she thought that they produced a "fine and imposing effect." In the evening she was taken to a hill above Lowell and she gazed down with delight on the buildings of the mill, "glittering with a thousand lights like a magic castle . . . And to think," she wrote rapturously, "and to know, that these lights . . . were actually symbols of a healthful and hopeful life . . . to know that within every heart in this palace of labor burned a bright little light, illuminating a future of comfort and prosperity . . ." Further on she notes, still in the same happy vein, that the "industrious and skillful can earn from six to eight dollars per week, never less than three, and so much is requisite for their board each week. The greater number lay by money . . ."

The reality was not so idyllic. The romantically twinkling lights were shining on girls who were required to tend as many clattering machines as their agility and concentration would let them handle, and to go on doing it for twelve hours with two half-hour periods for food. In the winter weekdays they saw the daylight only through the tall, dirty windows of the mill, or on their brief, regimented march to meals. After working twelve hours, their "leisure" was subjected to the control of house mothers, and they ate company food, slept in company beds, bought at company stores, all without any choice in the matter. The slow and inexperienced among them were able to earn just enough to pay the company for their board. The others were somewhat better off than the average working women of that day, who were lucky to earn two dollars in a week, but they were receiving only about half what men received for the same work and were confronted with rising prices, wage reductions and long periods of unemployment which in many cases more than canceled their gains. And if in their hearts there burned a "bright little light," it was more than likely to be a glowing spark of revolt.

They discovered the strength of concerted action, they learned to stand up to their bosses, and they became exceedingly articulate. The Lowell girls wrote articles for the company paper, the "Lowell Offering," in which they criticized company practices until the company refused to publish them. Thereafter, various groups of women workers set up their own publications, or were instrumental in starting them, and thus they became the creators of the labor press in America. In the pages of these publications they campaigned for a ten hour day, expressed resentment of the rose-colored reports of their foreign visitors, and replied to the employer's poets with some poetry of their own.

In 1846 the Lowell girls formed the Female Labor Reform Association

with Sarah Bagley, one of the first American women labor editors, at its head. The Association was short-lived, but working women had discovered the power which belongs to the organized and the Association became the pattern for other groups seeking similar reforms. Women in several trades in various parts of the North joined trade unions and supported the men workers in their drives for labor reform, though the attitude of the male union members was not always open-minded toward women in industry.

They also discovered that physical strength lay in numbers. A reporter wrote of the striking women of Lynn that "They assail the bosses in a style which reminds one of the amiable females who participated in the first French Revolution." There were innumerable instances of skirmishes between the women and their male superintendents, and on one occasion the girls of Lynn held one of them under a pump by way of expressing their displeasure.

The golden days when anyone could talk about a textile mill as a "philanthropical manufacturing college" were no more, and the public began to regard these militant mill women as a force to be reckoned with. In 1860 there was a spectacular shoemakers' strike in New England, in which the women joined the men strikers and staged two parades of their own. One, which took place in a heavy fall of snow, was recorded by an artist from Leslie's. They marched in hoop skirts, carrying parasols, grim of face, brawny and determined.

In this mood, the women workers arrived on the threshold of war. But behind this militant front was a strong current of philosophic thought and the beginning of an awareness of the larger aspects of the problems facing labor. They understood the threat of slavery to Northern labor and they gave their support to the Abolitionist cause not on humanitarian grounds alone but for economic reasons as well. The start of the war found the women workers strong, determined, informed and practiced in concerted action. They were women of will with a goal in sight.

In retrospect it seems as though women were prepared in many hidden ways to meet the challenge of the crisis, though as we know them from the fashion plates of *Godey's,* housed in their enormous skirts, they appear frail, unfit and all but totally immobilized. The lady of fashion came close to being all these things. If she were dressed in the height of fashion she could not maneuver her hoops through an ordinary doorway without using both hands and giving the operation her full attention. Dressing was almost as complicated as rigging a ship, and when she was ready to go out, she could do little more than negotiate the distance from

the front door to her carriage. If a strong wind were blowing she might have difficulty in doing even that.

Accommodating storekeepers brought their merchandise out to her and stood by her carriage while she made her choice. Dressed in a swaying hoop, a normal walking step was out of the question. She must move either in tiny steps or glide, and those who became expert gave the startling impression of being propelled on hidden wheels. It was in the evening, however, that the lady of fashion really bloomed. Her party dress might measure ten yards around the hem, and if it were flounced, a hundred yards or more of tulle or mousseline might have been used in its construction. So dressed, the women were a walking fire hazard and not a few of these lovely moths lost their lives because they came too close to a candle. One of them was Fanny Appleton, Mrs. Henry Wadsworth Longfellow, who was burned to death in 1861 when she was melting a stick of sealing wax to close a letter. Longfellow tried to save her, and the long beard familiar in his portraits was grown to cover the scars he received while trying to beat out the flames.

These were the women who have preempted the tradition of the period, but in reality there were few who dressed in the height of fashion. The majority never owned or ever saw a tulle gown made of a hundred yards of cloud-like material, and most women wore dresses of sturdy wool or calico trimmed with a little braid or white collar and cuffs. Their hoops were moderate, though many women felt immodest without them, and the style of their clothes was so conservative that they did not quickly go out of fashion.

A new dress was "best" the first year, "second best" the next year and eventually it was "turned," which meant that it was ripped apart and sewed together again, wrong side out. When a dress could be worn no longer, the good parts were used to line a cloak, and at long last the scraps went into a piece bag eventually to begin a new life in the pattern of a quilt. There were no dry cleaning establishments in those days, and a spot which could not be removed with water or fullers' earth was there to stay. Consequently, children and grown women wore aprons most of the time, plain ones for housework and fancy ones for the afternoons.

Except that the skirts were long—and they needed to be in the drafty winter houses—these modified everyday styles were practical. And there is something admirable about the attitude of the middle-class women toward dress. Their tastes were modest, but not prudish, simple but not austere, sensible but not to the exclusion of the pursuit of fashion which is every woman's pleasure. When war came, those who were going to

the front hung their hoops on a closet peg, filled a carpet bag with the barest essentials, added a shawl which was both coat and blanket, and they were ready.

War made severe demands on the physical stamina of hundreds of women, and if they had been the fragile, consumptive creatures they have often been pictured, the work they did would have been impossible. Fortunately for the nation, the day when it was fashionable to be frail was passing. About 1860, health became a craze, a mania. Picnics and outdoor excursions were the style, and Louisa Alcott wrote in her journal that the whole town of Concord, having "gymnastic fever," went about waving arms like windmills. That winter, skating, bobsledding and other sports which had formerly belonged to children, were taken up by young girls and mature women. Surprised by their own freedom and daring, they enjoyed themselves enormously and the frosty air rang with happy laughter.

Medically, however, these women were still under the shadow of the past. The cause and effect relationship between dirt and disease had taken firm hold on their minds, but they were ignorant of the part played by bacteria. They used drugs too freely and in startlingly large doses, even for slight ills. They knew no more about their dangers than the character in one of Mrs. E. D. E. N. Southworth's novels who remarks, "My dear, you are hysterical—I must give you some morphine." False modesty perpetuated the midwife and the woman "doctor" without medical training. The preference for women doctors was so strong that those who were qualified found their practices lucrative. Clemence Lozier of New York, the first woman surgeon to receive a degree, was earning fifteen thousand dollars a year before she had been in practice a dozen years, and by 1866 there were three hundred women doctors who had incomes of from ten to twenty thousand dollars a year.

Children were born in pain and fear, and because of the uninformed use of anesthetics and greater number of women attended by physicians (who through ignorance transmitted erysipelas and puerperal fever) it was less safe to bear a child in 1860 than it had been ten years earlier. An appalling number of the babies did not survive their infancy, and infant mortality was the largest factor in lowering the average of the years of life. That average being the life expectancy of a child at birth, a child born in Shakespeare's time had a life expectancy of about thirty-three years. By 1850 a baby had a life expectancy of only two years more— and that is only a little more than half of what it is today.

But though, medically speaking, women were still living in the dark

ages, in other respects than in childbirth progress was being made. Tuberculosis (then called consumption), which had reached a peak in the Thirties, had begun a long decline, though it may still have been the principal cause of women's death in the Fifties and Sixties. There is no way of knowing with certainty, especially as the United States Census for 1850 does not list consumption and gives dysentery as the chief killer of women. In 1860 cholera killed, according to this source, about 32,000 fewer people than in 1850; dysentery about 10,000 fewer, smallpox deaths were reduced by half and those from yellow fever considerably lessened.[8] This was a generation of women who knew the meaning of sickness, but also the value of health, and they carried their understanding with them into the wartime hospitals.

Perhaps the reason why these women so arouse our liking and sympathy is that they lived, not quite in the past, but on the brink of the modern world. The physical circumstances of their lives belonged to the one. Their hopes, their ambitions and their ideals had moved ahead of their power to realize them, into the other. It has been said many times, with the inherent inaccuracy of a generalization, that Victoria typified the women of the age to which she gave her name, but if she represented women as they were, it was not she but Florence Nightingale who symbolized women as they wanted to be.

Miss Nightingale had been confronted with most of the problems which beset the women of her generation and found the answer to them. She had been bound by convention and freed herself from the traditional subjugation of women. She had gone on to make herself a power in a man's world and to such purpose that men within and without her own country consulted her on aspects of the especially masculine province of war. She was, in a sense, a heroine of a novel come alive, virtuous, intensely feminine, suffering for a time under masculine dominance, but triumphant in the end by means of feminine virtues and with satisfactory completeness.

Nursing was a woman's province, and Nightingale transformed it from housework into a profession, endowing it with importance in the social scheme and with a highly skilled technique. Every woman who nursed the sick, whether at home or in an army hospital, felt herself of more consequence thereafter, and because Florence Nightingale was great by virtue of being a woman, every woman participated in her greatness.

The interest in Nightingale and her work in this country before the war was so intense as to amount to a cult. Every maxim which she

uttered concerning women, and she uttered a great many, was reverently cherished. An article in *Godey's,* in 1860, all but canonized her, and there were others in the same vein which women read with avidity. Nightingale's book, *Notes on Nursing,* published in England in 1859 and in Boston in 1860, was one of the most influential books ever to appear. Women all over America read it, conscious of the prestige it gave their work. They threw open sickroom windows and dedicated themselves to cleanliness.

Women, waiting for nursing appointments in war hospitals, read the little volume and carried it to the front in their carpet bags. The nursing techniques of the war, including those of the religious orders, were founded on it. Throughout the war years Miss Nightingale watched with intense interest the work which was being done here, and she corresponded with the Secretary of War and the officers of the Sanitary and Christian Commissions. Her advice was constantly asked and given, and there was some discussion of her coming to this country, which she might have undertaken to do had she been in better health. Her tenets permeate all the women's activities in the war, and the fact that she believed that women, organized as nurses, laundresses and cooks, should be with the troops in the field undoubtedly made this easier of accomplishment. It is possible that the frail little invalid with the sharp nose and acid tongue, lying on her couch in London may have been the most influential woman of the war.

That this generation of women stood between two eras, half in darkness, half in light, nowhere shows more clearly than in their position before the law. The more advanced women of the Forties and Fifties felt that they had a grievance in respect to their legal status, and their efforts to alter the laws which applied to them became one of the great reform movements. They did not, in the pre-war days, seek to become the equal of men in the eyes of the law. That was to come as a later phase of the woman's rights movement. Their crusade in the beginning was directed almost wholly against the traditional control of the husband over the property and the destiny of the wife. The leaders of this crusade were possessed at times with a frenzy of zeal; they were willing to make spiritual martyrs of themselves and their families in the interest of their cause and they were appallingly articulate.

One of these dedicated women was Lucy Stone, and on her wedding day she made a statement of protest against the plight of the married woman which summarized so succinctly the situation as the crusading women saw it that it became in a sense the articles of their faith. Lucy

was petite, supercharged with emotion which she poured into her crusades, eloquent, (she was the first American woman to make a public speech on woman's rights), and she dearly loved to fight for a good cause. This formidable little female was a leader in the group of liberal semi-intellectuals which was referred to in their own times as "the emancipated women," and history remembers her chiefly for one of her lesser crusades directed against the tradition which required a woman, when she married, to assume her husband's name.

In 1855 Lucy married Henry B. Blackwell, brother of the Elizabeth Blackwell who was the first woman in America to receive a medical degree. The marriage ceremony, which was a simple one, took place in the home of Blackwell's mother, with only a few guests present. Lucy and Henry began the formalities by joining hands and reading aloud their statement of protest against the laws which gave to the husband:

1. The custody of the wife's person;
2. The exclusive control and guardianship of their children;
3. The sole ownership of her personal [property] and the sole use of her real estate unless previously settled upon her, or placed in the hands of trustees, as in the case of minors, lunatics and idiots;
4. The absolute right to the product of her own industry [wages she might earn].

Lucy's words (it is easy to imagine that Henry had no great part in formulating them) were publicized by the newly organized national movement for woman's rights and they appear to have moved many women and some men to support the cause. In any event, they became famous. Some of the women who rallied to the standard of woman's rights had authentic grievances, though not so much, as will be seen, because of the law as because of the way the law was administered. Others— and they were undoubtedly the majority—had never before been aware that there was anything about their position as married women which needed reform, but they were nevertheless willing to support so likely sounding a cause.

Women orators, bold, sincere, persuasive, traveled through the North and West, pouring out a cataract of words to mixed audiences of astonishing size. Women writers sent out a blizzard of pamphlets. Out of all this there quickly emerged a well polished concept of the subjugation of women which was generally accepted as true in those days, and in the same form was passed on as a legacy to the following generations. The

formula of the subjugation of women has colored our thinking to such an extent that the "early Victorian" woman, more than the women of any other age, has become the symbol of feminine serfdom.

The formula, however, was not strictly accurate as a description of the status of the married woman in the two decades preceding the war. The women did not intentionally misrepresent the facts. The information, out of which they constructed their formula, they derived from Sir William Blackstone's *Commentaries on the Laws of England* and specifically from the chapter "Of Husband and Wife." In this chapter Blackstone describes the "legal death," as it came to be called, of the woman who married.

"By marriage the husband and wife are one person in law; that is, the very legal existence of the woman is suspended during the marriage, or at least is incorporated into that of the husband . . ."

Being legally dead, or merged with her husband, it followed that she could not own property, or money, except under special conditions, the appointment of a trustee, or by contract before marriage (the marriage settlement). She could not sign a contract—a fact which Mary Livermore and Mrs. Hoge discovered with astonishment when they attempted to contract for the construction of a building for the Chicago Sanitary Commission Fair. Nor could a married woman take custody of her child.

This was indeed the gist of the law. It came to be so because when this country severed its connections with England, our states adopted, with local modifications, the legal structure of the mother country. Blackstone, consequently, was almost as useful in the new world as in the old. His book was a single volume, his text was clear and simple. Law books in general were not always easy to come by, especially in the rural districts, and there was no indexing of court decisions for reference purposes.

All this insured the *Commentaries* a firm place in a country where a young man's legal education usually consisted of "reading" law, either unaided or under the supervision of a practicing lawyer. It frequently happened, in fact, that a lawyer set up in practice with little more to guide him than his study of Blackstone, and he retained for the rest of his life the conviction that the *Commentaries* were the end-all and the be-all of the law. Thomas Jefferson, deploring this state of affairs, thought that Blackstone was to many American lawyers "what the *Alcoran* is to the Mohametans, that everything which is necessary is in him and what is not in him is not necessary."

Sir William Blackstone had a concise mind and a liking for clear-cut

facts which could be neatly pigeonholed, and the *Commentaries* were, in effect, an attempt in the grand manner to pigeonhole the facts of the common law. There is, however, another function of law, more elusive of classification, known as equity, and for equity Blackstone had little liking. Equity is embodied in the decisions of courts aiming to correct injustices which may arise out of the harsh dicta of common law. Equity seeks to bring about justice when, for one reason or another, the strict application of the common law would work injustice. Its purpose is not to subvert but to supplement the common law.

It functions somewhat in this fashion. The common law declared a wife legally dead, and therefore unable to own property. In equity, however, if husband and wife agreed before and after marriage to the holding of funds or property in her own right, not subject to the demands of her husband or his creditors, then the harsh provisions of the common law could not deprive her. And as in the ownership of property, other facets of the common law, as it related to married women in those days, might similarly be modified.

If a practicing lawyer could be unaware (or only dimly aware) that the common law was susceptible of modification, the average layman most certainly was not. The "emancipated" women at the start of the woman's rights movement were not. The first meeting of the woman's rights movement, before it was on a national basis, was held at Seneca Falls in 1848. There were speeches, resolutions and a "Declaration of Sentiments," which was a resounding document, patterned after the Constitution. The ladies had read Blackstone, for the resolutions of the afternoon session state, "Whereas the great precept of nature is conceded to be, 'that man shall pursue his own true and substantial happiness', Blackstone, in his *Commentaries,* remarks that this is the law of Nature being coeval with mankind, and dictated by God himself, is, of course, superior to any other."

Obviously, the ladies were excited—too excited to pay adequate attention to their prose. And it seems clear that they were entirely ignorant of the safeguards which hedged the common law.

The year after the Seneca Falls meeting, there appeared a famous work by Justice Joseph Story, called *Commentaries on Equity Jurisprudence.* Whether Lucy Stone was acquainted with this book, when she presented her famous four points in 1855, it is impossible to say. There is evidence that the leaders of the woman's rights convention of that same year had read Story, for their attack is directed more against the administration of the law than against the law itself. However, qualification, modification, or even absolute accuracy were not part of the

stock-in-trade of the militant, reforming women. Belief that the status of women was exactly as stated by Blackstone, and implicit in Lucy Stone's "points," spread outward like rings on the disturbed surface of a pond, for if these women were not good students, they were most excellent publicists.

The extent of the discrepancy between belief and fact may be shown by matching Lucy Stone's points with excerpts from Story on the same topic, though that is a most unscholarly approach to a complicated and highly technical subject. Lucy's first point should probably be left out altogether, for it is not fully clear what she means by "custody of the wife's person." Here, then, is Lucy's summary of what she and her co-workers believed to be the subjugation of women, and a rough summary of her real position before the law.

Point two protests the law which gave to the husband "the exclusive control and guardianship of their children." Of this Story wrote, "Ordinarily, indeed, the father will be entitled to the custody of his infant children. Thus, for example, if the infant be a daughter and of very tender years, and the mother, under all circumstances, be the most suitable to take care of her person and education, a Court of Chancery will confer the custody on the mother; when, if the infant were of riper years, and more discretion, and, especially if a son, he would be entrusted . . . to his father, if no real objection to his character or conduct existed."

Lucy's third point protested that the husband has, under law, "the sole ownership of her personal [property] and the sole use of her real estate unless previously settled upon her, or placed in the hands of trustees, as in the case of "minors, lunatics and idiots." On this subject Story writes: "Courts of Equity have, for a great length of time, admitted the doctrine that a married woman is capable of taking real and personal estate to her own separate and exclusive use, and that she has also an incidental power to dispose of it." The subject is a complicated one, however, and how tedious it sometimes proved in settlement is remembered by anyone who has read Trollope's *The Eustace Diamonds*. Incidentally, the common legal phrase, "women, minors, lunatics and idiots," which so irritated the feminists of the day, merely implied that such individuals were especially liable to unjust treatment, and so were entitled to the watchful protection of those who administered the law.

Lucy's fourth point concerned what she called the "absolute right" of the husband to money his wife might earn. There are complications here also, but if certain technicalities were observed, there were no barriers either to her entering trade or to keeping the money she earned. Story writes, "So, if a husband should desert his wife and she should . . .

carry on a separate trade . . . her earnings in such a trade will be enforced by Equity against the claims of her husband." This statement was particularly pertinent, for the leaders of the woman's rights movement gave great publicity to a lurid story of a deserted wife who was hounded into starvation by her husband because he was able to collect her income at its source. The odd fact is that there may have been some truth in this story and in others of the same ilk, for women were reluctant to go to court for redress, partly because of modesty but mainly because of their unquestioning belief in the doctrine of the subjugation of women. And, since too large a proportion of American judges held the same views, the women might not readily have found the justice had they sought for it.

So it was that the great reform movement for woman's rights was planned in misconception, powered by misconception, and continued to nourish its growth on misconception long after the mists of all the breathy oratory should have blown away. Perhaps the reform movement would not have been either so great or so strong if those women who inspired it had more fully understood their position. Real understanding came slowly, and then only to the few. If they found the true situation not exactly what they had thought, neither was it greatly to their liking. These few, when they ceased fighting shadows, used their energies to attack specific laws of specific states in order that women need not depend to such an extent on the somewhat more nebulous equity. In this they made some slight headway, before the war, while at the same time they tried to educate the rank and file of the movement, in which they never quite succeeded.[9]

War brought these brave undertakings to a halt, and after long years of war the problem of woman's rights no longer had the same aspect, even to the former leaders. The movement started up again, though not from the point at which it had been abandoned. Too much had happened in those years to change the relationship of women to their environment, and to alter their status in masculine estimation and in their own.

One symptom of the change was that women less frequently found themselves classified with minors, lunatics and idiots as objects needing protection. On the other hand, in the new discussion of the rights of the Negro arising from his freedom, the rights of women tended to be included, not because of any similarity in the two problems, it is true, but because when the talk is of freedom, there is no logical place to stop. The significance of the new juxtaposition, however, is considerable for it signals the removal of the women, in the minds of men, from the category of the protected to the category of the free.

NOTES

[1] Mrs. E. D. E. N. Southworth, *The Deserted Wife* (T. B. Peterson and Brothers, Philadelphia, 1855).

[2] Van Wyck Brooks, *The Flowering of New England* (E. P. Dutton & Co., New York, 1936).

[3] Frank Luther Mott, *Golden Multitudes, the Story of Best Sellers in the United States* (The Macmillan Company, New York, 1947).

[4] Hawthorne to Tichnor, 1855.

[5] Frank Lee Benedict, *The Orphan's New Year's Eve* (Peterson's Magazine, January, 1864).

[6] Decision of Chief Justice Lemuel Shaw, Massachusetts, 1842.

[7] Philip S. Foner, *History of the Labor Movement in the United States* (International Publishers, New York, 1947).

[8] This is a good place to sound a warning about the too literal acceptance of medical statistics in this period and throughout the war. Diagnosis was uncertain, reporting erratic, and methods of collecting and processing data are, to say the least, open to question. Statistical totals should, therefore, be regarded as estimates which are always uncertain and often crude. Their value lies in the fact that, after allowing for a large factor of error, they are still more useful than a guess.

[9] For a full discussion of the relation of women to the law, see *Woman as a Force in History. A Study in Traditions and Realities* by Mary S. Beard (The Macmillan Company, New York, 1946).

1

THE IMPENDING CRISIS

★

CHRONOLOGY
1859

October 17   John Brown, with 18 men, attempted to start an insurrection of slaves at Harper's Ferry, Virginia.

November 2   John Brown sentenced to death.

December 2   John Brown executed at Charles Town, Virginia, (now West Virginia).

1860

November 6   Lincoln elected President, to succeed Buchanan. Lincoln received 180 Electoral votes, Breckinridge 72, Bell 39, Douglas 12.

November 10   The United States Senators from South Carolina resigned.

December 3   Opening of the second session of the Thirty-Sixth Congress.

December 10   Resignation of Secretary of Treasury, Howell Cobb, to join the secession movement in Georgia.

December 20   South Carolina seceded from the Union.

December 26   United States garrison moved from Fort Moultrie to Fort Sumter.

December 27   The Commissioners from South Carolina arrived in Washington. South Carolina seized Fort Moultrie, Castle Pinckney and various other properties of the Federal Government.

26

December 29   Secretary of War John B. Floyd retired to join the Confederate cause.

December 31   South Carolina seized the United States arsenal, post office and custom house in Charleston.

★

> Old Brown
> John Brown
> Osawatomie Brown
> He'll trouble them more when his Coffin's nailed down!
> —J. S. Reader

On FRIDAY, the second of December, 1859, John Brown stood erect and dignified upon the scaffold. He was dressed in carpet slippers and an ill-fitting suit; the noose was around his neck, and the black cap over his head. The ceremonies were waiting while three companies of badly drilled infantry were deployed into position, a process which seemed to take a great deal of time. The sheriff asked him if he would like to be warned the last moment before he fell, and John Brown replied that it did not matter if only they would not keep him waiting too long. For a moment nothing happened, but a growing sense of dignity and portent seemed to pervade the scene, emanating from the tall, stoical figure who was about to show a nation how a brave man dies. Then the hatchet in the sheriff's hands fell, severing the rope with a single blow, and the voice of authority rang out: "So perish all such enemies of Virginia. All such enemies of the Union. All such foes of the human race."

At this precise time, as nearly as he could calculate it, Longfellow was writing in his diary: "This will be a great day in our history, the date of a new revolution, quite as much needed as the old one. Even now, as I write, they are leading old John Brown to execution in Virginia for attempting to rescue slaves. This is sowing the wind to reap the whirlwind, which will soon come."

A goodly number of the New England intellectuals felt as Longfellow did. Emerson had called John Brown, before his execution, "that new saint, than whom none purer or more brave was ever led by love of men

into conflict and death—the new saint awaiting his martyrdom and who, if he shall suffer, will make the gallows glorious like the cross."

And to the booming voices of the great, Louisa Alcott, then in her late twenties, added her gentle reedsong:

> No monument of quarried stone,
>   No eloquence of speech,
> Can grave the lessons on the land
>   His martyrdom will teach.

Not all of the North, nor even all of New England thought John Brown a saint and a martyr. There were many who thought him a black murderer, and others, not willing to go so far, believed he had paid a just penalty for breaking the law. But the pro-Brown feeling was dominant enough to startle the South, where it was thought he had been trying to lead an insurrection of their slaves, and the shocked surprise in the Southern states was the greater because most of the reaction in the North did not occur until after the man was dead.

Concord held a martyr service at the Town Hall the day of his execution, and Louisa Alcott trudged through the mud to attend it. John Brown was more than a symbolic figure to the tall, plain young woman, for he had come to Concord to visit an old friend, the schoolmaster Frank Sanborn. Louisa had heard him speak on Kansas slavery, when John Brown's name was famous in connection with the "Pottawatomie massacre," and she had come away stirred to the depths with a desire to dedicate her life to the abolition of slavery. Louisa's father, Bronson Alcott, spoke at the martyr service (indeed, it was difficult to keep him from speaking on any occasion). Thoreau read one of his poems, and the congregation joined in singing a dirge which the schoolmaster had written for his friend.

A few months after the execution, John Brown's widow and some of his family came to visit in Concord, establishing a relationship which remained close, for the following year, after war had been declared, his daughter returned to board with the Alcotts.[1] Some of the people of Concord thought John Brown insane, some denounced him as a criminal, but to Louisa he seemed a selfless man who had sacrificed his life in a great cause. After the stirring martyr service, Louisa continued her normal life—if a life which combined poverty, Bronson Alcott, Emerson and an intellectual daily fare not equalled in any other town on earth, can possibly be described as "normal." There was no outlet for the emo-

tions which burned so fiercely in her. The normal way in Concord was peaceful enough—skating on the frozen river in winter, riding on the snowplow, excursions into the woods to gather wild flowers (where sometimes Thoreau was to be met on his solitary wanderings), nutting expeditions in the fall. There was as yet no sign that anything would ever alter the peaceful sequence of her days, but there was a foreboding. She felt the future to be alive with the promise of events which might change the destiny of the human race, and she cried out against the fate which had made her a woman.

Nothing better illustrates the range of emotions in those days than the different ways the news of the execution was received in that quiet town and in the nation's capital, where the affair at Harper's Ferry caused a wild flapping in the peaceful dovecote of Washington society. While the ladies of New England were donning their somewhat dowdy and faintly austere bonnets to go to lectures by Emerson, and the ladies of Cleveland and Chicago were picking their way through the mud of the unpaved streets to go to gatherings where politics were discussed, the ladies of Washington were leading an altogether different sort of life. Washington was (and to an extent still is) a city of Southern customs and attitudes. Southern ladies dominated the society—socially indefatigable little Mrs. Roger Pryor, Rose O'Neal Greenhow, who sent military information to the Confederates even after she was shut in Old Capitol Prison, Mrs. Clement C. Clay, the Alabama Senator's wife who was witty and clever and used a therapy machine to invigorate her for evening parties.

They were members of Mr. Buchanan's "court," and Mr. Buchanan was a Pennsylvania gentleman of Southern inclination, who was having trouble adapting his sectional views to his national role. They were the initiate, the arbiters by self-appointment. They discussed politics wherever they went—at the teas, the chocolate parties, the White House levees—and as the tension grew between North and South they mourned to see "poor Mr. Buchanan" so "bothered" by events he was utterly unfit to influence or control.

The social day in the capital was a busy one. In the morning the ladies went shopping to try on hats from Paris or to Mr. Gautier's, the confectioner who catered to all the best parties, to order some towering creation in sugar for the center of the table. State dinners took place at any time from late afternoon on. Home dinners for the family or a few friends were usually served soon after Congress had adjourned for the day, at about five o'clock. Mrs. Roger Pryor would send her children

up to the roof of the house to watch for the falling of the flag at the Capitol, the signal that the day's session was ended and that the hungry lawmakers would soon be home wanting their dinners.

The cooking was elaborate, rich, and not in the least to the taste of the Northern ladies. Terrapin stew and oysters in season were standbys, and stocks of them were kept in cellars against emergency. These Washington cellars would have given a Northern lady fits for they were awash with brackish water where oysters were "seeded" to be culled when wanted, and terrapin destined for the stew crawled in a darkness made odorous by an occasional bivalve which had given up the ghost.

Tea followed close on dinner (two lumps of sugar, two slices of lemon and a dollop of rum in the cup before the tea was poured in) and there might also be an urn of chocolate, and always wine for the gentlemen. Sometimes several tea tables would be visited in an afternoon, and Pennsylvania Avenue would be crowded with open carriages jouncing over bumps while smiling ladies in huge skirts waved to one another through clouds of dust.

Supper was late, light, and simple—chicken or chipped beef and biscuits—served buffet style. In the evening there might be a grand ball, with the dance floor decorated in designs of colored sands which had taken a day to create and were effaced in an instant by the first sweep of the great skirts. To these functions the ladies wore fresh flowers, on heads, bodices, waists and wrists—enough of them on one debutante to decorate a modest wedding of our times. The ladies smiled and flirted with their fans and talked the latest government gossip with the men until it was time to go home.

Most of these ladies had listened all their lives to talk of secession and even war, but if they thought about it at all, they were aware, as the men were, that such talk was only a safety valve for the emotional pressures engendered by the differing economies in the two parts of the nation. The affair at Harper's Ferry had on all this gaiety and charm the effect of a severe shock. It was not really the thing itself which caused the disturbance; for what, after all, did that brief attempt to incite an uprising amount to, and what signified the death, however courageous, of a strange fanatic who had made himself beyond question liable for that penalty? Moreover, the blacks had not responded to the call to revolt, so that the incident was without sequel.

It was not the event which so deeply stirred these charming ladies, but the sudden light it threw on the extent of the rift between the North

and the South, on the depth of hatreds and the irreconcilability of points of view. The Baltimore *Sun* of November 28, 1859 put this feeling into words: "That the South can afford to live under a Government the majority of whose subjects or citizens regard John Brown as a martyr and a Christian hero rather than a murderer and robber, and act up to these sentiments, or countenance others in so doing, is a preposterous idea . . . "

The pretty waltz music had stopped with a crash, the lovely dancers stood in a momentary tableau of fear. After the execution of that lonely man, nothing in Washington was ever the same again. Instead of one society, there suddenly appeared two hostile groups, the larger, which was made up of Southern sympathizers, looking at the loyal Northern ladies with mistrust and aversion, and with an even deeper emotion, for these Southern ladies had realized so swiftly that it seems to have happened almost overnight, that the war they had heard talked about all their lives might become a reality.

With that realization, much of the frivolity vanished from Washington life. The Southern ladies deserted the tea tables to go to the Capitol to hear the fire-eating representatives of the cotton states denounce the tyranny of the North. They went in such numbers that some of them were forced to sit on the floor or stand in the corridor, and they stayed for hours, keeping unnaturally quiet, leaning forward over the gallery railings spellbound. The scenes on the floor of the House and the Senate were intensely dramatic, the speeches ranging all the way from sectionally patriotic oratory to simple name-calling. At times the atmosphere grew so tense that it seemed certain the lawmakers would shortly come to blows. Once a pistol fell from under a representative's coat-tail and the entire feminine contingent caught its breath, fearful that shooting was about to begin.

One of the most violent of the fire-eaters was Congressman Roger Pryor of Virginia, a Southern aristocrat who believed that the ownership of slaves was tantamount to a patent of nobility and that all Northerners were tradesmen and shopkeepers. There were others of Pryor's stamp—Barksdale, Rust, Keitt, Hindman—all violent to the point of irrationality, but more than any of them Pryor has retained the power to irritate. Across the years we can still see him clearly as he strode by, tall, angry, powered by his own fierce ego, with adoring little Mrs. Pryor in his wake, her wide skirts sweeping the corridor, her sharp nose lifted high, as unshakably convinced of her husband's superiority as he himself. Pryor was well named, for he was fond of being the first to do or say a thing

of note. He laid claim to having originated that phrase which caught the attention of an entire nation, the "irrepressible conflict." He was the first to wear "the gray," a suit of Southern-made gray cloth, presented to him by his constituents, which drew from a Northern orator the sarcastic comment that "Virginia, instead of clothing herself in sheep's wool, had better don her appropriate garb of sackcloth and ashes."[2] It was Mrs. Pryor's nimble pen which ardently recorded these triumphs for posterity.

The ladies emerged from the fiery sessions at the Capitol with crinolines crushed and spirits exalted. There was no outlet for their intense patriotic fervor, however, save the snubbing of the ladies from the North. This they proceeded to do. They still considered that Washington society was theirs by right of preemption, and they made this plain to the interlopers by means which ranged from coldness to downright rudeness. Northern ladies could be dropped from visiting lists and private parties, but they could not be excluded from official functions, and these took place from this time on in a chill atmosphere of animosity.

The charm of Washington society had vanished, the gaiety had fled, the delightful afternoons on the White House piazza, the airy coquetry over the chocolate cups, were utterly spoiled. President Buchanan, it was noted by General Cass, who did not like him and may have been exaggerating, wandered among his disrupted court "pale with fear" that war would find him still in office, dividing his time "equally between praying and crying." The poor, befuddled Chief Executive, glancing apprehensively at the gathering war clouds, was heard to mutter, "Not in my time. Not in my time." Fortunately for everyone, his time was running out.

The Southern women in Washington during these trying days were showing the worst in feminine nature, but only because there was nothing in the stalemated situation which demanded anything better of them. When the break finally came and these Washington society ladies returned to their homes in the South, they faced hardships and personal tragedies as though they had never harbored a petty or frivolous thought. Mrs. Roger Pryor lost a son in the war and wrote of him that he had given to suffering humanity all that God had given him. Courageously, these ladies "propped the South on a swansdown fan" and the touching, tragic story of the metamorphoses of these butterflies has never fully been told.

From the scholar's point of view, the causes of the Civil War are abstruse, nor has the long perspective of time simplified the issues, but rather the reverse. To the masculine part of the population who lived through these days, however, the reasons for fighting seem to have

appeared clear and even simple. They knew, or thought they knew why they felt it imperative to go to war, though their reasons went through evolutionary changes as the nation took the steps toward war, and the time would come, as it has in every major conflict, when men would ask themselves "Why are we fighting this war?" But in those days, before fighting became a reality, most people could and did express their reasons in such simple phrases as "to prevent secession," "to prevent the extension of slavery," or (at the start a small but shrill voice) "to abolish slavery in the United States." And for a certain fairly large number the reason seemed even simpler, being merely a desire to "give the cur dogs a good licking." The differences in points of view were geographical, in the main, the West not being particularly interested in anything but whether or not slavery was to be extended into certain territories, the South predominantly concerned with their right to become a separate nation and New England with bringing an end to slavery.

Women also held these views, for it would be a mistake to think that the majority of them, in all classes, were not aware of the issues of the day. They listened to discussions of them, at home, at church gatherings, at social functions and at that Northern institution, the lyceum lecture. But then they used their feminine alchemy to translate the concrete into the abstract, and based their beliefs more on ideals than on political concepts. They tended to transpose "secession," "extension," and "abolition" into "rights," "freedom" or simply "patriotism," plain and undefined. In this respect the line between the sexes cannot, of course, be rigidly drawn. There were some prominent women who were as materialistically political in their views as any man, and some men who were motivated almost wholly by idealism. But the difference, which is certainly not peculiar to this war, went deep. What is peculiar to this war, is that the women found waiting for them a tremendous field for the expression of their ideals.

In New England and especially in Concord, which represented in a way the distilled essence of New England thought, the materialistic almost merged with the idealistic point of view. Here where the dominating reason for going to war was to free the slaves, tradition was strong and war seemed to be a renewal of the ancient fight for human freedom. On April 27th, eight days after the anniversary of the Battle of Concord, and the same number of days after the Concord volunteers departed to answer Lincoln's call, Oliver Wendell Holmes put these sentiments into verse:

Eighty years have passed, and more
Since under the brave old tree,
Our fathers gathered in arms and swore
They would follow the sign their banners bore,
And fight till the land was free.

Half of their work was done,
Half is left to do—
Cambridge, and Concord and Lexington,
When the battle is fought and won,
What shall be told of you?

The abolitionists were a small minority in those days. The time was not far distant when Lincoln would say: "I have no purpose, directly or indirectly, to interfere with the institution of slavery in the States where it exists. I believe I have no lawful right to do so, and I have no inclination to do so."

The Emancipation Proclamation was not issued until January of 1863, and then largely as a measure to revive the flagging support of the war at a time when people were beginning to doubt whether the Union was worth so protracted and bloody a conflict. By that time, the abolitionist sentiment had grown, but even in these early days just before the guns began to fire, this minority was so vocal as to convince the South that it represented very nearly the solid opinion of the northern half of the nation. It has, in a sense, been growing ever since and has come so to color the popular view of history that historians of recent years have been in doubt how to place the abolitionists in their proper perspective.

New England women did not wait for war to translate their abolitionist ideals into action. A number of ladies, whose views were wider and whose crinolines were narrower than those of Washington ladies, decided long before war was inevitable to strike a blow for freedom by turning their homes into way stations on the Underground Railroad. Since there was a law which enforcement officers, whatever their sympathies, were bound to respect, requiring the capture and return of escaped slaves, special hideaways for these black men had sometimes to be constructed. Some mysterious new building at the white, elm-shaded Emerson house in Concord was generally suspected to be for this purpose and Mrs. Alcott, who lived down the street, once hid a slave in her oven.

The whole proceeding was sometimes rather an open secret, but the conventions of secrecy were observed. The black man (or woman) usu-

ally arrived, very frightened, at night. Some families carried out the letter of the ideal and sat the confused black at the family table. He was a symbolic figure, a representative of the oppressed, an honored guest—which did not prevent the lady of the house from making use of his services to cut the kindling or do other chores if the coast were clear. At night he was sent to the next "station," usually in a wagon, half-smothered under tarpaulins or a load of hay. All this was just risky enough to be exciting and gave a number of women, including Louisa, the feeling of participating in great events.

Both in New England and in the nation's capital, during these weeks immediately preceding war, the legendary figure of John Brown seemed to grow larger and larger, like a vision in the sky. Then it began slowly to fade and another figure of more than human dimensions began to emerge. In some respects this new apparition, with rugged face and burning, sad eyes and fantastic, stove-pipe hat, was as improbable as the other vision had been and far more potent to inspire both terror and hope. Some in the North, seeing this emergence, spoke of the millennium. Some ladies in Washington saw in it the figure of doom and, calling their slaves, began cramming their pretty finery into trunks.

The exodus began, though in a small way, before the elections of 1860. Those who remained talked of Washington as the logical capital of the Confederacy if and when the South became a separate nation. Washington society was suffering increasingly from strain, and the adherents of both factions gazed at each other with growing suspicion. At official functions, where of necessity both sides were present, discussions of the issues of the day were strictly avoided, but at dinners and teas when all were of the same party, talk crackled like a brush fire with now and again the ominous word "treason."

When Election day, November 6th, arrived, Washington Southern society, for all the alarms and terrors of recent times, did not believe—could not conceive—that its rule was threatened. Reality did not yet seem quite real. On that night, far away in Springfield, Illinois, the ladies of the Republican party had prepared refreshments for the politicians and their wives. It was a noisy gathering, and when word was received that Lincoln had carried New York, everyone went wild. The crowd shouted and sang and wove around the room in a kind of snake dance, greeting the political victory in a spirit of levity and triumph. Presently Lincoln and a few friends slipped away to a dim little telegraph office, and there he stayed, receiving the returns, until nearly dawn.

When the election returns were all in, the results were of a sort to make

the thoughtful ponder. It was found that Lincoln would command 180 Electoral votes of a possible 303, but in fifteen states he had received no Electoral votes, and in ten states not one voter had cast a ballot in his favor. Lincoln had been elected by a large majority over Stephen A. Douglas, but if Douglas had been able to command the popular votes which were given to the Southern democrat, John C. Breckinridge, he could have defeated Lincoln with ease. Lincoln, therefore, was not elected by a majority of the American people. His votes were Northern votes and he carried almost all the free states, but he carried no others.

It took some time for the North to assimilate the significance of these facts. To thoughtful Northerners, war did not seem inevitable. Nevertheless, it was generally felt that the change of administration had released forces which were as yet incalculable.

It took no time at all, however, for the Southern political leaders to understand what had happened insofar as they themselves were affected. To them the new administration was as alien as a foreign power and the coming of the Republicans to Washington meant only one thing —immediate separation of Southern territory, to be enforced, if necessary, by war. This was discussed in an atmosphere of suspicion, unrest and conspiracy. Men spoke together in lowered voices or drank in moody silence at the Willard bar while eyeing their neighbors with suspicion.

The Southern women had received a second severe shock, for on the morning after the election they awoke to the realization that the Washington they had ruled and loved so long, their home, their guarantee of prestige, their dream of future glory, was theirs no longer. Washington had become a Northern city. With that realization, the exodus began in earnest. Day after day drays of trunks and household goods, and groups of slaves made their way to the Acquia creek steamer. All over the city shutters were being put up on empty, deserted houses, but the owners of these houses were telling each other confidently that soon they would return in triumph.

After the election, events began to move with the swift, deadly current of a mill race. On the tenth of November, the senators from South Carolina resigned and a thrill of excitement ran along Washington's taut nerves. On December third, the second session of the Thirty-Sixth Congress convened with bursts of belligerent oratory. Buchanan, trembling like a jelly-fish and obsessed with the desire to avert war on any terms, sent a message declaring his belief that a sovereign state could not be coerced by the central government. It was a doctrine which, if it had been accepted, would have dissolved the Union at once. On December

tenth, Secretary of the Treasury Howell Cobb resigned to join the secessionist party in Georgia, and about this time Buchanan, in a sudden burst of decisiveness, permitted General Scott to reinforce Fort Sumter.

On December twentieth South Carolina seceded. Buchanan was at a wedding when the telegram announcing the news was handed to him, and Mrs. Pryor, who had a knack for being present at historical events, was standing behind his chair. There was a commotion in the hall, and the nervous President turned to inquire of her if she thought the house was on fire. Mrs. Pryor's lively pen records the scene:

"I will inquire the cause, Mr. President, I said. I went out at the nearest door, and there in the entrance hall I found Mr. Lawrence Keitt, member from South Carolina, leaping in the air, shaking a paper over his head, and exclaiming, 'Thank God! Oh, thank God!' I took hold of him and said: 'Mr. Keitt, are you crazy? The President hears you, and wants to know what's the matter.'

"'Oh!' he cried, 'South Carolina has seceded! Here's the telegram. I feel like a boy let out from school.'

"I returned and, bending over Mr. Buchanan's chair, said in a low voice: 'It appears, Mr. President, that South Carolina has seceded from the Union. Mr. Keitt has a telegram.' He looked at me, stunned for a moment. Falling back and grasping the arms of his chair, he whispered, 'Madam, might I beg you to have my carriage called?'"

On Christmas Day the Richmond *Examiner* called for the men of Maryland to join with Virginians in seizing Washington, and a sudden horrified realization swept through the North that the nation's capital was isolated and vulnerable. Inside the city wild rumors were flying to the effect that there was a conspiracy to seize Washington from within. Guards were detailed to search the cellars of the Capitol each night for hidden explosives. Not one soldier had as yet been called to arms, but a Mrs. Almira Fales, living in Washington, was so certain of war that she began to scrape lint and gather hospital stores, and people said that Almira Fales was crazy. Eccentric she probably was, but she was certainly among the first of the women to recognize emergency and to begin to prepare for it.

On December twenty-seventh, South Carolina seized Fort Moultrie, Castle Pinckney, a lighthouse, a Federal schooner and various other government property. On December twenty-ninth John B. Floyd retired as Secretary of War amid the hissing of the word "treason." On the

thirty-first South Carolina added the United States arsenal, the post office and the customs house in Charleston to the spoils of her as-yet-undeclared war. Thus, in an atmosphere of increasing apprehension, the last year of peace drew to a close. Louisa Alcott, in her journal, called 1860 "The Year of Good Luck," but she was thinking of her career as a writer and her gratifying ability to buy bonnets and second-hand carpets for her family.

Lincoln, President-Elect, was in Springfield, and the hiatus in effectual government which of necessity existed until his inauguration, was proving a fine growing culture for the germs of sedition in Washington. Almost hour by hour the determination spread among his enemies to prevent his taking office and numbers of people believed he would never be inaugurated. Lincoln was thinking of other things, and as the year was dying he urged that there be no compromise on the extension of slavery: "On that point hold firm, as with a chain of steel."[3] By this time, among the war clouds, the vision of John Brown had faded wholly away.

NOTES

[1] Ednah D. Cheney, Editor, *Life, Letters, and Journals of Louisa May Alcott* (Roberts Brothers, Boston, 1892).

[2] Mrs. Roger A. Pryor, *Reminiscences of Peace and War* (The Macmillan Company, New York, 1904).

[3] "Private and Confidential" letter from Abraham Lincoln to E. B. Washburne, dated Springfield, Illinois, December 13, 1860.

2

THE DRUMS BEGIN TO BEAT

──────────────── ★ ────────────────

1861

April 4   The Virginia Convention refused, 89 to 45, to submit the secession ordinance to popular vote.

April 7   Communication with Fort Sumter cut off.

April 9   The expedition ordered by President Lincoln for the relief of Fort Sumter, sailed from New York.

April 12   Fort Sumter bombarded.

April 13   Fort Sumter surrendered.

April 15   President Lincoln issued a Proclamation calling out State militia and summoning Congress for a special session.

April 16   The Confederate Government called for 32,000 troops.

April 17   The Virginia Convention voted for secession, 60 to 53, subject to a referendum vote. The Sixth Massachusetts Regiment started for Washington.

──────────────── ★ ────────────────

"Take your gun and go, John,
Take your gun and go,
For Ruth can drive the oxen, John,
And I can use the hoe."
—Anonymous

T HE INAUGURATION WAS APPROACHING and the feeling was general in Washington that there might be rioting of serious proportions on that day. It was that which decided Mrs. Roger Pryor to take the children out of the capital, and she made a hasty departure, via the Acquia Creek steamer, leaving her luggage to be sent along after her. Pryor remained in Washington to keep his seat in Congress until after the Inauguration, when he too left for the South. There, as Mrs. Pryor fatuously recorded, "my young Congressman" became "my young Colonel."[1]

He immediately plunged into the politics of the Confederacy. The majority of the Virginia Convention were opposed to secession but Pryor and many of his associates were convinced that if war became a reality, Virginia would at once throw in her lot with the Southern States. Accordingly, Pryor undertook to bring pressure on the Confederate Government, then in session at Montgomery, to attack Fort Sumter in Charleston harbor. This was work to Pryor's liking, and to an immense audience at Charleston he shouted, "I tell you gentlemen what will put Virginia in the Southern Confederacy in less than an hour by the Shrewsbury clock—strike a blow."

Two deputations went out to Fort Sumter, in the entrance of the harbor, to demand of the commander, Major Anderson, that he surrender. Pryor, armed to the teeth with bowie knives and revolvers, went with the second expedition. At the Fort, he behaved with arrogance, as though he owned the place, and seeing a glass on the table filled with what appeared to be brandy, he seized it and tossed it down his throat. It was iodide of potassium, and a doctor who happened to be present, said, "Sir, what you have drank is poison. You are a dead man." Pryor survived, though he returned to Charleston very sick as a result of the emetics which were given him. It is hard to feel much sympathy.

When the bombardment was about to begin, Pryor was invited to fire the first historic shot, but Pryor, unaccountably it would seem for one who so loved to be first, refused, and the honor was given to an aging secessionist named Edmund Ruffin. The shot, which was fired from the Stevens battery on Cummings Point, sped across the water and lodged in the wall at Fort Sumter in uncomfortably close proximity to the head

of Abner Doubleday. Writing long afterward, Mrs. Pryor indulged in some speculation about how different her life might have been if Pryor had fired the first shot, but that was as nothing compared to the difference it would have made if the shot had struck Abner Doubleday instead of the wall beside him, for Doubleday, in addition to becoming a major general, became famous as the "father" of baseball. That shot was fired at dawn on the twelfth of April, 1861. It did indeed unify the South, but no one seems to have considered that in the North the effect would inevitably be similar.

It was known in the city of Charleston that if Anderson had not surrendered by four in the morning of the twelfth, the firing would begin. The excitement in the city was intense. Mary Chestnut, wife of ex-Senator Chestnut of South Carolina, passed some of the anxious time of waiting by writing in her diary: "I do not pretend to go to sleep. How can I?" Her husband was out in a rowboat on the dark water, having gone to Fort Sumter with additional instructions for Anderson regarding the surrender, and Mary counted the passage of time by listening to the bells from St. Michael's church. Four o'clock chimed, followed by deep silence, while she listened, knowing that the next few moments would decide whether there was to be peace or war. The silence continued and she began to hope. Then, at half past four, she heard the heavy boom of cannon. She arose from bed, dropped on her knees and began to pray.

The whole house was awake by this time and she heard the many people in it hurrying to the flat roof. She dressed herself quickly, seized a shawl and went there also. Shells were bursting like stars over the bay and she thought of her husband out there in the small boat. "The women were wild there on the housetop," Mary wrote, "and all the roofs were crowded with people. Prayers came from the women and imprecations from the men. And then a shell would light up the scene."

After the excitement, the next day seemed like anticlimax. "Nobody has been hurt after all . . . Not even a battery the worse for wear. Fort Sumter has been on fire. Anderson has not yet silenced any of our guns. So the aides, still with swords and red sashes by way of uniform, tell us . . . "

Fort Sumter surrendered on April 13th, which was a Saturday. Lincoln received the news on Sunday, and by that time it was clear that action of some sort must be taken by the government without a moment's delay, not only because the country was obviously at war, but because the city of Washington was perilously undefended against attack. Hotheads

in the South were urging with fiery oratory, the immediate seizure of the city, and Southern sympathizers within the city made no secret of their conviction that the government would soon be in their power.

Indeed, there was little to prevent their carrying out these threats. Most of the regular Army, which numbered only 16,000 men, was stationed in a long chain of small forts, far away on the Indian frontier. Actually on the spot, and available to meet the expected attack, were some local militia, known to be full of Southern sympathizers, and a few regular soldiers who had been brought to town for the counting of the electoral vote and remained to guard the President at the Inaugural ceremonies. Except for a handful of swivel-chair officers at the War Department, many of whom held secessionist views, that was all the force which could be mustered against the large Confederate army which people believed to be almost at the gates. Tension in the city mounted hourly; no man felt certain he knew friend from foe.

The President immediately called the Cabinet into session, and the members gathered with solemn faces. There was, in point of fact, only one course of action open to them and that was to call on the loyal states to send their militia in all haste, with the larger intention of putting down what was generally called the "rebellion" and the more immediate purpose of saving the threatened city. The outlook was not a cheering one, for these militia organizations were understrength, untrained, and unarmed. The troops thus raised would be a citizen mob rather than an army, their mettle and their temper unknown.

There was some hurried research in an attempt to find a legal precedent for the call, and the Militia Act of 1793, which had last been invoked at the time of the Whiskey Rebellion, was selected. A proclamation was then drafted which called on the governors of the states to furnish militia to put down "combinations too powerful to be suppressed by the ordinary course of judicial proceedings." The Proclamation stated the probable duty of the militia to be the repossession of forts and Federal property, and referred to the need for avoiding the destruction of private property, or the disturbance of peaceful citizens, and called for the convening of Congress on July 4th. The militia force was to number 75,000 men and the length of service, though not mentioned in the Proclamation, was to be ninety days.

The Proclamation was, in a sense, a trial of strength for the Administration and there were those who thought it would not succeed. It was given to the people on April 15th. "Monday dawned. Who saw that day will ever forget it?" wrote Mary Livermore.[2] This Proclamation was

like "the first peal of a surcharged thundercloud clearing the murky air." Mary was an intelligent woman of forty, who had the direct, unwavering eyes of one who makes thoughtful judgments about people. She was strong in body and mind, but at this time she had no idea of the demands the war would make on that strength.

Her reaction to the Proclamation was typical. First there was a tremendous burst of relief that the time of uncertainty was ended and that feelings could find release in action. And Bronson Alcott, who could be counted on never to let an event slip by without comment, proclaimed that "no greater calamity could befall a people than deliberating overlong on issues which imperilled liberty." There followed from the loyal states an overwhelming response. Governors of those states flooded Washington with telegrams begging to be allowed to raise double the number of men required, and so intense was the patriotic fervor that the entire quota might have been raised in New York City alone.

There were mass meetings in every city and village of the loyal states. Huge crowds attended and the women, who had no more idea than the men of the real meaning of war, mingled their shrill voices with the shouting. It was a delirium of patriotism, and it lasted for days. The nation's manhood responded. All over the land men left the plow and the ledger. They rose from desks and came out from behind counters. The scholar closed his book, the banker left his money bags and joined the long lines of dusty men going to the recruiting centers. They came from all stations of life, each to merge his identity in this would-be army.

Mainly the volunteers were young men, but a good many oldsters and some boys came along on the great adventure. Since this was a three months' lark, by which time the war was certain to be over, few questions were asked about the fitness of the volunteers for service, and when there were any medical examinations at all, they were of a most cursory nature. Just how cursory may be gathered from the fact that at one time or another, about 400 women found their way into the ranks and remained undetected by the authorities, for the most part, until they were wounded or killed in battle.

Since volunteer regiments were not mustered into the Federal service until they were complete and officered, the new soldiers often found themselves involved in something like chaos. The officers knew as little about soldiering as the men—which is to say, nothing at all. Some had become officers because they happened to be political favorites, or because they had helped to raise a regiment, or because they were promi-

nent citizens with influence. Some were elected by the men or appointed by other officers.

In Galena, Illinois, the evening of the fifteenth, there was a town meeting presided over, rather diffidently, by an ex-army captain who had seen service in Mexico and in consequence had suddenly found himself an arbiter of military matters in the town. He was Ulysses S. Grant and he conducted the meeting with "much embarrassment and some prompting."[3] There were speeches, followed by a call for volunteers. A company was formed with the vague intention of adding itself to some infantry regiment, and the men proceeded to elect their officers on the spot. The same sort of scene, the same amazing, spontaneous, haphazard self organization of this citizen-army was taking place all over the North in the days following the President's call.

The ladies of Galena who were, Grant recalled, "quite as patriotic as the men," conceived the idea of sending their company off to war properly uniformed, and as none of them had any idea what the uniform of a United States infantryman should look like, they besieged Grant for a description and followed his directions with care. Other women all over the North were banding together with the same idea, hiring tailors to cut the cloth while they stitched furiously on their whirring machines that their local soldiery might march to war properly garbed. A good many of these sewing groups, lacking such an authority as Grant to guide them, relied on their own creative imaginations with some wild and wonderful results. For the most part, however, the new army relied on their states or on the Federal government to clothe them, only to find themselves months later still wearing the tattered remnants of the civilian clothing in which they had marched away to war.

On the sixteenth of April, there began the tramp of marching feet. In Boston, on this day, bands of volunteers filled the streets. Here the organization of the new army was simpler and worked more smoothly than in parts of the West, for here where tradition was strong, the old regiments of the Revolution came to life, and sometimes the descendants took the same place in the same company that their forefathers had filled in the Revolution. Faneuil Hall, the "Cradle of Liberty," was opened for the volunteers. And as the new soldiers marched in, they were surrounded by crowds cheering vociferously. "Merchants and clerks rushed out from stores saluting them as they passed. Windows were flung up and women leaned out into the rain, waving flags and handkerchiefs. Horsecars and omnibuses halted for the passage of the soldiers . . ." Mary Livermore still felt the excitement of that day twenty-seven years later.

In nearby Concord, Louisa Alcott, a young woman of far more sensitive imagination than the practical Mary, was having a busy time getting the Concord company ready, but finding it a sad business, ". . . for in a little town like this, we all seem like one family," and she wrote, "I've longed to be a man; but as I can't fight, I will content myself with working for those who can."[4] Louisa did not view the war in the same light as the girls who ran with shrieks and laughter along the ranks of the marching volunteers, thrusting at them little beribboned bunches of flowers to tie on their gun barrels, or trading a kiss for a shiny new brass button snipped from a uniform.

In Washington, at this time, there was another New England woman, a clerk in a patent office, who shared Louisa's longing to be a man. Her name was Clara Barton, and in a few months she would step out of obscurity—in a few years she would take her place in history. At the time of the President's call for volunteers, she seemed a most unlikely subject for fame. She was homely, with a strong face, round and lumpy, like a bag full of apples. She had heavy unmanageable hair which she knotted on the back of her head. Her clothes were of necessity plain, and practical, but she had no trace of the style which can sometimes mitigate such things, and even in the days of her greatness, when she rather pathetically indulged in furbelows, she was never able to carry them off.

Like many other unattached women of her day, Clara was filled with the restless discontent which comes from having more to give than life demands, and of a clerk in the patent office, life demanded nothing but self-effacements and neat penmanship. But here was a woman bursting with physical and mental energy, well endowed with intelligence and common sense, warm-hearted and longing to give these qualities scope. The long repression of them had produced in her a personality which by this time, when she was forty, bordered on the neurotic. She was often seized with painful fits of shyness, and under emotional strain her voice grew weak and husky. Clara had been through one upset of a nervous emotional sort, and she was almost certainly heading for another. At the sudden shock of war, it seemed as though the frustration and the longing for life, found expression in the way she reacted. Clara took a pistol and went to the Monument grounds, where she put up a target. There she blazed away, "putting nine balls successively within the space of six inches at a distance of fifty feet." There are those, mostly soldiers, who are only great because their lives chanced to coincide with a war, who otherwise would have remained in obscurity. Clara Barton was certainly such a one.

Meanwhile, the volunteers continued to gather themselves into a happy, sloppy, eager mob. It was an army by spontaneous combustion. It was pathetic, but it was also glorious, for this extraordinary army had elements of greatness. And while the young men and oldsters and the boys were shuffling around in the dust, unarmed, un-uniformed, or dressed in fancy rigs, trying to teach themselves the rudiments of drill, a volunteer army of a different stamp was gathering in the South. Between the two were important differences which had an effect on how the war was fought, even after the armies on both sides had become veterans. In the North, the new army took its character largely from the characteristics of the men in the ranks, but in the South, the nature of the army was determined by its officers or by the young aristocrats in the cavalry troops whose daring has created much of the romance of Southern history. Sherman, who had lived among the young men of the South, and knew that they created one of the special problems of the war, described them to Lincoln: "The young bloods . . . who never did work and never will. War suits them, and the rascals are brave, fine riders, bold to rashness and dangerous in every sense. They care not a sou for niggers, land or anything . . . they don't bother their brains about the past, present and future . . . the best cavalry . . . the most dangerous set of men this war has turned loose upon the world. . . ." Even the romanticism for which both armies were conspicuous differed in quality. The special brand of Southern romanticism stemmed from tradition and an idealized concept of a way of life—a romanticism created and largely maintained by the male members of that society. Romanticism in the North, however, lacked tradition, except in the older sections, and lacked a way of life common alike to cities, farms and plains. Theirs was a romanticism based on many intangibles—on religion, literature, on youth itself. The priests were women and the temple was the home.

Mary Livermore was awed by the transformation from peace to patriotic frenzy which took place within twenty-four hours and by the headlong speed with which events were taking place. In Massachusetts, by six o'clock in the evening of April 16th, three regiments were ready to start for the protection of Washington, and new companies were forming all over the state. The first of the regiments to depart was the Sixth Massachusetts, and on Wednesday the seventeenth, an enormous crowd gathered at the railroad station long before the troops arrived. It was a quiet, deeply serious crowd, made up of families of the soldiers and prominent citizens, like Mary Livermore and Julia Ward Howe, who had come because they could not stay at home in stirring times like these.

The marching column of men appeared and a wild cheer went up from the waiting crowd. No one had an eye for the ludicrous that day, or instead of a cheer there might have been a great burst of laughter, for some of the soldiers still wore civilian clothes, some wore red pantaloons in imitation of the French. Company A's uniforms had not been finished on time but they had dressed themselves in blue coats, black pantaloons and tall caps surmounted by white pompoms. When General Butler, who commanded the troops from Massachusetts, had first seen the Sixth, he had begged Governor Andrew to find them gray overcoats to conceal, at least partially, the bizarre costumes, and this the Governor had somehow managed to do, but the effect of uniformity they produced was slight. The new soldiers, however, did not seem comic, either to themselves or to anyone else.

When they reached the station, they broke ranks and mingled with the crowd. A clergyman climbed up where he could be seen, and a hush fell. While he prayed, a long train was backed slowly in and came to a stop by the station platform. The prayer ended and orders rang out for the men to fall into line. There were tearful farewells as the soldiers tore themselves from the arms of the women who loved them. The companies formed, began to march and to disappear into the train. A whistle blew, the train jerked and began to move, and suddenly the air turned white with waving handkerchiefs. Men leaned out of the train windows waving and shouting until the crowd at the station was out of sight. The Sixth was on its way to save the city of Washington, but before they reached their destination, two days later, some of them would be dead and blood would have stained the bright new uniforms of many more.

NOTES

[1] Mrs. Roger A. Pryor, *Reminiscences of Peace and War* (The Macmillan Company, New York, 1904).

[2] Mary Livermore, *My Story of the War* (A. D. Worthington and Company, Hartford, Conn., 1888), p. 89.

[3] *Personal Memoirs of U. S. Grant* (Charles L. Webster & Company, New York, 1885), p. 230ff.

[4] *Louisa M. Alcott, Life, Letters, and Journals.* (Roberts Brothers, Boston, 1892), p. 127.

3

THROUGH THE STREETS
OF A CITY

CHRONOLOGY

1861

April 18   Four hundred and sixty volunteers from Pennsylvania arrived in Washington. The Arsenal at Harper's Ferry was burned to save it from Confederates. Robert E. Lee declined the unofficial offer of the command of the Union forces.

April 19   The Sixth Massachusetts Regiment was attacked by a mob in Baltimore. Four were killed and about 31 wounded. Miss Dorothea Dix was unofficially appointed head of army nurses. Southern ports were blockaded.

★

Low let the city lie
That thus her guest receives;
A smoking ruin to the eye
Be marble walls and eaves!
—Julia Ward Howe, written
in commemoration of the
dead in the Baltimore
riot.

I N WASHINGTON fear was growing stronger hour by hour. Any unusual noise, any disturbance in the streets, convinced people the attack had begun. Rumor swept through the city like a brush fire. Men stood in groups on the sidewalks outside the Willard Hotel, or in front of the Treasury, where news was sometimes posted on the bulletin board. Women stayed at home, parting the lace curtains to peer fearfully out, or scurried through the streets to a friend's house where they drank their chocolate nervously and talked of what to do when the enemy came.

Some of the soldiers who were already in the city had been moved into the White House giving it, thought John Hay, the President's young secretary, the appearance of a barracks. Sentries patrolled the Capitol, and people stared at them as though they were too strange a sight to seem wholly real. Though it was too soon to expect any part of the volunteer army, many people went to the railroad station where they stood for hours disconsolately gazing down the tracks in the direction from which the troops would come. But though every loyal citizen longed for the arrival of the volunteers, no one outside the War Department had given thought to the fact that an undisciplined, largely unarmed mob made up of people like themselves, is not an army. In the evening of the eighteenth, 460 unequipped volunteers from Pennsylvania put in an appearance and were loudly cheered. They had met an angry secessionist mob on their way through Baltimore, which was an unruly city even in peacetime. The mob had thrown a few stones at the volunteers, but no real damage was done, and no one took the demonstration seriously.

The professional soldiers in the War Department did not look forward to the arrival of the great citizen army for the military men knew that the three-months term of service was too short a time in which to transform this rabble-in-arms into a disciplined force fit to take the field. There was a hope, though a faint one, that the mere size of the citizen army might awe the rebels into submission, but General-in-Chief Winfield Scott, who had a low opinion of volunteers, thought that it was useless to

attempt any offensive operations and that the new army should be used merely as a line of defense along the Potomac.

In the War Department the anxious hours of waiting were spent largely in talk, paper work, and the study of large but inadequate maps of the country south of the river. No one made any preparations either to feed or shelter the horde which would shortly pour into the city, or took account of the fact that green officers would not know how to requisition these necessities. In the little brick building which housed the war offices there seemed, in fact, to be a paralysis of action, as though the professional soldiers had been trapped in a trance-like state.

The truth was that the War Department was wholly unfit to cope with the emergency. General Scott, gallant old hero of the Mexican War, was close to his seventy-fifth year—infirm and dropsical to such a degree that his day had to be punctuated with naps, after each one of which two aides were summoned to hoist him off his couch. There was no retirement provision in the army regulations of those days and the War Department was full of sexagenarian officers. General Scott's second in command, General Wool, was two years older than his chief, though considerably more spry, the Surgeon General, Thomas Lawson, was over eighty and a veteran of the War of 1812. The Commissary and Ordinance Departments were in charge of officers respectively seventy-eight and seventy years of age. In some instances the work of these ancient officers had been done by young Southerners who resigned at the outbreak of hostilities. Every department was inadequately staffed and tangled in red tape.

Though neither side of the conflict could be said to possess a military caste in the true sense of the word, old General Scott, who was a Virginian, had long held the theory that Southern men were better fitted by nature and tradition for military careers than men from the North, and he had favored them to such an extent that, when war broke out, most of the desirable army positions were held by Southerners. A number of West Point men from the North, including Sherman, McClellan, Burnside, Halleck and others, had come to believe that this attitude of Scott's would be too serious a handicap to their careers, and had retired to civilian life. When war came, Scott's policy had immediate and disastrous results, for nearly one-third of the commissioned officers of the Regular Army resigned and went over to the Confederate side, taking with them a great part of the scant military knowledge the country possessed.

Lincoln was fully aware of the dolorous state of affairs in the War Department and on the eighteenth of April, Robert E. Lee was sum-

moned to Washington from his home in Arlington across the river, by a message from Francis P. Blair. Behind closed doors, Blair, in President Lincoln's name, offered Lee command of the Union Army. Lee, declining, said that though he was opposed to secession and deprecated war, he could take no part in an invasion of the Southern states. Lee was Scott's favorite, and a personal friend, and Lee went directly from Blair House to see the General. Perhaps the infirm old soldier saw himself living again in the younger man and hoped through him to influence the future. Each of these two men understood the other's quality, each was moved by true affection. When they greeted each other, warmth, for a moment, overlay every other feeling. Then Lee told the General his decision, and Scott replied, "Lee, you have made the greatest mistake of your life, but I feared it would be so." They parted and Lee rode out of Washington for the last time.

The city spent that night in wakefulness. In the White House, those who listened for sounds in the stillness could hear the occasional grunt of a sleeping soldier as he shifted his position where he lay on the rich carpeting. Clara Barton, in her bare room, listened to the first mosquitoes of the summer horde, humming against the cotton netting she had tacked in her windows. Stanton, who had a genius for quarreling, closed his shrewd little eyes and tried to shut out anger and anxiety. On Sixteenth Street, a lady in need of darkness, Rose Greenhow, was perhaps awake, for she was hatching plots against the Union as fantastic as any melodrama. Care was the President's bedfellow that night, and no one knows how Mary Lincoln rested. She had half-brothers in the Confederacy, and she saw suspicion in most of the eyes which met hers, so her sleep could not have been in peace. Lights burned late in the War Department. Sometimes in the city, one heard the clank of accoutrement as a sentry passed, but no one else was abroad that night. Through the dark empty streets the spring breeze rustled, blowing dust and debris into the doorways of the deserted houses. The river glinted silently by.

The next day, which was Friday, the nineteenth, and the anniversary of the Battle of Lexington, the Sixth Massachusetts Regiment arrived in Baltimore to keep its rendezvous with fate. The officers had been warned that a mob, roaming the streets in Baltimore, might cause some trouble. It would be necessary for the troops to cross the city from one station to another, a crossing which Colonel Jones, commander of the Sixth, naturally assumed would be made on foot. No one really believed an unarmed mob would attack an armed (though incompletely armed) regiment, but nevertheless Colonel Jones gave the order to load and cap rifles. From

here on the story is full of those discrepancies which are always found in eyewitness accounts of swift moving action, so that what follows is, perhaps, only approximately correct.

What the Colonel did not know was that the practice in Baltimore was to move the whole train from one station to the other, on tracks, a car or two at a time, drawn by teams of horses. On arriving in Baltimore, he was about to order the regiment out of the train when, to his surprise, the car he was in and five others, began to move rapidly away, separating him from a part of his command. A large and sullen crowd of Southern sympathizers watched the six cars depart. The street where this was taking place had been torn up for repaving; there was a pile of bricks and cobblestones conveniently to hand. Some men in the mob helped themselves, and as cars numbers five and six moved away, they hurled the brickbats. Then car number seven began to move and the mob was suddenly violent. A hail of cobblestones broke windows and some of the soldiers were cut and bruised. There was the sharp crack of gun fire, and the officer in command ordered the men to lie down on the floor of the car. By this time the mob, which had grown large enough to be really dangerous, had surrounded the remaining cars. Barricades suddenly appeared across the street and the tracks in front of the cars were ripped up. The air was full of missiles and the noise could be heard half across the city. With the rails destroyed, the soldiers were forced to leave the shelter of the cars and to try to rejoin the rest of the regiment on foot.

From this time on, all was confusion. The mob captured some of the rifles and fired on the soldiers, who returned the fire with what was, under the circumstances, remarkable restraint. Step by step the soldiers fought their way across the city for a mile and a half, dragging some of their wounded with them, and at last reached the station where their comrades were waiting. A train of sorts had been made up and the battered soldiers crammed themselves into it in such confusion that the standard bearer could not manipulate the pole of his flag and ripped the colors off. After some delay, the train pulled out.

One car, containing the band and its instruments, was left behind. That car was still back at the starting point, surrounded by the mob, and the unarmed, terrified musicians inside were having a hot time of it. Rioters swarmed all over the car, and when the bandsmen succeeded in barricading the doors, they smashed a hole in the roof. Hand-to-hand fighting followed in a shambles of smashed instruments. The musicians, who were no match for the toughs in the mob, were driven from their stronghold, whereupon they took to their heels. They could run better than they

could fight, and after a wild chase through the streets, they left the mob behind.

The street in the part of the town in which they found themselves was filled with women, who had heard the noise of the fighting and had come out of their houses to find out what was going on. Whatever the women's politics may have been—and some of them may have had husbands among the rioters—the battered and frightened boys aroused their sympathy. Acting quickly for fear the mob would arrive on the scene, they led the boys away to the shelter of their homes. Here they ripped off the bright, betraying stripes from the bandsmen's trousers and completed their disguise with various pieces of old clothing.

They were the first women to help embattled soldiers and they are all, save one, nameless. The one whose name has survived was Ann Manley, whom the Boston *Saturday Evening Courier* daintily referred to as "an outcast and polluted being."[1] Whether her help was more effective than that of the other women, or whether her name has survived only because she had considerable notoriety in Baltimore, we do not know. But thanks to these women, the band, wearing its disguises, was able to go into the street safely, where it counted its members and generally took stock. One of them was missing but turned up, days later, back in his home in New England where he was telling everybody that he was through with war forever.

Toward evening Baltimore grew quiet. The littered streets where the riots had taken place were empty, police patrolled the city, emergency hospitals were set up to care for the wounded. At dusk, Sister Adeline Tyler emerged from the building which housed the Order of Deaconesses over which she presided. Sister Adeline was a Boston woman, tall and commanding, and she was concerned about the safety of those wounded men of her native state who had been left behind in the hostile city. Some of them, she had been told, were at one of the police stations and she went there. A station house in the Sixties was a rough place where no women of reputation ever went, and her going there is a good example of the readiness with which these astonishing women of the war put aside tradition, training and prejudice to do work which no one summoned them to do, with no precedent but the Nightingale ideal to guide them.

The door of the station house was locked. She knocked and was refused admission, but after some delay she was taken to an upstairs room where the Massachusetts men lay. Two she thought were dead. The others, who lay on cots, stretchers, or on the floor, had been given heavy doses of sedatives, but their wounds had not been dressed. The two

most seriously wounded were a man named Coburn who had been shot in the hip, and a Sergeant Ames who had been hit at the base of the brain with a bottle, pieces of which were still protruding from the wound. Sister Adeline decided to remove these two soldiers to the Deaconess Home. A stormy argument with the police ensued, but finally she was permitted to take the men away in a furniture van which she summoned, one wonders how, at that time of night.[2] At the Home they were nursed back to health.

A wall of eulogy obscures Sister Adeline so that it is difficult to see her as a human being. She gave the war years to the care of soldiers, becoming "Directress in charge of lady nurses" at the Naval School Hospital in Annapolis. It was to this hospital that the skeleton-like prisoners from Andersonville were brought, and by her order, the first photographs, which shocked the world, were taken.

News that the Sixth Regiment was on its way to Washington, and would shortly arrive, flew around that city, bringing a large crowd of people to the railroad station. Clara Barton was one who went there, for this regiment was from her own state and some of the men she had taught when they were boys in school. The train pulled in and the men climbed down onto the platform. They were a shocking sight. Their fine new over-coats—those coats which Governor Andrew had provided for them—were soiled and torn. Many heads were bound with bloody handkerchiefs and faces smeared with dirt. Clara Barton made her way rapidly along the lines of men, searching for familiar faces. Some of the men recognized her and called out to her, and she forgot her shyness in the warmth of their greeting. They surrounded her, shaking her hand, delighted to find a friend at the close of this nightmare day.

Some of the men who were badly wounded and needed hospital care, were sent to the Washington Infirmary; the rest were directed to make the Capitol their temporary barracks. No food had been provided for them but the men still had bacon and bread and coffee in their knap-sacks. With cheerful adaptability, they lit fires in the Capitol furnaces and pushed their frying pans through the narrow doors, and presently the smell of bacon was floating through the marble halls above.

Subsequently there was a ceremony for the dead at King's Chapel in Boston. Julia Ward Howe, sensitive, not happy in her marriage, moved to deep sorrow by the war, stood in the crowd. There, perhaps, she would not have been noticed by any but her friends for, except on rare occasions she was withdrawn, meek, with a perpetual droop to her head. Her bright hair was tarnished by gray, her eyes cast down and heavy

lidded, her expression so subtle that bonnet bows effaced her and she seemed all hat and shawl and ribbon. But after the ceremony, her spirit blazed, as it always did when she held a pen, and she wrote:

> Weave no more silks, ye Lyons looms
> To deck our girls for gay delights
> The crimson flower of battle blooms
> And solemn marches fill the nights
>
> Weave the flag whose bars today
> Droop heavy o'er our early dead
> And homely garments coarse and gray
> For orphans that must earn their bread . . .

After the riot, but on the same day, Dorothea Dix, a lady well known for her work in reforming insane asylums, arrived in Baltimore. She was on her way to Washington to offer her services in organizing care for the wounded. Miss Dix was already well known in the capital, for she had discovered the plot to seize the Philadelphia, Wilmington and Baltimore Railroad in order to prevent Lincoln from going to Washington to take the oath of office, a plot which possibly intended the assassination of the President. The plot may or may not have been real but many people in the Administration and the Army took it seriously and Miss Dix was highly regarded by them.

The train which carried Miss Dix to Washington on April 19th was the last to go to that beleaguered city for a long time, for southern sympathizers tore up the track, leaving Washington without rail communication with the North. Miss Dix could not have had either a comfortable or a rapid journey, for bands of secessionists threw ties across the rails and attempted in various ways to delay the train. When she reached Washington, darkness had fallen. She found a hack and told the driver to take her to the War Department.

Miss Dix is one of the few women who, because of some quality of personality, stand out clearly in history, so that whenever she appears she brings with her a sharp sense of reality. As she sat erect in the redolent interior of the shabby hack, a woman nearing sixty, dirty and rumpled from the journey, fatigued and anxious, she still must have been an arresting figure. She had the controlled manner of royalty, and the uncertain lights from the streets would have shown her face to be grim with determination—a grimness which could on occasion, however, degenerate into stubbornness. It was the face of a sensitive person

compelled by her own nature to face the world's hardness without shrinking, and to combat its cruelty. She was a reformer without the true reformer's toughness of spirit, and when it happened, as it sometimes did, that her control was not equal to her determination and some obstacle drove her into high-voiced anger, she suffered agonies of remorse. When the blows of life struck her, they sank deep. The expression of her eyes showed the suffering and the weariness these blows had caused her.

In her pictures there is sometimes a lift to her chin, a distant look in her eyes, as though she were more aware of her goal than her surroundings. It was the detachment of one who was conscious of seeing more in life than others see, and when in pursuit of her reforms, others saw this detached superiority in her and they found her more than a little exasperating. She never learned the dimensions of the national stage on which she was this night about to make her entrance. She had reached her full maturity and there was little that even war could do to change her nature, though her war work brought some of her traits, and not always the most pleasant ones, into sharp relief. But the war left a permanent scar, for it taught her the bitter lesson of her own inadequacy. Miss Dix had great courage, but the most courageous attitude of her life was that with which she met the knowledge of her own failure, and at the end, when the whole of her endeavor lay exposed to the pitiless light of history, she uttered a cry from the heart, "It is not the work by which I would be judged."

On the night of April 19th, however, this already-too-tired woman was still confident of herself. And she was dreaming of great things, for she was about to propose that she carry forward in this war the work which Nightingale had begun in the Crimea. When she arrived at the War Department building she found it crowded with officers. One imagines their look of surprise and curiosity as they flattened themselves against the walls of the narrow corridors to let the somberly dressed woman pass. She went at once to see Surgeon R. C. Wood who, in the absence of the old Surgeon General Thomas Lawson, who was on his deathbed, had become Acting Surgeon General.

Wood was a much harassed man, facing the crisis with an inadequately staffed Medical Department, which in peace times had consisted of thirty surgeons and eighty-three assistant surgeons. Of these, three surgeons and twenty-one assistants resigned to join the Confederacy and three more were subsequently dismissed for disloyalty. Most of this small force was stationed at distant army posts, and at headquarters in Washington, the staff consisted of four surgeons and three clerks. All the bureaucratic

procedures of the Department were intricate and antiquated, but Wood was less concerned with unsnarling red tape than with inspecting the knots to be sure they held secure.

Miss Dix told Wood that she proposed to organize under the official auspices of the War Department, an Army Nursing Corps made up of women volunteers, with herself at their head. Perhaps Wood realized the potency of the Nightingale legend, or perhaps Miss Dix helped him to understand that women could not be prevented from nursing the wounded and that the nursing should be subject to regulation. Wood obviously believed that Miss Dix' work of reform in the insane asylums qualified her for this new undertaking without, perhaps, stopping to consider that her past work had not required organizing and administrative ability, which would be of the first importance in creating an army corps of nurses. He accepted her proposal at once, though official confirmation had to await the action of the Secretary of War. When Miss Dix left the War Department that night, she faced a task as difficult as any which had ever fallen to the lot of a woman in wartime. She was far from realizing its magnitude.

NOTES

[1] Frank Moore, *Rebellion Record* (C. P. Putnam, New York, 1861-1866), I, p. 38.

[2] L. P. Brockett, M. D. and Mary C. Vaughan, *Woman's Work in the Civil War* (Ziegler, McCurdy & Co., Boston, 1867), pp. 241-250.

4

FEAR IN WASHINGTON

————————————★————————————

CHRONOLOGY

April 20   Miss Dorothea Dix started her work as Superintendent of Army Nurses, and Miss Clara Barton began her work among the soldiers. A committee from Richmond offered General Scott command of the forces of Virginia. Confederates seized the United States arsenal at Liberty, Missouri. Confederate Provisional Congress met at Montgomery, Alabama. Railroad communications were severed between Washington and the North, leaving the city isolated and without mail or newspapers.

April 21   Federal Government seized the Philadelphia and Baltimore Railroad. Rioters in Baltimore cut off the telegraph communication between Washington and the North. Flour in Washington, $7.50 a barrel. Norfolk navy yard destroyed. Troops sent from Chicago to establish a base at Cairo, Illinois.

April 22   The New York Seventh Regiment joined the Massachusetts Eighth Regiment at Annapolis. Arsenals at Fayetteville, North Carolina, and at Napoleon, Arkansas, seized by the Confederates.

April 24   Virginia proclaimed a member of the Confederacy. Fort Smith, Arkansas, seized by the Confederates.

April 25   The Seventh New York Regiment reached Washington.

————————————★————————————

The dwellers in Manhattan's isle saw
bloody Treason stalk,
Like the deep growl of thunder answered
the sons of York
—Anonymous

FEW IN WASHINGTON believed that the night of the nineteenth of April would pass without a Confederate attack on the city. The Secretary of War spent the night on a couch in the War Department, and many through fear or with last minute preparations to make did not go to bed at all. When morning dawned without the expected attack having taken place, there was almost a sense of anticlimax, but the city was in a state of siege, for not only were the rail connections with the North cut off, but there were no newspapers and no mail. The sense of isolation seemed to grow throughout the day.

There had been another wave of panic among those Southerners who still remained and the transportation facilities being overcrowded, many departed on foot. A few stayed stubbornly on, confident that the capital would soon be in Confederate hands, but these were mostly men, truculent in manner and easily identified as Southerners by their long hair. The city teemed with spies who had no trouble sending out their messages, for the Post Office Department, amazingly enough, did not discontinue mail service to the Southern states until the twenty-seventh of May, and all a secret agent had to do to send a dispatch was to buy a stamp.

Miss Dix, who was without fear and who scorned panic, set out to make a survey of the medical facilities of the city—a task which could not have occupied her long, since they were almost nonexistent. In theory, each of the volunteer and militia regiments, which would shortly arrive, would bring with them surgeons, medical supplies and hospital tents. It seems not to have greatly disturbed the officers of the Medical Department, if they gave it any thought at all, that civilian doctors in uniform could not be expected to understand the special problems of military medicine or the sanitation of camps. The *laissez-faire* policy of the Surgeon General's office toward the medical requirements of the new regiments was grounded on the belief—which was general throughout the War Department—that citizens in uniform could not be subjected to the same discipline as the Regular Army. No one, in fact, was quite sure how far the authority of the War Department extended over political soldiers and states' militia, and no one was anxious to trespass in the

shadowy realm of states' rights. This constituted an area of doubt which was to affect profoundly the conduct of the war in its early stages, and in the field of medicine the leaving of the new medical officers more or less to their own devices was to have disastrous results.

The Medical Department planned, however, to create a system of general hospitals, in Washington and throughout the North, which would care for cases which the regimental hospitals could not cope with, either for lack of facilities or because the regiment would be on the move. Some buildings in Washington were to be converted into general hospitals as soon as possible, and a small quantity of medical supplies had been ordered, though they had not arrived. It was with the general hospitals here and elsewhere that Miss Dix was to be concerned. They were to be staffed by her nurses, and to a large but undefined extent, their organization was in her hands.

While Miss Dix was going about the city, laying her plans, Clara Barton was enjoying the feeling of being more intensely alive than she had ever felt before. She thought the dirty, sprawling city "grand, noble, true and brave." She felt certain, like everyone else, that the Confederates would try to seize Washington and she wrote to a friend, "If it must be, let it come and when there is no longer a soldier's arm to raise the Stars and Stripes above our Capitol, may God give strength to mine." She was in an almost exalted state. "This conflict is one thing I've been waiting for . . . I'm well and strong and young—young enough to go to the front. If I can't be a soldier, I'll help soldiers."

Clara went to the Capitol to visit her friends in the Sixth Massachusetts Regiment, and she found the men lounging in the comfortable chairs in the Senate Chamber, or sprawled on the velvet carpeting. The weather had turned warm, the boys were suffering in long winter underwear, and all their baggage had been lost. She visited a while and then she went home to turn herself into a one-woman soldiers' aid society. She tore up sheets and towels to make handkerchiefs, she assembled baskets and filled them with everything she could lay hands on that she thought the men might want. That night, while Washington slept the restless sleep of fear, she must have worked on and on, happy, at last, with work to do and work to look forward to. She was already dedicated.

The next day, which was Sunday, enforced a degree of quiet on the war frenzied North, a pause which allowed time for reflection and stock-taking. People went to church and listened to sermons which dwelt on the need for strength, endurance and determination in wartime, so that, after this Sunday, there was no general return to war hysteria, and the passing

of that phase left the country hard with determination, men and women alike.

In Brooklyn that Sunday, Henry Ward Beecher read during the church service an appeal to the women of his congregation to prepare themselves to nurse the wounded.[1] There were many such appeals in these early days, from pulpit and press, but mainly they did more harm than good, for there were as yet no organizations ready to receive the volunteer nurses, and no hospitals in which they could work. Six women who had listened to an appeal made by Henry J. Raymond of the New York *Times* at the Cooper Institute did, in fact, manage to get to Washington where they stayed until their funds ran out and only one found work in a small-pox hospital.[2] They were among the first of an army of women who would shortly invade every hospital and military encampment in the land.

One of the astonishing facets of this astonishing war was the wide-spread and apparently spontaneous belief that women should, for the first time in history, carry the burden of wartime nursing in hospitals and camps. There were a few dissenters, mainly among men, who thought that a woman must sacrifice her modesty, if not her virtue, to become a nurse. Dr. Howe, Julia Ward Howe's husband, was one of them. He refused to let his wife do any more unconventional war work than the making of lint and bandages, and, toward the end, some hospital visiting, though it was he who, many years before, had encouraged the young Nightingale to take up a nursing career. When charged with inconsistency he justified his stand by saying that it was Miss Nightingale's not being married which made all the difference. He told his wife that, "if he had been engaged to Florence Nightingale, and had loved her ever so dearly, he would have given her up as soon as she commenced her career as a public woman." By "public woman" Dr. Howe seems to have meant any female who had any activities outside home and church, but Howe was trying hard to straddle two cultural epochs and his effort to keep a foot planted firmly in each made it impossible for him to take a step forward.

Washington, on this April Sunday, was a strangely silent city, and there was a sense of conspiracy going on behind the closed doors of the houses. In Baltimore, the mob was still in control, and the telegraph, the last link with the outside world, ceased to function. The capital was without knowledge of what was being done elsewhere to save the city. The silence and isolation had a nightmare quality. Citizens, government and White House began to sink into the apathy of enforced inaction. Crowds stood still at the railroad station, gazing into the distance, emo-

tion narrowed down to intense longing for the arrival of more troops.

Even then, unknown to Lincoln, the fashionable New York Seventh Regiment, its knapsacks packed with sandwiches from Delmonico's, was in seasick discomfort on the high seas, bound for Washington, via Annapolis, ignorant that the Annapolis branch of the railroad had also been destroyed.

All that day, wild rumors flew around the city of a large army rapidly approaching, and so close that the advance scouts had been seen. General Scott, torpid with age like a turtle on a log, planned the defense of the city in the form of a retreat, from building to building, street by street, working it out in minute detail, like a war game. In preparation for the street fighting, ten-foot-high barricades had been built on Capitol Hill out of the iron sheets intended for the still unfinished dome. To those around him, the President seemed calm, and it was in these days of trial that the city began to be aware of the stature of the uncouth Westerner who was all but a stranger.

Another night closed in on the city. A light burned late in Clara Barton's room, for she was packing more baskets for her boys, and she was happy. Miss Dix' indefatigable pen flew over her paper, writing, writing, writing in her hurried, nervous script.

Little happened the next day in the city which was beleaguered by an imaginary army. Acting Surgeon General Wood succumbed to sudden panic for fear the supply of lint and bandages he had ordered from New York would not arrive soon enough. He thought he saw a crisis building up, like a storm cloud in the sky, and he ordered his carriage and rushed off to ask Miss Dix to help him. Miss Dix was not at home, but the little incident throws a startling light on the antiquated procedures of the Medical Department.

The next day Wood wrote Miss Dix a letter,[3] "Dear Madam: I called to see you yesterday and also spoke to Mr. Cameron. A very large quantity of medical supplies has been ordered from New York and will ultimately come through. We are deficient in lint and bandages. I would most respectfully suggest that you institute primary measures for those important items of surgical necessity. Most respectfully, Your obliging servant, R. C. Wood, Acting Surgeon General."

That phrase, resounding with hollowness, "institute primary measures," was part of the bureaucracy argot of the day. Miss Dix translated it into an appeal to the self-mobilized army of war workers. The blockade of Washington was still effective, though a belated mail did reach the city Tuesday, and subsequently, there were various roundabout ways

of communicating with the loyal states. In time, Miss Dix' appeal was answered, and so bountifully that she was forced to acquire a warehouse in which to store the supplies which were addressed to her.

General Wood had been chivied into unusual activity since the nineteenth of April, but he found time to take up the question of Miss Dix and her proposed group of nurses with Secretary of War Cameron. The Secretary responded with a most astonishing document:

Document 213

TO VOLUNTEER NURSES

War Department, Military Hospital

Be it known to all whom it may concern that the free services of Miss D. L. Dix are accepted by the War Department, and that she will give at all times all necessary aid in organizing military hospitals for the care of all sick and wounded soldiers, aiding the chief surgeons by supplying nurses and substantial means for the comfort and relief of the suffering; also, that she is fully authorized to receive, control and disburse special supplies bestowed by individuals or associations for the comfort of their friends or the citizen soldiers from all parts of the United States.

Given under the seal of the War Department this twenty-third day of April, in the year of our Lord one thousand eight hundred and sixty one, and of the independence of the United States the eighty-fifth.

Simon Cameron, Secretary of War

Literally interpreted, this document gave Miss Dix unlimited powers in the organization of military hospitals, put her in control of the entire nursing personnel and made her the receiving agency for all supplies sent by volunteer war workers. Florence Nightingale herself had no such sweeping authority, and it went far beyond the power which Miss Dix had wanted.

Miss Dix' personal commission did not emerge from the slow-grinding mill of the War Department until the tenth of June. By that time, control of hospital organization was slipping out of her hands and much of her paper power over supplies vanished when the President activated the Sanitary Commission. There was only one clause of the original document which the War Department consistently attempted to uphold (and which Miss Dix fought with fury to uphold) and that was the one which gave her control of women nurses in Army hospitals. The struggle over

this control was to become a minor war in itself, with fierce partisanships, skirmishes, retreats, triumphs and bitterness.

Some of the officers and wounded men of the Sixth Massachusetts Regiment went to call on the President, and he said to them, "I don't believe in any North. The Seventh Regiment is a myth. Rhode Island is not known in our geography any longer. *You* are the only Northern realities." Now and again the President would wander alone down to the gates of the White House, or out into the streets. Often he crossed the lawn by the gravel path which led to the War Department where the telegraph room alone was silent in the midst of activity. Once, aimlessly loitering by himself, he came to the city's arsenal, found no guard present, tried the doors and discovered they were unlocked.

Had Lincoln but known it, the Seventh New York Regiment, in company with the Massachusetts Eighth Regiment, were beginning their march from Annapolis to Washington. The Seventh Regiment, composed of wealthy young sophisticates, was sometimes referred to by less gilt-edged organizations as the "kid glove regiment," and they had not lost the fine sheen of fashion in the seasick days at sea. The Eighth had many mechanics and railroad men in the ranks. There was instant cordiality between the two regiments and somehow the decision was made between them not merely to go to Washington but to repair the railroad as they went. Marylanders had dismantled the locomotives to prevent their use by Union troops. A Massachusetts soldier surveyed the scattered parts and said, "I made this engine and I can put it together again," which, to the admiration of the New York Seventh, he proceeded to do.

This fine gesture of repairing the railroad delayed the start for the capital where people might have preferred to see them a little sooner. The dashing Seventh was wildly cheered by the ladies. Washington society became gay once more, but it was the hectic, overstimulated gaiety of wartime. Rail communication via Baltimore was not restored until the thirteenth of May, but the arrival of the Seventh was followed by other regiments in such number that the flood of troops reminded one observer of taking the bung out of a full barrel. A semi-circle of white tent camps grew up around Washington and the volunteers took possession of the city as surely as though they had been an invading army.

Outside of Washington, there was no paralysis of thought and action like that in the capital city. All through the North incompetent drill sergeants were yelling themselves hoarse and citizen soldiers were learning how to make tent pegs hold firm in the spring mud. The Western

theatre had come alive, and in Chicago new troops had taken the oath, saying in unison, "I do solemnly swear, in the presence of the Almighty God, that I will faithfully support the Constitution of the United States and the State of Illinois. So help me God." Then they had gone off with bands playing and flowers tied to their muskets, to occupy the dismal little town of Cairo just before the Confederates had the same idea. Cairo was of military importance because it was at the joining of the Mississippi and Ohio Rivers and the southernmost point of the Illinois Central Railroad, but it was a mudhole which Anthony Trollope had called with feeling, "The most desolate of all the towns of America."

And all over the North the women were busy, almost feverishly so, to an orchestration of whirring sewing machines and the chop-chop of heavy blades cutting material. They were turning out hundreds of articles, some of them as fanciful as their ideas of war. There were pillows stuffed with milkweed down and quilts with lines of poetry embroidered on the squares. But about the usefulness of such items as these the women were beginning to feel a little uncertainty, like a cold draft in the great halls where they worked. The uncertainty was to grow, until the women war workers sent representatives to the camps to find out what the soldiers really needed—but that was to happen a little later. At this time, two weeks after the first gun was fired, they were thinking of the men, not as an army, or even as regiments, but as individuals with names like John and Hal and Jo, who had become strangely transfigured because they had gone to war.

NOTES

[1] Mary A. Gardner Holland, *Our Army Nurses* (B. Wilkins & Co., Boston, 1895), p. 167.

[2] *Ibid.* Pp. 455-58.

[3] R. C. Wood to Dorothea Dix, Surgeon General's Office, April 23rd, 1861. (Letterbook, 1861), p. 2.

5

THE WOMEN MOBILIZE

————————————— ★ —————————————

1861

April 15   From this date, Soldiers' Aid Societies were organized throughout the North.

April 17   Cleveland Soldiers' Home established to care for the disabled.

April 19   Miss Dix appointed unofficially to head an army corps of nurses.

April 23   Miss Dix' services accepted formally by the Secretary of War.

April 25   A meeting at the New York Infirmary for Women and Children where the first move was made toward coordinating women's work.

April 29   A meeting at Cooper Institute of between three and four thousand women. The "Woman's Central Association for Relief" was organized, out of which grew the Sanitary Commission.

May 13   Dr. Henry W. Bellows, Dr. Elisha Harris, Dr. W. H. Van Buren and Dr. Jacob Harsen, representatives of the affiliated women's organizations, left for Washington, arriving the following day.

May 15   Surgeon General Thomas Lawson died and Dr. C. A. Finley became Surgeon General.

June 9   The Secretary of War issued an order sanctioning the Sanitary Commission.

June 13   The Sanitary Commission's plan of organization approved by
President Lincoln over the signature of Secretary of War
Cameron.

———————————————————— ★ ————————————————————

The daughters enter into the Council.
—Ancient Hebrew

WHEN THE WOMEN all over the land turned away from the railroad
stations to face their empty lives, there began another mobilization, the
mobilization of the army of war workers. It was remarkable in that no
proclamation had summoned them and the more remarkable in that
there was no precedent for the widespread response to the self-imposed
call. Some hundreds of thousands of women (their number cannot be
calculated) formed themselves into groups, which they called Soldiers'
Aid Societies, of which, at one time or another, there were in existence
about ten thousand.

"It is not unusual for women of all countries to weep and to work for
those who encounter the perils of war," wrote Bellows, who loved to
adorn his style with literary curlicues. "But the American woman, after
giving up, with a principled alacrity, to the ranks of the gathering and
advancing army, their husbands and sons, their brothers and lovers, proceeded to organize. . . ."[1] The key word is "organize" for it was that
which was new and amazing and that which established the pattern of
women's war work for generations to come. The aid societies came into
existence with startling speed.

The President's Proclamation, calling out the States' militia, was issued
on April 15th. The Bridgeport aid society was founded April 15th, the
Bunker Hill society of Charleston, Massachusetts, on April 20th, the
Cleveland society on that same day, the Concord society on April 23rd,
the Philadelphia society on April 26th. These are only selected inci-
dences, for during these early days germination was going on in many
places.

The Concord society met wherever it could for a time and then proudly
established itself in permanent quarters over the engine house, a Mrs.
Simon Brown sacrificing her parlor carpet to keep the cold drafts from
coming through the floor. Louisa Alcott became an active worker after a

brief rebellion against her fate in being a woman, which took the form of a good cry on the motherly bosom of the attic ragbag. On the first day of May, there were 200 women present at the meeting (in her enthusiasm Louisa recorded the number as 300) out of a total town population of 2232 people. The regular members numbered 140, among them Mrs. Emerson and her two daughters, Mrs. Alcott, Mrs. Horace Mann and Mrs. Frank Sanborn, wife of the schoolmaster who had befriended John Brown. About a dozen men were members also, and they took charge of packing and shipping the boxes. After the shooting began, the ladies were proud to learn that their bandages were in great demand by the surgeons, who called them "Concords," and there is a brief glimpse of Mrs. Emerson scurrying off to Boston in search of English pins (which did not rust) with which to fasten the rolled bandages. The Concord society was not greatly different from other societies everywhere in the North, except for the echoing names of its members and perhaps for a greater awareness of history which led them to preserve the records of the society for posterity.[2]

The Soldiers' Aid Societies came into being smoothly for the framework already existed throughout the country in the sewing circles, church societies and town meetings. "Soldiers' Aid Society" was sometimes merely a new name for an old organization, and though these existing groups were barely a skeleton of the structure, because of them a good many women had already become practiced in the difficult art of working together for a common aim. Concerted effort, for this nucleus, was already natural and easy.

In having this structure to build on, the North was more fortunate than the South. There, several conditions proved a handicap, among them the distance which separated the plantations, the lack of a large middle class accustomed to work and the difference in the status of women. The novelist, Mrs. E. D. E. N. Southworth wrote in 1855 that "sewing circles and other useful Yankee inventions" were unknown in the South,[3] a statement which was almost, if not quite, literally true. When war came, soldiers' aid societies sprang up rapidly in the South but not in the same proportionate number and not so smoothly as in the North, and there never developed a coordinating central control comparable to the Sanitary Commission.

Since there had never before been a large army of women determined to participate in a war, the techniques, the inter-meshing organization and the basic philosophy of war work had still to evolve. There was general confusion about the extent of the government's responsibility for uniforming and equipping the new troops (a confusion in which

both the State and Federal governments shared) and some of the societies made uniforms, some, hospital garments, and some took contracts from the government for various items of clothing. Little bags called "comforts" in the East and "hussies" (short for "housewives") in the West, were made literally by the thousand. They contained needles, pins, buttons, quinine, tape and any other item the feminine mind might fancy. They were enthusiastically received by the men in camp, and on Saturdays whole regiments might be seen, their "hussies" open beside them, industriously preparing themselves for the routine Sunday inspection.

Sometimes the work of the aid societies was done with a speed which would have been a credit to a factory. Miss Dix appealed to the ladies of Boston to produce five hundred hospital shirts. Her request was received on a Thursday (May 1st). By Friday night the shirts were on their way to Washington.

One of the major industries of the aid societies was the making of lint and bandages, and ragbags were ransacked for soft pieces of old linen. The bandages were cut in strips, rolled, and fastened. There was a universal belief in the virtues of lint as a material for packing wounds, though actually its chief function was to transmit infection. Lint was made by unraveling the material, or by scraping it with a sharp knife blade or the edge of a piece of glass, and all over the North, in parlors and meeting halls, the scratching scrapers filled the air with fluff. Machines were invented for bandage rolling and lint scraping, but after a time surgeons lost their enthusiasm for lint, and its manufacture was almost abandoned.

The women of the South also scraped lint in prodigious quantities. Cotton wool had not been invented and for various reasons unprocessed cotton could not be used. When the shortage of fabric grew acute, bandages were washed and used again, and lint was salvaged by baking it in an oven, and so by accident, they were more or less sterilized.[4]

The ambition of every aid society was to own at least one sewing machine. It was, in fact, the greatest weapon of the home front, and the output of some truly mechanized sewing circles was astounding. To make a soldier's shirt by hand required about fourteen hours of steady work, but the same kind of shirt could be made on a foot-treadle machine in a little over an hour. Of the two popular makes of sewing machines, Wheeler and Wilson, and Singer, there were about 38,000 in use at the start of the war, and the demand was so great that the number rose to around 63,000 before the war had come to an end.

To the camps which were growing up all over the North went boxes,

crates and barrels in incredible numbers, containing jars of "jell," fresh eggs packed in oats, butter wrapped in damp leaves, homemade bread, pies, pickles, sauerkraut, fried chicken. One of the amazing things about these early days is how the express company managed to handle it all and to locate individual addresses in the confusion of the new camps. Eggs and jelly jars were prone to break, chickens to spoil, butter to melt in the sun. When some stinking, leaking box was dumped outside a tent, the recipient wrote home describing the ruin, so it was not long before the shipment of food was given up as impractical.

There were other mistakes, the result of zeal accompanied by total ignorance of what the boys in the camps required. The greatest of them was a form of headdress for the soldiers, called a havelock. This was a cap with a piece of white material stitched to the back and sides which hung down to the shoulders. The havelock seems to have been inspired by a romantic article about General Havelock, fussy little martinet hero of the Indian Mutiny, whose troops wore them as a protection against the sun. The ladies reasoned that since the army was going south, the havelocks would be indispensable, and many thousands of them were turned out. The havelock mania spread like an epidemic, and "havelock societies" were created to manufacture nothing else.

It was about the time the havelock mania was at its height that doubts began to assail the women workers concerning the true value of some of their efforts. There were also some disturbing reports of the misappropriation of hospital supplies; and all over the country, at about the same time, the aid societies decided to send their own inspectors to the camps to see what the situation really was and to make reports—a procedure which was so successful that it was continued, in one form or another, until the end of the war.

Mary Livermore, whose good judgment and executive ability were already making her a leader among the war workers, was one of those selected to visit the camps. There she found that the soldiers had christened the havelocks "the white nightcaps" and that they tore them up to use for rags to clean their guns, cleaned frying pans with them or used them to cover the mud of their floorless tents. Then the Nineteenth Illinois Regiment ended the havelock craze almost overnight. A contingent of women bearing food baskets came to visit the regiment. It was the opportunity the Nineteenth had been waiting for. Mary Livermore was present and saw the Nineteenth scrambling out of their tents to greet the ladies *en havelock,* but wearing them as turbans, sunbonnets, nightcaps, in every absurd way but the one for which they had been intended. The

ladies gasped. A great shout of laughter went up from the officers and then the ladies began to laugh too. They laughed until they had to wipe tears from their eyes, and, still laughing at the memory, they told their friends in the soldiers' aid societies. There were similar incidents in most of the camps. The havelock was no more.

In Philadelphia, the ladies discovered a new sort of war work. A train arrived with ninety of Sherman's men en route for Washington. When the train stopped in Market Street, between Fifteenth and Sixteenth, some ladies brought the soldiers bread, meat pies and cakes. Before anyone knew what was happening, a large crowd of women and pretty girls from the neighborhood were vying with each other to feed the soldiers. Some of them had taken the family dinner off the stove, and storekeepers joined in the crowd, carrying baskets filled from their shelves. The scene was a bedlam of shouting and laughing. Men leaned out of the train windows and girls stood on tiptoes while hoop skirts swayed dangerously. The men said they were thirsty, and a bevy of girls rushed for water, which may not have been precisely what the men had in mind. Cigars followed, and the party ended with cheers for the girls. It had all been such a success that a permanent canteen was established which continued to operate until the end of the war.

Preparing a son for a war which would last three months, or a very little longer, was, except for the emotions of parting and the remote possibility of danger, not so different from preparing a boy to take part in the school play. There were the costumes to make, the parting injunctions, the pride and hope. It was understandable under the circumstances that in the early days the women worked mainly for individuals, men who belonged to them or men whom they knew by name, or at most for a company which came from their home town. It would not be long before women everywhere would enlarge the purpose of their work to include all the soldiers from a certain state, but they were a long way, even then, from the final, mature concept of working for all the soldiers, without discrimination, for one army and for one nation.

The change came when the representatives of the aid societies went to the hospitals to distribute various articles which often made the difference between hardship and comfort to the sick and wounded boys. The supplies might be intended only for the men of a certain state or a certain regiment, but the men and boys from Maine and Wisconsin, from Ohio and Rhode Island, from every loyal state and from the Confederacy lay side by side, and the woman in charge of the gifts would go slowly through a long ward, singling out these men, while the others watched

her with disappointment plain on their faces. Some of the women could not do it. Many times it happened that the suffering and the need broke her down so that she disregarded her instructions and gave to all. Then she would return to the aid society and beg that there be no more discrimination in the face of universal need.

The change in attitude was deeply significant. In putting nation before state, the women were developing, for the first time in the country's history, a feeling of belonging to one country. Men also were arriving at a new understanding of the true meaning of a central government, though by a different route, but for the women the road to national consciousness lay through the narrow aisles between the hospital cots.

On Thursday, the twenty-fifth of April, the first step was taken to bring together the mushroom-growth aid societies and to organize their work into a concerted, nationwide plan. The end was great but the beginning was insignificant. On this day Dr. Elizabeth Blackwell called a meeting of managers of the New York Woman's Infirmary to discuss that already burning question, the need for women nurses in the war.

Elizabeth was a little person with neatly parted dark hair and one disfigured eye, blinded by an infection during her internship, or the equivalent of an internship in a Paris hospital. Her good eye had the direct, searching look of the clinic, her hands were precise. She had traveled a hard road since her first appearance in the Geneva Medical School had been greeted with derisive yells by the male students, and her manner—in fact her whole outlook on life—was reserved and thoughtful. She considered herself the trustee of the professional standing of women in medicine. And rightly, for the little white-coated figure was watched by the whole profession, and her chief concern, along with the quality of her work, was to create an unchallengeable standard for the women doctors who would follow her.

The Woman's Infirmary, which is still in operation—now known as the New York Infirmary and located on Stuyvesant Square—had been started in 1853 by Dr. Elizabeth and her red-haired sister, Dr. Emily Blackwell. It was not Dr. Elizabeth's intention to open the meeting to the public, but Henry Raymond, indefatigable patriotic writer for the New York Times, put a notice of it in the paper. The result was indicative of the anxiety of women to take part in the war, for not only was the Infirmary crowded to capacity, but a queue formed in the street.

Elizabeth, who knew all too well the jealousy men doctors felt of women who entered their profession, was anxious to avoid friction, and to this end she kept herself in the background, not only in these

early days, but throughout the war. Her decision certainly had elements of wisdom, but perhaps it was not ultimately wise, for her intelligence, experience, administrative ability, and even her close friendship with Miss Nightingale suggest that she might have been a better choice to head a wartime nursing organization than the wholly inexperienced Miss Dix.

There were a number of men at the meeting in the Infirmary, among them Henry Whitney Bellows, Unitarian minister and champion of many causes. Bellows was a fluent talker whom some found charming, others irritating. His energy was boundless, and his restless interest in human affairs carried him into the fields of sociology, sanitation and various reform movements. He was one who, if he did not love his fellow men, assuredly loved to be with them, and he became one of the founders of the Union League, Century and Harvard Clubs. He had a knack for success and a knack for being in the public eye. It was the most natural thing in the world for such a man to attend a meeting where plans were to be made for women's participation in the war. He was no businessman and no organizer, but he liked the atmosphere of business and the foment of organization, and he had a gift for making people work together which made him welcome wherever plans were forming. The meeting at the Woman's Infirmary was his element. He could be counted upon to take the broadest possible view and to include the widest possible territory—qualities which were to have an important effect on women's activities in the war. Bellow's instinct for scope, plus Elizabeth Blackwell's practical grasp of the problems involved, were an ideal combination.

Another man at that meeting was Dr. Elisha Harris, a physician with a positive passion for sanitation in all its aspects. He was more aware than most people of the problems of army sanitation as illustrated by the tragedies of the Crimean War, and he was deeply concerned lest those tragedies be repeated in this war. The meeting, with its unexpectedly large attendance, resulted in the drafting of a letter for the newspapers, defining women's war work, and calling for a larger meeting on April 29th. The letter is credited by Stillé, the contemporary recorder of these events, to the Rev. Dr. Bellows, and the style, the wordiness and grand scale of the project it outlines are all characteristic of this espouser of causes. But there is certainly more than a trace of Elizabeth Blackwell's experience and intelligence in it also, and through a phrase or two we surely catch a glimpse of that enthusiastic sanitarian, Dr. Harris. The letter is one of the most remarkable documents of the war, a milestone in the long history of philanthropic effort.

". . . Numerous societies, working without concert, organization or head—without any positive instructions as to the immediate future wants of the army—are liable to waste their enthusiasm in disproportionate efforts, to overlook some claims, and overdo others, while they give unnecessary trouble in official quarters, by the variety and irregularity of their proffers of help or their inquiries for guidance.

"As no existing organization has a right to claim precedence over any other, or could properly assume to lead . . . it is proposed . . . that the women of New York should meet in Cooper Institute, on Monday next at eleven o'clock A.M. . . . to appoint a General Committee, with power to organize the benevolent purposes of all into a common movement.

". . . The form which woman's benevolence has already taken . . . is, first, the contribution of labor, skill and money in the preparation of lint, bandages, and other stores . . . second, the offer of personal services as nurses.

"In regard to the first, it is important to obtain and disseminate exact official information as to the nature and variety of wants of the army . . . so as to avoid superfluity in some things and deficiency in others; and . . . to come to a careful and thorough understanding with the official head of the Medical Staff, through a Committee . . . To this Committee should be assigned the duty of conferring with other associations in other parts of the country and . . . through the press, to keep women of the loyal states everywhere informed how their efforts may be most wisely and economically employed and their contributions . . . concentrated at New York . . .

"In regard to the second form of benevolence—the offer of personal service as nurses—it is felt that the public needs much enlightenment, and the overflowing zeal and sympathy of the women of the nation, a careful channel, not only to prevent waste of time and effort, but to save embarrassment to the official staff . . . The result of the experiences in the Crimean War has been to prove the total uselessness of any but picked and skilled women . . .

"A central organization is wanted, therefore, to which all those desiring to go as nurses may be referred, where a Committee of Examiners . . . may . . . decide upon the fitness of the candidate. Those accepted should then at once be put under competent instruction (for which it is understood a thorough school will be opened at once) . . .

". . . many may be rich and many poor . . . Some may wish to go at their own charge, and others will require to be aided.

. . . But the best nurses should be sent irrespective of these distinctions, as only the best are economical on any terms.

"It will appear that, without a central organization . . . there can be no efficiency, system, or discipline in this important matter of nurses . . . and there can be no organization, except it originates in the common will and becomes the genuine representative of all the women of New York and of all existing associations having this kind of aid in view . . . all the women of New York, and of the country . . . will have a direct opportunity of giving support. . . ."[5]

There followed the signatures of ninety-one women, most of them prominent, a number of them wealthy, but Dr. Elizabeth's name is not there and Dr. Emily's name is not there.

This letter, written ten days after the President's call to arms, encompasses the whole modern concept of volunteer aid in wartime. It was directed to the women of New York, but the wording is in effect an appeal to loyal women war workers to link their groups and societies into a unified endeavor. "Our plans," wrote Bellows with characteristic self-satisfaction, "have a breadth and height and depth which no military philanthropic undertaking ever had, since the world began." Dr. Bellows liked to stand where he could contemplate his horizons stretching into infinity, but his statement is literally true.

The letter points out the need to coordinate the womens' work with the supply and relief work of the Army—a long forward step since no such need had as yet been generally recognized, but it betrays a naive ignorance of Army titles and organization and makes the still more naive assumption that the Army would be willing to cooperate. New York was chosen as the central depot where the output of the volunteer societies would be collected because access to Washington was at that time virtually impossible. As the war work broadened, the plan for one central depot was abandoned in favor of a number of storage and distributing centers nearer the widespread scenes of action.

The influence of Nightingale is obvious, especially in the passages about nursing, an influence of which those present at the meeting must have been strongly aware through the medium of her long-time friend, Dr. Elizabeth. Apparently the meeting was ignorant of Miss Dix' appointment, but these women (or at least the Blackwell sisters) seem to have had a better grasp of the problem of organizing a corps of nurses than Miss Dix, who was operating on the principle that, aside from the nursing staff, she herself was all the organization that would be needed.

Miss Dix' plan did not include preliminary training of her nurses, though she often invited her novitiates to spend a night or two at her house where they received what amounted to a brief indoctrination concerned more with deportment than technique.

The letter, however, shows a real understanding of the need for some sort of training, and in these passages Elizabeth Blackwell seems to speak. At this time Elizabeth still hoped to establish a nurses training school in connection with the Infirmary, and this project may have been synonymous with the school mentioned in the letter. In the end, a plan for a special school was abandoned and the nursing candidates, selected by Elizabeth, went either to her Infirmary or to Bellevue Hospital for a short period of work in the wards. By modern standards this training amounted to little, but it insured, at the least, some experience. After training, the nurses were under the direction of Miss Dix, for Elizabeth, perhaps because she preferred to work in obscurity, was one of the few to whom the head of the army nursing corps was willing to relinquish even a modicum of her authority.

The meeting at Cooper Institute, which took place on the twenty-ninth of April, attracted between three and four thousand women, eager for guidance in their war work, Dr. D. D. Field was in the chair and there were speeches by various prominent men on how women could serve in time of war. An organization, to be called "The Women's Central Association for Relief," was formed, which continued to meet and to work at the Institute throughout the war. Once more the Reverend Dr. Bellows was in the thick of things, drafting a Constitution for the new organization.

It was agreed that the first essential was to establish working relations with the medical branch of the Army in order to find out what actually were the needs of the new troops. Accordingly, Bellows, as representing the Women's Central Relief Association, called on the Medical Purveyor of the Medical Department of New York. The Medical Purveyor was a Dr. Satterlee, old-time soldier, thoroughly incrusted with army tradition, deeply convinced that war was a soldier's business and that any interference from civilians constituted unwarranted meddling.

The army man and the charming Reverend seem to have had a stormy session. Satterlee stated flatly that the things the women were proposing to do could be of no sort of practical value to the army. Bellows attempted to present Satterlee with questions about the possible wants of the volunteer soldiers. Satterlee brushed them aside with the statement that he

did not think cooperation between the Medical Bureau and the ladies would be either possible or desirable.

This was the first contact between medical authority and organized volunteer workers and the army man made it clear that he thought "the zeal of the women and the activity of the men assisting them, superfluous, obtrusive and likely to grow troublesome. . . ." Bellows was not fitted either by character or by experience to deal with a man like Satterlee and the good Reverend caved in completely. He listened meekly to the voice of bureaucratic authority and rushed away to make a public statement that the plans of the women were "ill-advised and uncalled for."

Bellows' capitulation was ignominious, and the women would not accept it. They diagnosed Satterlee's attitude as a sample of bureaucratic obtuseness and decided to go over his head to the Surgeon General's Office in Washington, whereupon Bellows, like a weathercock, veered again. How he managed to keep in the good graces of the women is something of a mystery, but he shortly reappears, confidence restored, as one of the delegation bound for the nation's capital. The other members were Dr. Harris, Dr. Van Buren, representing the "Physicians and Surgeons of New York" and Dr. Jacob Harsen, representing "the Lint and Bandage Association." The women had chosen well, for these were all distinguished men, well known in Washington. They boarded the train on the fifteenth of May and arrived the next day.

On that long trip there had been ample time for talk. Before the train pulled into the station these men had clarified their position in their own minds, and since Bellows was one of their number, there was nothing narrow or limited about their views. The delegation descended from the train, not merely a group of men charged with seeing how the work of Northern women could be made effective, but determined to put into operation an American Sanitary Commission.

Just whose idea it was to transform the project into a Sanitary Commission is not clear. Bellows and Harris seem to have discussed the need for such a Commission sometime previously, so that with them, at least, the idea was not altogether new. As the plan emerged, there was to be a Commission somewhat on the British lines, but dedicated primarily to measures which would prevent or reduce illness and hardship among the troops—to care for a soldier in health as well as in illness. Such a concept was of course foreign to the thinking of the Surgeon General's Office where the ancient belief was still in force that a medical officer's duties did not begin until after a soldier was wounded or had contracted some disease and that the government had but slight responsibility

for his rehabilitation. Dr. Bellows and his associates believed that the new Commission should be largely composed of civilians and that to be effective, they must be endowed with authority to enforce acceptance of their recommendations. With the broad outlines of these plans agreed on, the delegation was ready to propose them to the Acting Surgeon General and to the Secretary of War. The members of the self-appointed, and not yet officially recognized, Sanitary Commission arrived in Washington on May 16th. They went first to visit General Scott in the hope that they could persuade the old gentleman to eliminate from the volunteer army the large number of physically unfit. The physical examination of the applicants for enlistment had been cursory, or nonexistent, and those who had proved unequal to soldiering were now a burden on the government. General Scott listened courteously, but again the barrier of states' rights was in the way, and no one was quite sure whether federal authority extended to the discharge of state militia soldiers for reasons of physical disability. The delegation received assurances, however, that some action would be taken, but in the end little was accomplished, for it was feared that the sudden discharge of so many men would alarm the country.

The delegation went next to call on Acting Surgeon General Wood and outlined to him the reasons underlying the need for a Sanitary Commission. They were again given the courteous attention due to distinguished citizens. Wood, however, was not willing to acknowledge that the Surgeon General's Office needed any outside help, and he assured the delegation that the Medical Department could be expanded to meet all needs. The delegation was equally convinced that the Medical Department was pitifully inadequate, and nothing that its members had so far heard indicated that the Surgeon General's Office was even remotely aware of that fact. They had the uncomfortable feeling that they were regarded as impractical visionaries who were attempting to use the war emergency for purposes of social reform. Nevertheless, they succeeded in winning Wood over to the extent that he wrote to the Secretary of War endorsing in principle the delegation's plan. It was not a victory but an example of the ancient army technique of "buck passing."

The delegation also wrote to the Secretary of War. They began by stating the crucial fact that: "The present is essentially a people's war," and pointed out that a war of that nature required "organized popular participation." They stated that: "We (the American people) wish to prevent the evils that England and France could only mitigate and deplore . . ." They included their own endorsement of the use of women

as nurses in Army hospitals. The letter to Secretary of War Cameron was based on the premise, already presented to General Wood, that the work of a Sanitary Commission should be preventive, and its purpose to forestall the ills which had overtaken great armies in the past. Pointing out that no provisions were being made to care for the soldier's health, but only for his sickness, the delegates asserted that a Sanitary Commission must be endowed with authority to make its recommendations effective.

There followed a time during which the delegation waited anxiously, while government lapsed into a devastating bureaucratic silence. The plan was now being considered by the higher echelons where no one seemed to understand what the delegation had in mind. Some officials, Stillé records, "more than insinuated that the scheme was a cunning device to gain power for selfish ends." Lincoln did not question the good intentions of the delegation, but he thought a Sanitary Commission might prove to be "a fifth wheel to the coach." There were hours of waiting in anterooms, hours spent in trying explanation and argument.

The women in New York, who had sent this delegation, were kept constantly informed about the turn of events, and they too waited anxiously. Dr. Bellows began to waver once more and Mary Livermore thought that, "But for the zeal, intelligence and earnestness of his numerous women constituents, it is more than probable that Dr. Bellows would have retreated before the rebuffs and hinderances opposed to his humane efforts."

Surgeon General Lawson, who had been in the service for forty-eight years, had died on the fifteenth of May. Wood had hoped to succeed him as Surgeon General, but until Wood was officially appointed there was necessarily an element of uncertainty in the dealings of the Surgeon General's Office with the Sanitary Commission delegation. Wood did not receive the appointment, and in the midst of the delegation's uncertainties, Dr. Clement A. Finley became Surgeon General. General Finley was sixty-four years old, a white-haired, whiskered, red-cheeked military man who did not care either for reforms in Army medicine or for civilian interference in Army matters, and who was said to be opposed to women nurses in Army hospitals. He promptly informed the Secretary of War that he could not endorse the Acting Surgeon General's tentative approval of the plan for a Sanitary Commission.

The delegation continued to bring pressure on the Administration and eventually an agreement was reached which neither side regarded with satisfaction. The government, convinced that a Sanitary Commission could do no good, was primarily concerned that it should do no harm.

The authority which the delegation thought essential to the work of the Commission was denied, and the activities of the Commission were restricted to inspection and advice. The Commission was to work only among the volunteer troops and to have no duties in connection with the soldiers of the Regular Army.

There was obvious reluctance on the part of government to grant even this limited permission, and the withholding of any actual authority was a bitter blow to the members of the delegation. The restrictions seemed to make the work of the Sanitary Commission almost impossibly difficult, in that tact and diplomacy would be needed at every turn, and the good it could do would depend on the whim of commanding officers. That the Sanitary Commission not only succeeded in spite of these limitations, but succeeded brilliantly, is a tribute to the Commissioners and to their women backers.

On June 9th the Secretary of War issued a sanctioning order officially creating the Sanitary Commission and naming the men who were to act as Commissioners. The Commission was permitted to add other members at its own discretion. In the original form the list included one minister, one professor, four doctors (not all in active practice), and three military men. They were: Henry W. Bellows, D.D., A. D. Bache, L.L.D., Jeffries Wyman, M.D., W. H. Van Buren, M.D., Wolcott Gibbs, M.D., Samuel G. Howe, M.D., husband of Julia Ward Howe, R. C. Wood, Surgeon, G. W. Cullen, U.S.A., and A. E. Shiras, U.S.A.

Wyman declined to serve, and other members were appointed by the Commission from time to time, including Dr. Harris and Frederick Law Olmsted. Bellows became President and Olmsted, who must be given credit for much of the subsequent success of the Sanitary Commission, became Secretary.

The newly constituted Commission met in Washington on June 12th and adopted a plan of organization which had been prepared for them by Lincoln. This document, which was in effect a constitution, created two committees, one for "inquiry" and one for "advice." The next day the Commission in a body went to the White House, where the plan of organization was signed by the President and the Secretary of War. The birth struggles of the Sanitary Commission were at an end, and the Commissioners were free to begin their nebulous duties in an unfamiliar field. Within a few weeks, Sanitary Commission agents had been sent to camps and hospitals all over the North and were sending back reports which were submitted to the women backers of the Sanitary Commission for approval and to the government with recommendation for action. At the

same time, plans were made for Sanitary Commission regional headquarters through which the work of the women's groups could be transformed from independent units into a network of supply which was to produce results from volunteer work of a quality never before imagined.

NOTES

[1] Introduction by Henry W. Bellows, D.D. to *Woman's Work in the Civil War* by L. P. Brockett, M.D. (Zeigler, McCurdy & Co., Boston, 1867).

[2] Information about the Concord Soldiers' Relief Society was supplied by Mrs. Herbert B. Hosmer from the Concord Common Archives.

[3] Mrs. E. D. E. N. Southworth, *The Deserted Wife* (T. B. Peterson & Brothers, Philadelphia, 1855).

[4] Sister Charles Marie Frank, *Historical Development of Nursing* (W. B. Saunders Company, Philadelphia, 1953).

[5] Charles J. Stillé, *History of the United States Sanitary Commission* (J. P. Lippincott, Philadelphia, 1866).

6

A HUNDRED CIRCLING CAMPS

---★---

CHRONOLOGY

1861

May 3   President Lincoln issued a proclamation calling into the service of the United States 42,000 volunteers for three years' service, and increasing the Regular Army and Navy.

May 6   The Arkansas Convention adopted an Ordinance of Secession.

May 7   The Tennessee Legislature submitted an Ordinance of Secession to a referendum vote.

May 8   Richmond made the capital of the Confederate States.

May 10   St. Louis seized by Union forces. Lincoln suspended writ of habeas corpus on part of the Florida coast.

May 13   The British Government issued a proclamation of neutrality. Baltimore seized by General Butler's troops. Railroad communication restored with the North via Baltimore.

May 14   William Tecumseh Sherman appointed Colonel of the Thirteenth Regular Infantry and summoned to Washington.

May 20   North Carolina adopted an Ordinance of Secession.

May 23   Virginia voters ratified the Ordinance of Secession.

May 24   Colonel Elmer E. Ellsworth of the Eleventh New York Regiment
          (The Fire Zouaves) was shot by James T. Jackson, proprietor of
          the Marshall House in Alexandria after Ellsworth pulled down the
          Confederate flag. The Kentucky Legislature adopted a resolution
          of neutrality.

--------------------------------★--------------------------------

Father and I went down to camp,
Along with Captain Gooding,
And there we see the men and boys,
As thick as hasty pudding
—Edward Bangs (?)

T HE NEW SANITARY COMMISSION found the problems of health and
sanitation in the camps of the volunteer army to be serious indeed. The
magnitude of the problem was increased when on May 3rd, Lincoln,
who had never shared the belief in a ninety-day war, issued a call for
42,000 volunteers for three years' service. The country responded with
enthusiasm, tempered by the realization that war, after all, was not to be
a summer excursion, and the scenes at the railroad stations were enacted
all over again, with perhaps more tears and fewer cheers.

No one instructed the medical officers of the volunteer and militia
regiments about the need for locating the camps on high ground beyond
reach of the dangers of swamps and drainage water. No one told them
how to arrange the sanitation facilities of the camps, and, being civilians,
the regimental medical officers not only did not know how to deal with
such problems but for the most part were not even aware of their existence. Moreover, they could at best only persuade in matters of sanitation,
for they lacked the authority to enforce.

Some of the camps were comparatively clean, many were not. In most
of them debris was allowed to collect in piles outside the tents, and
litter was thrown into the camp streets where, in dry weather, the dust
was over the tops of the men's shoes. Garbage was left to rot in open
dumps which lured armies of rats into the camps. Latrines were no
more than open trenches into which earth was supposed to be shoveled
each day. Some camps did not have trenches and the men were allowed
to foul the surrounding land, often in such a way as to affect the water

supply. Diarrhea, dysentery and typhoid were the inevitable consequences, and it was small wonder that anyone approaching a camp could smell it half a mile away.

The odor of frying grease perpetually hung heavy in the air—grease that was used again and again, long after the hot weather had turned it rancid. It was the universal cooking medium. Each man was issued rations of meat—usually salt pork—hardtack, coffee, sugar and beans. No issue of fresh vegetables was regularly provided. A soldier was supposed to do his own cooking or to pool his resources with his comrades. The meat and hardtack he fried. The beans he baked, or semi-baked in the dirt under the campfire, and sometimes, if any were left over, he pounded them into cakes and fried them too. If cooking was too much trouble, or his regiment was on the move, he made a sandwich of hardtack and raw salt pork, or cold, fried, and half-baked bean cake. Few of the men had ever experienced such fare as this, and they were attacked by all sorts of intestinal disorders and food poisoning.

The water supply was usually inadequate and frequently contaminated. When the men were thirsty, they drank whatever they could find, which might be swamp water or deceptively clear surface water they accumulated by digging shallow holes in the ground to collect seepage. Rivers and streams near the camp smelled like the sewers they were, but thirsty men are not particular, and if the water looked clear, that seemed enough. Many of the men came from rural districts and had not been exposed to children's diseases, but in the crowded camps they came down with measles by the hundreds. Too often, a doctor failed to make a correct diagnosis, and when he saw a man with ominous red spots on his face, he was sent off to a smallpox hospital where he usually died.

In addition to sickness, there were many accidents with firearms in the hands of those unused to them, casualties of this sort were so frequent that there was mention of them in the newspapers almost every day. The regimental hospital tents, under their yellow flags, were full and the regimental matrons were busy from morning to night. In Washington, those who could not be cared for in this way were sent to one or another of the hospitals in the city, but the men feared these hospitals, and with some reason. Many preferred to remain in their own tents, trusting to the rough and ready care of their comrades, believing in this way they had a better chance of recovery. Considering the conditions in some of the hospitals at this time, there was much to say for this point of view.

Sickness, dirt and bad food began to take their toll of morale, and not

all the disabling gunshot wounds were accidental. There were other things to undermine the morale of the troops in these hot spring days. Many of the men had gone to war as a romantic adventure, only to find that it was neither romantic nor adventuresome. Others, who had enlisted from motives of purest patriotism, could not understand how the country was being served by their idleness. The men neither felt like soldiers nor looked like them. Some of the troops were clothed in government-issue garments, and these were of more or less standard design, though there was no real uniform until 1862. The government clothing was manufactured by contractors who were not required to meet standards of quality, a situation which resulted in what has been referred to as a "saturnalia of graft." The material used was called "shoddy," a sub-stance which was not real cloth, but "the refuse stuff and sweepings of the shops, pounded, rolled, glued and smoothed to the external form and gloss of cloth."[1]

> Worthless waste and worn-out woof
> Flung together a spacious *sham!*
> With just enough of the "fleece" to pull
> Over the eyes of poor Uncle Sam.

The shoddy, hymned by the anonymous poet, literally dissolved in a rainstorm, and General Butler, to demonstrate its defects to William Russell, the British war correspondent, scratched a hole through a soldier's coat with his fingernail.[2] Shoes were often of so poor a quality as not to survive a day's march, and like the cloth, they dissolved when wet. Wet feet and inadequate clothing added colds, pneumonia and various respiratory diseases to the long list of soldier maladies.

The city of Washington itself contributed to the health hazards of the new troops, for Washington in the Sixties was one of the most unhealthy towns in the country, and one of the dirtiest. The low, swampy land along the river hummed with mosquitoes, some of them malaria carriers, though their connection with the disease was not known in those days. The filth could not have been much worse in a medieval city. At the foot of the monument, which was then an unfinished stump, was a government slaughter house. The refuse from the slaughtering was thrown onto piles and left to decay, the liquid putrefaction draining into the sluggish canal which wound through part of the city. Slops were emptied into the streets where the paving had long ago disintegrated into danger-ous sink-holes, full of mud and water when it rained.

Only the more pretentious houses were equipped with drains, and

privies of the most unsanitary sort were everywhere, their stench mingling with that from the manure which was piled in the alleys behind the houses. As the spring days grew warmer, the stench became "the rankest compound of villainous smell that ever offended nostril." Flies covered everything—the meat in the markets, the food on the tables and the faces of the sick. Beds were equipped with mosquito net curtains (though only some of the hospitals had them) and there were no screens on the windows. In every house, up toward the ceiling of each room, a small, humming cloud of flies hung in the air through all the summer months. Typhoid, malaria, smallpox, dysentery and various forms of cholera were endemic, and though the residents of the city had developed a certain amount of immunity to these diseases, summer was considered a time of sickness. The new troops had no such immunity, and summer was at hand. In May, thirty percent of the volunteer army was on the sick list (the miracle is that the figure was not higher). Some of the regiments were reduced to half their strength, and experienced men, like Dr. Elisha Harris, knew that pestilence threatened.

The city which had greeted the troops with cheers and gaiety, and treated them as though they were heroes, soon began to tire of the noise, the overcrowded streets and the constant brawls. The ladies still made pets of certain regiments, like the Fire Zouaves, that were well drilled and romantically uniformed. They still clustered like a bouquet around certain handsome officers, like the dashing Colonel Ellsworth who commanded the Fire Zouaves. But to be crowded off the sidewalk by bands of sloppy, impudent soldiers, to be spattered with mud when a cavalry troop dashed past, or choked with dust when a gun caisson with its yelling riders went crashing over the holes in the pavement, was becoming wearisome. By the first of May the welcome had cooled, by the middle of the month the troops had driven the city to the verge of distraction. The soldiers were depressed by this attitude on the part of the citizens, and especially of the women of Washington. To be shunned and to have nothing to do is a hard lot for a homesick boy barely out of his teens, and of leisure there was a great deal too much. The volunteers added boredom to their other woes.

Until a Mrs. Elida Rumsey Fowle opened a reading room for soldiers some time later, there was no organized amusement. The Fire Zouaves and a few other regiments which had some pretense of style staged reviews at which the pretty girls cheered and clapped and threw roses, but the gaudy uniforms, the gaiety, the devil-may-care pose only further depressed the men who belonged to less fortunate regiments.

There were plenty of drinking places in the city and there were plenty of brothels. Madams from far-flung places had answered the call to war and herded their girls into the capital where they were doing a thriving business without any serious interference from the authorities. The liquor and the ladies were the cause of a good many fights, some of them spectacular enough for the newspapers. The rowdy element, however, though conspicuous, was not large. The average soldier who did not drink or frequent brothels spent his spare time wandering around looking at the half-built disappointing city, or just standing, brooding and wondering whether the lassitude he felt was a combination of boredom and the abominable climate or whether it might not be the onset of some disease.

This state of affairs dragged on and on until it seemed to both citizens and soldiers that boredom, disease and waiting was all that would ever come of war. Then on the twenty-fourth of May an event occurred which jolted everyone out of lethargy. A small force, which included handsome Colonel Ellsworth and his crack regiment of Zouaves, was sent across the river to establish a line of defense on the high ground around Alexandria. While the engineers laid out the lines of fortifications, the troops rested under the trees and Private Theodore Winthrop reflected that: "Nothing men can do—except picnics with ladies in straw hats with feathers—is so picturesque as soldiering."

In Alexandria, on the flagpole of the Marshall House Hotel, the flag of the Confederacy floated on the spring breeze. Colonel Ellsworth saw it and determined to pull it down. He entered the Marshall House, dashed up the stairs, hauled down the flag and was coming down the stairs again with the flag under his arm when he was shot in the breast by the secessionist innkeeper. As the Colonel fell, Private Brownell, who was accompanying Ellsworth, killed the innkeeper with his bayonet.

Colonel Ellsworth became the second hero of the war. Young ladies who had danced with him, shed tears and draped black crepe over lithographed pictures of him which were on sale everywhere within twenty-four hours. Pieces of the flagpole and of the woodwork of the Marshall House became treasures. Ellsworth had been a friend of the President and funeral services were held in the White House and Mrs. Lincoln placed one of the pictures and a wreath of laurel on the coffin.

After the services, the funeral cortege, which included President Lincoln and a number of notables, wound slowly through the streets to the railroad station. Beside the driver of the hearse sat Private Brownell displaying the captured Confederate flag and his bayonet stained with

the assassin's blood. Crowds lined the route. Women moaned and wept hysterically. Clara Barton had found a place for herself on the steps of a public building and it seemed to her that the President appeared shrunken by the universal grief to the stature of other men.

NOTES

[1] Frazer Kirkland, *Anecdotes of the Rebellion* (J. H. Mason, St. Louis, 1889), p. 567.
[2] William Howard Russell, *My Diary North and South* (Harper & Brothers, New York, 1863).

7

THE TOWN NOBODY LOVED

———————————— ★ ————————————

1861

May 27   McDowell took command in northeastern Virginia. The Postmaster General issued an order suspending mail service from May
31st to Virginia, North Carolina, South Carolina, Georgia, Florida,
Alabama, Mississippi, Louisiana, Arkansas and Texas.

May 29   Capital of Confederacy moved from Montgomery, Alabama, to
Richmond, executive departments following later.

June 1   First Confederate battle death—Captain John Q. Marr, Warrenton
Rifles, in skirmish at Fairfax Court House, Virginia.

June 8   Tennessee ratified the Ordinance of Secession.

June 9   Mother Bickerdyke arrived at Cairo with supplies, donated by
Galesburg, for the volunteers encamped there.

———————————— ★ ————————————

Ever been to Cairo? It is the dolefullest, cussed-
est place. If a man is excusable anywhere for
drinking himself insensible, it is at Cairo, Illinois.
—John William deForest

THE DEPLORABLE CONDITION of the camps in Washington repeated itself in Cairo and every other place where troops were concentrated.
In the encampments which paid some attention to sanitation, the sickness
rate was comparatively low, in the majority it mounted and kept on
mounting. And from all of them carloads of mail went home to families
in the North, letters filled with accounts of bad food, the purloining of
gifts from the aid societies, of discomfort, disillusion, of sickness and the
death of comrades.

These letters caused a wave of anxiety throughout the North. Women
began to journey to the camps, women who perhaps had never traveled
before, packed carpet bags and set out on a trip which to many of them
seemed perilous. In every encampment they were shocked at what they
discovered. They could see plainly enough that it was true that the men
were growing sick from filth and bad food and that when this happened,
they were cared for at inadequate hospitals or simply left to lie in a tent
on some straw, ministered to by their comrades. The women knew
nothing about army sanitation, but they knew bad housekeeping when
they saw it, and the conditions in the camps seemed to them bad housekeeping on a colossal scale.

That was the spirit in which they approached the problem when they
went home again and told their stories. The aid societies began to buzz
like angry hornets. The women and girls lost interest in gaily supplying
the soldiers with jam and picturesque sartorial appurtenances. They had
waked up to the realization that little luxuries were not what the situation called for. Food, and good food was needed—substantial, practical
clothing and medical supplies, and it was necessary to see that these
things reached the men without being pilfered. If the government would
not or could not meet the needs the women considered it was up to
them to supply the men. If the magnitude of the task appalled them,
there is no record of it. They simply went to work, all of them, all over
the country. The aid societies that had not already heard about the
Sanitary Commission, learned about it now, and most of them hastened to
affiliate with the central organization.

The women interpreted the role they were to play as twofold. Part of
the task, as they saw it, was to supplement government and to be ready

with supplies and nursing care when the government failed to produce them. The other part of the task was to bring pressure on government, through the Sanitary Commissioners, to reform its antiquated practices. The women, however, placed the blame for the hardships in camps and hospitals more on the traditions of warfare than on Washington, and in these early days there was little bitterness toward government for its failure to provide for the troops. In part because camp and hospital sanitation had something in common with housekeeping, and in part because they were determined that not even war should break the ties with home, it seemed natural to these women to take on themselves the burden of reform. The degree of responsibility of a national government for a citizen army had never been defined. It was the women themselves who were beginning to define that responsibility and in so doing were creating standards of humanitarianism in war which ultimately all governments were compelled to adopt.

The shifting of responsibility for the welfare of the soldiers and for the care and rehabilitation of the disabled from a largely volunteer enterprise to a recognized duty of government has had a gradual development. It began in Europe before 1861. The Civil War was the great period of growth, and the process is not yet wholly complete. But the ultimate fixing of the major responsibility on government was the legacy of these women volunteers.

A letter describing the suffering in the hospitals of Cairo, Illinois, written by Dr. Benjamin Woodward, came into the hands of Dr. Edward Beecher. Dr. Beecher (brother of the famous Henry Ward Beecher) was pastor of the Brick Congregational Church of Galesburg, Illinois,' and he read the letter aloud to his congregation. There followed an open discussion of the best means of alleviating the suffering in Cairo, which resulted in the sending of a woman named Mary Ann Bickerdyke to Cairo. Mrs. Bickerdyke was famous for her ability as a nurse, and taking with her a quantity of medical supplies, she went south to meet Dr. Woodward.

Cairo at this time was a fever-ridden campsite of volunteer regiments who were hurriedly building gun emplacements to guard the river traffic. Debris and dead dogs littered the streets, which turned into wallows of sticky mud whenever it rained. The great rivers were a majestic sight, but they were hidden from view of much of the town by the levees, which formed breastworks against attack on the river front. On the other sides the town was surrounded by swamps filled with stagnant pools of black water.

When Bickerdyke arrived in Cairo, she wasted no time before visiting the hospitals. The conditions she found were shocking beyond words. Any tent or empty building was considered good enough for a hospital. Beds were sacks filled with corn husks, usually laid directly on the ground. There were no pillows or sheets. Some hospitals had no medicine or medical supplies, and some regiments had left for war without doctors, without surgical instruments and without any means of caring for the sick. Some of the doctors were not fit to practice. The nurses were convalescent soldiers, too weak and too ignorant to fulfill their duties. The food was the same unpalatable kind given to the men on active duty, and it was served on half-washed tin plates. Filth and grime were everywhere. Unwashed men had nothing to wear but their dirty underclothing. Inside the wards, the smell of sick, dirty bodies, of excrement and grease was all but overpowering.

Bickerdyke was filled with horror by the scenes of suffering and neglect which confronted her. She rolled up her sleeves and went to work. She scrubbed, she cooked palatable meals out of the disgusting rations, in old kettles on any broken-down stove she could lay hands on. She was not a young woman, but her energy was boundless. Her work-worn hands soothed the sick and contrived ways of making them comfortable. They called her "Mother," which was their way of paying her high honor.

Bickerdyke was that rare combination, a good bedside nurse and a good executive. She reorganized the wards, had the men's filthy clothing washed, bossed the male nurses in vigorous, ungrammatical language and brushed out of her way ladies in hoop skirts and doctors who demanded to be told by what right she had invaded their hospitals.

She had no authority whatsoever for the things she was doing beyond the slight amount that Dr. Woodward could give her. But lack of authority never stopped Mother Bickerdyke. If there was work to be done, she did it, not bothered by the fact that she made enemies right and left. She had no patience with slovenliness and no respect for rank. For officers who did their duty she found room in her ample affections, but if she thought one of the medical men was neglecting his duty, she gave him a tongue-lashing in words that stung like a whip. One of the doctors complained that a "cyclone in calico" had struck the hospital. Others tried to oust her, but if she was ushered out the front, she came in at the rear. She did not quite hate all authority, and some officers (among them Grant and Sherman) she counted as good friends, but she enjoyed a good quarrel and she bristled like a porcupine with righteous indignation. Her sympathies were always with her "boys" whatever their rank might be.

Kind ladies of the town came to these filthy places with jellies and custards, tracts and bits of cold chicken. The benevolent ladies with their baskets Bickerdyke tolerated, but did not like because they did no real work. But among the lady visitors whose great hoop skirts blocked the narrow hospital aisles, Bickerdyke's bright, observing eyes saw one she approved. This was a young lady named Mary Safford, who had been coming to the hospitals since they were opened, bringing food which she had prepared with judgment and care, food for a sick man. To Bickerdyke it seemed that Mary possessed the qualities which would make a good nurse. Bickerdyke detached her from the ornamental flock of amateur Nightingales, put her to work and taught her that true nursing is not charm, but a combination of love and soap suds.

These two women differed in every way. Mary was rich by standards of Cairo. Bickerdyke was a poor widow. Mary was young, ornamentally educated and as frail as a church lily. Bickerdyke was forty-four years old, stocky, vigorous, used to hard work, and possessed of an arsenal of ungrammatical eloquence which she used whenever an obstacle blocked her path, as when a doctor asked her by what authority she was appropriating hospital supplies. She replied, "From the Lord God Almighty. Do you have anything that ranks higher than that?"

Mother Bickerdyke and Mary became more than ordinary friends, and the picture of these two women working together, is an appealing one. And it may be that Mary's association with Mother Bickerdyke was the most important influence on her life. Working with Bickerdyke in the hospital tents, Mary learned to set aside the inhibitions and artificialities of the traditional lady. She learned to discard superficialities, as symbolized by her basket of jellies, and to come to grips with the essentials of life in the dirt and blood of the wards.

One can well believe that at first Mary was astonished by Bickerdyke, but there followed the gradual realization that behind Bickerdyke's brusque, earthy manner was a truly great personality. There would be admiration, then love, then the comprehension that Bickerdyke exemplified an ideal, that she was the manifestation of a philosophy of life.

The accounts of Mary Safford usually picture her as delicate, gentle and refined, but these aspects of her personality hid more important qualities, for she had the fortitude to carry her through Fort Donelson and Shiloh, where she saw some of the bloodiest scenes of the war. The record shows that Mary tried to imitate Bickerdyke's accomplishments but she lacked the older woman's stamina. She drove herself until her health failed, but the ideal captured in those days with Mother Bickerdyke

never left her. After the war ended and Mary recovered from a protracted illness, she found her own way of giving it expression. She
entered a medical school, received a degree, and became a practicing
physician. Mary's was not the only life on which Mother Bickerdyke left
a permanent impression.

The nursing done by Bickerdyke and Mary Safford was of high
quality, but it was accomplished, in these early days, without the backing
of an organization. There were certain distinct advantages in this, the
principal one being their freedom from red tape and bureaucratic control,
but as individuals they could only alleviate, not remove, the deplorable
conditions in the wards. The fact that these two women succeeded so
well must be attributed to their own qualities; for the work of many
volunteer nurses, who were without guidance or control, was showing
more of the faults than the virtues of individual effort.

Like Bickerdyke, a number of the women who went to the camps remained there. Most of the hospitals allowed a wife or mother to take
over the nursing of her soldier, and sometimes she was allowed to make
the hospital her living quarters, for what these hospitals lacked in technique, a good many made up in kindness. Usually the woman undertook the care of three or four other boys in cots near to her own patient,
and some of these volunteer workers, discovering in themselves an
aptitude for nursing, continued in the work.

A surprisingly large number of women, wives of both officers and men
in the ranks, were permitted to stay with their husbands, not only in
camp, but on the march, when the regiment moved toward the front and
to remain, supposedly in the rear, while a battle was being fought. Mrs.
Grant was with her husband a good deal of the time, and the wives of
a number of generals followed their husbands on the campaigns. There
was Mrs. Colonel Turchin. Riding a great horse side-saddle she flashed
past, stern, lady-like and leaving behind her the impression of a personality slightly larger than life. There was Mrs. Ellis, wife of the Commander of the First Missouri Regiment, another hard-riding lady with
military dispatches in her keeping. She wore a fanciful uniform with a
red sash, and two orderlies accompanied her wherever she went. Belle
Reynolds was commissioned a major because of her bravery at Shiloh
(her husband was a lieutenant) and though a commission in a state
militia is not the same as a commission in the Army of the United States,
the citizens of Peoria, her home town, were so impressed with the honor
that they formally thanked the Governor. There was an Irish girl called
"Michigan Bridget," whose real name was Bridget Divers, and a Mary

Owens who fought in three battles and was wounded twice. A girl named
Georgianne Peterman from Ellenboro, Wisconsin, went to war as a
drummer boy when she was seventeen and served for two years.

The most famous of these vaguely official women (if we except Major
Pauline Cushman, who was a spy and in a class by herself) was Kady
Brownell. Kady was the wife of an orderly sergeant of the First and
later the Fifth Rhode Island Infantry. She was the daughter of a Scot-
tish soldier serving in the British Army and had been born in a military
camp. We will meet Kady again, dressed outlandishly in a short skirt
over trousers and a red sash, wildly waving her company colors while
the bullets were flying around her.

There was an astonishing number of these military ladies who went
openly to war, some were respectable and some, it seems, were not. That
these two groups, the respectable women and the females of tattered
virtue, should go off on the great adventure more or less in each other's
company is not the least amazing aspect of this whole unusual business.
Both sorts often acted as nurses and, in the lower ranks, they met over
the washtubs, for they both filled that time-honored role of the camp
follower, the laundress.

Most of these women went with the troops into battle. Some carried
water for the wounded, some rallied the men. Michigan Bridget used to
step into the ranks to fill the place of a fallen soldier; Kady's position as
company colorbearer was official, and we see Mrs. Major Reynolds, a
pistol in each hand, putting a stop to a panic.

In addition to these fighting furies, there were various "daughters" of
this or that regiment. The "daughter" in this incurably romantic army
appears sometimes to have been the choice of the men, sometimes of the
officers, or she may have been appointed by the officer in command.
Kady Brownell was an official "daughter" appointed by Burnside who had
great liking for her. The position was semi-official and ill-defined, rating
somewhere between an honor and a job. Perhaps the "daughter" was a
child, or a popular young army wife, or simply an adventuresome young
lady who had come out with the regiment for the fun of the thing. The
Sixth Massachusetts had a daughter named "Little Lizzie," but they left
her behind when they marched off to war. The regiment usually gave their
daughter a gay uniform and she was supposed to have style, in a pert,
drum-majorette sort of way.

The "daughter" was a European institution and she flourished principally in the wars of the eighteenth Century. Sometimes she resembled
the girl in Donizetti's opera, *La Figlia Del Reggimento,* sometimes she

belonged more truly in the category of the *vivandieres,* women, virtuous or not as the case might be, who accompanied the army as cooks, which is the origin of their name. She was the regiment's mascot, their showoff, and her duties, aside from being petted and admired by several hundred homesick men, included riding at the head of the regiment on parade.

From four to six women went to war with most of the regiments in some semi-official capacity, the most useful undoubtedly being that of matron. There were customarily two matrons to a regiment, vigorous, home-town young women, for the most part, some with husbands in the ranks. To these women it seemed the most natural thing in the world to go to war with the men they had known all their lives. They were the nurses in the regimental hospitals, but they were not above doing all sorts of tasks, including washing, to make the men comfortable. On them Miss Dix declared instant and unremitting war, but all her efforts, backed by the Secretary of War, were powerless to eradicate them wholly from the regiments of the citizen army.

Like every other army in history, this one had its camp followers, ladies of easy virtue who clustered like flies around the mustering-in camps. A good many of them added liquor smuggling as a sideline, carrying forbidden spirits from the nearest city into camp. Crinolines were ideal for such purposes and one woman had a tin bustle made in which she could transport five gallons on each trip.[1] When the army moved, a sluggish mass of these women moved with it—notably on the route to Antietam—and when the army came to a halt, more of them swarmed out of the nearest towns. The prostitutes, however, were not a prominent feature of camp life as they had been in some of the European wars, for on the whole, this was an astonishingly moral army. Most of the regimental commanders drove them out of camp, and it is not unusual to run across a reference to some little band of them being deported from the district, indignant, ruffled and exceedingly vocal about their wrongs.

Perhaps no army in history has ever been so surrounded by women as Lincoln's volunteers. In addition to the officers' wives, the soldiers' wives, the regiments' daughters, the hordes of female relatives that visited every encampment, the girl friends, the nurses, the laundresses and the ladies-of-joy, there were the women in the ranks, that mysterious four hundred who went to war in disguise. If the astonishing figure of four hundred is correct,[2] that is the number of women who were discovered either because they were killed or wounded or because their disguises proved inadequate, as in the case of the girl who was found out

because she did not put on her shoes and socks like a man. How many more there may have been, we do not know.

One day in the summer of 1861, Mary Livermore went to the camp of the Nineteenth Illinois to see how the soldiers were faring and to report their needs to the busy women workers back home. "I was watching companies that were drilling," Mrs. Livermore wrote, "a good deal amused at their awkwardness and their slow comprehension of the orders given them. One of the captains came to me, with an apology for intrusion, and begged to know if I noticed anything peculiar in the appearance of one of the men, whom he indicated. It was evident at a glance that the 'man' was a young woman in male attire, and I said so. 'That is the rumor, and that is my suspicion,' was his reply. The seeming soldier was called from the ranks and informed of the suspicions afloat, and asked the truth of them. There was a scene in an instant. Clutching the officer by the arm, and speaking in tones of passionate entreaty, she begged him not to expose her, but to allow her to retain her disguise. Her husband had enlisted in this company, she said, and it would kill her if he marched without her. 'Let me go with you!' I heard her plead. 'Oh, sir, let me go with you!' She was quietly conducted outside the camp, when I took her in charge. I wished to take her to my home, but she leaped suddenly from the carriage before we were halfway from the camp, and in a moment was lost amid the crowds hastening home from their day's work."[3]

Sometimes these women, when discovered, caused embarrassment all around. One of them was wounded and picked up by the Confederates at the battle of Chickamauga. When they discovered her sex, they returned her, under a flag of truce, to the Union lines, with a message to the effect that, "As the Confederates do not use women in war, this woman, wounded in battle, is returned to you." She had been with her regiment for more than a year.

Two women soldiers were discovered in Sheridan's command, one a teamster in the division wagon train and the other a private soldier in a cavalry company. They had joined the army at different times, had seen through each other's disguise and become friends. One day on a foraging expedition, they acquired some applejack, drank too much, and fell into Stone's River. They were nearly drowned, and in the process of reviving them their sex was discovered. One was a large, coarse featured, masculine woman, the other Sheridan thought "rather prepossessing." The discovery that they had been in the ranks for some time seems to have given Sheridan something of a shock and to have "to some extent

demoralized" the men. The women were hastily sent to headquarters, where they were ordered to put on dresses and escorted beyond the lines.[4]

Most of the accounts of the women *travesti en soldat* assert that their sex was not known to their masculine comrades-in-arms. There need be no hesitation in saying that such a thing is utterly impossible under ordinary conditions of warfare. Under special conditions it is just conceivable that the women might disguise themselves successfully for a time. It is possible also that the officers might not be aware of a woman's presence, but that the men with whom she lived, slept, ate and washed in the lack of privacy of an army should not be aware of her sex is beyond credibility.[5]

Miss Dix' strongly disapproving views on the subject of women with the regiments, even though their participation in military life might be strictly moral, had some justification. No one saw more plainly than she that the conduct of those women who called themselves "matron" or "nurse" could, unless above reproach, turn public opinion against nursing careers for women, and damage the prestige of her own organization. The fear of this haunted her. Brooding over this possibility, she set herself two goals. The first was to create a set of requirements for admission to the Army Nursing Corps that would keep out women whose conduct might undermine the repute of the corps. The second was to bring all unregulated nursing activities everywhere under her control.

She wrote her requirements in the form of a press release which was published throughout the North. The release, after appealing to women to become nurses, continued: "No woman under thirty years need apply to serve in government hospitals. All nurses are required to be very plain-looking women. Their dresses must be brown or black, with no bows, no curls, no jewelry and no hoop skirts." To these requirements, she added a personal prejudice in favor of Protestants, for she believed they would be less likely than Catholics to try to convert their patients. (Experience was to prove that one group was no more likely than the other to force religion on the men in the wards.) Her requirements did not include nursing ability or experience.

The original plan to have the corps composed of unpaid volunteers was soon abandoned. Nurses were to receive twelve dollars a month, army rations and free travel at the discretion of their superior. Miss Dix preferred to interview candidates in person, but when this was not possible, they must send pictures and all were required to give references. After the candidates were approved by Miss Dix and the Surgeon General's Office (this latter being merely a matter of form) it was

usually up to the nurse herself to find a hospital where her services were needed. The surgeon in charge must then formally request that she be assigned to him, and he held the power to dismiss her from his service.

These requirements and regulations produced many good nurses, but the age limit excluded a number of young women who, subsequently, working outside the Dix organization, contributed some of the finest nursing service of the war. To many others, the rigid regulations were distasteful. The net result was that the greater number of nurses whose outstanding work has made their names remembered were not under the authority of Miss Dix. Among them were Clara Barton, Mary Safford, Helen Gilson, Cornelia Hancock, and the great Mother Bickerdyke.

A serious fault in the qualifications required by Miss Dix was that they resulted in the acceptance of a large number of women who, because of age, were not fully equal to their duties. The patients thought these older women bossy as well as unattractive. The doctors often complained that they were set in their ways, given to impudence, would not follow instructions and tended to give the patient what they thought would be good for him and not what the doctor had prescribed. Miss Dix, however, achieved the aim she held so dear, for no scandal ever tarnished the Army Nursing Corps, and no Dix nurse was ever dismissed for moral laxity.

On May 4th Miss Dix fired her opening gun in her private war against the nursing activities which were being carried on beyond reach of her authority.

"The great number of humane persons impelled by self-sacrificing benevolence to offer their services as nurses, in the event of necessity, in the military hospitals, makes it proper to communicate a few facts briefly through the medium of the press:

"1. It is the wish of the acting Surgeon General that qualified persons communicate their names and residence to the writer; and, as no serious sickness exists at present, they are respectfully requested not to proceed to headquarters at Washington or elsewhere till such time as their valuable aid may be needed, when immediate notice will be given.

"2. It is believed that all who offer as nurses do so with the understanding that this is a *free* service—looking for no pecuniary recompense; and the writer earnestly and respectfully suggests that all who enter upon this work be provided with the means of sustaining all their personal expenses—especially as, by the army regulation, no provision is made for such service.

"The matrons allowed each regiment are laundresses for special work, and in the hospitals have charge of the linen, bandages, etc., which they wash and prepare for use.

With respectful consideration,

D. L. Dix

"NOTICE.——Benevolent ladies desiring to furnish means for increasing the comforts and benefit of hastily established military hospitals, will insure success by consulting surgeons of practical knowledge and experience in their vicinity.

"Pillows of various sizes and of various material for various purposes will be of much use.

"At present the stock of flannel body garments and of warm socks is quite deficient and already in request.

Very respectfully,

D. L. Dix

505 Twelfth Street, Washington"

The statement that no serious sickness existed in the army at that time is either true or false according to the angle from which it was viewed. The amount of sickness was slight, for example, compared to the worst days of the Crimea, and as illness reports were not yet functioning properly, the Surgeon General may not have realized that the cause for alarm lay in the fact that sickness figures were beginning to rise rapidly. The notice at the end, to the effect that benevolent ladies should consult with surgeons about supplies for the soldiers, must have caused some irritation among those who, like the women of New York, had been snubbed for doing precisely what she advised. The purposeful paragraph, however, is that in which she states that the regimental matrons are laundresses, with the additional privilege of working in hospital linen rooms. The matrons had no objection to doing laundry work or any other service needed by the men, but when the men fell ill, especially if they were to be cared for in the regimental hospital tent, there was no power in Miss Dix' possession which could keep the matrons from nursing them.

Miss Dix never realized this and never gave up the struggle. Eventually, the post of regimental matron was abolished by order of the Secretary of War and some of the women left the service. Many remained, staying with their regiments in winter quarters and moving with them on their campaigns. Division and corps commanders also appointed matrons and these too proved to be beyond Miss Dix' control. Once, on a Southern inspection tour, she encountered one of

these unauthorized military matrons, and said to her with some crispness, "You are the regimental woman, I suppose." "No, *mam,*" was the reply, "I'm the Brigade woman," and she made it clear by her manner that Miss Dix was no superior of hers.

Perhaps there was more animosity in Miss Dix' fight against independent nursing than the abuses it fostered would seem to justify. The bitterness may have been a reaction to a tendency on the part of various people in authority to hold her responsible for the failure in a situation she had no power to control. In addition, the government plainly regarded the disposal of the many unqualified volunteer nurses who were coming to Washington in great numbers, as part of her duty. Not only would-be nurses but female relatives of the soldiers came to Washington in considerable numbers during the month of May. Many were without funds, many could not find a place to stay, and some discovered too late that the regiment they sought had been sent elsewhere. There was no organization to care for these helpless, distracted women, and somehow it came about that she was more or less responsible for them. On May 29th she issued another of her many statements to the press.

"All persons are respectfully and earnestly requested not to send to Army Headquarters, or moving stations, women of any age in search of employment, unless the need is announced by either letter or advertisement, there being no provision made by the government or otherwise for such persons. There are many who are anxious to join their friends who believe they will readily find remunerative employment. They arrive without means either of support or defraying return expenses, and so far from meeting fathers, brothers, or husbands, may learn that their regiments are on the march to distant stations. The expense for providing these ill-counselled but well-intentioned and helpless persons in Washington falls inconveniently on individuals who are not willing to witness needless exposure or suffering."

Miss Dix' position was an almost impossible one. On paper, she had more power than any woman other than a ruler ever had in wartime, but her actual commission had not been signed, and was not signed until June 10th. Her real difficulty, however, all through the war, but especially in this crucial month when permanent decisions and policies were being formed, was that her authority was half-heartedly enforced

or not enforced at all. The War Department left her duties and her jurisdiction, possibly deliberately, vague and uncertain.

She was painfully aware that, in the eyes of the country, the Nightingale mantle had fallen on her shoulders, and that if a good many people had expected her to carry on the great tradition, they were already experiencing disappointment. In some ways Miss Dix was startlingly like Miss Nightingale; so much so, in fact, that it is impossible not to believe that she consciously attempted to imitate Miss Nightingale even in insignificant ways. She had pursued Miss Nightingale halfway around the world and never encountered her, but she must have heard about her mannerisms for she had acquired the same commanding manner, the same trick of carrying her head high and the same rigidity of pose, even the same recurring periods of nervous collapse.

Miss Nightingale was in the habit of presenting the young nurses of St. Thomas Hospital with money, presumably for hack fares, when they came to see her, even though she knew some of them came from wealthy homes.[6] Somehow, Miss Dix must have learned of this habit, for there is a similar incident about her told by the sprightly pen of a young schoolteacher of Auburn, New York. Her name was Sophronia Bucklin and at the time Miss Dix was attempting to extend her jurisdiction over the hospital where she worked as a volunteer. Sophronia was summoned to appear before Miss Dix.

"I found her busy with letters," Sophronia wrote, "and, after watching her in uneasy nervousness, as she dashed off two or three, I gathered courage enough to say, 'Miss Dix, I should like to return as soon as possible to my duties.'

"She replied, 'You can go, dear.' At the same time she opened a drawer in her table and took therefrom a five-dollar bill, which she handed me, saying, 'This is not pay—only a little present from me.'

"I took it in confusion, and, as she bade me a kind 'Good morning,' I hastened back to the hospital."[7]

Though Miss Dix may have resembled Miss Nightingale in certain respects, she lacked Miss Nightingale's ability to establish a sound working relationship between herself and government. She lacked conspicuously Miss Nightingale's farsightedness. The organization problem which Miss Dix was facing was greater, because of the multiplicity of hospitals and extent of territory involved, than that which confronted Miss Nightingale. But Dorothea Dix was essentially a lone worker and not a born organizer. She never fully grasped the Nightingale precept

that "management is the art of multiplying oneself, so that what is well done when one is there, is equally well done when one is not."

Though organization was not Miss Dix' strong point, she resembled Miss Nightingale in that her inclination was toward administrative, rather than bedside nursing. She was not a ministrant but a reformer. For the war wounded, as for the insane, she felt pity rather than sympathy. In the presence of suffering Miss Dix remained aloof.

When the Sanitary Commission was formed, Miss Dix failed to comprehend either the nature or the scope of its work. She did not concern herself to any great extent with camp sanitation, it is true, but she added hospital inspection to her other activities. There was real justification for this in the wording of her commission which appeared to designate, or at least to permit her to enter areas assigned to the Sanitary Commission. The situation could easily have been straightened out by Miss Dix either with the Sanitary Commission or with government. But any compromise with the Sanitary Commission would have been a curtailment of her authority, and Miss Dix was not one to risk a loss of authority, however shadowy it might be.

Sometimes she would appear at a hospital, and, without introducing herself, carry on her inspection. If she did not like what she saw, she reported to Secretary Stanton, with whom she was on excellent terms. In the course of her activities, there were a number of clashes with the chief surgeons who resented her interference, and it sometimes happened that Miss Dix lost her temper and a scene ensued which, later, she must have sincerely regretted.

Policy dictated that outwardly her relations with the Sanitary Commission should appear amicable, and there was no trouble between Miss Dix and the Commission members of any serious sort. There were, however, exasperations on both sides. Commissioner George Templeton Strong kept a diary which throws a light, albeit from one angle, on Miss Dix and her relations with the Commission. Strong was a New York lawyer, small in stature, large in intelligence, energetic, judgmatic, and possessed of a style of writing which brings the characters of his time alive. One of his journal entries reads, "Extricated ourselves from an entanglement with that philanthropic lunatic, Miss Dix . . . " And again, "Miss Dix has plagued us a little. She is strong, energetic, benevolent, unselfish, and a mild case of monomania. Working on her own hook, she does good, but no one can cooperate with her, for she belongs to the class of comets and can be subdued into relations with no system whatever."[8]

As late as the end of September Miss Dix had not yet clarified her task in her own mind, for on the twenty-third Strong wrote, "General Fremont seems to have set up a local Sanitary Commission of his own to act under the direction of Miss Dix! . . . This has doubtless been got up by that indefatigable woman. She is disgusted with us because we do not leave everything else and rush off the instant she tells us of something that needs attention. The last time we were in Washington she came upon us in breathless excitement to say that a cow in the Smithsonian grounds was dying of sunstroke, and she took it very ill that we did not adjourn instantly to look after the case."

Miss Dix is one of those whose work is of sufficient importance to deserve the tribute of criticism, but as a woman she inspires great pity. She was lonely, tired, and working, as it seemed to her, without support, toward a distant goal which neither she nor anyone else could clearly see.

NOTES

[1] Margaret Leech, *Reveille in Washington* (Harper & Brothers, New York, 1941), p. 271.

[2] Mary A. Livermore, *My Story of the War* (A. D. Worthington and Company, Hartford, Conn., 1888), p. 120.

[3] *Ibid*, pp. 113-114.

[4] P. H. Sheridan, *Personal Memoirs* (Charles L. Webster & Company, New York, 1888), I, p. 253.

[5] One of these female soldiers, Sarah Emma Edmonds (alias Franklin Thompson) wrote a book of reminiscences, but her adventures as she relates them are not believable and it seems clear that her story is of more interest to the clinician than to the historian.

[6] Told to the author by one of the nurses who later became head of the St. Thomas' Nurses Training School. Miss Nightingale was confined to her couch but she insisted on the students coming to her home to be interviewed.

[7] Sophronia E. Bucklin, *In Hospital and Camp* (John E. Potter & Co., Philadelphia, 1869).

[8] *The Diary of George Templeton Strong* (The Macmillan Company, New York, 1952).

8

THE ARMY MOVES

---- ★ ----

1861

June 10   Miss Dorothea Dix received her commission as superintendent of Army nurses from Secretary of War Cameron. Harper's Ferry abandoned to the Confederates. Action at Big Bethel, Virginia.

June 13   Order creating the Sanitary Commission approved by the President.

June 29   President Lincoln met with his Cabinet and military commanders to discuss the advisability of an immediate attack on the Confederate Army concentrated at Manassas.

July 2   Lincoln suspended the writ of habeas corpus from Philadelphia to New York.

July 4   The first session of the 34th Congress convened.

July 11–13 Union victories under General George Brinton McClellan in western Virginia.

July 16   The Union army, under General Irvin McDowell began its advance into Virginia.

July 18   Action at Blackburn's Ford.

July 19–20 General McDowell maneuvered his forces into position in preparation for the Battle of Bull Run (First Battle of Manassas).

---- ★ ----

Move on the columns! Why delay?
Our soldiers sicken in their camps.
—W. D. Gallagher

THERE WAS NOW NO LONGER any novelty left about the encircling camps at Washington and every discomfort the troops caused that city was growing worse. There was more sickness in the city than usual and the encampments received the blame. Even the flies exceeded anything that fly-infested city had ever before experienced, and George T. Strong of the Sanitary Commission wrote in his journal that they "blackened the table cloth and absolutely flew into one's mouth at dinner." Everyone longed for the day when the great, sprawling army would gather itself together and roll off into the green hills of Virginia.

That day seemed to be postponed beyond reason. The public in general had no doubt that the army they had raised was vastly superior to any fighting force the enemy could put into the field. Richmond, the capital of the Confederacy, lay only a hundred miles away. Why, then, the delay? William Russell, the British war correspondent, who had seen other armies and shared the misgivings of the professional military men about this one, said that the people believed that "an army is like a round of canister which can be fired off whenever a match is applied." However, most of the newspapers of the North shared the general opinion, and "On to Richmond" became their battle cry.

The Administration found it more and more difficult to resist the pressure for an advance, though General Scott did all he could to prevent the politicians from taking precipitate action. Russell was shrewd enough to recognize in the rising tide of public sentiment a force which a democratic government could not long withstand. At the time he reached this conclusion, Russell was making a leisurely tour of the South, and he turned northward in order to be in Washington at the opening of the campaign, not because of any sympathy with the Union cause, but because his dispatches to the *London Times,* if sent from the North, would not have to run the tightening blockade of the Southern ports.

He entered Union territory at Cairo, Illinois on the nineteenth of June. The thermometer stood at 100 degrees and he could not understand why sane men had built a town in such a location. Though he had come openly up the river from enemy territory, on a Confederate steamer, no one stopped him on the dock to enquire his business. He spent a miserable night at the one hotel, his room humming with mosquitoes, and went

north next day by rail. From Chicago, Russell turned eastward, a river of words flowing constantly from his pen.[1] He noted that everywhere people talked of little but the coming campaign. Everyone believed that the Confederacy would crumble at the first attack, but the crest of patriotic fervor had passed and enlistments had fallen off, in part, perhaps, because victory seemed certain, but also because of alarm over the sickness in the camps. Women, whose patriotism had been so powerful a factor in creating the volunteer army, were no longer urging their men folk to go to war.

When Russell arrived in Washington early in July he called on Secretary Seward whom he thought more worn and haggard than he had seemed three months earlier. General McDowell, who was to command the army in the coming campaign, was subjected by Russell to a press interview in much the modern style. The General was quite willing to talk about his troubles, and of these he had plenty. McDowell was a Regular Army man with a contempt for what he termed "political generals," and he put little trust in volunteer troops, deploring their lack of discipline. He complained that he had no maps fit for use in the coming campaign and no reconnaissance officers worthy of the name. They walked together to Russell's lodgings, and Russell noticed that not one of the soldiers they met took the trouble to salute the General.

By this time everyone knew that there would shortly be a great battle somewhere on the other side of the Potomac, and that knowledge intensified every phase of Washington life. As early as the second week in July there began the ominous gathering of the war correspondents in the city. They were to be found wherever news might be in the making—at the Willard bar, in the gallery at the Capitol, and standing in the narrow, crowded corridors of the War Department. They wrangled with officials about the freedom of the press, asserting their right to publish information about troop movements, armed strength, and other military matters of considerable use to the enemy. In the absence of news, they filled columns with rumor and anecdote, the scratching of their busy pens producing a vivid record of the tension and suppressed excitement which permeated those hot July days.

The order to advance was finally given on July 9th, and quickly countermanded when it became obvious, even to the politicians, that the army was not ready. Russell thought the army was short of nearly everything which would be needed in the coming fight. "And it is with this rabblement," he wrote, "that the North proposes not only to subdue

the South, but according to some of their papers, to humiliate Great Britain and Canada afterward."

Meanwhile, Rose Greenhow was making her own estimate of the situation, and in the face of coming hostilities she was assiduously gathering information to turn over to the Confederate command. This information she put in a message for General Beauregard which read, "McDowell has certainly been ordered to advance on the sixteenth." On July 10th Rose summoned one of her devoted women agents, a beautiful young lady with bright, dark eyes and long, shining black hair, improbably named Betty Duvall. Betty took the message, which was written in cipher, rolled in a piece of silk, and hid it in the coils of her hair. Then, dressed in the clothes of a farm woman and riding in a wagon, she drove to the house of friends near the river, outside of Washington. Here she spent the night. The next day she changed to a fashionable riding habit, rode across the river at Dumfries and on to Fairfax Court House.

There for the first time she was stopped by a sentry, a Confederate guard outside the headquarters of General M. L. Bonham. After some argument, she succeeded in having herself brought to the General. She told him that she was the bearer of an important message which must either be sent to General Beauregard at once, or she must be given a pass to deliver it in person. General Bonham, astonished and impressed, agreed to dispatch the message, whereupon Betty Duvall pulled out her comb and her shining black hair fell down, creating an effect the General remembered for the rest of his days. Betty handed him the silk-wrapped message, and not long afterward Beauregard was in possession of the vital information.

Meanwhile Russell had grown tired of waiting around the over-crowded, malodorous city for a campaign which did not commence. He heard that some members of the Sanitary Commission, including Commissioner Strong and President Bellows, were going to Fortress Monroe to inspect the hospital there. Russell cared little about hospitals, but the fortress and the garrison, under the command of the energetic General Butler, did interest him and he decided that he could go and return before the army started to move.

It was not a compatible party that set out for the fortress. Everybody got on everybody's nerves right from the start. Russell's attitude toward the work of the Sanitary Commission, which seems to have been one of indifference tinged with snobbery, irritated the easily irritated Commissioner Strong. Russell recorded his slightly pompous thought that Bel-

lows was a believer, "not in the perfectibility, but in the absolute perfection" of the New England character. The party wandered around the fortifications and watched the troops drilling. On such occasions, the Reverend Dr. Bellows did undeniably have a tendency to pontificate, while Russell let it be known that he was bored and contemptuous.

The tour of inspection included a visit to the Hygeia Hospital, a large institution, destined to play an important part in the war, which had been a short time previously a fashionable hotel. Strong was impressed by the busy staff of women nurses, mainly from Massachusetts, who were giving the hospital a cheerful, efficient air. Russell also noticed them, as well he might, since a military hospital full of women nurses was the outward and visible sign of a change in the social order, but all he could find to say about it was the faintly supercilious comment that the nurses were there, "let us believe as I do, out of some higher motive than the mere desire of human praise . . . " He then adds an account of a pretty young nurse who was having trouble making an amorous Scotsman eat his bowl of soup.

Russell returned to Washington by train from Annapolis, arriving on Tuesday the sixteenth, the day the army was scheduled to advance. At the station he met General McDowell who had come there to look for two missing batteries of artillery. McDowell, having only the rank of a brigadier, though he commanded an army, had been denied an adequate staff and he was, therefore, obliged to do errands which should have been the work of a junior officer. To Russell, the General said, "You are aware that I have advanced?" and offered the correspondent a lift in his carriage. He had, he told Russell, made arrangements for the correspondents to take the field with him and had suggested that they wear white uniforms to symbolize "the purity of their character."

Russell had returned none too soon. The excitement in the city had grown noticeably. The last vestiges of southern sleepiness had gone, and everyone moved more quickly, talked more loudly. People glanced often across the river where, hidden by the rolling hills, the enemy waited. Noises of the heavy military traffic in the streets seemed more purposeful, the rumble of the wheels had the sound of fate.

Long trains of wagons and ambulances had already crossed the river. The troops had begun to march. Along Pennsylvania Avenue crowds collected to see the marching columns pass on their way to battle. They filled the sidewalks, they jostled each other on the steps and leaned from windows, waving flags. The road shook under the rhythmic pound of marching feet. Clara Barton, loving military show, loving excitement,

had found herself a place from which she could watch the men marching away, a strange solitary girl who loved the soldiers and wished she could be one of them.

Clara and the hundreds of other women who watched the troops go out to war, saw them in a rosy mist of patriotism and romance. In sober truth, they were a bizarre sight, for most of them still wore the fanciful uniforms created by the women in the days of their enlistment or designed by themselves to express some vague notion of martial style. The 79th New York Regiment, which appeared at dress parades in kilts and sporans, had dressed for battle in fatigue trousers of bright plaid. General Sherman's command included some New York Guards wearing uniforms of the design of 1812, there were Wisconsin troops in gray, confusingly close to the color of the Confederate uniform, and the 69th New York Zouaves—who were Irish to a man—wore red Turkish trousers and fezzes and marched under an emerald-green flag. There were Garibaldi Guards with bunches of iridescent cock feathers on their broad-brimmed hats and the New York Fire Zouaves, angry men since the death of their hero, Colonel Ellsworth, wore spotless white gaiters below their brilliant, baggy pantaloons.

It was a Fourth of July home town parade on a national scale, brimful of naiveté, bravura, and a kind of brash self-confidence which was enough to bring tears to the eyes. The ridiculous uniforms were perfect targets for the enemy (who were little if any better uniformed themselves), but blending into the landscape was not considered soldierly in those days. Indeed, there was no point in not wearing bright colors in an army that marched into battle in parade formation and charged the enemy strong points in closed ranks.

Clara Barton, who was an intelligent young woman and always aware of what was going on around her, had from the beginning of the war felt sure that Washington was full of spies and traitors. She was wholly justified in that view. Of all the women spies of North and South—and there were many—Rose Greenhow was the boldest. Unlike most of the others, she did not work alone, but sent her agents hither and yon, while she remained in the little house in Sixteenth Street, like a general in his headquarters.

It was there, on the morning of this day, that a former government clerk, who had crossed the river from the Southern side by night, sought her out and handed her a message in cipher. The message was from her associate, Jordan, and it read "Trust bearer." Rose knew that the information Jordan was seeking concerned the strength of the army

which was being sent across the Potomac into Virginia, and the time of the move against the enemy.

Later, when Rose herself revealed all these dealings, she claimed to have seen the actual order for the advance. She wrote out a reply for the messenger to carry back to Jordan: "McDowell with 55,000 men, will advance this day from Arlington Heights and Alexandria on to Manassas via Fairfax Court House and on to Centerville."

The estimate Rose gave of the strength of the Union forces was more than double the actual number, but the rest of the information was substantially correct and of great value to the Confederates, since it gave the precise route of the advance. General Beauregard, Commander of the Confederate Forces, received Rose's message that evening and the next morning he telegraphed to Richmond, asking that General Johnson, and the large force in the Shenandoah, be sent as reenforcements to Manassas. As a result of Rose Greenhow's hastily written words, Johnson's army was moved up, arriving fresh and in prime condition in time to throw their weight against the weary Union force.

That night, after the departure of the troops, the city of Washington seemed quiet and empty. Across the Potomac campfires glowed in the summer dusk, and bugles sounded taps, the long notes floating over the hills. The First Rhode Island Regiment, with Kady Brownell, color bearer for her company of sharpshooters, was in camp near Annandale, east and a little north of Fairfax Court House. Kady had marched with the men most of the day, in the broiling sun. Her heavy standard would have been rolled in a leather case, not to be unfurled until just before the start of the battle, and it is said that she herself carried it for the entire march.

The next day, the seventeenth, the regiment moved on toward Fairfax Court House. The day was intensely hot, and the troops which went before tramped the dry dirt of the road into dust so that those who came behind walked ankle-deep in soft, burning hot powder. The dust rose around the marching men, clinging to their faces and their clothing, parching their throats with every indrawn breath. It hung in a cloud over their heads, so thick that through it the fiery sun looked like a luminous ball. The men continually broke ranks to dash, shouting, into the water of every stream they passed. They gathered around the wells in the dooryards and drank them down to the mud, so that every well along the line of march was dry.

The men were not used to marching, which had not been part of their training in camp. Seven miles was about all they were equal to, and all

day long they threw away their energy in a wild exuberance of spirit which was in part an expression of release from the monotony of camp, in part a way of dealing with the dread which every man must feel on going into battle. Each incident of the road was an excuse for horseplay. They stopped at blackberry patches, filling their caps with berries and smearing the dust on their faces with purple juice. Yelling, they chased chickens and pigs across fields, and when they caught them, hung their carcasses on the points of their bayonets to be roasted over the evening campfires. A soldier chasing a pig was an excuse for half a regiment to stop and cheer him. One man, stealing honey from a hive, got his hair full of bees and ran screaming to plunge into a stream while his comrades howled with laughter.

Livestock was not the only prize of war on the long days of marching. Houses were entered and various articles appropriated, only to be abandoned later by the roadside. Sherman, who was at that time a colonel in command of a brigade, and had not yet realized the military value of vandalism, was inspired by the sight of the plundering soldiers to remark that "No curse could be greater than invasion by a volunteer army." Sometimes frantic officers rode up and down the ranks, commanding the men not to leave their places. Their commands were met with hoots and jeers. Sometimes the officers joined the men, behaving in a way that filled the Regular Army men who saw them with disgust.

Russell had spent a large part of Tuesday the sixteenth in an unsuccessful search for a saddle horse to carry him to the scene of the coming battle. So many congressmen and private citizens had decided to drive out to see the glorious victory that all the horses had already been taken. On Wednesday, when Russell finally located a man who had a spavined, ringboned animal for sale, he was told that the price would be a thousand dollars.

It was on this Wednesday also that Russell called at General Scott's headquarters, where he found, as he had expected, that the universal optimism about the coming engagement was not shared. Many people believed that the old General would himself take the field in a buggy and command the troops in battle. The General was resting when Russell arrived, so he talked for a while with the headquarters staff, "plodding pedants with maps," and some "ignorant and very active young men."

The night of the seventeenth the First Rhode Island Regiment went into camp near Fairfax Court House, and Governor Sprague was a guest of the Regiment. Sprague was enjoying himself thoroughly. Young, handsome, overflowing with the romance of war, and beginning to be much

in love with Kate Chase, the belle of Washington, the world must have seemed nearly perfect that night as he ate and drank with the officers and later, in the cool of the evening as the moon rose, listened to the men singing around the embers of their fires.

On Thursday the eighteenth, the Rhode Island men moved on toward Centerville. The heat of the day had the still intensity that precedes a storm, and men began to drop out of the ranks with sunstroke and heat prostration. In the afternoon, the regiment heard firing in front and to the left, the heavy thud of artillery and rapid bursts of gunfire which indicated an engagement of some importance was in progress. They were hearing the sound of the fight at Blackburn's Ford, on Bull Run, where General Tyler was making a feint at Manassas.

The Second Michigan Volunteer Infantry, under a Regular Army officer, "Fighting Dick" Richardson, had been sent forward as skirmishers. The purpose of the expedition was to feel out the enemy's position, and it was not McDowell's intention to become involved in action. Almost before anyone knew what was happening, however, the Second was in the midst of a severe fight. The regiment was spread out through the woods and on the level bottomland along the Run at Blackburn's Ford, and some miles away, the men of the First Rhode Island, gazing in the direction of the sound of firing, could see the blue smoke of the powder drifting upward through the trees.

There, was a woman in the midst of the fighting at the Ford. Her name was Anna Etheridge, "Gentle Annie," the men called her, daughter of the Regiment. She rode a horse and dressed in a long side-saddle skirt with two revolvers thrust through her belt, and she carried saddle bags filled with lint and bandages. Anna had an aversion to the revolvers, which were there to be used only in the event that she fell into the hands of the enemy. Anna's mission was not to fight, but to give first aid to the wounded where they fell.

The Second Michigan charged the enemy position, the charge carrying them forward with such momentum that two mounted officers rode through the lines and were killed inside the enemy earthworks. Anna rode with the charge, for she considered part of the duties of a daughter of a regiment to be the setting of an example of courage in battle. She was not wounded at Blackburn's Ford, but she displayed a reckless indifference to danger, and when the charge was over she dismounted and, under heavy fire, she unpacked her saddle bags and set about caring for the wounded.

By the twentieth, which was Saturday, it was clear that the battle would

be fought the next day. Washington, still anticipating victory, was tensely waiting, but doing little to prepare for the great numbers of wounded who would arrive in the city. Russell had given up trying to find a saddle horse and was hunting for any kind of conveyance to take him to the front. Ever since the army had moved into Virginia, sight-seers had been crossing the Potomac in large numbers to see the novel spectacle of a large army on the eve of battle. Ladies in floppy hats and billowing muslin skirts, accompanied by well-tailored gentlemen, wandered among the tents or stood on the heights of ground gazing into the distance in the hope of catching sight of the enemy. Most of the parties had come with elaborate lunches packed in wicker hampers by Washington's best caterer. The picknickers sat on the ground under the trees, gay and excited, passing each other cold chicken and sandwiches, the ladies looking like groups in a painting by Winterhalter.

Sometime that day Russell had a windfall, for he found not one horse, but three. He hired them all. Two were for hitching to a hooded gig in which Russell with a friend from the British embassy and a driver would ride. The third, with a small colored boy in the saddle, was to be held in reserve for Russell to use when they came near the lines of battle. His adventures subsequently found their way into some fairly scurrilous poetry, for Russell's unpopularity reached its peak after he had been a witness to the humiliating defeat:

> "Tomorrow's sun will see a fight
> On Bull Run's banks they say;
> So there, my friend, we'll early go,
> All in a *two-oss shay.*

> "I'll also take a saddle-horse
> To bear the battle's brunt
> Whereon, in my Crimean style,
> I'll see the fight *in front.*"[2]

On the night of the twentieth, most of the Union Army was camped in and around Centerville, a village of a few poor houses and a bleak stone church where the wounded from Blackburn's Ford lay moaning. The enemy was at, or near, Manassas, seven miles away to the southwest. On the nineteenth and twentieth, Kady Brownell's regiment remained in camp. The intense, enervating heat continued and the men built small shelters of brush to shield themselves from the sun.

Evening came, and for an hour or two the smell of cooking hung in the still, hot air. When the evening meal was finished there was nothing for the men to do but to get through the hours of waiting as best they might. All felt the strain. Some relieved their apprehension by horseplay, shouting and pummeling each other with their fists. Sometimes real anger would flare up, and for a few minutes they would fight each other viciously. In the Irish regiments, men knelt on the ground with bowed heads, listening to the sonorous roll of Latin words as the priests blessed them and blessed the regimental flags. Protestant chaplains read psalms and prayed that Almighty God would lead the army to victory. As the light faded, many men wrote letters home. Others wandered off alone to watch the stars come out. Somewhere in the camp of the First, Kady and Robert Brownell were together. The men of the First began to sing. The sound floated over the hills, and, for some who heard that singing, was never wiped from memory.

At dark, the long drawn notes of the bugles hushed the camps into silence. The embers of the campfires glowed in the still night, and candlelight shone through the open flaps of tents where officers bent over crude maps unrolled on folding tables. Sometimes in the silence a night bird would cry out, and a sentry would shift his gun nervously. Sometimes there would be the thud of a horse's hoofs as some messenger, riding hard by the eerie light of the moon, passed along the road. Sometimes an outpost, thinking he saw a bush stir, would fire and at the crack of the shot sleeping men would leap to their feet and officers would come to the openings of their tents to peer into the night. There would be angry voices and swearing which would die down to murmurs as the men settled back to sleep once more.

That night in Washington the great again slept fitfully. There was old General Scott, at the end of his career, at the end of his usefulness and of his strength, facing the next day's uncertainty. There was Secretary Cameron, conscious perhaps that a finger dipped in blood would next day write the sum of his achievements for the pages of history. Cameron was to lose a son in that day's battle and his term in office was drawing to a close. There were many others in Washington who were powerless to shape events but whose whole lives would be shaped by the morrow, among them the women whose sons and husbands and lovers had gone across the river. And there was William Russell in his lodgings, an outsider to all of this. Russell, too, slept fitfully that still night in the empty city and dreamed that General McDowell was standing by the table in his room.

NOTES

1 William Howard Russell, *My Diary North and South* (New York: Harper & Brothers, 1863).

2 "The Modern Gilpin—A Ballad of Bull Run" by "Chanticleer" from *Personal and Political Ballads*, edited by Frank Moore (New York, George P. Putnam, 1864).

9

FIRST BULL RUN

————————————— ★ —————————————

1861

July 21   The First Battle of Bull Run (Manassas) began about ten o'clock in the morning. Toward the end of the afternoon, the Union lines broke and a disorderly rout ensued. Union killed were an estimated 480, wounded, 1500. Confederates killed were 380, wounded, 1500. This is a total, in round numbers, of 3,360 killed and wounded. The same estimated total after Gettysburg was about 40,000.

————————————— ★ —————————————

> *While the mad rout at Manassas was surging,*
> *When those around her fled wildly, or fell,*
> *And the bold Beauregard onward was urging,*
> *Who so undaunted as Kady Brownell!*
> —Clinton Scollard

GENERAL MCDOWELL WAS FACED with the decision of whether to move his divisions closer to the enemy that night of the twentieth, or whether to wait until morning and march them straight into battle. He left that decision to his commanders but few of his officers were qualified to advise him. Two of his three division commanders had never seen a battle, and of his nine brigade commanders, only two had any battle

117

experience. They thought that the men were too exhausted and too unused to marching to go further, though the distance they would have to march next morning before going into battle would not be much shorter, for some of the regiments, than the distance they had covered that day. McDowell then issued orders that each man was to carry three days' rations in his knapsack. That night McDowell ate some canned peaches for supper, which probably played a part in history. The peaches were tainted, and when morning came McDowell was a sick man.

At two A.M. there sounded through the camps the roll of drums, rousing the men from sleep. The moon, sinking in the west, still cast a pale, silvery light and a chill dawn wind tossed the branches of the trees. Some of the men made campfires and put coffee on to boil, others, too apprehensive to eat, stood about shivering and waiting for the order to march. The order came at two-thirty and the men, accoutrements rattling, formed into line. The divisions were to move forward at once, but Tyler's division, which blocked the way, was slow to start, and there followed a delay which McDowell, in his official report of the battle, called "a great misfortune."

The First Rhode Island marched in silence, except for occasional words of command. Whatever Kady Brownell had done with her heavy standard on previous days of marching, she was carrying it now. Somewhere, separated from her, Kady's husband marched with Company H. Up ahead, Governor Sprague rode on a fine horse. Dust rose from the road and hung in ribbon-like clouds just above the tops of the trees, marking too plainly the line of the advance.

The First was moving out on the Warrenton Pike toward Centerville, but after two miles they were halted by the road jam caused by Tyler's late start. There followed one of those waits common to all wars when no one knew what had happened or why they were halted there. The men broke ranks and sat on the dusty grass. Some, who had eaten no breakfast, opened their emergency rations. Others had disregarded the order to carry provisions and had left their emergency rations in the abandoned camp. The sun rose, and with it the intense heat returned.

Presently the roadblock was cleared, the order to fall in was given, and the regiment began to march. But by this time, the whole plan of battle had been disrupted. The men were already tired and for the most part, hungry. Some had not filled their water canteens; others had used their supplies unwisely. At Cub Run they drank, filled their canteens and splashed water on their dusty faces. They crossed where a narrow stone bridge arched its back over the little stream, and tramped on up

Mrs. Mary A. Bickerdyke

Louisa May Alcott

Mrs. Mary A. Livermore

Culver

Major Pauline Cushman

the turnpike. Progress was slow. When the command was given for the regiment to leave the turnpike and to proceed cross country through fields and woods, the men were marching doggedly, heads down, gasping in the dusty heat.

When they reached Bull Run near Sudley Church, which was soon to become a field hospital, the men were thirsty again, and aware that they would soon be in the fighting. During the halt they relieved their strained nerves with horseplay, broke ranks, ran shouting into the water, splashing each other, stirring up mud so that it was hard to find any clear water for the canteens. Horses stood knee-deep in the stream, heads down, making sucking noises, their riders lounging in their saddles. Men sitting on the banks, took off their shoes and bathed their burning feet.

In the midst of this scene, there was a commotion and a fast-driven carriage surrounded by mounted officers pulled up. It was General McDowell and his staff. The General looked pale and ill. Sitting a horse was agony to him and he was attempting to keep in touch with his army by negotiating the clogged roads in a carriage. Someone heard him say, "The enemy is moving heavy columns from Manassas." Then he was gone and the First began to climb out of the muddied waters of the Run. The air was still and stifling. Looking toward the heavens for relief, the men saw great white storm clouds piling up.

Thick woods lay ahead, obscuring the view, and on the ridge, out of sight, the enemy waited. Confederate officers with glasses had watched the narrow ribbons of dust creep slowly through the green treetops as the troops advanced. The main attack had been expected nearer Centerville, but when the dust betrayed the massing of troops in the neighborhood of Sudley Church, the Confederates wheeled their forces to receive the shock of the attack.

The First Rhode Island formed in line of march and began to move across Bull Run. The Second Rhode Island ahead of them, but hidden by the trees, had spread out on either side of the road in battle formation and were advancing. The Confederates, tense and quiet, waited, scanning the edge of the woods for the first appearance of moving men. The First, nervously awaiting its own command to advance in line of battle, heard fighting. The battle had begun.

By this time, Kady Brownell's standard, drooping in the heavy air, was held high. From the moment the regiment started to advance, it must be a visible guide and rallying point for the men of her company during the fight. The command to advance was given, the regiment fanned out into the long lines in which they would walk into the enemy's fire,

with Kady and her flag approximately in the center. The lines began to move forward as Kady and the First went into battle.

While the First was advancing, William Russell was driving rapidly toward the scene of action. He had rigged himself for battle in something called a "Himalayan suit," Italian boots, cord breeches and an old felt hat. He had armed himself with a flask and a revolver, a bottle of water, another of cold tea, and some unpalatable sandwiches. His friend from the embassy overslept, so that they were late in leaving Washington and the sentry at the Long Bridge informed them that "plenty of congressmen" were already on their way to see the battle.

The country through which they drove was quiet, and from the windows frightened, sickly-looking women with children clinging to them, peered at the passing carriage. Near Fairfax Court House, Russell heard the sound of distant artillery fire, "like taps with a gentle hand upon a muffled drum," and fearing to be late, the party pushed on. A little further, and they met a large body of troops straggling along the road, their backs to the beginning battle, heading for Alexandria. They were the men of the Fourth Pennsylvania, a regiment of three-month volunteers whose time had just expired and they were going home. The men were cheerful, if a trifle reticent about where they were going, and their baggage wagons were piled high with tables, chairs and other household goods looted from the houses along the route. Nearer to Fairfax Court House, Russell and his party were startled to see in the middle of the road a huge blue dome as high as the tree tops, which heaved gently like a lung. It turned out to be an observation balloon hopelessly wedged in the trees, and the terrified horses were with difficulty maneuvered around the fantastic obstacle.

Russell had forgotten to wind his watch (a strange oversight for so meticulous an observer) and his friend appears not to have had one, but they probably arrived at Fairfax Court House about the time that Lincoln, back in Washington, was leaving church. The firing had increased in intensity, and the President paused for a moment to listen to the distant sounds before stepping into his carriage and hurrying back to the White House to wait for dispatches from the front.

At Fairfax Court House, Russell began to meet the carriages of the sight-seers who had come out from Washington. Near Centerville, the road went over a rise of ground and on the crest Russell saw a line of civilians, their backs toward him, all gazing toward the valley. Behind them in the fields was a strange assortment of carriages, wagons and saddle horses. Russell joined the spectators on the ridge. Most of them

were men, but there were women also, though probably not as many as tradition would have us suppose. All were talking excitedly, pointing, and raising field glasses to their eyes.

From his place in the line, Russell could see the thin, frayed lines of blue smoke which rose above the muttering roll of musketry and the large white puffs from the fieldpieces. Through the smoke and dust he saw flashes of light as the sun gleamed from a bayonet. There was an unusually heavy burst of artillery and a lady with opera glasses standing near him, quite beside herself with excitement, cried out, "That is splendid. Oh my! Is not that first rate? I guess we will be in Richmond this time tomorrow." The whole line shared her enthusiasm. Then a mounted officer came dashing past and reined up to shout that the Union troops were victorious all along the line. Wild cheers broke out from the civilians on the crest of the hill.

The hilltop where they stood was too far distant from the fighting for Russell's purpose, and he was becoming irritated by the constant demands for the loan of his glasses. He had the saddle horse brought up, and leaving his embassy friend (whom he never saw again that day) at a place of rendezvous with the carriage, Russell mounted and rode off toward the firing.

Now Kady Brownell was advancing with the First, carrying the flag. Kady was stocky and strong, and she had to be. Her black hair was long and straight and it must have been damp with sweat and thick with dust as she went plodding up the hill toward the enemy. Kady's company of sharpshooters held a position to the left of the line as the regiment advanced. The men were ordered up as skirmishers to feel out the enemy strength. The company moved through a pine wood and took up its position at the edge of a clearing, facing the enemy lines. The men advanced by fours, stealthily, until they made contact with the enemy, then they fired and retreated to reload and another four would repeat the same tactics. Kady carried no gun that day. She stood with her flag out in the open to guide the men who were struggling through underbrush and trees, back to their line.

Shells were screaming overhead most of the time, but they were aimed at the Union artillery positions and at the regiments still coming into line. About one o'clock there was a burst of musketry, aimed directly at the colors which Kady carried. Kady stood firm. Then suddenly the carefully planned skirmishing gave place to fierce fighting all along the line. The battle was at its height, and Kady was in the midst of it. Six times the colors she displayed were the focal point of attack. The men

around her could at least fight back. Kady, holding the heavy colors in both hands, stood her ground. The hillside was now a bedlam of noise, dust and smoke. Men near Kady, their faces blackened beyond recognition by gunpowder and dirt, fell and lay still, or called for help, or tried to crawl toward the rear. Gunfire crackled, fieldpieces boomed, bullets whined as they ricocheted from the trees, wounded men and horses screamed.

Until afternoon the battle seemed to be going in favor of the Union troops and there was rejoicing among the picnickers on the ridge. Word traveled fast to Washington, where flags were flown and men and women, celebrating victory, filled the streets. For a while, the men in the line also believed they were winning the day. Then the time came when they could advance no further. The lines of Confederates which wavered and crumbled under the Union fire, seemed always to be replaced by fresh troops in wave on wave.

About three-thirty in the afternoon, the Union line far to the right of the spot where Kady stood with her flag, began to hesitate, then to break. Before anyone had time to realize what was happening, men were running toward the rear. The first small break in the line spread and became a general rout. Men pelted down the hill, throwing away their guns, deaf to the shouts of officers to stand and fight. Some regiments stood their ground better than others; some were completely demoralized, the men in panic, the officers giving up any attempt to command, and running with the men.

Nearer and nearer to where Kady stood, the line gave way. The First Rhode Island did not immediately yield to panic, but as men from other regiments ran past and through their ranks, the men of the First succumbed and followed. Kady and a few men from her company stood their ground.

The Confederates, seeing the break, crashed through the underbrush in front of the spot where Kady and her comrades were standing. Kady could see them and hear their shouts. They came within a few hundred yards, wheeling a battery of fieldpieces into place. Kady and the few men with her were all that was left of the First Rhode Island's skirmish line. The battery opened fire, hurling shells into the masses of men who were fleeing to the rear. Kady was in the line of fire.

While she and the men with her stood there, a little island of defiance, a Pennsylvania regiment, fleeing obliquely from her right, began to run past her. One of the men saw her, realized she was a woman and yelled at her—words which, coming out of the din and confusion, still

have the ring of reality: "Come, sis, there's no use to stay here just to be killed—let's get into the woods."

He grabbed her hand and dragged her along, and they ran down the slope toward a pine thicket. There, feeling safe in the shelter of the trees, they stopped to catch their breath. It was in that moment that a shot struck Kady's rescuer. He fell against her and she caught him in her arms. His head rested on her shoulder and his blood poured down over her dress. She spoke to him. There was no answer, and she eased him gently to the ground. She bent over him and saw that he was dead.

When she straightened up and looked around, she found that she was alone and that shots were still coming into the wood. She left him there and ran on. Presently, in another part of the wood, she found some men of her own company, and they went on together heading toward Centerville. The Confederates were moving up behind them and shots still ripped through the leaves of the trees.

By this time Kady must have been near exhaustion, for she had started the day at two in the morning and had been under fire for more than five hours. In the neighborhood of Sudley Church, she came on an ambulance whose driver was apparently making for safety as fast as the congested road would permit. The few ambulance drivers who came this close to the front had given up all thought of collecting the wounded. Some of the drivers had taken the horses out of the shafts and were riding them back toward Washington. One ambulance, the horses gone, hung crazily over the bank of the stream. Others had been seized by men and officers trying to escape, and were caught in the hopeless blockade of vehicles on the road. The one Kady found seems to have been empty, or at least to have had room for one more passenger, and she climbed inside.

The Confederates were close behind her, already in possession of the wood she had just left. (About thirty minutes after this they were in possession of the spot where she now was.) Shots fired by their advance skirmishers were tearing into the congestion of men, horses and wagons on the road. One of them ripped through the canvas side of the ambulance in which Kady had taken refuge, and Kady climbed quickly out again.

Then she saw a riderless horse and she ran after him and captured him. She rode him into Centerville where she was safe, though she did not know this, but realizing the enemy were no longer in close pursuit, she went on her way more slowly. But now that she had time to think, she

was tortured by anxiety about her husband, whom she had not seen or heard from all this long time.

When she turned her horse from Centerville toward Alexandria, she was in the midst of the full tide of the retreat. The road, the ditches and the fields were a solid, crawling, snake-like mass of wagons, gun caissons, horses and demoralized men, shouting, cursing and driven on by panic. Broken down equipment, abandoned fieldpieces and the smashed light carriages which had brought the sight-seers from Washington littered the roadsides. All vestige of organization was lost and every man was convinced he was fleeing for his life. Here and there an officer, sword in hand and hoarse from shouting, planted himself in the road and tried to turn back the terrified men. Other officers, all decency and responsibility thrown away, fought with their men for places in ambulances and wagons. There were scenes to haunt the memory of a lifetime. Men attacked each other with fists and bayonets. A man, losing his hold, fell screaming under the rolling wheels of a gun caisson. Two officers on the back of one mule whipped him to a gallop. Men on stolen horses were riding down anyone in their path.

Kady made her way through scenes like this, not so much of her own volition, as swept along by the retreat. When she came across any members of the First Rhode Island Regiment, she asked for news of her husband. One man had seen him fall dead, another knew that he had been carried to a building which was being used as a hospital, and that the enemy had set fire to the place and all inside had been burned to death. Still another told her with convincing sincerity that his body lay on the edge of the pine wood not far from the place where she had stood with her flag.

Kady probably lost her horse, or had it taken away from her, somewhere along the route. Perhaps the animal was worn out and had to be abandoned, so that she entered Alexandria on foot. The town was in a turmoil. The broad main street and all the side streets were filled with soldiers, many of them resting on the curb and on the steps of the houses before struggling on their way to Washington. They were a sorry lot, dirty, bloody, unarmed, a rabble in retreat. Somehow, in this crowd and disorganization Kady found another horse.

Kady, the homely, un-feminine woman who loved her husband, made up her mind to go back and look for him. It was an incredible decision, and to arrive at it she had to fight down the contagion of panic, her own exhaustion, and the fear of entering alone the territory of the enemy.

She mounted her horse and was on her way when she met General

Burnside, commander of the First, who had commissioned her regimental daughter. The General was fond of her and no doubt he was glad to know that she was safe. But more important, he knew that her husband was alive and unhurt. He told her that they would be together soon.

The First Rhode Island Regiment had not behaved badly when the line had broken. They had retreated in disorder, but not in panic. Governor Sprague, Kate Chase's handsome lover, had stayed to spike the guns which had to be abandoned and had escaped unhurt. Burnside had won himself a reputation, as had Colonel Sherman, who had shown his brilliance as a field commander, and characteristically came out of the melee with two more guns than he had in the beginning.

Most of the sight-seers had adventures they would never forget. Congressman Ely was taken prisoner and spent the night in a barn behind the Confederate lines. Another member returned to Washington ignominiously riding on a mule. William Russell never came close to the fighting, for as he was approaching the lines he was overtaken by the retreat and swept with it back toward Washington. He was seen by one of the correspondents riding his horse in the midst of the confusion, his broad face beet red and he was wearing a bright colored silk handkerchief under his hat which hung down like a havelock.

How many women beside Kady Brownell were in the battle and the retreat is not known. There was Augusta Foster from Maine who had a horse shot from under her, and escaped to Alexandria where she helped to nurse the wounded. Probably there were several more—daughters or matrons of regiments whose names and adventures were never recorded and there were certainly some women who fought that day disguised as men. Annie Etheridge and her big horse were not on the field because the Second Michigan Regiment was being held in reserve, though at the end it was moved in to cover the retreat, but for both Annie and Kady the life of adventure had just begun.

All night long the demoralized, tattered, disorganized army straggled into Washington. Russell was back in his lodgings writing his report for the London mail. Presently exhaustion overcame him and he laid down his pen and slept with his head on his half-finished dispatch. About six in the morning he awoke, heard strange sounds outside and, rising stiffly, went to the window to look out. Torrents of rain were falling and the air was chill. The street below was filled with the men of the defeated army and they were pouring like a river down Pennsylvania Avenue. Russell wrote all that day. Toward evening the rain slackened

and the river of defeated men had overflowed into all the principal streets of the city. Commissioner Olmsted of the Sanitary Commission was watching that scene also, and he too picked up his pen and wrote:

"Groups of men wearing parts of military uniforms and some with muskets were indeed to be seen; but upon second sight they did not appear to be soldiers. Rather they were a most woebegone rabble . . . No two were dressed completely alike; some were without caps, others without coats, others without shoes. All were alike excessively dirty, unshaven, unkempt, and dank with dew. The groups were formed around fires made in the streets, of boards wrenched from citizens' fences. Some were still asleep at full length in the gutters, or sitting on the curbstone resting their heads against the lampposts. Others were evidently begging for food at house doors . . . There was no apparent organization: no officers were seen among them . . . At Willard's Hotel, however, officers swarmed. They, too, were dirty and ill-conditioned; but appeared indifferent, reckless, and shameless, rather than dejected and morose."[1]

Around every liquor shop there were crowds of men terrorizing the proprietors with their wild, haggard appearance and their savage demands for drink. All of them were famished, filthy, hang-dog. They had no idea where their officers were or how to re-form into regiments, or even where to go to get in out of the rain. All that day and into the next night the women worked in the streets caring for the wounded soldiers. Some walked for hours searching for husband, son or lover. Others went back and forth through the rabble, carrying hot coffee and food to the men where they sat on the curbstones, or helped them to rise and stagger to the shelter of some house. They brought bandages and dressed wounds there in the street or turned their own homes into hospitals. The next day the whole North would feel the shock of the defeat.

NOTES

[1] William Law Olmsted, Report to the Sanitary Commission, Document No. 28, *op. cit.*, Stillé, p. 91.

10

AFTERMATH

———————————————————— ★ ————————————————————

CHRONOLOGY

1861

July 22   General George B. McClellan summoned to Washington.

July 27   General McClellan assumed command of Union forces in Virginia.

August 3   Female nursing made legal in Army hospitals by Act of Congress and pay set at forty cents a day. Medical Department increased by ten surgeons and twenty assistant surgeons.

August 6   Confiscation Act passed by Congress. Adjournment of Congress.

August 12   Surgeon Charles S. Tripler succeeded Surgeon King as Medical Director of the Army of the Potomac.

August 29   Fort Hatteras and Fort Clark in North Carolina surrendered to the Union forces.

August 30   General Fremont, in Missouri, proclaimed martial law and the emancipation of the slaves.

September 11   President Lincoln revoked Fremont's proclamation of August 30th.

September 12   Commissioners of the Sanitary Commission voted to request the removal or retirement of Surgeon General Finley.

October 21   Defeat of Union forces at Ball's Bluff, Virginia.

———————————————————— ★ ————————————————————

By our Northern host betrayed,
At Manassas' bloody raid,
By our losses unatoned—
   Our dead heroes, heart-enthroned,
    Miserere, Domine!
      —Sarah Helen Whitman

THE MEDICAL DIRECTOR OF THE ARMY in the field, W. S. King, never quite succeeded in making up his mind what his duties consisted of on that day of battle. This was not altogether his fault, since no one in the War Department had thought through the problem of caring for the wounded, the general plan being that each regiment would care for its own with its own surgeons and equipment. King had no central organization directly under his authority, and there was more than a little doubt as to whether the regimental surgeons would take orders from him or from his assistant, D. L. Magruder.

It was the old, vexing question of the extent of Federal control over volunteer and militia troops. King avoided the issue and resolved the problem of what to do with himself by considering himself a member of General McDowell's staff. He spent the greater part of the day galloping around after the General, a course of action which made it virtually impossible for him to observe, or to take part in the handling of the wounded. He had stuffed his saddle bags with surgical dressings, and when he came on a wounded man he would dismount and give him first aid. After a time, while the fighting was in progress, he was suddenly struck by the thought that no provision had been made for listing the casualties. That seemed immensely important to him and he took out a notebook and a pencil and wrote down the names and addresses of every wounded man he came across. That self-imposed and futile task occupied him for a large part of the day.

King was no administrator. Perhaps the most useful thing he did that day was to send Magruder to organize an emergency hospital at Sudley Church, where a group of regimental surgeons, pooling their resources, were attempting to deal with a flood of wounded men. There had been two days before the battle during which King might have made preparation for some sort of general field hospital. When the wounded arrived at Centerville he had helped to prepare a church to receive them, though not in advance of the need. He had ordered the establishment of a hospital at Alexandria, which proved woefully inadequate, and he ordered additional medical supplies from Washington which never arrived, though

through no fault of his. King waited to cope with an emergency until it was upon him.

During the battle, nothing connected with the care of the wounded worked out according to plan. That plan had been made on the assumption that slightly wounded men, who could walk to the rear, would seek out their own regimental surgeon for aid. Regimental stretcher-bearers were to search the field for the men of their own regiments who could not walk, and bring them in. First aid was to be given by the regimental surgeons, and those who would need prolonged care were to be sent by ambulance to the general hospitals in Washington. There was no provision for field hospitals, and it was assumed that no important surgical work would be done on the spot.

As soon as the heavy fighting began, it was plain that the plan to sort out the wounded according to regiment could not work. Stretcher-bearers and ambulances seemed to have vanished mysteriously from the scene, and not all the regiments were equipped with the prescribed number of stretchers. Regimental hospital tents were too far in the rear. The confusion was too great, the work too urgent to distribute the wounded to their own regiments before giving them surgical aid, though for a time some of the surgeons kept to the letter of their instructions and refused help to men of other regiments.

When a man was wounded, it usually happened that his comrades came to his aid. If a stretcher was needed, they made one out of a shutter, or a door, or lacking these they tied the four corners of a blanket to four muskets and carried him in that. Wounded men were often brought to the rear without delay, but for every wounded man, two or four fighting men left the line. Some of them never returned, and as the day wore on and the men grew weary, a man with an inconsequential wound who was quite able to walk, was often tenderly escorted out of the fighting by as many as six of his comrades.

Certain places behind the lines developed naturally into concentration spots for the wounded, the most important being Sudley Church. In the absence of ambulances to take the wounded to Washington, it was necessary to perform operations never intended to be done in the field, and the surgeons, throwing regimental discrimination to the winds, pooled their resources to improvise a field hospital.

There was no real ambulance corps. Each regiment had, in theory, two ambulances for the use of its own wounded, but few of them were so equipped. The small fleet of ambulances which was to transport the wounded from the battlefield to Washington belonged to the Quarter-

master Corps, and neither King nor any other medical officer had any authority over them. The drivers were civilian teamsters hired expressly for the battle, and they had but one thought among them: to keep as far as possible away from danger.

Apparently, no ambulances ever encroached on the edges of the battle-field, except in the neighborhood of Sudley Church, though a few of them, with their panicky drivers, were caught in the retreat. After the battle the Sanitary Commission held an investigation, but was unable to find a single instance in which one of these ambulances carried a wounded man to Washington.

The Army had never formally approved a type of ambulance, though two kinds had been in experimental use since 1859. One was a high contraption shaped like a wagon, with canvas sides and four large, fragile wheels. This had space inside to carry four wounded men. The other, which was slung between two large wheels and was designed to accommodate two men, developed in motion a formidable fore-and-aft pitch. Neither one was comfortable, though the second was far the worse of the two. When driven over rough roads, by drivers trying to gallop their horses out of range of shellfire, the men inside could be heard screaming and begging to be taken out and left on the roadside to die. This unique implement of torture remained in use for some time. The Army was aware of the defects of these two styles of ambulance, but no steps to improve them had been taken, and at the outbreak of war several hundred of them were built with a speed which seemed to William Russell remarkable.

The problem of removing the wounded from the field of battle was not solved satisfactorily in all the years of war. In time, there was an ambulance corps, and a system of field hospitals. Each regiment had ten stretcher bearers, who continued to show a talent for being elsewhere when needed. The regimental bands were removed from the firing line, on the theory that musicians made poor fighters, and given stretchers to carry. As bearers, the bandsmen were a conspicuous failure, and in the end they were ordered back to the lines.

Early on the day of battle, when King discovered that a great many wounded had been collected at Sudley Church, and that a number of regimental surgeons had gone there to care for them, he sent Magruder to take charge of converting the church into a hospital. Magruder went to work with so much energy as to imply that something constructive to do was a relief to him. Sudley Church was a stone building on a rise of ground, surrounded by a grove of tall trees and located near the princi-

pal crossing of Bull Run. Magruder had the pews removed, operating tables improvised, and part of the floor covered with blankets on which to lay the wounded. He had hay carried in for bedding and saw that a supply of water was at hand. Then he departed, leaving the surgeons at work.

The wounded came in so rapidly that within two hours the church was filled and wounded men were being laid on the ground under the trees outside. Before Magruder left he had commandeered three nearby buildings and some of the wounded were taken to them. In the end, there were 286 wounded men at Sudley Church, seventy of them lying on the ground.[1]

The surgeons working in the church—five of them from volunteer regiments and two from the Regular Army—moved among the men lying on the hay, passing by the slightly wounded and the mortally wounded, to care for those who could be saved by surgery. The church was strangely quiet, for most of the wounded were suffering from shock and were not yet feeling the full pain of their wounds. Here and there men called out to a surgeon, "Come to me. Please come to me." Sometimes there was a shriek of agony as a man was lifted onto an operating table. Sometimes men groaned as they tried to ease themselves on their hard beds. In the heat the blood-soaked blankets soon began to smell, sickish-sweet and heavy, and mixing with the odor of chloroform from the soaked rags being held over the faces of the men on the tables, the stench began to fill the buildings.

The surgeons worked with quiet concentration, paying little attention to the progress of the battle on the hill above. About four in the afternoon the noise in the direction of the crossing of Bull Run rose to a tumult. The road past the church was suddenly jammed with vehicles of every description. There were shouts, crashes and the sound of splintering wood. The retreat had begun. Soldiers ran past, throwing away their guns and equipment as they ran. Their faces were grimy and black with gunpowder, their eyes wild with panic. Some of them paused, panting under the shade of the trees where the wounded lay and seeing the buckets of bloody water which had been used to wash the wounds, they snatched them up and drank.

After a while the noise diminished; the crest of the retreat had passed. About five o'clock Confederate troops appeared on the road below the rise of ground where the church stood. Some of them came up through the grove of trees and surrounded the building. Sudley Church had fallen into the hands of the enemy.

Inside the church, the surgeons continued to work over the operating tables. According to the accepted usages of war, they had the status of noncombatants, but whether they knew this or not, they were not willing to desert the wounded. Presently about fifty Union prisoners were driven into the church by their guards, to be held there until they could be sent to Manassas. Among them was a young man named E. P. Doherty of the 71st New York Regiment. Doherty, who was an enterprising young man, had no desire to spend the rest of the war in a Southern prison, and he began to look around him for a means of escape. The fifty prisoners, the wounded lying on the floor and the line of operating tables crowded the church to its limits, and for a little while there was considerable confusion. Taking advantage of it, Doherty crawled under a bloody blanket and lay still.

After a while the prisoners were ordered out of the church and Doherty, keeping very quiet under his blanket, heard them being marched off down the road. When he was sure they had gone, he crawled out and offered to help one of the surgeons at an operating table.

About seven-thirty that evening the Confederate commander, General Beauregard, rode up to the church accompanied by some of his staff. He stayed long enough to give the church a cursory inspection and rode off again, leaving orders that the wounded should be well attended. A few more prisoners arrived and a guard was placed in charge of them and of the church. The rush of operating was beginning to subside. Night came, bringing comparative quiet to the church. Medical supplies were running short and the only food at the church was what little some of the men happened to have with them.

On Monday, Sudley Church had settled down to a hospital routine. Some of the wounded had died during the night. The rest lay moaning with pain and fever. Everyone was hungry except those who were too sick to eat. During the day someone, scouting around for food, found enough corn meal in a nearby house to make about a cup of gruel for everyone. Doherty was making himself useful as a self-appointed hospital orderly. Then some rebel officers arrived and demanded that the Union surgeons sign a parole of honor not to take action against the Confederates. Five of them refused. No one was sure how the rules of war applied in a situation like this, and the five surgeons were declared prisoners of war and taken away to Manassas.

The little hospital was now in desperate straits, without supplies and without food. The cold rain had begun, and those of the seventy men still alive who had been left outdoors, now lay on the soggy ground with

no protection but the trees. The remaining surgeons and those who were able to work, hunted among the debris of the retreat for discarded rubber blankets, and found enough of them to build shelters over these wounded men. During the day the five captured surgeons returned, having been sent back by General Beauregard. This incident, which arose from ignorance of military usages, was made much of in the North as demonstrating the brutality of the Southerners.

The next day the surgeons put the useful Doherty in charge of nursing and allowed him to choose twenty helpers from among the Union prisoners. One of the war correspondents, seeing how such willing but inexpert nursing had worked out at the Centerville hospital, thought:

> "What a blessed comfort a Nurses Department would be, following the Army. For some kind gentlewoman to come in there to bind up wounds . . . would be invaluable. Then, if she had authority to draw for tea and little niceties on the Quartermaster, and could carry them in her own wagon—say an ambulance—making her bed in this at night, and having all her little stores ready, so that in the confusion after a battle, she could at once bring forth tea and comforts for the sick, the field hospital would have a very different aspect and comfort to the poor fellows. . . ."[2]

Meanwhile, there was a desperate need for food. On Wednesday morning a woman of the neighborhod appeared with a bottle of wine and two dozen eggs. That noon the surgeons were able to buy twelve dozen more eggs from a wandering sutler. News of the wounded lying at Sudley Church had begun to spread around the countryside and kind-hearted farmers and their wives began to bring in food—soup, a whole pig, meal, milk. The orphaned hospital lived off the country, but there was never enough to give anyone a square meal.

Doherty was beginning to worry about the day when the Confederates would remember the prisoners at the church and return to get them. With two companions he planned his escape, and one dark night, they slipped past the Confederate guards and headed for the Potomac. The first part of their journey was easy, then they were seen and pursued by some mounted Confederates. Doherty hid close to a fallen tree, covered with some underbrush and one of his pursuers came so close that the horse's hoof touched his sleeve. In the end, Doherty reached the Union side of the river and safety, bringing to Washington the first news of the wounded at Sudley Church.

In the weeks following the battle, the country began slowly to emerge

from the profound shock of the defeat. The women had a new and deeply disturbing concept of the horrors, privations and sufferings of war. The condition of the wounded at Sudley Church and other improvised hospitals, within and without enemy lines, gave them the first revelation of the problem with which they would have to deal—the double problem of lack of preparation and neglect. After the defeat, the women of the North saw their role in the war in a new light which was reflected in the renewed vigor with which they set about the work of the Sanitary Commission and of the aid societies. (A curious symbol of the new grimness was a fashion of dark brown, unornamental aprons worn by the women war workers from this time on.) The number of women who sought nursing positions both under Miss Dix and outside her jurisdiction increased during July, August and September. Plans for the care of the soldiers were made on a more permanent basis and the women's work began to take on the character and proportions of a great enterprise, for no one any longer doubted that the war would be long.

Miss Dix threw all her fine standards to the winds and asked her applicants just one question: "Are you ready to go to work?" She was everywhere, issuing orders, watching her nurses as they knelt on the floor beside the wounded men or struggled to create a workable kitchen in some room not equipped for such use. She must have been a striking figure, bedraggled, proud, her face showing exhaustion and stubbornness, her eyes burning.

Her nurses were not always welcome to the surgeons. She fought for them. To the women themselves she gave orders to disregard the surgeons and do the work she told them to do. And these women, most of whose names were never recorded, worked as long as they could stand. Then, if they had no homes near enough to go to, they slept for a while in some corner, on the floor, in their bloodstained clothes. Their morning toilet was a dash of cold water on their faces, a little soap, if there was any, on their hands, and they were ready to work again. They washed wounds and fed the helpless, they wrote letters for the men who could not write and listened to the last words of the dying. They made many mistakes, they often got in the way of the surgeons, some were inefficient, some stupid, all lacked experience and training. But in the main, their work was on the credit side of the ledger. Gradually, and to a considerable extent through their efforts, chaos became order, filth gave place to cleanliness, so that before a week had passed unfit buildings had become workmanlike hospitals.

The smoke of battle, clearing away, revealed some strange scenes. Out

on the rain-drenched battlefield, for days after the fighting had ceased, little groups of people moved slowly about, watched by the Confederate sentries, bending over the bodies lying on the ground. They were the relatives of missing men, and they had driven out from Washington in carriages, hoping to find the one they sought still living. Sometimes their hopes were realized, for some of the wounded lay on the field for two or three days after the battle.

In the hope of rescuing those who were still living, Surgeon King went out from Washington with a train of ambulances but, feckless as ever, he had neglected to arrange for permission from the Confederates to pass their lines and he and his train were refused access to the battlefield. He and his ambulances drove for a while up this road and down that and finally turned back to Washington.

Often weeks passed before the families of missing men were able to learn their fate. Realizing this, Clara Barton (who had turned her own rooms into a nursing home) worked hard on a file of names and addresses of the men. Often hers turned out to be the only records in existence, and she was sometimes able to give the family of a missing man information about him which the military men did not possess. Her special concern was for the boys from home and people from all over New England wrote to her for help. Before the year was out, her name was widely known as one who could be relied on to take charge of all sorts of personal matters for the men and for their relatives.

One of the women who was driven to desperation with anxiety about her missing husband was Fanny Ricketts, wife of young and handsome Captain James B. Ricketts of the Regular Army. Fanny was living in Washington and for two days after the battle she was not able to find out what had happened to him, though several contradictory stories about his fate were told to her. An officer of his regiment had seen the Captain fall and repeated his dying words to her. A sword, said to be his, was put into her hands. Fanny would not believe he had been killed.

Then an officer who had visited the Confederate army with a flag of truce told her that her husband was badly wounded and a prisoner somewhere behind the Confederate lines, and Fanny was convinced this story was true. She went to General Scott and begged for a pass and he gave her one which would take her through the Union lines, from which point she would have to rely on her own resourcefulness. She persuaded an officer of the Quartermaster Corps to lend her a carriage with a driver who took her as far as the first Confederate outpost and left her there.

She handed the outpost sentry a note she had written to a former army

friend of her husband's, J. E. B. Stuart, now a Confederate cavalry officer. After a time a reply came from Stuart, giving her permission to go through the Confederate lines to Fairfax Court House, where he would be waiting for her. They met like friends and talked a while. Then Fanny told him what had brought her there and asked to be allowed to search for her husband. Instead of replying, Stuart picked up a pen and started to write. When he had finished, he gave her the paper and, holding out the pen, told her to sign.

He had written a parole-of-honor which pledged her not to carry back any military information to the Union command. Fanny's reply, if history has quoted her correctly, was in the best literary tradition of the day: "I am no spy but the wife of a wounded officer, and I will go as your prisoner, but I will never sign a parole." Thereupon, her eyes blazing with anger, she tore the paper into little pieces.

Amused, perhaps, by her fiery spirit, Stuart gave her a pass and, after crossing a part of the still corpse-strewn battlefield, she found the Captain, badly wounded, in a house that was being used as a hospital. Near the house was a pile of arms and legs, the product of two days of the surgeons' work, and to enter she had to step around a severed arm which lay on the front steps. She established herself in this crude hospital and began to nurse her husband and other wounded men. The only food was bacon, hardtack and coffee, and water had to be brought from a spring half a mile away. After a time, hospital gangrene, a blood-poisoning disease, appeared, and the wounded including Captain Ricketts, were moved to Richmond. Fanny went with him. There followed a series of harrowing adventures, including a stay in Libby Prison during which Captain Ricketts was selected for execution as a hostage for thirteen privateersmen who were being held in New York. He was sent to the condemned cell, but was saved at the last minute. Shortly after this experience, the Captain was exchanged, and he and his wife returned to Washington together.[3]

Union women who had crossed the lines presented something of a problem to the Confederates, who were never sure how they should be handled. A Mrs. Hindale was captured and made a prisoner at Blackburn's Ford. She was attached to the Second Michigan Regiment, the same to which "Gentle Annie" belonged, and at the time of her capture she was searching for her husband, who was in the same regiment.

The Confederates sent her to Manassas and put her to work nursing the wounded in the hospital there. Somehow, she managed to see General Beauregard, who gave her permission to return to her own side. She

arrived in Alexandria, foot-sore and covered with dust, on the Friday following the battle. She had traveled the whole distance on foot, and as no one had asked her to sign a parole-of-honor, she brought back with her some useful information about the strength of the enemy and the disposition of their forces.

Women in military dress, such as that worn by the daughters of the regiments, were an especial problem to the Confederates, who were not sure whether to treat them as soldiers or civilians. A Mrs. Custis, who was a "daughter" from Rochester, New York, was captured and sent all the way to Richmond, where she caused considerable interest and excitement. She was young but, said the Richmond *Whig,* "by no means prepossessing." She had velvet chevrons on her sleeve and her hat was cocked up on one side with a brass ornament in the shape of a bugle. She was not in the least frightened by her predicament, and having a fluent tongue, she told her captors in detail what she thought of them and their cause. As they could not very well send her to the military prison, they were for a while at a loss to know what to do with her. In the end, they solved the problem, somewhat expensively, by renting a room for her in a private house.

The defeat and the disgraceful behavior of most of the troops during the retreat did not altogether take the members of the Sanitary Commission by surprise. They had for some time suspected the existence of a positive correlation between sanitary conditions in the camps and the quality of discipline and military administration on the one hand, and on the other, the behavior of troops in battle. It was a thing well known to army men who had commanded troops in the field, but that clean camps and discipline might have any connection with courage in battle seems not to have occurred to the Surgeon General's office or to most of the administrative officers of the War Department—or at least not to have impressed them sufficiently to make them attempt to extend Federal control into these fields.

Immediately following the defeat, the Sanitary Commission took steps to test the truth of such a relationship by methods which would remove the question once and for all from the realm of conjecture. A questionnaire was prepared to be given a sampling of officers and men who had taken part in the battle. There were seventy-five questions concerning strength of regiments, the time of the last meal before battle, the vigor of troops at the start of the fighting and the presumed causes of exhaustion and of the final defeat. The answer-taking was handled by seven field inspectors of the Commission. Their work was completed

within a week of the battle and became Document Number 28 of the Sanitary Commission.

The results were so clear as to leave no doubts that the suspected relationship did in fact exist. Those regiments which had come from comparatively clean camps, where the men had not been allowed to remain idle, and discipline was enforced, showed a distinctly better record in battle than those who had lived under opposite conditions. The inference was plain that the battle had been lost in the camps before ever the volunteer army had moved across the river into Virginia. Nor did it seem that War Department squeamishness about the independence of volunteer and state militia troops was an adequate excuse for the laxity which had been permitted.

The original intention of the Sanitary Commission had been to make their report public, in part in order to use the power of public opinion, as a substitute for the authority the Commission did not possess, to force the Surgeon General into action, and in part to influence the state governors to better the quality of militia officers. The findings embodied in the report were so devastating, however, that the Commissioners decided it would not be wise to publish them while the country was still stunned by the defeat. From this time on, however, the Sanitary Commission was regarded within government circles as a force which could not be ignored, and though the friction between the Commission and the War Department continued, Sanitary Commission recommendations were hereafter listened to with considerably more respect. The Sanitary Commission had emerged victorious from its first real trial of strength.

NOTES

[1] Estimate by Captain Louis C. Duncan—*The Medical Department of the United States Army in the Civil War.*

[2] New York *Times,* Wednesday, July 24, 1861, p. 2.

[3] Moore, Frank, *Women of the War* (Hartford, Conn., S. S. Scranton and Co., 1866). Captain Ricketts became a General and left a record of distinguished service.

11

WOMEN OF THE WEST

CHRONOLOGY

1861

November 1   General McClellan replaced General Scott as General-in-Chief.

November 7   Battle of Belmont, Missouri. Port Royal, South Carolina, taken by Union forces.

November 8   Mason and Slidell, Confederate envoys to Great Britain, seized on the British steamer, *Trent*.

November 19   General Henry W. Halleck assumed command of the Department of the Missouri, General Don Carlos Buell of the Department of the Ohio. Julia Ward Howe wrote *The Battle Hymn of the Republic*.

December 2   The second session of the 37th Congress convened.

December 8   Beaufort, South Carolina, taken by Union forces.

December 9–10   A joint committee on the conduct of the war was created by the House and Senate.

December 28   Mason and Slidell released.

1862

January 14   Resignation of Secretary of War Cameron. He was replaced by Edwin M. Stanton.

January 28   The Christian Commission organized.

February 2   Expedition of 9000 men left Cairo for Fort Henry, Tennessee, under command of General Ulysses S. Grant.

February 6   Fort Henry captured.

February 7   Roanoke Island, North Carolina, captured by Union troops.

February 12   Expedition under Grant set out for Fort Donelson, Tennessee.

February 16   Fort Donelson captured.

February 25   Nashville, Tennessee, evacuated by the Confederates.

March 6–8   Union victory at Pea Ridge, Arkansas.

March 8–9   Union shipping in Hampton Roads destroyed by the Confederate ironclad, *Merrimac,* which was subsequently forced to retire by the *Monitor.*

March 9   Confederates abandoned Manassas, withdrawing toward the South.

March 11   General McClellan removed from Supreme Command. General Halleck made Commander of all forces between the Rockies and the Alleghenies.

March 14   Battle of Newbern.

March 17   The Army of the Potomac embarked at Alexandria for the Peninsula under command of General McClellan.

March 23   Stonewall Jackson's attack on Kernstown, Virginia, repulsed by Union troops.

April 2   General McClellan arrived at Fortress Monroe to begin the Peninsula Campaign.

April 4   General McDowell in command of a corps assigned to the defense of Washington.

April 5   The siege of Yorktown began.

———————————————— ★ ————————————————

It seems as though a few energetic women could
carry on the war better than the men do it so far.
—Louisa May Alcott, October 1861.

THE FUTURE OF THE NORTH did not look bright after Bull Run. In the fall of 1861 the Confederates held a long front which extended from the Potomac to Mill Springs, to Bowling Green, and westward to Fort Donelson on the Cumberland River and Fort Henry on the Tennessee, finally touching the Mississippi at Columbus. These points were strongly fortified, and all the territory southward to the Gulf was in Confederate hands. From the Mississippi the line continued westward, dipping a little, until it was lost in a territory so vast that it could be held only by outpost forts and fast moving raiders. The problem, strategically, came down to the question of where this vast front could be attacked in such a way as to drive a wedge into Confederate territory. The attempt to do this in the East by capturing Richmond had failed.

The day following the Battle of Bull Run, young, vigorous General George B. McClellan was summoned from some spectacular successes in West Virginia to replace McDowell in command of the troops which were now being designated the Army of the Potomac. The transforming of the citizen army from a sloppy, demoralized mob into a veteran fighting machine was one of the great feats of the war, and would still have been notable had it not been accomplished in so brief a time. McClellan worked the men unmercifully and they gave him affection and loyalty such as few commanders have inspired. Cheers for "Little Mac" followed his progress through the camps.

Drill improved, sloppy uniforms vanished, accoutrements shone and the men saw their changed appearance and grew proud. McClellan had no squeamish fears about states' rights and the camps grew clean and orderly. Army food was not so easily improved, but with improved living conditions and more exercise the men were better able to tolerate it. The new atmosphere of professionalism extended into every branch and department, even to maps, which for the first time showed detail and elevation.

The renovation of the army was complete but the months slipped by and McClellan did not take the field. Lee once said of him that he had no reason to think that McClellan ever omitted to do anything that was in his power, but however sound may have been the little General's reasons for delay, criticism mounted rapidly. Many within the Administration thought him unduly arrogant, and contemptuous of the authority

of old General Scott. McClellan was a professional military man through and through and he despised politician-soldiers, but he carried his independence even to the point of rudeness to the President, whom he sometimes kept waiting in the anteroom.

Time slipped away, the President fretted, and McClellan insisted that his men were not ready to fight. Since apparently nothing could be expected in the immediate future from the Army of the Potomac, the attack must be made to the westward and there were other urgent reasons why the Western theatre should be the scene of action.

The spirit of secession was strong in Southern Illinois and Indiana and a Northern victory was essential to hold them in line. Kentucky, after trying to maintain an impossible neutrality with part of the state in Confederate hands, had, on November 28th with Missouri, joined the Confederacy and the usefulness of the considerable Union element within the state was rapidly being destroyed. The Union hold on vast stretches of territory was almost visibly crumbling. For all these reasons, the next act of the drama was destined to take place in the West.

But the West too was suffering from lethargy, and nothing much had been accomplished there except by Brigadier General U. S. Grant, who was already showing a talent for aggressive action. He had seen the strategic value of Paducah at the juncture of the Ohio and Cumberland rivers and occupied the town on his own initiative. He had fought and won the battle of Belmont. But he was not possessed of sufficient authority to control the strategy of the campaign which was every day becoming more important.

That strategy—the question of where to drive the wedge into Confederate territory—was the chief concern of War Department generals and politicians alike. In choosing the location for the campaign, there were several vital considerations. The blow must be struck at a point that would do maximum damage to the Confederacy. It must take place where the enemy defenses were weak enough to make success likely, and it must penetrate at a location where lines of communication with the base could be maintained, either by rail or by water.

There were various plans under discussion, the most obvious from a military point of view, as well as from the standpoint of the damage to the Confederacy which would result, being an attack down the Mississippi River from the base at Cairo. There were a number of reasons, however, which made the wisdom of this plan doubtful. The attack on the strong points which held the river would have to be mainly a water attack, since the Confederates held the country behind, country which

was swampy and difficult, in any event, for a large body of men to negotiate. The water attack would have to be made against strong points, literally bristling with heavy artillery which could bring an invading fleet of boats under fire and make landing operations difficult, if not impossible. Moreover, the chances of a successful water attack, unsupported by an attack from the rear, were greatly affected by the character of the river banks which, in most places were steep and difficult to scale. There were a number of tributary streams which offered an opening into the back country for the flat, shallow-draught river boats, but they were subject to sudden, treacherous flood and their banks in many places were impassable marsh. It was small wonder that the military commanders on the spot and the War Department generals in Washington looked with trepidation on a campaign involving such hazards.

President Lincoln, who wanted action, but who had been unsuccessful in prodding his generals into starting a campaign against the enemy, had seriously taken up the study of military strategy. He was fully informed of the perils involved in an attack straight down the Mississippi into the heart of strong enemy country, but he was aware that the temper of the North would not long tolerate idleness in both of the great theatres of war. Moreover, the question of the basic strategy of a campaign was inextricably bound up with other problems which plagued Lincoln greatly—problems having to do with personalities and administration in the Western war. All sorts of reports and information came to him, some contradictory, some he suspected of being erroneous or misleading, most of it filtered through the prejudice, ignorance, or personal ambition of interested parties. Being more and more convinced that he must make himself Commander in Chief in more than name, and take an active part in directing the war, he was coming to feel that he must form his own opinions. But before he could do that effectively, it was urgently necessary to clear the air of the miasma of confusion.

Perhaps he felt the need to send to the Western theatre his own observer, a person who would study the whole complicated mess of personalities, political interests and inefficiency in high places which were delaying military action. Perhaps his ideas were not so clear cut. But if such a person were to be sent on a long inspection tour, that person must be highly intelligent, and free from any self-interest, either political or military. The person who finally went to the Western theatre, not quite unofficially, but not openly as a representative of either Lincoln or the War Department, was a woman.

She was Anna Ella Carroll, a member of the famous Southern family

of that name. Anna, the daughter of a former governor of Maryland, had been interested in politics and public affairs since her girlhood. She was an able and fluent writer on current political problems in a field not often invaded by women in those days. Her style was a trifle wordy, but if her writing might have benefited by revision, her thinking usually penetrated through complications to the heart of the question she was discussing. As a consequence, her work, plus the fact that she possessed sense and tact, won her many friends and sincere admirers among the prominent men in Washington. Her sympathies were wholly with the Union cause and to commemorate Lincoln's election in 1860, she had freed her slaves, a gesture she could ill afford financially. Because of her family connections and her own abilities, her influence was considerable and she is credited with doing much to insure the adherence of Maryland to the North. She had been engaged by Lincoln and the War Department to write in support of the Administration, and some paragraphs (which she later expanded) on the war powers of the President had attracted much attention.

Anna was small, with curly brown hair and blue eyes. Her face was too full, her neck too short, but she had beautiful shoulders and could wear to advantage the revealing evening dress of the day. Her blue-stocking tendencies were evident in her serious expression, but she had a radiant smile which made her attractive enough as a woman to excite Mrs. Lincoln's easily aroused jealousies. This was the woman chosen by Lincoln to send to the Western theatre, and she probably was asked, among other assignments, to look into the feasibility of the much-discussed attack down the Mississippi. She left for the West in the fall of 1861, ostensibly as a woman writer, but with prestige enough to gain her entry wherever she needed to go. She went everywhere, making a slow and inquisitive progress, inspecting military installations and talking at length to anyone from whom she could gather information.

At Cairo, Anna met Grant, whom she found sitting on a nail keg, dressed in most unmilitary attire. He had recently been promoted to the rank of brigadier general and ordered a new uniform which had not yet arrived. At this period he was sending military expeditions here and there at the direction of his superiors, and restlessly biding the time when he could take real initiative. It came in the battle of Belmont on November 7th, while Anna was still in the West.

Belmont was a battle which was not intended. Grant had no orders to attack the enemy—the object of the expedition to Belmont, across the river from the heavily fortified town of Columbus, being to show suffi-

cient force to prevent the Confederates from detaching troops from their garrison. "After we started," Grant wrote, "I saw that the officers and men were elated at the prospect of at last having the opportunity of doing what they had volunteered to do—fight the enemies of their country."

Belmont was an uncertain victory claimed by both sides, but it accomplished the purpose of preventing the enemy from detaching troops from Columbus. Losses were high, by the early war standards. The wounded of Grant's forces were carried to houses in the rear, then transferred to the river boats which formed part of Grant's expedition. It was not possible to rescue all the wounded, and some were left on the field where they fell. Those on the boats were taken to Cairo and distributed among the hospitals there.

Anna did not involve herself with the wounded of Belmont, for there was nothing in her intensely intellectual make-up which ever led her far from her desk, and when she laid down her pen it was only to seek out people who might be useful to her in her work, and nursing the wounded was no part of her mission in the West. But there were two other women waiting at the docks when the boats carrying the wounded arrived. One of these women was Mary Safford and the other was Mary Ann Bickerdyke.

While Bickerdyke was dealing with the Belmont wounded in her own way, and Anna's manuscript was piling up, sheet on closely written sheet, Mary Safford did an extraordinary thing. She went alone to the battlefield after the fighting was over. She was the only woman there. No flag-of-truce agreement was in effect when she arrived in the morning after the battle, though Grant made one later that day. Mary went out on the field, stopping by each fallen man to see if he still lived and if so, what might be done for him. Absorbed in the work and paying little attention to where she was going, she came close to the enemy lines. Perhaps she assumed she was safe, and under ordinary circumstances she would have been. Perhaps the light was poor, or a picket grew nervous. Whatever the reason, she was fired on. She did not retreat. She made her own flag of truce by tying her handkerchief to a stick, and while this fluttered in the cold November wind, she continued to care for the wounded.

Belmont caused a wave of excitement all through the North, but Anna Carroll continued to concentrate on her work, not only writing but studying maps and interviewing people. The more she learned about the problems and risks which would be involved in a campaign down the Mississippi River, the less that plan recommended itself to her. But in this

view she was not alone, for some of the military men were of her way of thinking. Then one day a great idea came to her. Why, instead of running head-on against the enemy's finest defenses, could not the wedge be driven into the Confederacy along the Cumberland and Tennessee Rivers?

The plan had a great deal in its favor. Both rivers, she discovered, were navigable for a considerable distance. Their waters flowed north, which would aid the low-powered gunboats in extricating themselves from uncomfortable situations. The rivers were fortified, but not so formidably as the Mississippi. A successful attack by this route would endanger the Memphis and Charleston Railroad, important to the Confederates because it linked Memphis and the Mississippi River, and eventually make possible attacks on the Mississippi strongholds from the rear.

The evidence is that the plan was truly her own in that she arrived at it by her own thought processes, though she must have discussed a number of plans of attack with numerous military men. Certainly she believed herself the sole originator. Filled with the energy of excitement and an almost crusading zeal, she returned to Washington and, on November 30, 1861, she presented her plan, not to Lincoln, but to Thomas A. Scott, Assistant Secretary of War. Her report, which still exists, accompanied by a map which has been lost, was undoubtedly the first recommendation in written form advocating a campaign along the Tennessee River, to reach the high command in Washington.

Anna made no public claim to authorship of the plan at this time, which was certainly wise though possibly necessary as events then stood, but her reticence eventually cast a shadow of doubt on her place in history. Years later, when she was much in need of money, Congress was petitioned to grant her compensation for the work she had done for the government, her authorship of the Tennessee River campaign plan being an important element in the claim. A controversy of some dimensions ensued. In 1881 a bill was printed giving Anna the pay of a Major General from November 1861 to the end of her life. The bill in this form was never enacted. In that same year a bill was passed which granted her a simple pension, from date of passage, of $50 a month "for the important military service rendered the country by her during the late civil war." That final judgment on her worth by the government she had served was a great grief to her, but she never renewed the struggle and the bill filled her last days with bitterness.

Anna was the victim of a situation common enough not only in the

field of military strategy, but in the development of science and the healing arts. The time was ripe for her plan. Perhaps she really was the first to whom it had occurred, or perhaps others had conceived the same plan then or earlier and she was merely the first to record the proposal and to place it in the hands of those in command at Washington. Grant, who actually launched the campaign, makes no mention of her in his memoirs, and says that the idea for the campaign first occurred to him in January, 1862, as a result of a report from General C. F. Smith concerning the defenses in this section of the theatre. "This report of Smith's," Grant wrote, "confirmed views I had previously held, that the true line of operations for us was up the Tennessee and Cumberland Rivers."[1] Mary Livermore, who is a consistently reliable writer and who had a first-hand knowledge of many of the events in the Western theatre, gives Anna full and unqualified credit for originating the strategy which resulted in winning the war in the West.[2]

Whether Anna Ella Carroll was the only effective influence in the adoption of the Tennessee River campaign, or whether she was the first to conceive the plan, will probably never be settled. In the final analysis, it is of less importance that she did or did not originate the plan than that the campaign took place successfully. And the truth or falseness of her claim has nothing to do with the fact, which no one has disputed, that hers was a recognized first-class intellect, which influenced many people of importance in various ways.

Grant presented his plan of attack along the Cumberland and Tennessee Rivers to his commanding officer, General Halleck, but at that time Halleck scarcely gave it his attention. On February first, however, Grant received instructions to move against Fort Henry, on the Tennessee River. Grant set out from Cairo the next day in a flotilla made up of some idle river boats which had been tied up at Cairo since the start of the war, and seven gunboats, four of them ironclads, under command of Flag Officer Foote. The waters of the Tennessee were high and the Fort was in some danger of being flooded. The attack was largely from the river and the victory was comparatively easily won.

There remained the far more formidable fortifications comprising Fort Donelson on the Cumberland, eleven land miles distant. Fort Henry had fallen on the sixth of February. On the twelfth Grant began the overland march to Donelson, while in the meantime Foote and his gunboats steamed back down the Tennessee and up the Cumberland in order to rendezvous at the Fort. The twelfth was a deceptively mild day, almost like spring. A good many of the volunteers, lacking the wisdom of

veterans, left their blankets behind in camp. The air was saturated with humidity from the soggy ground, and as the morning grew warm and steamy, many of the marchers hung their overcoats on trees, intending to retrieve them on their return.

Grant's forces reached the Fort about noon and positions were assigned the regiments on the surrounding hillsides. That night a chill rain fell. Since Grant was anxious not to betray the size of his expedition to the enemy, campfires were forbidden. Tents had been left behind in order to march quickly, without encumbrances. That night there was much discomfort among those who had foolishly dispensed with blankets and warm clothes. The next day dawned cold and sullen. On the fourteenth there was sleet and snow and the cold was intense. The suffering among the men was extreme, for many of them lay in the open on the frozen ground without covering of any sort. By this time, the sick list, mainly comprising men with respiratory infections ranging from colds to pneumonia, was lengthening rapidly. There had been considerable fighting and some of the wounded had been left beyond the lines where they fell. All night long, that bitter night of the fourteenth, they could be heard crying for help.

Various sheds and small houses had been taken over for hospitals, but these were soon filled. Hospital supplies began to give out and there were too few surgeons, so that emergency operations which should have been performed at once had to be postponed, sometimes for days. The wounded left on the field were in a pitiable condition, for the mud, mingled with their blood, froze hard and when they were finally rescued they had to be chopped out of the ice.

When it became probable that Fort Donelson would fall into Federal hands, two of the senior Confederate Generals, Floyd and Pillow, fled. Floyd had good reason for taking unceremonious departure for, prior to the war, when he was a strong secessionist and Secretary of War, he had transferred arms from Northern to Southern arsenals. About this and other actions which were construed in the North as violations of his oath of office, his conscience was troubling him and he feared trial before a court of law in case of capture. About General Pillow's abrupt departure, the most charitable thing that can be said is that in the early days of the war the policy of the Federal government concerning the war guilt of captured general officers was not clear.

One other officer escaped, though without the opprobrium attached to the flight of Floyd and Pillow, for he was not in command of the Fort. He had found a gap in the Union lines, and in the night he slipped

through it, taking his men with him. He was Nathan Bedford Forrest—then only a colonel—as able a fighter as the war produced who would, before the war was ended, prove himself a sore trial to Grant. Forrest's manner was rough and uncultured, but he fought his cavalry command with an unconventional brilliance unequaled by any other cavalry officer in either army.

On the sixteenth, General Buckner, who had inherited the mess from the fugitives, Floyd and Pillow, sent a note to Grant asking terms of surrender. To this Grant made his famous reply, ". . . No terms except unconditional and immediate surrender can be accepted. I propose to move immediately on your works." At noon the Stars and Stripes floated over Fort Donelson.

Toward evening of that day a large river boat steamed majestically into view. She was of the very latest design, her paint gleamed white, her brass shown, and fancy gold leaf letters on the side proclaimed her the *City of Memphis,* most luxurious of the Mississippi passenger boats built for fashionable travelers just before the war. While everyone watched this incongruous apparition, she nosed gently up to a wharf on the opposite bank and came to rest.

In this dramatic manner the Sanitary Commission made its appearance at Fort Donelson. The *City of Memphis* had been equipped as a hospital ship by the Commission, and long rows of cots were crowded into her salon, where thick carpets still covered the floor and fine curtains hung at the windows. She was staffed by members of the Sanitary Commission, all of them men, and this expedition to the battlefield was supposed to be; from start to finish, a Sanitary Commission undertaking. But somehow, no one quite knew how, Mother Bickerdyke, who at that time had no connection with the Sanitary Commission, had got herself aboard. She was not an accredited nurse, she had no sort of authorization from anyone, but there she was, the only woman on the ship.

When the wounded, many with frozen feet and hands, were carried on board, she was there to welcome them, as bossy, efficient and bustling as ever. Her loud, harsh voice could be heard in every part of the ship giving orders and demanding food for this new aggregation of "her boys." She worked until any ordinary person would have dropped with fatigue and until every one of the wounded and sick had been made as comfortable as it was in her power to make them.

That night an extraordinary thing occurred. At midnight, or after, Colonel John A. Logan, Congressman from Illinois, who had been slightly wounded, gazed out the entrance of his tent and saw a light mov-

ing erratically, close to the ground, across the recent battlefield. There had been stories going around about robberies of the dead and wounded. Colonel Logan thought that something of the sort must be going on out there in the cold darkness. He called his orderly and told him to go and catch whoever it was who was carrying that light, and bring him to the tent.

The orderly was gone a long time, and when he returned, he had Mother Bickerdyke in tow. The possibility that among the dead who lay frozen into the mud there might be some who still lived had haunted her so that she could not rest. She had no great faith in stretcher-bearers and she knew that some of the wounded fell in inaccessible places, in thickets and small ravines where the bearers, themselves weary and numb with cold, might not have looked for them. She decided to go and see for herself and, taking a heavy shawl and a lantern, she set out. It was her light that Colonel Logan had seen as she held it close to the faces of the dead in the hope of finding that some life remained. The story captured the imagination of the newspaper correspondents and various versions of it found their way into print. Mother Bickerdyke became mildly famous, and found herself the subject of an emotional poem by Eliza Pitzinger:

> "Behold the light! It moves around
> Through all the dreary night!
> Whence comes that slow and muffled sound?
> Who bears the charmèd light?
>
> 'Twas neither angel, sprite nor elf,
> Nor spectre; it was like
> The dear, good, kind and loving self
> Of faithful Mother Bickerdyke!"

The *City of Memphis* steamed down the swollen river with its load of wounded but Mother Bickerdyke stayed behind to do what she could for the men still awaiting removal from the wretched field hospitals.

The conquest of Fort Donelson was the first important decisive victory for the Union forces, and its effects were far-reaching. It opened up the country all the way to the southern border of Tennessee and freed the upper Mississippi. The Memphis and Charleston Railroad, on which the Confederates relied heavily, now lay exposed to attack and Nashville was evacuated. The real attack on the Mississippi could now begin.

When the news of victory reached the North, the people responded

Anna Ella Carroll

Clara Barton

with a wave of wild enthusiasm such as had not been seen since the early days of the war. Bells rang, flags flew high and bonfires were built in the streets at night, and people eagerly told one another that the war would soon be at an end.

But following the news of victory came the stories about the terrible suffering of the wounded. Looking back years later, Grant thought that the care of the wounded had been as good as it could be under the circumstances, but the country was shocked, and horror replaced rejoicing. Most of the wounded were boys from Illinois and trainloads of relatives and volunteer workers, both men and women, came into Cairo. Some of them found places on the Sanitary Commission boats which were steaming up the river to Fort Donelson. Some hired boats of their own.

The Chicago Board of Trade gathered together $3,000 worth of supplies and sent them, in charge of a citizens' committee, to the front. Sanitary Commission supplies which for some time had been arriving in crates at the Cairo docks at the rate of $1,000 worth a day, were opened and distributed to any who needed them. Many families and philanthropic people, among them doctors who had come to volunteer their services, disembarked below the captured Fort and went to visit the miserable shacks where many of the wounded still lay, and it sometimes happened that a volunteer civilian doctor worked beside some army surgeon by the light of a flickering lantern far into the night.

Mary Safford arrived early and was given a warm welcome by Mother Bickerdyke, who did not take time to take off her bloodstained dress for the ten days following the battle. The two women worked day and night through scenes of indescribable horror until Mary, who never learned to endure suffering in others without emotion, began to fail in health. Mrs. Bickerdyke, who loved the gentle girl, took her away from the field hospitals, out of the dirt and the cold, into the order and comparative quiet of the *City of Memphis*. Together, Mary and Mother Bickerdyke made five trips from the Fort on the laden hospital transport, delivering wounded to be cared for at Cairo, Mound City and St. Louis. Mary Safford was ill, and it became clear that even the lighter work of the hospital ship was too much for her rapidly failing strength. After the fifth trip she was forced to remain at home in Cairo and to resume the less arduous role of hospital visitor.

The Sanitary Commission had done a gigantic and efficient job of providing supplies, and they had been at the scene with the first of the great hospital boats, but these things had not been enough. Influential workers in the Sanitary Commission resolved to review the whole prob-

lem of medical and nursing care with special attention to methods for evacuating the wounded promptly. Plans were made to convert a number of unused river steamers into permanent hospital ships, staffed by women nurses, which in future battles would follow close behind the gunboats as they moved into action. Work was begun on replacing the supplies consumed for the wounded of Donelson and augmenting the quantity available for future use. The burden of the work fell on the Western branch of the Sanitary Commission, and the Chicago office on Madison Street became a bedlam of noise and activity. Drays with crates from local aid societies drove up all day long; the crates were opened, their contents sorted, repacked and directed to the proper destinations. Letters by the ten thousand were written by hand, and circulars by the hundred thousand were sent out from these rooms.

This headquarters of the Sanitary Commission was under the supervision of Mary Livermore and Mrs. A. H. Hoge, who had both so organized their private lives as to make this work a full-time undertaking. The two women were friends, and they usually agreed about the work, so that theirs was an ideal and highly productive partnership. Mrs. Hoge was more sentimental, more emotional and more easily swayed by the drama of war work than the common-sense Mary, but she was highly intelligent, quick to perceive ways in which the relief system might be bettered and, like Mary, she possessed an almost incredible energy.

After Fort Donelson, when the first wave of work in the Chicago rooms of the Sanitary Commission had subsided, these two women were sent on an inspection trip to the scene of the Western campaign. They received their instructions from Mark Skinner, foster father of the Northwestern branch of the Sanitary Commission, and its treasurer, E. W. Blatchford. Part of their work was to ferret out misuses or misappropriations of Sanitary Commission supplies, for there had been a number of complaints from the field. But the really important phase of their work was to visit hospitals and supply depots in order to work out ways to improve the methods of handling the wounded at each successive stage.

The two women went first to St. Louis, where they visited the Fifth Street Hospital, which had a ward assigned to the wounded of Fort Donelson. It was Mary's first visit to a military hospital. She had heard, like every war worker, of the horrible sights in these places and of the nauseating smell of blood and suppurating wounds, but the reality was almost too much for her. She attempted to help a surgeon dress a face wound, but when the bandages were lifted and she saw the wreck of a face exposed, she came near to fainting, and hurried from the ward for a

breath of pure air. This happened to her twice more before that visit was over, but the emotional Mrs. Hoge, surprisingly enough, was the less affected of the two.

In time, Mary was to become accustomed to the shocking sight of the wounded and even to the horror of seeing dead limbs protruding from shallow graves on former battlefields, but she long remembered her emotions on this first day. Passing through a ward, she heard one young lad cry out, "I can't die. I can't die!"

"But perhaps you may not die," she said, though it seemed plain to her that death was not far off. "I went to the surgeon and enquired about the man," she wrote, " 'He was horribly cut up,' the surgeon said. One leg had been amputated, the other had suffered two amputations, the last one taking off the leg between the knee and the hip, the right arm had been broken, a caisson had crushed the lower left arm, and he had been shot twice through the abdomen. 'All you can do is help him die easy.' I returned to the fellow whose anxious eyes were following me.

"Why are you afraid to die?"

"I ain't fit to die. I shall go to hell."

"I drew a campstool to his bedside and spoke as to an excited child. 'Stop screaming. Be quiet. If you *must* die, die like a man.' I told him of Christ's mission on earth, and assured him that however great his sins had been, they would be forgiven.

" 'Can't you get a Methodist minister?' he asked. 'Oh, send for a Methodist minister!'

"One of the attendants remembered that the hospital steward was also a Methodist minister and hastened to find him.

"Can't you sing, chaplain?" I enquired. Immediately, in a rich, clear tenor, he sang.

> "When cold, the hand of death
> Lies on my marble brow,
> Break forth in songs of joyfulness,
> Let heaven begin below."

"A second and a third time he repeated the song. Patients, attendants, surgeons, glowed under the melody, and the dying man's face grew rapturous. My friends came to say that it was time to go.

" 'Don't go! Stay!' whispered the fast sinking man, and I promised to remain with him to the end. The end came sooner than anyone thought. Before the sun went down, he had drifted to the immortal shore. The

mutilated corpse was carried to the dreary 'dead house,' and preparations made for burial next day."

Except that this was the only man Mary ever encountered in her long years of hospital visiting who feared death, the story with its gentleness and simple religious faith, is typical of the experience that every woman hospital worker encountered. Most of the boys in the volunteer army were young men, on the average only twenty-one or twenty-two years old, or possibly even less. Many of them were away from home and mother for the first time in their life, and the role of substitute mother which the women nurses and visitors performed was one of their most useful services.

While Mary was in St. Louis, she saw 15,000 troops march out on their way to the front. Many were without muskets, some regiments were without surgeons or surgical instruments. They were undisciplined and their officers were untrained. Most of them had never fired a gun or had the remotest idea how to load one, but they were on their way to take part in the battle of Shiloh, or Pittsburg Landing, one of the bloodiest battles of the war.

From St. Louis the two ladies, who, after their hard initiation, had become experienced hospital visitors, went on to Cairo. Mary thought that "from the levee the town looked like an immense basin . . . partially filled with water; and the incessant activity of the steam pumps alone saved it from inundation. Vile odors assailed the olfactories, as one walked the streets . . . the glutinous, tenacious mud held one by both feet. . . . I went down a flight of crazy stairs, across a bit of plank walk, around a slough of unknown depth, behind somebody's barn, across somebody's backyard, over an extempore bridge of scantling that bent under my weight, then into mud at the risk of losing my rubbers, boots, and I sometimes feared for my feet, and, at last, ferried over a miniature lake in a skiff, I reached my destination."

In Cairo, Mary was impressed with the poor quality of the regimental hospitals of which there were a half dozen or more in sheds, stables and small houses, but she found that the men preferred them to the general hospitals, where they were separated from their comrades. The residents of Cairo eventually protested so strongly against the foul conditions in these regimental hospitals that they were abolished.

The one general hospital in Cairo, the "Brick Hospital," was run by the Sisters of the Holy Cross, and here, as elsewhere, Mary noted the quality of the nursing care given by the Catholic Sisters. But she, stout

Protestant that she was, found herself sympathizing with the sick boys who disliked the Sisters' great headgear, describing it as "a cross between a white sunbonnet and a broken-down umbrella."

The quality of Catholic nursing had so impressed the surgeons of Cairo that Mary found an almost universal prejudice against nurses of any other faith. All sorts of reasons for this attitude were given and some of them, like the claim that the Protestant women were less amenable to discipline, were undoubtedly justified. But the most original was probably the complaint that Protestant nurses wrote too many books and articles for the press, and their writings did not always present surgeons in a flattering light.

Mary Livermore found Mary Safford in Cairo, recovered to an extent from the fatigue of Fort Donelson, and the two women went about their hospital visiting in each other's company. The town was full of military activity, for Cairo was the base for the expected attack down the river. One day the two women entered a hospital where everyone seemed so low in spirit that Miss Safford finally asked if anything especial had happened. The reply was that "Mother Bickerdyke went down the river this morning and we shall all die now." Mother Bickerdyke, who could tell that a battle was brewing as well as any General, was determined to be on the spot, and she was now on her way to Pittsburg Landing.

The impending battle made Mary Livermore hurry her inspection trip, for she knew the rooms of the Sanitary Commission had more work than they could handle, but she took time to visit the hospital at Mound City, six miles from Cairo, then on to Paducah and Bird's Point. Mound City she found to be an exception to the chaos existing elsewhere. The Mound City hospital, administered by Dr. E. S. Franklin and staffed, like the Brick Hospital in Cairo, by the Sisters of the Holy Cross, was, at that time, considered the best military hospital in the North. The Mother Superior was Mother Angela, a cousin of General Sherman's wife; in her, in spite of religious differences, Mary recognized a kindred spirit, possessing energy, intelligence and an organizing ability to match her own.

Mary and Mrs. Hoge knew they were urgently needed at home, for the Cairo Sanitary Commission had requisitioned supplies for 20,000 men, and the battle-relief stores were already arriving from Chicago in tremendous quantities. So the inspection tour, which was to result in many administrative changes and considerable improvement in the handling of the wounded, came to a hurried end. Before the two ladies reached Chicago, the battle of Shiloh had begun.

NOTES

[1] U. S. Grant, *Personal Memoirs* (Charles L. Webster and Company, New York, 1885), I, 286.

[2] Livermore, Mrs. Mary A., *My Story of the War* (A. D. Worthington and Co., Hartford, Conn., 1888), p. 174.

12

BLOODY SHILOH

CHRONOLOGY

1862

April 6–7   Battle of Shiloh or Pittsburg Landing, Tennessee. Union
troops were under the command of General Grant, the Confederates under General Albert Sidney Johnston. Contact between the armies was made about five A.M. on the sixth. On
that first day the Union forces were driven back. Late in the
day, General Buell arrived with re-enforcements. The next day
the Confederate forces retreated. The battle was characterized
by fierce, stubborn fighting on both sides, convincing Grant
that the war would not easily be won.

★

The Son of God goes forth to war,
A kingly crown to gain,
His blood-red banner streams afar:
Who follows in his train?
                                        —Bishop Heber

AFTER THE FALL of Fort Donelson, the Confederates were forced to
abandon large areas of country around the Tennessee River. They
selected for their new stronghold and base of operations, the town of
Corinth, Mississippi, which was located south and east from Memphis

157

and about twenty miles back from the river. Travelers going to Corinth by water up the Tennessee, went ashore for the overland journey at a dismal spot on the west bank of the river known as Pittsburg Landing. Here there were some old warehouses at the foot of the steep, yellow river banks, a line of rotting wharves and little else.

Not much traffic came by this route, however, for two railroads had their junction at Corinth. One was the Memphis and Charleston Railroad, which was the link with the eastern part of the Confederacy, the other, the Mobile and Ohio, ran south through the cotton country, and it was these two roads which gave Corinth its military importance and made it the logical point of attack by the Union army. In the spring of 1862 the Confederates had gathered there, in anticipation of attack, a force of 40,000 men. On the tenth of March, General Halleck began to move the Union forces southward, sending them by river in a flotilla of eighty transport steamers. Grant, who so recently had been hailed as the hero of Donelson, and was the logical field commander for the expedition, had been relieved of his command by Halleck because of some supposed failure to comply with orders, and was sitting in moody solitude at Fort Henry. Sherman, who had himself but recently come out from under a cloud, and now stood in the full sun of Halleck's favor, had gone up the river in advance of the flotilla of transports.

When Sherman arrived at Pittsburg Landing, he sent back word to Halleck that this was a suitable place to land the troops and concentrate them for the attack on Corinth. Sherman selected as a camp site for his own command, a hill on which there stood a small church, known as Shiloh Meeting House. It was a lovely spot, with peach orchards all about, which were just coming into bloom. Birds sang their spring songs and the warm air was languorous. A spot less suggestive of war would have been hard to imagine.

The day after Halleck had sent his flotilla on its slow progress up the swollen river, he was made Supreme Commander of all the forces between the Rockies and the Alleghenies. At the same time Lincoln, who recognized in the victor of Donelson military talent which the country could not afford to lose, gave Grant the rank of Major General. Grant came out of retirement to resume command on the thirteenth and, following the flotilla up the river, set up headquarters at the river town of Savannah, on the east bank, eight miles north of Pittsburg Landing. Grant chose Savannah for his headquarters because he was expecting General Buell to arrive from Nashville with a force of 40,000 men, and it was at Savannah that he would come to the river. Buell's force was of

the utmost importance to Grant, who was anxious to confer with Buell at the earliest possible moment.

The little town of Savannah, sleeping on its remote river bank, was transformed into a busy army post. Here the surgeons set up hospitals and began the accumulation of medical supplies. No one expected an attack in this neighborhood, so that these were not conceived as field hospitals, and they were already beginning to fill up with boys who could not stand the damp and their own cooking. Members of the Sanitary Commission continued to move medical supplies into the neighborhood and to prepare the hospital ships for the day of need.

Mother Bickerdyke was on the scene also, though nobody wanted her. She had no sort of authority from anyone except a pass which she had previously wangled from General Grant, by means of which she attached herself to the 21st Indiana Volunteers and procured herself a free ride to her destination on the gunboat *Fanny Bullet*. But she went bustling around wherever the sick boys were, doing what she thought needed to be done, and, as usual, paying no attention to enraged surgeons who demanded that she take herself off. Perhaps it was at this time that the odd friendship began to develop between Mother Bickerdyke and General Grant. Mother Bickerdyke who had no respect for authority as such respected his because it made sense to her practical mind when often the rulings of other officers and of the surgeons did not. Grant, on the other hand, was able to see past her crudeness and ungrammatical explosions of indignant anger, to the woman who had something of his own ability to get things done. He liked her vigor, her way of brushing aside obstacles, and, as time went on, he admired the way she grew with the growing tasks which faced her, so that she never lost herself in detail, but as a true commander should, dealt in the grand manner with the broad aspects of a great undertaking.

By the first of April most of the force had gathered, mainly at and around Shiloh, and Grant was waiting anxiously for Buell to arrive from Nashville in order to launch the joint attack on Corinth. And the peach blossoms were in full bloom, looking like drifts of pink mist over the rolling hills.

Among the regiments present there were detachments of the 17th Illinois Volunteers, with Sherman's Fifth Division. With them was a young wife, almost a bride, since she had married not long before the start of the war. She was Belle Reynolds and her husband was Lieutenant W. S. Reynolds in the 17th Regiment. Sometime before Belmont she had come, with a trunk, to visit her husband, and when the regiment moved

she was given permission to go along. Sometimes she walked with the men along the dusty roads, carrying a musket on her shoulder. There is a picture of her still in existence, in which she looks startlingly like Florence Nightingale, for she had the same thin features, the same long, rather sharp nose and the same look of observing intelligence. There is another picture showing her riding a horse on a side saddle, elegantly dressed. Her skirt falls almost to the ground and a veil is over a stylish hat, but that picture was posed much later, after Belle had received her commission as a Major in the army.

After the battle of Belmont, young Mrs. Reynolds watched with beating heart as the ranks of the regiment re-formed and was filled with a surge of joy to see her husband step into his place. By the time the regiment reached Shiloh, she was almost a veteran, used to tent life and hardened to long days on the march. There was another woman camping under the peach trees whom Belle identifies only as Mrs. N., and Belle thought they were the only women present, but about this she was mistaken.

There had been skirmishing since the first of April, whenever some of General Johnson's roving forces, riding out from Corinth, came in contact with Union outposts. This was expected, but neither Grant nor Sherman expected the Confederates to attack. The day before the battle Sherman wrote to Grant, "I do not apprehend anything like an attack upon our position." That night, with 40,000 Confederates deployed in the woods less than two miles from the picket lines at Shiloh, Grant telegraphed to Halleck: ". . . the main force of the enemy is at Corinth . . . I have scarcely the faintest idea of an attack being made upon us. . . ." In his memoirs, written long after the event, Grant qualified the element of surprise by saying that as late as the evening before the battle, the Confederate leaders were still undecided about whether to attack and that the battle was actually begun by the Union troops opening fire on the enemy.

The first of Buell's forces, a division under the command of General Nelson, arrived at Savannah on April 6th and Grant moved them up the east bank of the river. As the Tennessee, unlike the Mississippi, flows from south to north, they moved in the direction of Pittsburg Landing and Shiloh, but on the opposite side of the stream.

Buell himself arrived in the neighborhood of Savannah that evening, but Grant did not know this until some time later. On the morning of the sixth, Grant was at breakfast in Savannah when he heard firing in the

direction of Pittsburg Landing. The firing was heavier than usual and Grant, leaving a note for Buell, set out for Pittsburg Landing.

At Shiloh, the morning of Sunday the sixth of April seemed in its early hours like any other peaceful morning, and the soft spring air was filled with the smell of bacon frying on campfires in front of hundreds of tents. The tent which Belle Reynolds and her husband occupied was next to the one belonging to a "Mrs. N." Belle and Mrs. N. shared a campfire and made a joint undertaking of cooking breakfast in long-handled frying pans—breakfast which included pancakes, coffee and probably other good, solid fare.

While the women cooked, they heard the sound of musket fire in the distance, but they paid no attention, for often in the morning the pickets fired their muskets to see if the night dews had dampened their powder. Suddenly a cannon ball flew over the heads of the two women and crashed into the trees beyond their tents. Belle was startled, but she did not leave the fire, even when more balls followed, then she heard the long roll beginning—that ominous roar of sound from the drums which kept on and on, tightening the nerves and making the blood tingle, warning of danger and coming action.

In a moment the camp was in confusion. Men who had wandered off, half-dressed, into the woods, came dashing back yelling that the Rebels were coming. Boys who had never fired guns in their lives came tumbling out of their tents with muskets in their hands, gazing wildly about them as though they thought the enemy was already among the tents.

The enemy very nearly was, but almost no one believed it was a real attack, especially when it was discovered that the long roll had been ordered by Colonel Appler of the 53rd Ohio, a nervous man who had several times ordered the long roll sounded when he had seen some moving shadows. Even his own men failed to fall in and Sherman sent word to Appler, saying, "You must be badly scared over there."[1] Then some wounded pickets came running into camp, screaming that the Rebels were chasing them. Sherman turned his horse, dug in his spurs, and rode off after re-enforcements, while Appler, screaming like the wounded men, ran for the rear.

When the order to fall in was given and Belle Reynolds' husband called for his horse, Belle finished cooking the pancakes, dumped them into a napkin, and thrust them into his haversack. The musket fire was closer now. Shells were shrieking overhead, and each time a shell came over Belle dodged instinctively. The Lieutenant mounted his horse and she came to stand beside him. He looked down on her and said, "What will

you do, Belle?" There was no way to answer that question, and he rode away.

Belle watched him go, while the noise and confusion increased all around her. Now there was the thud of heavy artillery, felt as much as heard, as though the ground underfoot had been struck a giant blow, and the sound of tearing canvas as the small, round cannon balls ripped into the tents. The musket fire was close now, and it had a crackling sound. Veterans of Belmont and Donelson were forming into line and advancing on orders from their officers. The raw recruits, some of whom had only received their muskets the day before, were trying to find out how to load them and quite a number, giving it up, threw their muskets on the ground and ran for the rear. When Lieutenant Reynolds had gone from sight, Belle looked around her at this scene and was startled to see the Rebels running down a hillside at no great distance away.

There is no accounting for what people will do in time of danger. With the Rebels coming toward them and shells bursting near them, these two women, Belle and Mrs. N., walked into their tents and methodically began to pack their trunks. That they had taken trunks with them on an expedition certain to end in battle, throws into sharp relief the extraordinary character of this war in which women played so unusual a role. The two women were still folding up clothing when the regimental wagon master yelled at them to run for their lives. Even then they took time to get their traveling baskets and their bonnets. When they were all prepared, as though for a train journey, they came out of their tents to find the camp deserted, all the men from their own regiment departed and no Rebels in sight. It must have been an eerie experience to find themselves alone in the camp, with the shots still coming over, and not a living person to be seen.

They left then, suddenly feeling the need to hurry, passing the parade ground where some cavalry was trying to form under shellfire, shells bursting among them, and the horses rearing and plunging. They went on, clutching their traveling baskets, their bonnets neatly tied under their chins, until they came to General Ross' headquarters. Here they found a deserted tent and went in to rest, though the canvas was no protection against the bullets which were streaking through the camp. Here an astonished Lieutenant found them and said, "For God's sake, run for the river. The Rebels are coming!" The next instant a shell exploded close outside and pieces of it came tearing through the tent. Belle and Mrs. N. moved on.

The road to the river was a wallow of mud, churned up by wagons and

heavy gun caissons. The women found themselves in the midst of heavy traffic, fresh troops being moved into the fight and a ragged, disorderly mass of wounded and frightened men moving in the other direction. The women, hampered by their full skirts and their baskets, made slow progress in the deep mud. They had not quite reached the river when they came on a place where several ambulances were drawn up around an open-air dressing station, and surgeons were at work. Belle and Mrs. N. stopped, took off their bonnets, and began to dress wounds.

They had only been working about ten minutes when an orderly dashed up with orders to load the wounded back into the ambulances at once and take them to the river, for the Rebels were not far away. The road was now close to impassable, for panic was spreading through the army and the raw troops were making for the river in increasing numbers. They were gathered in terror-stricken masses around the warehouses and under the river banks, impeding the wagon drivers who were trying to get ammunition to the front and the surgeons who were working among the wounded on the wharf. As all able-bodied medical assistants had been sent into the fight to bolster the wavering battle line, the surgeons tried to impress deserters into service, but they were too terrified to be of any use.

One of the surgeons told Belle and Mrs. N. that the best place for them would be on one of the river boats which were hovering around the docks, and if they wanted to work, they would find plenty to do among the wounded on board. They chose the *Emerald,* and just as they were going up the gangplank, they saw Grant and his staff, all with anxious faces, arrive on a river boat and hurriedly depart for the scene of action.

On the *Emerald* Belle found a lady, whom she, after her maddening habit, calls "Mrs. C.," who was probably a nurse with the 17th Illinois, which was Belle's own regiment. Mrs. C. had just arrived, bringing with her some hospital supplies, and as the failure of the army medical men to make proper provision for the wounded was becoming apparent even at this early stage, they were put to immediate use.

The battle moved closer while the women worked aboard the *Emerald.* The noise grew to an uproar, clouds of acrid smoke drifted over the river and sometimes when their work took them along the docks where the wounded and dead were laid out in rows, spent balls pattered like hail around them. Meanwhile, some of the frightened recruits had begun to regain their courage and there was a slow, but appreciable movement of men back toward the fighting. Sometimes whole units returned to-

gether. Sherman, looking like an apparition from hell, with his red hair standing on end and his face black with powder, was rounding up wavering men like herds of cattle, and driving them back into the lines. Sherman had four horses shot from under him that day and Grant, riding along the lines to inspect his command, thought that here was an officer who needed no help from anyone.

The men remained in the battle, and those who conquered their fear and returned from the river, fought with an almost unbelievable tenacity and determination, and they faced a like determination in the enemy. Boys whose only previous fighting experience had been behind barns and in schoolyards, walked into the face of withering fire, to fight at point-blank range, or hand to hand. One small field was so thickly strewn with their dead bodies that Grant thought a man could walk on them like stepping stones and not touch the ground.

Buell at last arrived in Savannah and was proceeding up the river to Pittsburg Landing at a pace too leisurely to suit his own command, who could hear the terrific din of the battle and were impatient to get into it. He arrived at Pittsburg Landing in advance of his troops some time about the middle of the afternoon and found some 8000 terrified men still cowering under the banks. Seeing them, Buell concluded that the day was lost. Grant and Buell met on a dispatch boat and had a brief discussion about getting Buell's forces from the east to the west bank of the river. Then they went ashore together, Buell pausing to rail at the panicky stragglers and threatening to have his gunboats fire shells at them. On the deck of the *Emerald,* Belle Reynolds paused in her work to watch this scene.

The miserable stragglers were milling about on the shore like herds of frightened sheep, trampling rations and hospital supplies into the mud. They believed themselves to be caught in a trap between the flooded river and the banks, as indeed they would have been if the Confederates had descended on them. Buell's tirade and his threat to have them shelled only added to their terror. Some tried to swim the river. Some rushed toward the *Emerald,* intending to find safety on board. Such a rush could easily have swamped or capsized the low-lying river boat. Captain Norton, who made his headquarters on the *Emerald,* seeing the danger, stationed himself at the gangplank, a revolver in each hand, and threatened to shoot anyone who tried to board. One man against so many might easily have been rushed. It was a dangerous moment and he called Belle to aid him. He gave her a revolver and told her to go up to the hurricane deck and shoot when he gave the order. The necessity

never arose. Gradually the panic subsided and Belle went back to her work among the wounded on the boat. It was for her bravery on this occasion that the governor of her State gave her the commission of Major.

When night fell, the Union forces had not been defeated, nor were the Confederates victorious. Three hundred and fifty wounded had been carried aboard the *Emerald,* and other hospital ships were preparing to leave for Savannah with full loads. All other available craft were being used to ferry Buell's troops across the river. In the darkness, the scene was awesome and fantastic. Blazing pine torches on the shore turned the shadows of men into grotesque, leaping giants. Buell's troops in long columns marching down to the river on one side and up on the other, looked like a huge, undulating, black snake. Teamsters, struggling through the night to carry ammunition to the front, brought their empty wagons to the top of the bank, let their mules skeeter down, four feet planted, sliding on their haunches with the weight of the wagon shoving them down. A storm came up with torrents of rain, rolling thunder and intensely brilliant flashes of lightning. Two gunboats, the *Tyler* and the *Lexington,* which had escorted Buell's forces to Pittsburg Landing, had opened fire on the enemy and the heavy boom of their six-pounders shook the ships on the river.

Toward morning, the *Emerald,* with Belle on board, dropped down the river, riding easily with the sweeping current, to unload the wounded at Savannah. About four A.M. another hospital ship steamed into the crowd of boats which were hovering around the Landing and maneuvered up to the dock, her paddles thrashing the muddy water. Her hospital staff consisted of a surgeon and three women nurses, one of whom, Annie Wittenmyer, was shortly to be known throughout the Western theater. This is the scene on the river banks as she saw it when the light of day began to dawn.

"Our hospital boat was lying alongside of other steamers. The rain was falling steadily. We could hear the heavy guns, the screaming of the shells, the thunder of the battle going on near by. As the light increased, we shivered to see the wounded lying on bags of grain and out on the guards, and the dead, who had been carried from the boats, lying mangled and bloody along the shore of the river. At first we could only cover our faces with our hands in a shiver and chill of agony, in the attempt to hide the horrid sights of war from our eyes.

"But as we stood there a feeble hand was lifted, and a feeble voice called out,

'Say lady! Can't you bring me a drink of water?'

"Immediately a hundred hands were lifted. We could scarcely see them in the faint light of the early morning, but we could hear the voices.

'Bring me some water.'

'Bring me something to eat.'

"I called out cheerily,

'Yes, yes; *we'll help you all we can.*'

"It was a great relief to have something to do. We went with gladness to our work. I was the pioneer, and went right onto the boat lying nearest.

"The surgeon in charge of our hospital boat had gone off to the field. There was no one in authority left on the boat, and we took possession.

"I had several boxes of canned oysters, and three or four barrels of crackers, but we soon exhausted these; then we began on the beef in the storeroom.

"Barrels of soup were made and distributed. The other two ladies made the soup, and I distributed it from boat to boat, and from one to another. Oh, the sights and scenes I witnessed that day!"[2]

Mrs. Wittenmyer worked all the next day of battle, scarcely pausing to rejoice when word came in the afternoon that the Confederates had been driven back. She had been foolish enough to put on a new dress for her work among the wounded. On Tuesday she took time to make her toilet and discovered herself to be covered with mud and blood, so she carried the dress to the rail of the ship and watched it float away on the muddy stream.

The hospitals in Savannah were overcrowded before the first day of battle and would have been without supplies if the Sanitary Commission had believed the belligerent assertions of the army doctors. A few women nurses were already at work and Mother Bickerdyke was there, making her witches' brew of gruel and liquor and handing out hospital supplies which she had wangled, as usual, without authority.

The *Emerald* stayed at Savannah Sunday night and the next day she was back at the dock at Pittsburg Landing. There the three women, Belle Reynolds, Mrs. N., and Mrs. C., who had not been to bed all night, were attempting to care for the new load of wounded as fast as they were carried on board. It was not for thirty-six hours that Belle could find any

time to sleep. Word reached her that her husband was safe, but she did not see him for days.

One day she was attending the surgeon at an operating table in a shore hospital, watching as suffering men were laid out on the bloody boards after being given a mixture of whiskey and chloroform which put them into a state of semi-insensibility. The shrieks, the glittering knife, the spurting blood and the severed limbs were finally too much for her, and she felt herself beginning to faint. One of the doctors gave her some brandy, and she shook off her weakness, but she had done all she could do that day.

She was on the point of leaving when a hand was laid on her shoulder. She turned to face a rough-looking man, whose clothing was torn and muddy and whose haggard face was covered with grime, and she did not at once recognize him as her husband. They were almost shy with each other, and very gentle. They had been through so much.

How many women there were at Shiloh that spring morning of April 6, 1862, will probably never be known. There were a number who, like Belle Reynolds, were accompanying their husbands on the campaign, and others who were there in the capacity of regimental nurses. Some of them we know about. There was Modenia Weston, who "did up" wounds on the field and on a hospital boat. On Tuesday after the battle she went on the boat to Savannah, where the wounded were transferred to an empty building. She told the story, told by so many others, of inadequate facilities and shortages of food and supplies until the arrival of relief boats, sent by the Sanitary Commission.

Mrs. Jerusha Small was on the field during the battle, doing her best to bind up the wounds of her husband and other members of the Twelfth Iowa Regiment. She had a narrow escape when the Confederates invaded the camp, and spent days nursing the wounded. She contracted the disease known in those days as "galloping consumption," and at her own request was sent home to die.

Another nurse, Anna McMahon, lost her life because of her work after Shiloh. Anna came down with the measles, which still plagued this boy army, and lived only five days. Mrs. M. V. Harkin, one of the little group of nurses to which Anna belonged, recalled later that, "We could not procure a coffin, but a carpenter took some cracker boxes, from which he made as decent a one as possible. We wreathed it with flowers from the battlefield, and buried her beneath three large trees that grew on the bank of the Tennessee River. A rude board headpiece, bearing her

name, was erected, and we left her there to take up our work as best we could."[3]

Mary Safford was there, having risen from a sickbed when she heard that help would be needed. She was on board the hospital ship *Hazel Dell,* and when she met her old friend, Mother Bickerdyke, she was given a loving welcome. Mary made several trips on the *Hazel Dell,* wearing herself out, not eating enough and sleeping little. She never learned the necessity to spare herself, but as one of the men she nursed said afterward, "The biggest sort of men obeyed her. She was the only one who seemed to know what to do on that boat."

There was a little cricket of a woman at Shiloh, named Lucy Kaiser, Lucy L. Campbell Kaiser, she signed herself. Lucy was sharp, shrewd, tireless and tough-minded, and she had a talent for righteous indignation when nursing conditions were not to her liking. She had been staying in and around St. Louis, paying her own board at hotels, and helping out in hospitals whenever she could get a foot in the door. Eventually she persuaded Miss Dix to accept her services, and went to work in earnest— busy, quarrelsome, and of doubtful usefulness.

She was at Benton Barracks, interpreting her commission in the Nursing Corps as a license to do battle with the staff, when the concentration of troops commenced at Pittsburg Landing. Lucy decided to go there and, armed with a pass which only permitted her to go to the other side of the river, she took her trunk and went up the gangplank of what seems to have been a hospital ship carrying a regiment to the front. Lucy boldly held out her pass to the guard, who motioned her on without bothering to read what it said.[4] There were some sick soldiers already on board, and Lucy went to work. An officer appeared and shouted the order, "All females will immediately come ashore." Lucy simply stared at him and stayed where she was.

Presently she felt the boat beginning to move, heading out into the stream, and she left the sick boys in order to find herself a comfortable cabin. When she found one she liked, she moved in. When on Saturday the fifth, the boat arrived at Pittsburg Landing, Lucy followed the regiment ashore and through the windy darkness to their camp because, she said naively, "I knew of nowhere else to go."

On the fateful Sunday morning, Lucy and a helper were giving breakfast to the sick of the regiment when the long roll sounded. Almost at once several shots came ripping through the hospital tent and Lucy began to prepare the men for transfer to a safer place. If Lucy is to be believed, somebody was criminally negligent for, she says, "The regiment had

no ammunition and must soon fall back. . . . We had gone there in the dark and had not taken the trouble to find out our position, and what to do we did not know."

She found a lieutenant, who at least knew that the camp was on the edge of a ravine, and he told Lucy to move the sick there. She and her assistant managed it somehow. Then an orderly appeared with orders to get the men into ambulances, which Lucy interpreted as relieving her of further responsibility, so she took someone's rifle and set out to find the battle.

Oddly enough, it was hard to find, or perhaps she arrived in one of those periods of quiet which are perpetually occurring in battles in one sector or another, and did not realize she was in the fighting line. She found some wounded, however, and tore up her handkerchief and underskirt for bandages. Then, finding nothing else of interest, she wandered off until she reached the river. There the deserters were milling about, and she went up to a surgeon who was working with some wounded. He told her to go and work on one of the boats (no doubt to rid himself of her) and she took his advice.

By this time, Lucy was tired, so she sat down on the floor in a passageway, with her back to a partition, to rest a while. Presently a woman came along and said, "Why don't you get to work?" And Lucy, who never let anyone get the better of her in a tongue battle, replied succinctly, "Why don't you go to work yourself, and see how you like it?"

Lucy got up after a while, located the kitchen and elected herself boss until she lost interest in coffee and hardtack. Then she went off to help the surgeons dress wounds. For all her exasperating traits, Lucy was a worker. She worked all night long on Sunday, all day Monday, and all but two hours, spent in sleeping, on Monday night. She continued to work with the wounded until Thursday. By that time her dress was a mass of dried blood and dirt and her trunk was lost, so she took time out for a trip to Cincinnati to replenish her wardrobe.

When she returned, she went to call on General Grant, who gave her permission to live on one of the boats until a hospital steamer should arrive. That gave her a little time in which to poke around among the various temporary hospitals, and in her exploring she encountered Mother Bickerdyke. Two cats on a back fence could not have displayed more instant animosity. Bickerdyke was, as usual, working hard, and Lucy offered to help. Bickerdyke refused the offer "in a way," said Lucy, "which to me was rather amusing." Bickerdyke did not invite Lucy into

the hospital tent, but Lucy went in anyway and interested herself for a while in making notes about the patients.

The number of women of Lucy's stamp, who were free-lancing around the theatres, living off the government, was rapidly convincing both the members of the Sanitary Commission and the Surgeon General's Office that more stringent regulations were in order. Some, in theory, were already in effect, notably the Government's order of December 1861 abolishing the position of regimental matron. Various field commanders had issued orders governing the activities of women, or excluding them altogether. All of this availed little. Regiments kept their matrons and their daughters. Women continued to follow their husbands to war. Women volunteers, without authority from anyone, continued to rush to the scenes of conflict. Sometimes they made inexcusable nuisances of themselves. Sometimes, and probably more often than not, in these early days, their work was of great value when there was no one else on the spot to do what needed to be done.

Gradually most of the wounded were removed from the temporary hospitals to general hospitals in St. Louis, Cairo, Mound City, Keokuk and other places, where they could receive better care. General Halleck, who had arrived at Pittsburg Landing to take command a few days after the battle, was opposed, in the first instance, to this removal and his consent for so obviously wise a move was finally wrung from him, after he had refused permission to many others, by Mrs. James Harlan, wife of a Senator—a woman, it would seem, of some executive ability and quite possibly possessed of charm. There remained for the Sanitary Commission and the Surgeon General to review the failures and advances demonstrated by the handling of the Shiloh wounded.

On the credit side of the ledger was the fact that the hospitals close to the lines at Shiloh approached more nearly the true field hospital than those connected with any previous battle. This was especially true of the hospitals set up by Surgeon Irwin in vacated tents on the field of battle. Hospitals behind the lines had been prepared in advance, albeit they proved inadequate. The collection of the wounded was better handled, though much improvement was still necessary. The hospital ship, an institution which had proved its value at Donelson and was indispensable at Shiloh, took its permanent place in the advance, instead of in the aftermath of battle convoys. (The *City of Memphis,* gaudy heroine of Donelson, was there.)

On the debit side was the continuing shortage of surgeons and of supplies. They never, throughout all the years of war, proved adequate

to cope with the mounting casualties. Walt Whitman, writing in 1864, said:

"I have seen many battles, their results, but never one where there was not, during the first few days, an unaccountable and almost total deficiency of everything for the wounded—appropriate sustenance, nursing, cleaning, medicines, stores, etc. (I do not say surgical attendance, because the surgeons cannot do more than human endurance permits.) Whatever pleasant accounts there may be in the papers of the North, this is the actual fact. No thorough previous preparation, no system, no foresight, no genius. Always plenty of stores, no doubt, but always miles away . . ." Whitman, hypersensitive to suffering, was, in the main, correct.

The tragic deficiency of supplies at Shiloh, however, was mainly chargeable to the Army medical bureaucracy, still mired in the policies which produced too little, too late. True, there were difficulties. Many ambulances, hospital tents and their equipment were captured by the enemy in the first day of battle. Mud and rain hampered the handling of the wounded. But these are conditions which may arise in any engagement and must be provided for with the same care with which a general plans a possible line of retreat. The medical work at Donelson was bad; that of Shiloh was close to a disgrace.

On the Thursday following the battle, Belle Reynolds encountered a shocking example of Army Medical Department mismanagement when she went aboard one of the hospital ships which was in charge of an army surgeon. This surgeon told Belle and Mrs. N. that he "wanted no women around," but they were searching for boys from the Seventeenth, and they chose not to hear this remark. On board, they found men, many of whom had been wounded on Sunday, with their wounds still untended. The two women went back to the *Emerald* for supplies and to the Sanitary Commission boat in charge of Dr. Warriner. When they returned to the government boat, which had four hundred wounded and only two doctors, they set to work washing the men and dressing wounds. Mrs. N. came to a cot on which lay a man with a coarse woolen blanket over him, covering his face. Supposing him to be dead, Mrs. N. pulled back the blanket, and was horrified to see that the man who lay beneath had an active case of smallpox.

Shiloh was a Confederate failure but not a Union victory. Of the 62,600 Union troops engaged, there were 1700 killed and 8400 wounded.[5] The Confederates constructed a new line of defense with the grim determination which had led Grant, when he observed it in the

green recruits of both armies during the battle, to believe the war would be long and hard-fought. From this time on, Grant's policy was one of ruthless aggression and the destruction of enemy property, both public and private, which might be used for military purposes, believing that such a policy was necessary to bring the war to an end.

The country at large came slowly to hold similar views about the probable duration of hostilities. The result was the re-establishment, on a more permanent basis, of the various relief organizations and a tightening of the ties between them. After Shiloh, the leaders among the women of the North carried on the business of relief unemotionally, professionally, and on an ever larger scale, in a spirit which suggested that this work might prove to be the great preoccupation of their lives until the end of time.

NOTES

[1] Lloyd Lewis, *Sherman, Fighting Prophet* (Harcourt, Brace and Company, New York, 1932), p. 220.

[2] Mrs. Annie Wittenmyer, *Under the Guns* (E. B. Stillings & Co., Boston, Mass., 1895), pp. 30-31.

[3] Mary A. Gardner Holland, *Our Army Nurses* (B. Wilkins & Co., Boston, Mass., 1895), pp. 490-491.

[4] The failure to examine passes seems to be a weakness of guards in all wars. One of the women workers in the author's organization in World War II found that the guards had been admitting her, through her mistake, to the War Department for a week on the strength of a recipe for veal *scaloppine*.

[5] Rounded numbers based on data in *Numbers and Losses in the Civil War* by Thomas L. Livermore (Indiana University Press, 1957). Obviously, these figures, like all-armed-strength data, even relating to present-day armies, must be regarded as estimates rather than literal totals.

13

LADIES OF THE TRANSPORT SERVICE

————————————————— ★ —————————————————

CHRONOLOGY

1862

January 31   Lincoln ordered the Army of the Potomac to take to the field.

March 17   Embarkation of the Army of the Potomac at Alexandria for the York River, under command of General George B. McClellan.

April 25   The Hospital Transport Service of the Sanitary Commission inaugurated with the commissioning of the first ship, the *Daniel Webster*.

May 4   Union troops entered Yorktown.

May 6   Union troops entered Williamsburg.

May 16   Advance of Union Army reached White House Landing.

May 20   Advance of Union Army reached Chickahominy.

May 31–June 11   Battle of Fair Oaks, or Seven Pines.

June 12   J. E. B. Stuart, with about 1200 troops, began his encirclement of McClellan's forces.

June 25   Battle of Oak Grove, or Second Battle of Fair Oaks; prelude to the Seven Days' Battles.

June 26–July 1   The Seven Days' Battles: June 26th, Mechanicsville; June 27th, Gaines Mills or Cold Harbor or Turkey Hill Ridge; June 28th, Garnett's and Golding's Farms; June 29th, Peach Orchard and Savage Station; June 30th, White Oak Swamp; July 1st, Malvern Hill or Crew's Farm.

June 23   Dr. Jonathan Letterman made Medical Director of the Army of the Potomac.

July 2   Withdrawal of Union Forces under General McClellan to Harrison's Landing.

July 22   The President called a meeting of the Cabinet to consider a proclamation to free the slaves. It was decided not to issue the proclamation until a victory of the Union forces had changed the growing apathy toward the war.

August 2   Order of this date by Letterman created an ambulance corps for the Army of the Potomac.

August 3   Order issued by General Halleck for the withdrawal of the Army of the Potomac from the Peninsula.

★

A lady with a flask shall stand,
Beef-tea and punch in either hand,—
Heroic mass of mud
And dirt and stains and blood!
    —Katharine Prescott Wormeley

A MONTH AFTER THE disastrous defeat of Bull Run, the Army of the Potomac at Washington had recovered from its panic and despair. They idolized their new commander, George B. McClellan, and they had every confidence that he would lead them to victory. Immediately upon assuming command, McClellan began the laborious process of instilling discipline into this tatterdemalion citizens' army, and Washington became once more an armed camp, but with a difference. "Little Mac" was a perfectionist in matters of military deportment. Under his rule veterans of Bull Run, and the new recruits with which the ranks had

been replenished, rapidly became well-drilled, soldierly battalions of infantry, batteries of artillery and squadrons of cavalry—a citizens' army still, but an army of which the nation might be proud. Three months after McClellan took command, it seemed that his force of 168,000 men was as ready to launch a campaign as ever an army could be.

Time passed, the perfect machine McClellan had created continued to go through its precise maneuvers, and McClellan continued to receive the adulation of the country and his men, and to attend cabinet meetings where he felt bored and annoyed by what he considered the interference of the politicians in matters beyond their ken. Nothing else of any importance occurred. There was, by this time, a growing feeling of impatience that this beautiful army did not take to the field and fight. For some time Lincoln defended his General against the increasing criticism until he himself, growing impatient, made the famous remark: "If General McClellan does not want to use the army for some days, I should like to borrow it and see if it can not be made to do something."

On January 27th Lincoln, using for the first time his powers as Commander in Chief, issued an order directing all land and naval forces to prepare for a general movement. On January 31st he issued a special order to the Army of the Potomac to take the field, putting an end to McClellan's inactivity. The military objective in the East was still Richmond, but there was a difference of opinion between the President and General McClellan as to the line of advance the Army should take. There were four possible routes to the Confederate capital. The first was along the line of the railroad through Manassas Junction, which had been evacuated by the Confederates, and on through Gordonsville. The second was by way of the Potomac through Fredericksburg. The third lay by way of Chesapeake Bay and the York River. The fourth by Chesapeake Bay and the River James.

The first route was the longest, but by taking it, the army could move against the enemy while, at the same time, covering Washington from attack. This was substantially Lincoln's plan. McClellan preferred the route which led to the York River, and Lincoln yielded to him on the stipulation that a force be left behind to guard Washington.

There were more delays before the Army of the Potomac began to move, and meanwhile Fort Henry and Fort Donelson had fallen into Union hands. Finally, on the seventeenth of March, McClellan's forces set sail from Alexandria, for the York River, and there began the arduous advance up the narrow, muddy strip of land between the York and the James, and the series of battles known as the Peninsula Campaign.

When preparations for the Army's departure from Washington were being made, it became evident that even the reorganized Surgeon General's Office would not be able to cope with the medical problems which would arise. These problems included not only the care of the men wounded in battle but of the sick, and because much of the country over which the campaign would be fought was unhealthy, malarial swamp and river land, the number of sick was expected to be high.

The Sanitary Commission, with these things in mind, applied to the Secretary of War for the use of some steamers to be fitted up as hospital boats, to gather the disabled from the regions around the James, the Pamunkey and the York Rivers and transport them to the great base hospitals at Fortress Monroe and Washington. It was not the intention of the Sanitary Commission to assume full responsibility for the disabled, or to relieve government of the duties which it should assume, but to supplement the work of government and especially to be ready in case the medical department once more proved unequal to the task. Their activities were to be confined to the ships—the sick and the wounded on land being the responsibility of the army medical authorities—but in actual practice, the Sanitary Commission women were, a number of times, called on for duty on shore when the medical department was unable to meet the crisis. With the cordial relations which now existed between the members of the Sanitary Commission and the Surgeon General's Office, the arrangements for steamers were not difficult to make. The Quartermaster General, under whose jurisdiction the coastal and river steamers came, was ordered to make available to the Sanitary Commission as many boats as would be necessary to transport a thousand men. This was the beginning of the great Hospital Transport Service, and the opening of a new field of activity for women.

The first of the steamers to be commissioned was the *Daniel Webster,* which was turned over to the Sanitary Commission on April 25, 1862. Frederick Law Olmsted, Secretary of the Sanitary Commission, took charge of her himself. Mrs. William Preston Griffin, a woman of sense and energy, became matron. Hospital supplies and a staff were sent on board and the ship set sail, the work of preparing for the sick and wounded being done on the voyage southward. The *Daniel Webster* arrived at the mouth of the York River on the thirtieth of April. There Olmsted and part of the hospital staff went ashore to establish headquarters, and the *Daniel Webster* sailed again, bound for New York with 250 sick men on board.

The trial run had been wholly successful. The *Daniel Webster* left

New York on her second trip to the York on May 9th, an exceedingly fast turn-around time. Mrs. Griffin was still in charge, and she had with her three carefully chosen young women. The Surgeon-in-Chief of the *Daniel Webster* was Dr. Grymes, an able man, but suffering from consumption, who alternated periods of tense, feverish activity with extreme languor. The rest of the staff consisted of eight medical students, or "dressers," and twenty volunteer male nurses and ward masters.

One of Mrs. Griffin's three assistants was a sprightly woman of thirty-two, named Katharine Wormeley. Katharine was English, but she had been in this country since she was eighteen, living with her parents in Boston and Newport. She moved on the fringes of the literary world (she must have known Julia Ward Howe, who also had a house at Newport) and she found life interesting and gay. She herself had a fluent, readable style, which might have made her a writer had she chosen to be one. She had none of the conventional sentimentality of the day, she was friendly, obliging and she possessed an unusual ability to see below the surface aspects of the passing scene.

There was little for Katharine to do on the first southward voyage of the *Daniel Webster* but to sit on deck enjoying the scenery and the spring sunshine. The only real work was bed-making and she wrote home, "How you would have laughed to see me, without a hoop, mounted on the ledge of the second tier of berths, making the beds on the third tier." On the morning of the eleventh of May, the *Daniel Webster* was again off Yorktown and Katharine rose at five to have everything in order for the load of typhoid patients that would be taken on in the afternoon. Then she sat down to write another of her charming, warmhearted letters home. Everyone in the ship was rushing around with great activity. Surgeons were arriving in tugboats and rowboats, demanding beef tea, lemons, brandy and many other things for the men who would shortly be sent out to the ship. It was bedlam and Katharine loved it. She finished her letter, "Good-bye! *This is life.*"

Katharine and Mrs. Griffin having, obviously, proved themselves workers of special merit, did not go north when the *Daniel Webster* sailed, but became special workers sent by Mr. Olmsted wherever intelligence, energy and courage were needed. They packed their carpet bags (no trunks for these fast-moving ladies) and Katharine expressed herself feelingly about these compartmentless pieces of luggage in which things were perpetually lost, making it necessary to up-end the contraption and shake everything out.

Katharine and Mrs. Griffin (who was an older, statuesque woman with

a sharp intelligence and a lovely peaches-and-cream complexion) were ordered to board a tiny river boat, the *Wilson Small,* headquarters of the Sanitary Commission. But before taking up their posts they explored Yorktown, which had recently fallen into Union hands. The two women went "shuffling about" without hoops, which Katharine thought made them look quite medieval. At the hospital they found Miss Dix, also without hoops, and it may have been that Katharine was well pleased not to be under that lady's jurisdiction.

They had no more time for sight-seeing. The *Wilson Small* shuttled back and forth, picking up sick and wounded men and transferring them to the larger hospital ships. Katharine wrote home that "it is an immense piece of work to get the patients (many of them very low, or in great agony) on board and into their beds, and stimulated and fed and made comfortable. So much is needed—quick eyes and ears, and, above all, some one to keep severe order in the pantry, or rather the kitchen, for the sick-food. Mrs. Griffin is magnificent at that. I never saw her hurried or worried for a moment . . . "[1]

The hospital ships, large and small, came and went. The *Elm City,* a river boat which could not brave the open ocean, but could carry 400 men up the Chesapeake Bay to Washington, the ocean-going *S. R. Spaulding,* the river steamboat *Knickerbocker,* especially designed for surgical cases, the busy little supply boat *Elizabeth,* her decks piled high with crates and boxes, churning the muddy water in her hurry to get from boat to boat, the *Wilson Small,* called by the ladies the *Collida* because of her knack for being run into by other boats (she was finally demolished), and the *Wissahickon,* known affectionately as the *Wicked Chicken.* There were others on the crowded river—the big boats resting in stately dignity at anchor or tied up along the wharves—the little tugs and supply boats, their decks barely above water, always in a hurry, waddling like demented ducks here, there and everywhere.

All these steamers had busy women on board, and Katharine learned to know them as only people know one another who share hardships and hilarity and danger. They were perhaps the most outstanding group of women front-line workers the war produced. All were educated women, many with wide experience of the world. Katharine thought them "just what they should be—efficient, wise, active as cats, merry, light-hearted, thoroughbred, and without the fearful tone of self-devotion which sad experience makes one expect in benevolent women."

Some of them still stand out clearly across the widening gulf of years. There was Miss Whetten, a tall, pre-Raphaelite young woman and the

only one whom the hoopless skirts seemed to become. Another lady, a Mrs. Reading, had nursed under Florence Nightingale in the Crimea, where she had learned to be an excellent surgical nurse, knowledge which she gladly shared. There was Helen Louise Gilson, who was one of those not-very-robust women who could nevertheless endure hardships like a boot soldier. Helen was not so gay in temperament as the other women—she seems never to have learned the sustaining power of laughter, as most of the others had, but she had a lovely singing voice and when she stood with clasped hands singing to a ward full of wounded men, she never failed to bring them peace. Her voice was low and rich, her manner always quiet. This was Helen Gilson's first, but not her last appearance at the fighting front.

There was Mrs. Joseph Howland, whose husband was a Colonel in the 16th New York Regiment. One of her patients, a private in the same regiment, was so moved by her care that he wrote a poem to her:

> "To one borne from the sullen battle's roar,
> Dearer the greeting of thy gentle eyes
> When he, a-weary, torn, and bleeding lies,
> Than all the glory that the victors prize."[2]

Mrs. Howland had a sister, an irrepressible young woman named Georgeanna Woolsey, affectionately known by all the women of the Transport fleet as "Georgy." Katharine Wormeley first heard of her aboard the *Wilson Small,* while the women were working frantically preparing to take on some of the wounded from the battle for Williamsburg. There were perpetual cries of "Where is Georgy?" "Oh, if only Georgy were here!" Georgy, it seems, had been accidentally carried off on one of the big boats, with some other ladies. Georgy showed up again, in a day or two, the ladies having put in their time giving the boat a thorough housecleaning from hurricane deck to hold.

The little boats, like the *Wilson Small,* which were permanently assigned to the malarial river districts, were chronically short of all sorts of supplies and when one of the big ships arrived from the North, beautifully equipped, the river ladies developed shameless kleptomaniac talents. Georgy was especially good at this sort of pilfering, and after a visit to one of the big steamers, she would joyfully empty her huge pockets of knives, forks, spoons, corkscrews, nutmeg graters and other assorted items. The women had no conscience about this method of acquiring what they needed, since the big ships were going back north

where they could re-stock, and Katharine herself became adept at walking off, in an absent-minded way, with a tin pail in either hand.

Sometimes the big boats were tied up side by side, and the women would scurry back and forth from one to another. Katharine wrote home that "there is so little to mark time, or even to distinguish day from night, on these vast ships. They are strange places, and I often feel like a cockroach, running familiarly into all the dark corners." But Katharine loved best the little *Wilson Small*. Here their dining table was the top of an old black stove or a board across the railings of the stairwell. There were no chairs and the ladies and the doctors plumped down on their carpet bags with their backs to the wall. They were forever short of knives and forks. Their drinking cups were tin, and their soup was made in a tin wash basin. One of the ladies had brought her French cook to war with her—an adaptable person named Maurice, who enjoyed himself thoroughly, served in style with a white rag draped over his arm and passionately insisted on the strict observance of conventional table manners.

On most of the boats, there was a chronic shortage of water (the river water being too muddy for use most of the time). If none were available, the ladies made their toilets with rags and the bottles of cologne or bay rum, without which no woman ever went to war. In bathing the patients, Katharine made one basinful serve for as many men as possible. Once, when she was about to throw some very dirty water overboard, a soldier called out, "Stop, marm! That water will do for several of us yet. Bless you! I make my coffee of worse than that." The ladies seldom had real mattresses to sleep on, the more usual arrangement being a sack stuffed with hay. These sacks were not always clean, and once Katharine was filled with gratitude toward one of the men, who brought her a fresh one, because the one she had been sleeping on was last used by a soldier with typhoid.

On the whole, the women stayed surprisingly healthy in this active, outdoor life, and the doctors saw to it that they dosed themselves regularly with quinine to ward off malaria. Most of the sickness among the men was either malaria or typhoid or a sickness having some of the symptoms of both. Once there was a flurry of excitement over a case suspected of being the dread typhus, and the doctors gathered on one of the big ships for an autopsy. It is not clear what the disease was—perhaps some form of meningitis—but typhus, miraculously, was not one of the scourges of the Civil War.

On May 16th, General McClellan's forces reached White House, and

began to establish there one of the great field bases which is the special genius of American armies. White House was at the juncture of the Pamunkey and the Mattapony, where these rivers, coming together, form the York. Richmond, the goal of the campaign, was twenty-four miles away, and here the Richmond-York Railroad crossed the Pamunkey River. White House was not a town, but a landing with wharves where the muddy river was deep and broad, serving the 5,000 acre property, owned by General Lee, known as the Custis Estate. The White House (which was not at this time white, but chocolate brown) was a six-room wooden house surrounded by great trees and a beautiful garden, on the site of the house where Martha Custis Washington had lived.

On May 18th, Katharine arrived at White House on the *Spaulding,* a boat so big that it sometimes brushed the branches of the trees on the river bank as it passed. Katharine found the landing full of activity, the clover fields around the solitary house looking like a vast fairground, with soldiers, tents and sutlers' stands and commissary stores everywhere.

She and the ladies with her went to visit the little house, sad and deserted in the spring sunshine, and found a note in a woman's writing, pinned to the wall beside the front door:

"Northern soldiers! who profess to reverence the memory of Washington, forbear to desecrate the home of his first married life, the property of his wife, and now owned by her descendants."[3]

The note was signed, "A granddaughter of Mrs. Washington." McClellan posted guards around the house and garden, but Katharine and her friends were allowed to enter. They found that the carpets and some of the furniture had been removed, but enough remained to give them a sense of the quiet charm of the life that had once been lived here.

There was little time for sight-seeing, however, for the work was very nearly incessant. Katharine made the discovery common to all who have taken part in a campaign or a battle that she was isolated in the world of the hospital ships and had no idea what was going on, in a larger sense, around her. Wild rumors would flare and fade, but beyond knowing in a general way whether the army was advancing or retreating, these women, working in the very center of the campaign, were all but oblivious to anything but the work to be done. All their work was done with speed and concentration. Their ship might collide with another near some crowded wharf and they would not so much as glance outside to

see what had happened. Once Katharine tried to find out what the day of the week might be, and no member of the staff could tell her.

The medical work of the army had not so much broken down, as failed to establish itself in any effective way. These intelligent women often talked about it, wondering bitterly "why a Government so lavish and perfect in its other arrangements should leave its wounded almost literally to the care of themselves . . . " Without enough surgeons, lacking equipment, with hospital boats that were nothing but empty shells, the army medical authorities would have been involved in a national scandal concerning the care and transportation of sick and wounded had it not been for the Sanitary Commission.

In the early days of the campaign, the Sanitary Commission task, though arduous, was not colossal. Perhaps the medical director would receive a telegram that 150 men sick with typhoid were lying on a river bank some distance up stream in the rain. If they were not picked up at once, some would inevitably die of exposure before the next day. The medical director would simply hand the problem on to Mr. Olmsted, who would send one of the small river boats, usually with Katharine, Mrs. Griffin and Helen Gilson on board, out to rescue the sick men. This is the way Katharine describes one of these missions of rescue:

"We were called to go on board the *Wissahickon* [a river tug], from thence to the *Sea-Shore,* and run down in the latter to West Point, to bring off twenty-five men said to be lying there sick and destitute. Two doctors went with us. After hunting an hour through the fleet for the *Sea-Shore* in vain, and having got as low as Cumberland, we decided (*we* being Mrs. Griffin and I; for the doctors were new to the work, and glad to leave the responsibility upon us women) to push on in the tug, rather than leave the men another night on the ground, for a heavy storm of wind and rain had been going on all day. The pilot remonstrated, but the captain approved, and if the firemen had not suddenly let out the fires and detained us two hours, we might have got our men on board and returned comfortably soon after dark. But the delay cost us the precious daylight. It was night before the last man was got on board. There were fifty-six of them—ten very sick ones.

"The boat had a little shelter-cabin. As we were laying mattresses on the floor, while the doctors were finding the men, the captain stopped us, refusing to let us put typhoid fever cases below the deck—on account of the crew, he said—and threatening to push off at once from the shore. Mrs. Griffin and I looked at him. I did the terrible, and she the pathetic, and he abandoned the contest.

The return passage was rather an anxious one. The river is much obstructed with sunken ships and trees, and we had to feel our way, slackening speed every ten minutes. If we had been alone, it would not have mattered, but to have fifty men upon our hands unable to move was too heavy a responsibility not to make us anxious. The captain and pilot said the boat was leaking (we heard the water gurgling under our feet), and they remarked casually that the river was 'four fathoms deep about there,' but we saw their motive, and were not scared. We were safe alongside the *Spaulding* by midnight, but Mr. Olmsted's tone of voice as he said, 'You don't know how glad I am to see you,' showed how much he had been worried. And yet it was the best thing we could have done, for three, perhaps five, of the men would have been dead before morning. We transferred the deck-men (who were not very ill) at once to the *Elm City,* and kept the others on board the tug till the next morning (Sunday) when they were taken on board the *Spaulding,* all living, and likely to live. Later in the day the *Spaulding* filled up to three hundred and fifty very sick men."[4]

With its base at White House, the Army of the Potomac now began to move toward the Chickahominy River—a sluggish, muddy, reptile-filled stream which flowed across the route to Richmond. The roads were bottomless pits of mud, the countryside one vast, treacherous swamp. Bridges had to be built as the Army advanced, and corduroy roads were made by felling trees, laying them side by side crosswise and throwing a little dirt on top. The air of the swamps was stagnant and stank of rotting vegetation. The mosquitoes hummed in clouds, though inaudible above the humming in the ears of those fortunate enough to have a store of quinine. In the semi-darkness under the trees, whitish mists, dank and sinister, hung over the black swamp water.

The Federal forces came out of this vast morass onto the banks of the Chickahominy on the twentieth of May. On the Richmond side of the stream where Nine Mill Road intersects the Williamsburg stage road, at a distance of about seven miles from the Confederate capital, there grew a fine stand of trees, know as the Seven Pines. Nearby was a farm called Fair Oaks and not faraway, on the Richmond-York Railroad, was a station of the same name. It was these land marches which gave to the engagement which followed the name of the Battle of Fair Oaks, or Seven Pines.

That day, while the Army of the Potomac was maneuvering across the Chickahominy, Katharine, unaware that a battle was impending,

was on board the *Knickerbocker* with some of the other women. Katharine was sitting, as usual, on the floor, trying to write a letter, but being constantly interrupted by the laughter and gaiety of her friends. Georgy was sorting socks and pulling out of them the little balls of darning wool and long needles. She was making a fringe of the threaded needles across Katharine's back, and Katharine wrote, "Do spare us the darning-needles! Reflect upon us rushing in haste to the linen-closet and plunging our hands into the bale of stockings!"

That night (the thirtieth) while the two armies faced each other in the certainty of an engagement the next day, a storm of great violence came on, with torrents of rain driven by high winds. The *Knickerbocker* plunged and rolled at her anchorage and the little *Wilson Small* (the Collida) added yet more to her collection of scars. For the men bivouacked along the Chickahominy, there was no protection from the downpour.

In the very worst of the storm, word came to the *Knickerbocker* that a steamer was aground up the river with 200 sick men on her, without food, and no one in charge. Katharine, Georgy and Mrs. Reading, the Nightingale nurse, accompanied by Dr. Ware, set out at once, taking tea, bread, brandy and beef extract. They went in a small, open boat, which tossed and dipped over the stormy black water. Katharine, who was afraid of nothing else, feared these little boats and feared the horror of climbing, often in darkness clutching her skirt, up the tall bulging side of some monstrous ship on a rope ladder that swayed and sagged with every step.

The next day, in the afternoon, the fighting began. A telegraph station had been set up on the *Knickerbocker* and the women had the unusual experience of knowing, hour by hour, the progress of the battle. All available hospital ships were gathered in the broad river to receive the wounded, who began to arrive in great numbers—and the women of the fleet had no sleep that night.

Five days later, Mr. Olmsted asked the ladies for volunteers to go to the *Vanderbilt*, a government boat, filled with wounded, but without staff or provisions, or mattresses. Katharine and Mrs. Griffin, though they had worked all through the preceding night, were among those who answered the call.

"We went on board," Katharine wrote, "and such a scene as we entered and lived in for two days I trust never to see again. Men in every condition of horror, shattered and shrieking, were being brought in on stretchers borne by 'contrabands,' who dumped them

anywhere, banged the stretchers against pillars and posts, and walked over the men without compassion. There was no one to direct what ward or what bed they were to go into. Men shattered in the thigh, and even cases of amputation, were shoveled into top berths without thought or mercy. The men had mostly been without food for three days, but there was *nothing* on board either boat for them; and if there had been, the cooks were only engaged to cook for the ship, and not for the hospital.

"We began to do what we could. The first thing wanted by wounded men is something to drink (with the sick, stimulants are the first thing). Fortunately we had plenty of lemons, ice, and sherry on board the *Small,* and these were available at once. Dr. Ware discovered a barrel of molasses, which, with vinegar, ice, and water, made a most refreshing drink. After that we gave them crackers and milk, or tea and bread. It was hopeless to try to get them into bed; indeed, there were no mattresses on the *Vanderbilt.* All we could do at first was to try to calm the confusion, to stop some agony, to revive the fainting lives, to snatch, if possible, from immediate death with food and stimulants. Imagine a great river or Sound steamer filled on every deck,—every berth and every square inch of room covered with wounded men; even the stairs and gangways and guards filled with those who are less badly wounded; and then imagine fifty well men, on every kind of errand, rushing to and fro over them, every touch bringing agony to the poor fellows, while stretcher after stretcher came along, hoping to find an empty place; and then imagine what it was to keep calm ourselves, and make sure that every man on both those boats was properly refreshed and fed. We got through about 1 A.M., Mrs. M. and Georgy having come off other duty and reinforced us."[5]

Among the women on board the *Vanderbilt* that night was Mrs. John Harris of Philadelphia, an active war worker and able executive. With the others, she carried buckets of tea and stacks of sliced bread to the wounded. Most of the men had not eaten anything but hardtack for some days, and Mrs. Harris was filled with "shame, indignation and sorrow" because of the failure of the government to provide even food for the wounded.

After some days of nursing the wounded on various transports (during which she worked in a dress stained from kneeling on bloody decks beside the wounded, having torn up all her spare clothing to make bandages) she went to the bloody field of Fair Oaks. Here she pitched

a tent at Dudley Farm, near Savage Station, close to one of the field hospitals where she worked until the retreat began.

Fair Oaks was a Union victory, though by a narrow margin, and the men who had toiled for so long through the dreadful country were exhausted. Richmond lay almost within their grasp—four miles from the advanced Federal outposts. But that four miles was not to be transversed. Word came that Washington was threatened by a Confederate force moving through the Shenandoah Valley and that re-enforcements, on which McClellan counted heavily, had been withdrawn for its protection. Without those re-enforcements, the Union position was untenable, and there began a slow and painful retreat of the Army of the Potomac. The series of engagements known as the Seven Days' Battles now started, while McClellan retreated toward the mouth of the James.

There was at least one woman with the Union Army in the seven days' retreat, walking knee deep in the mud with the troops. She was Amanda Colburn Farnham from St. Johnsbury, Vermont, and no doubt there were others with her whose names have long since been lost.

The medical direction of the Army of the Potomac had proved unsatisfactory from the start and a new director, Dr. Letterman, arrived at White House to take command. He was perhaps the most able medical administrator the war produced. He had need to be, for he inherited chaos. Medical supplies were almost used up, ambulances and other equipment were in bad condition, one-fourth of the Army of the Potomac was in hospitals, deaths had risen from 30 per 1,000 to 50 per 1,000, and there were not enough doctors.

Letterman arrived in the midst of the confusion which followed the order to abandon the base at White House. The ancient pine trees along the river, which formed much of the beauty of the landscape, had been cut down to permit the gunboats to cover the plain with their big guns and to protect the evacuation if the enemy arrived on the scene. Everyone knew that fighting had been going on for two days not far away, but no one knew the result. All the night before, supplies and materiel were carried on board the transports. The Sisters of Charity, who had set up a hospital in the White House, were evacuated along with their patients, and a guard set on the house. There were many sick men in the 250-tent hospital not far away, and not enough ambulances to move them to the waiting ships. Some were carried on stretchers and those who could walk were more or less left to their own devices. As soon as the sick men were evacuated, the tents came down and with their going, the scene became a dreary wasteland.

Not all the supplies could be moved and these and the wooden store-houses were burned. Bales of hay were dragged around them, whiskey poured on them and ignited. A corral of seven hundred invalid horses and mules was opened and the animals let loose. Word came that the enemy was only three miles away. A gun was fired as a signal for all on shore to go on board the ships. After that, the scene was sheer madness. Instead of complying, the soldiers rushed on the sutlers' tents, those mobile general stores run by adventurous merchants who followed the army, and, helping themselves to everything they could lay hands on, staggered down to the wharves.

Katharine Wormeley was on board the *Wilson Small,* which was standing out in the river. She watched this wild scene with amusement. "We have," she wrote, "just enjoyed the fun of seeing the last of the shore-people rushing on board schooners and steamers,—the former all yelling for 'a tow.' I never laughed more than to see the 'contrabands' race down from the quarters and shovel into barges,—the men into one, the women into another."

The great gun of the *Sebago* boomed, all the crowd of ships slipped their moorings and began to slide down the river. The *Wilson Small* forming part of this strange parade, passed by the gunboats drawn up in line of battle, the guns already manned and pointed toward the shore. Fires were still being set by the few remaining troops and stores of ammunition were exploding. Katharine looked toward the White House— a farewell look—and saw General Casey sitting on the piazza while signal men on the roof wigwagged with their colored flags. Katharine had a special fondness for the charming, pathetic little brown White House.

As the river twisted, the masts of the advance boats could be seen through the trees no more than a stone's throw away. "And now we are streaming down the winding river; the *Elm City* ahead, with two or three schooners; the little *Wissahickon* racing along as fast as she can go, like a crab, and blessing herself that she is too little to be detained for 'a tow.' By and by we come, hauling slowly two big schooners; then comes the *Daniel Webster,* towing ammunition-barges; after her the *Vanderbilt,* towing something of which I can see only the masts above the trees as the river winds. At each bend there is an excitement. Somebody is sure to be within an ace of getting foul of somebody else. The smoke at White House is growing denser and denser, and we hear cannon, —which we take to mean that the gunboats are getting a chance at the enemy."[6]

Katharine did not see the burning of the little White House and

perhaps she never knew of it. General Casey had tried to protect it, but the time came when the guards had to be withdrawn and the lawless element—the "bummers" who were responsible for so much of the wanton destruction all through the war, set it on fire. Katharine arrived at Fortress Monroe on June 28th and for her the Peninsula Campaign was at an end. "May I never see the pretty, poisonous Pamunkey again," she wrote. "Keep my room ready for me; I may be home any day."

The Peninsula Campaign was very nearly over for everyone. McClellan's army marched to a new base at Harrison's Landing on the James and rested there to recuperate from the heavy losses of men and supplies suffered during the Seven Days' Battles. In some sense the army, though it had failed in its objective, the capture of Richmond, had improved as a fighting machine, for men and officers had gained in military knowledge and in hardihood. From the Confederate point of view, the Campaign was a disappointment, for though Richmond had not been destroyed, the Army of the Potomac, which should have been destroyed, had escaped safely from the trap between the rivers.

For a time the new base at Harrison's Landing became a turmoil of activity.[7] Letterman, the new medical director of the Army of the Potomac, on July 1st took over the Harrison House which as a hospital was less than adequate, but the only building available, and from there could be heard the firing of the famous semi-circle of guns at Malvern Hill. The next day there were downpours of rain and the wounded began to arrive in great numbers. Only those who were seriously wounded could be given shelter, and Letterman and the rest had to provide for themselves as best they could. Letterman, noting this with the observing eye of the reformer, saw the need for hospital tents for such emergencies, as he had already made note of the need for a trained ambulance corps.

About three weeks later, 300 hospital tents, which Letterman sent for, arrived, and the hospital settled down into a routine of orderly efficiency. Meanwhile Lincoln, who now concerned himself more directly with military management, had become convinced that Harrison's Landing was not practicable as a permanent base and orders were issued for the complete withdrawal of the Army of the Potomac from the Peninsula. The evacuation of the wounded by ship began on the third of August and Letterman noted that by August 14th over 14,000 had departed, more than 5,600 being sent away in a single day. Letterman was beginning to prove his worth.

The Sanitary Commission had covered itself with glory. The Commission had not undertaken to transport all the wounded, but the 8,000

disabled who were handled by its workers was a smaller number than had been anticipated. Nevertheless, it was a tremendous undertaking and one which proved to have been indispensable. Stillé thought the work of the Transport Service "the most arduous and harassing duty performed by the Commission during the war." But perhaps of greater importance than the actual accomplishment was the ideal implicit in the whole undertaking—that the people of a nation would not, at this point in the world's history, any longer permit the inefficient, haphazard care of its disabled soldiers.

NOTES

[1] Katharine Prescott Wormeley, *The Other Side of the War* (Ticknor and Company, Boston, 1889), p. 29.

[2] L. P. Brockett, M.D., *Woman's Work in the Civil War* (McCurdy & Co., Philadelphia, 1867), p. 325.

[3] Wormeley, *op. cit.*, p. 51. Letter of May 18, 1862. There appear to have been two separate houses on the same site; the first, the original Custis house which disappeared, no one knows why or how, and the second, built about 1820, burned in 1862. A third house was built after the Civil War and destroyed about 1888. See Virginia Magazine of History and Biography, April 1936, pp. 129-130.

[4] Wormeley, *op. cit.*, pp. 75-77.

[5] Wormeley, *op. cit.*, pp. 103-105.

[6] Wormeley, *op. cit.*, p. 172.
There is a discrepancy in the dates and times of the events in some of the eye-witness accounts of the evacuation of the base at White House— understandable in those who worked so hard that, as Katharine said, they did not always know the day of the week.

[7] The following is a partial list of the women who were active during Harrison's Landing: Mrs. Arabella Griffith Barlow, Miss Amy M. Bradley, Mrs. Sarah P. Edson, Mrs. Almira Fales, Mrs. Isabella Fogg, Miss Helen Louise Gilson, Miss Maria M. C. Hall, Mrs. John Harris, Mrs. Mary Morris Husband, Mrs. Mary W. Lee, and Miss Anna Lowell.

14

THE WAR MOVES NORTH

---★---

1862

August 9	Battle of Cedar Mountain.
August 16	McClellan's army withdrawn from Harrison's Landing.
August 22	First regiment of colored troops mustered in at New Orleans.
August 27	McClellan's Army of the Potomac landed at Alexandria. In the days which followed, units of the Army of the Potomac were taken away from McClellan, leaving him virtually without a command.
August 28–30	Battles of Gainesville, Groveton and Second Bull Run.
August 30	Secretary of War Stanton issued a call for volunteer nurses to go to the battlefield.
September 1	Battle of Chantilly.

---★---

CLARA BARTON, in spite of her interest in ○
been to the front. She had been busy in W○
compiling her endless records of names and ○
to hundreds of homes. It is interesting to w○
the knowledge that she was to found an org○
and on an international scale would do precisely wha○
Thousands of women all over the world would follow the pattern ○
worked out—"comforts" for the soldiers sent from home, records which
would tell anxious families where their soldier son or husband might be,
and letters, letters, letters,—for him, from him, about him would pass
through their hands. The only part of the pattern which Barton did not at
least sketch in during the war was the sending of letters through a neutral
nation from prisoners to their homes.

Clara had made herself a link between home and the soldier, work
which was outside the scope of government, but of which the whole
country was in need. She kept to her aim with singleness of purpose, and
though she was tempted from time to time to abandon it for regular nursing duties, fortunately she never did. No one else during the war
attempted what she was doing on the same scale or with the same
persistence. No one had seen the need as clearly as she.

Clara—forty, vigorous and determined—was in constant touch with
a large number of aid societies, and often supplies were sent to her
rather than to the Sanitary Commission because she tried to deliver packages to individual soldiers, while the Sanitary Commission had to concern
itself mainly with transferring large quantities of supplies to places
where they were needed without taking special account of individuals.
There was a need for both types of service, and so her relations with the
Sanitary Commission were friendly and cooperative. Her self-appointed
task had grown to enormous proportions, but in August of 1862 Clara
was restless and dissatisfied. Women were going to the front in increasing
numbers. Clara knew some of them and heard their stories about the
hardships and suffering of the men in the wretched field hospitals, and
she too wanted to go to the field. It was becoming increasingly difficult
for a woman not a member of the Dix organization to get a nursing
appointment, but it could still be done through a state government and
Clara asked Governor Andrew of Massachusetts to send her to General

vision because forty of the men had been her former pupils.
Andrew vetoed her scheme—fortunately, since the position of
nurse would have changed the character of her work and nar-
her scope.

While Clara was in this mood of restlessness, the war came close to
er once more when the Confederates threatened Washington in order
to relieve the siege that McClellan was laying to Richmond. The protection of the city was assigned to General Pope, who had won fame in the
west at New Madrid and Island Number Ten in the Mississippi River.
He assumed command of a three-corps army, known as the Army of
Virginia, on June 26th. McClellan, whose glory was more than a little
tarnished, was ordered on August 3rd to evacuate the Peninsula and to
join General Pope on the Rappahannock, an order not at all to Mc-
Clellan's liking.

The clash between the Union and the Confederate forces came, as the
Confederates intended, before McClellan arrived. Jackson, commanding
the rebel forces under Lee, was in a position on the slopes of Cedar
Mountain near Culpeper, seventy-five miles from Washington, and Pope
ordered General Banks to attack him there. Banks had less than 8,000
men, Jackson three times that number. Banks' approach to the mountain
slopes lay across open fields within full range of the Confederate artillery.
He made that dangerous attack on Saturday the ninth of August, and the
battle which followed was one of the most devastating the Union forces
were to suffer. Much of the fighting was hand-to-hand so that the dead
and wounded of both sides lay together and many of them could not be
removed until the battle had ended.

News of the battle reached Washington on Monday. Clara had already
been to the Assistant Quartermaster General, Major Rucker, to get
transportation to take a load of supplies to the front. She had found the
Major harassed and cross, and when he spoke sharply to her she burst
into uncharacteristic tears. The tears, or her description of the supplies
she had ready to transport, won the Major over so thoroughly that he
not only gave her an order for wagons and mules, but took time to steer
her through the red tape involved in getting passes. On Monday she went
to the rooms of the Sanitary Commission for a conference, and when she
came away she had the promise of more supplies. Then she packed,
which, considering the number of packages, parcels and boxes she
planned to take with her, must have consumed a great deal of time, but
Clara never seemed to find such work burdensome. The next night she

and her wagons pulled into Alexandria, and the following day she arrived at Culpeper, the temporary base near the scene of battle.

At midnight Brigade Surgeon James L. Dunn, exhausted and covered with blood, looked up from his work and saw a startling sight. Outside the door of the building which was being used for a hospital, was a wagon drawn by four mules, and standing up in it a sturdy-looking woman, a scarf tied over her head, wearing a plaid jacket and a sensible dark skirt without hoops. Occasional shells were still falling near the hospital, but she seemed to be oblivious of them. She wanted to know if the hospital needed anything in the way of medical supplies. It certainly did. Dr. Dunn was out of practically everything, and he left his work with alacrity to help with the unloading of some of the boxes. Then, still amazed, he stood in the doorway and watched her drive off through the darkness in the direction of the next field hospital.

Clara, recalling her adventures later, remembered that she worked in and around Culpeper "five days and nights with three hours sleep—a narrow escape from capture—and some days of getting the wounded into hospitals at Washington . . ." She did some nursing, but she did not fully realize that work with the wounded was not the most useful contribution she could make. She thought of it then and later as an escape into a larger field, for she wrote, "When our armies fought at Cedar Mountain, I broke the shackles and went to the field." That field work was only a necessary experience in an undertaking of far greater significance, she did not understand. Looking back, however, she saw herself in perspective, and she wrote, "And so began my work."

For most people who have taken part in a war, the war days forever remain the high point of their existence. Also for many, especially women, war service is likely to prove the most valuable, and the war days the most productive of their lives, though there are not many, like Clara Barton and Florence Nightingale, whose work continues to grow after the war has ended. The war work of the greater number—women whose names have survived only by accident and whose lives follow a downhill path after the war—is like a single stone dropped on a cairn, significant only because there are so many.

Such a one was Mary Phinney Olnhausen, a widow from New England. She could not afford war work unless it paid her a wage, and the Army Nursing Corps seemed to be the answer. Mary applied to Miss Dix for a position and was accepted even though, like so many other Dix nurses, she had no nursing experience. Miss Dix, who might better have spent her energies in devising some sort of training course, however rudi-

mentary, was once more spending hours interviewing each candidate, keeping them with her as her guests and paying them long calls in the hospital where she sent them to work. Having accepted Mary, Miss Dix assigned her to the Mansion House Hospital in Alexandria and went with her to see her installed. One imagines them in some sort of conveyance, probably an ambulance, jolting over the cobbles of the old town, two middle-aged women with "duty" written on their serious faces. Mary was nervous and a little in awe of the somberly clothed Miss Dix, who seemed "a stern woman of few words."

The Mansion House was a grim, unlovely brick building. When Mary and Miss Dix arrived, there was a crowd on the sidewalk in front of the building and the street was full of ambulances from which the wounded from Cedar Mountain were being unloaded. The two women worked their way through the door past a double procession of the wounded being carried in and the dead being carried out. It was a grim initiation for one unused to the sights of war.

After presenting Mary to the authorities, Miss Dix unbent a little and took a kindly leave of her. Then Mary was led away to the ward where she was to serve. This consisted of a broad corridor off which opened many small rooms, the old hotel bedrooms, now so filled with cots that there was barely room to move between them. The ward was dirty, and the smell, the famous "hospital smell" of blood and sweat and pus, must have been close to overpowering in those stuffy rooms in the August heat.

Mary met the chief surgeon and his assistant, and was at once aware that their attitude toward her was one of hostility. She was peremptorily ordered to follow them while they went on their rounds, changing dressings. Next to operating room duty, the changing of dressings was the most harrowing a nurse had to face, but Mary stood the ordeal without any outward sign of the horror she felt. Afterward one of the nurses told her that the chief surgeon had said that he would "make things so hot for her that she would not stay long." And Mary learned that the animosity was directed against her because she had been forced on the hospital by Miss Dix, whom the surgeons disliked greatly and feared a little. Moreover, there were no other Dix nurses in the hospital, and Mary was regarded—correctly, as it turned out, as Miss Dix' first move in a fight to gain control.

Since the two head surgeons could not force Miss Dix to remove Mary, they did everything they could to make Mary's life so difficult that she would leave. She was not told what her duties were, but if she failed to do what was expected of her, she was severely reprimanded. She was

given no instruction in bandaging or in any other nursing technique. The cooks were surly to her, probably having heard the hospital gossip that she was to be forced out, and she had difficulty persuading them to give her the food she needed for her patients. Worst of all, she was given no place to sleep, though the other women nurses all had rooms of their own. At the end of the day, when she had worked as long as she could stand, she would drag a bag of hay, if she could find one, into a corner and sleep there. Once in a while one of the nurses would let Mary sleep on the floor in her room, but this did not happen often, probably because the other nurses were afraid to help her.

This miserable life went on for some weeks, and then Miss Dix came to inspect the hospital. Mary complained of the treatment she was receiving, but Miss Dix said, "You must bear it a while, my child. I have placed you here and you must stay."[1] Mary stayed. There was a tough grain of stubbornness in her nature and she hated defeat. Moreover, she honestly liked Miss Dix and was willing to give her loyalty. Perhaps Miss Dix, tired, conscious of hatred on every side, grimly fighting her own battle, was grateful for this small glow of warmth, for she was kind to Mary and as gentle as her unbending nature would permit.

Mary worked on. The hospital seemed to her to be in a state of confusion caused by lack of organization, and no doubt this was true to an extent, though as Mary discovered years later when she had become superintendent of a training school for nurses, administrative problems appear simpler to those in the ranks than they do to those in charge. Hospitals like this one worked under tremendous difficulties, with inadequate equipment and untrained staff, and the women nurses were liable at any time to be called on without warning to feed and care for a flood of badly wounded men.

Like most nurses, Mary was only dimly aware of events outside, for the hospital became her world. Rumors were news and tales of wounded men were history. One day she heard a commotion in the direction of the wharves and paused in her work to look out of the window. Boatloads of soldiers, tough-looking veterans with tanned faces and stained uniforms, were debarking and marching up the hill. It was the twenty-seventh of August and these were McClellan's veterans arriving from the Peninsula too late to help Pope at Cedar Mountain.

Mary was fitting into the hospital routine, or perhaps it would be more correct to say that she was creating a routine for herself in the midst of the general confusion. "I speak to nobody," she wrote home, "get what [food] I can, and buy the rest." Eventually Miss Dix won her

battle with the surgeons for control of the nursing in the hospital, and gradually all the other nurses were replaced by those selected by Miss Dix. The two head surgeons, making the best of what they could not help, dropped their hostility toward Mary, and by the end of September conditions had so far improved that she was given a room of her own.

When the ambulances carrying the wounded from the second battle of Bull Run rumbled over the paving stones of Alexandria, Mary was once more made aware of the world outside the hospital. She looked at the dust-darkened faces of men whose wounds had not been cared for, and at the dead who should not have been allowed to die, and she was filled with anger that such things should happen. "Did not the government do shamefully to let so many men lie there and die?" she wrote. "I am so indignant I can't hear of it."

An increasing number of women were feeling resentment like Mary's, but their anger was not directed against the administration so much as against the more comprehensive, more permanent, more impersonal bureaucracy they called "government." It was the slow germinating of the resolution, which was to keep on growing in strength through the war years, as a similar feeling had grown in England during and after the Crimean War, that no government on earth should be permitted to neglect its soldiers. It would seem that women, who were both more vague and more emotional in their blame than men, were also, in general, more determined to bring about permanent reform. However true that may be, the repeated disasters to the Union forces had brought grief and anxiety to all, and in these dark days of 1862 there was general disaffection with the war. People everywhere were beginning to wonder whether the saving of the Union was, after all, worth the price in blood.

By July of this year, the President had reluctantly concluded that if the war were to continue to receive popular support, some other objective must be introduced to bolster the waning desire to fight secession. With every failure of the Union armies, the anti-slavery supporters had been growing more powerful and more demanding of recognition in the policies of the Administration, and in their demands Lincoln saw a possible way to dissipate the war apathy. On July 22nd he called the Cabinet together to consider the draft of an emancipation proclamation. The Cabinet was amazed by the proposed step and Seward questioned the wisdom of raising such an issue at a time when the country might interpret it as "the last measure of an exhausted government." Lincoln, struck with this point of view, agreed to wait for a victory before issuing the Proclamation.

Instead of victory, there were further defeats, and the future seemed steadily darkening in both theaters of war. On August 20th, Horace Greeley attacked the President in an editorial in the New York *Tribune* for not pursuing a vigorous anti-slavery policy. In his reply to Greeley, Lincoln made his own position clear:

"My paramount object in this struggle is to save the Union, and it is not either to save or to destroy slavery. If I could save the Union without freeing any slaves, I would do it; and if I could save it by freeing all the slaves, I would do it; and if I could save it by freeing some and leaving others alone, I would also do that."[2]

He had concluded that the only possible way to save the Union was by freeing the slaves in the rebel states but at the end of August he still awaited victory. After the battle of Cedar Mountain, Lee arrived with the remainder of the Army of Northern Virginia, to join forces with Jackson. Pope was forced to fall back, and Lee, hoping for a decisive victory before McClellan and the Army of the Potomac could come to Pope's rescue, divided his army and sent Jackson around Pope, through the Shenandoah Valley to Manassas. Jackson made a brilliant two day march, destroying the railroad and Pope's supply base at Manassas Junction, and Pope turned to attack Jackson near the old battlefield of Bull Run. McClellan, meanwhile, had arrived at Alexandria, and part of his army was detached and sent to support Pope.

There followed on August 29th and 30th a bloody battle, fought over the old battlefield in the vicinity of Centerville and known for that reason as the Second Battle of Bull Run. On Friday, the first day of battle, gunfire could be heard in Washington and to the citizens anxiously waiting for news it was like living over again the emotions of the first Bull Run. A huge crowd filled the street in front of the Treasury where war news was posted on a bulletin board, but little news reached the public that day.

Lights burned late at the War Department for there, that night, a dispatch was received from Pope announcing that he had won a victory but that there were 10,000 dead and wounded lying on the field. The statement about the wounded filled the War Department with consternation, for it was known that Pope was almost without medical supplies. He had been moving rapidly through the country, out of touch with a base, and his men were hungry. He did not have vehicles in which to carry the vast number of wounded to hospitals, his horses had been in harness for ten days, and without food for two. It was clear to everyone at the War Department that unless the wounded received help from some-

where, a major disaster would ensue and a storm of national wrath would break over the Administration.

The question was, where was help to be found? McClellan's medical department was disorganized by the evacuation of the Peninsula and of no use in the emergency. The Surgeon General's Office was, as usual, unprepared. The Sanitary Commission had medical supplies but no means of transporting them to the battlefield. Stanton was fully aware of the political threats inherent in the situation, and Stanton was a nervous man, prone to losing his head in a crisis. He lost it now. Trembling with fear, he ordered notices prepared calling on the citizens of Washington to volunteer as nurses and directing them to be at the railroad station, with stimulants and supplies, at five o'clock, where they would find a train to carry them to the front.

The next day, Saturday, the notices were posted in all the hotels of the city, and the response was overwhelming. Long before five o'clock a huge crowd of "nurses" converged on the railroad station, most of them carrying bottles of whiskey. They were men for the most part, but there were a few women and only a fraction of them had any qualifications for the work they were supposed to do. The greater number regarded the whole business as a glorious, free sight-seeing excursion and the crowd was in gala mood, laughing, shoving, shouting witticisms. No passes were required and there was no supervision of any sort. It was an ideal situation for an enemy agent who might want to cross the lines without detection and inevitably a number of them took advantage of it. Long before five o'clock the station and the street were jammed. Five o'clock came, but no train appeared and by this time a large proportion of the crowd had taken to drinking the "stimulants" they were carrying to the wounded.

That was the day that Lee unexpectedly struck hard at Pope's army, and, unknown to the crowds at the station, Pope's imagined victory had become a disastrous defeat. Even while the noisy mob of volunteer nurses waited for the train which did not appear, the army was in full retreat.

Meanwhile, a telegram had been sent from the War Department to Colonel Haupt, superintendent of railroads and telegraph for the Army of Virginia, directing him to send a train to Washington to pick up the volunteers. Haupt is one of those whom it is a relief to encounter in the pages of history. In the midst of inefficiency and chaos he remained cool and in command of any situation in which he found himself. The problems of a transportation chief, always harassing, would, under the circum-

stances of that day, have driven a lesser man to distraction. Whole sections of his railroad were being swallowed by the Confederate advance. Demands for the immediate shipment of matériel were pouring into his headquarters, and unauthorized officers were taking it on themselves to move his trains, thereby causing blockades and snarls which the patient Haupt had to untangle.

Haupt had been director and chief engineer of the Pennsylvania Railroad before the war and he knew railroading through and through. Back in Alexandria he knew, all through that confusing day, what was going on at the front more accurately than the generals on the spot. Lincoln discovered this and sent Haupt laconic wires asking for news, and Haupt replied characteristically, in precise detail. He never seemed hurried, and he had the good administrator's ability to surround himself with able men.

Haupt was shocked when he received the order for the train and learned of Stanton's panic-stricken call for volunteers. He saw at once, what had not occurred to Stanton at all, that most of the volunteers would be sensation-seekers, but to Haupt an order, however foolish, had to be obeyed. He replied to the War Department that the Washington track was tied up by the movement of military baggage and that he would comply with the order for a train as soon as it could be cleared. He added that he thought surgeons should, by all means, be allowed to go to the front, but he questioned the wisdom of sending out several hundred volunteers, for fear, if the army were forced to retreat, they would stampede.

The War Department by this time probably thought so too, but Haupt was informed that the notices having been posted, could not very well be withdrawn. The more Haupt thought about what would happen if a mob of sightseers were turned loose on a battlefield with the battle still in progress, the less he liked the prospect. "It seems to me," he wired Assistant Secretary of War Watson, "that if the battle is over, we have men enough to act as nurses; if it is not over, we do not want any citizens to skedaddle and create a panic."

When the Washington tracks were clear, Haupt reluctantly sent a train of sixteen boxcars, which pulled into the Washington station after dark, amid a scene which was a cross between a jamboree and a riot. The crowd, mostly drunk by this time, rushed the train which was not long enough to hold nearly all those who wanted to go. About 800 fought their way aboard, some squeezing inside, some clinging to the roofs. Amid cheers from those on board and howls from those left on the plat-

form, the train pulled out—as madly fantastic a trainload as ever rattled over the rails.

At Alexandria, Haupt had the train stopped and sent an inspector on board. The inspector returned in great excitement and begged Haupt to have the train run onto a siding. Haupt's regard for orders prevented him from doing what his judgment told him was wise, and he allowed the train to go on to its destination, which was the station for Fairfax Court House, pointing out to his inspector that he, Haupt, was not responsible for what happened after it arrived. Nevertheless, he sent a wire to the officer in charge at Fairfax Station requesting him to arrest all drunks and return them by the next train to Alexandria.

No doubt the officer did his best to comply, but confusion reigned everywhere, and as soon as it was light a good many of the volunteers wandered off in search of food and whiskey, few of them attempting to relieve any suffering but their own hangovers. When they were exhausted, and had seen enough, most of them returned to the railroad station and demanded to be taken back to Washington.

Colonel Haupt, however, had received no orders to transport the volunteers home. The military situation had gone from bad to desperate, with every probability that Fairfax would fall into the hands of the enemy in the near future. Every available train was needed for essential military supplies and in addition the wounded must be promptly moved to Alexandria or Washington. Rain was falling, and though Haupt thought it might be cruel to make the volunteers walk home in the mud, he felt it would be far more cruel to leave the wounded lying on the ground.

The volunteers were driving Major G. O. Haller, the officer in command at Fairfax Station, to the brink of distraction. He wired to Haupt, saying: "Send no more citizens." He followed this with another wire, asking that the wounded at Fairfax be evacuated to Alexandria as fast as possible, and saying that the volunteers "have overwhelmed us, and they retard instead of, as they intended, assisting us." But Haupt had already begged Washington not to send any more citizens and to put a guard on Long Bridge to keep them from going across. His advice was taken in the matter of the guard, but since the first trainload, there had been others, and steamersful had been arriving at Alexandria, and now Alexandria also was full of drunk and disorderly volunteers.

Somewhere out on the battlefield on the twenty-ninth, Annie Etheridge, trim and elegant as ever, was riding her great horse. Annie had been with the Transport Service for a while, but now she was back

with the regiment she loved, and it must have seemed strange to her to be riding once more over this familiar country, with the noise of battle all around her. She still wore the two murderous-looking pistols thrust through her belt, and this time the emergency for which they were intended almost occurred, for while she was occupied with the wounded, she narrowly escaped being captured.

Annie was never more alive than in the midst of fighting. Danger excited her and she seemed to have no fear. General Phil Kearney, who was recklessly brave himself and admired the same quality in others, came on her when she was looking after some men who had fallen. Bullets were flying past her, and he was so impressed with her cool disregard for her own safety that he promised her that he would have her made a sergeant.

That battle came close to being Annie's last, for while she was kneeling beside a young wounded boy, holding a flask of water while he drank, he was struck by a cannon ball and almost literally torn to pieces. Annie never received a sergeant's commission. Two days later Kearney was leading a charge at Chantilly, in a downpour of rain when he was shot almost within the enemy lines.

Meanwhile, Clara Barton had been preparing for another trip to the front, and on the thirty-first she arrived at Fairfax Station with three carloads of supplies. How she persuaded the military authorities to let her go there with the army in full retreat, or how she managed to have her supplies transported is a mystery. She made her appearance at Fairfax in a boxcar, perched on a pile of crates along with two women she had brought with her. These lieutenants of hers were Mrs. Ada Morrell and Miss Lydia F. Haskell. A third, Mrs. Almira Fales, had missed the train and Barton sent an ambulance back to pick her up. Almira Fales was a tall, spare woman who always dressed in black and stalked through the field hospitals here and at Cedar Mountain looking like an image of death, but though her presence was not likely to cheer the wounded, she was a good and efficient nurse.

The women in the freight car climbed down to find the ground around the station covered with wounded men, some lying on piles of hay, others on the wet earth. Many of them had not had any food for some time, and the women started a fire and began opening crates of food. Then Clara learned a lesson she never forgot, for with 3,000 hungry men to be fed, her only utensils were two buckets, a pan, a kettle, five tin cups, four knives, a dish and three plates. She had with her a supply of canned goods and preserves, and as fast as these containers were

emptied, they were put into use to hold soup and coffee. It was hard, slow work, and not the least of it was the constant bending and stooping while long, full skirts dragging in the mud grew heavy with moisture. Clara's heavy hair, wet with rain, came down and hung around her shoulders.

The wounded were being loaded into freight cars to be hauled to Alexandria and Washington, but it was a slow business. Night came and the rain stopped. Clara lit a candle and continued to work among the wounded, but she was filled with fear of setting fire to the hay on which they were lying and she dared not set her candle down.

All this time it had been becoming increasingly clear that Fairfax would have to be abandoned; and on the next day, the first of September, the evacuation of military supplies and personnel was begun. Rain began to fall in torrents, with flashes of brilliant lightning, and between the loud claps of thunder she could hear the boom of artillery at Chantilly, where Phil Kearney was leading his last charge. The wounded were being moved out by wagons now, and Clara undertook to climb up on the wheel of every one to see to the comfort of the men and to give them a last word of encouragement.

Before the day was ended, Clara was exhausted. Almira Fales had long since gone back to Washington, and Miss Haskell had left also. Mrs. Morrell had found a dry spot on top of some boxes in a tent and was sound asleep there. Clara, too worn out to care much about comfort, lay down in a puddle on the tent's dirt floor and slept until she was awakened two hours later by the arrival of the wounded from Chantilly. She saw the dead General carried in and watched the remnants of his command pass by on the road to Alexandria. Word came that Confederate cavalry had been seen in the neighborhood of Fairfax Station, and an officer stopped Clara to ask her if she knew how to ride, for if not, she must leave at once by train. Clara told him that she could ride with or without a saddle, and he said that in that case she could stay and trust to her horsemanship to escape when the time came. He seems to have neglected to tell her where she could find a horse, and as it turned out his warning, though dramatic, was unnecessary, for Clara and Mrs. Morrell left in good order on a train which was carrying wounded.

In Washington, on the day after the battle, excited citizens were still demanding their "right" to be taken to the front. When any conveyance appeared which seemed to be going in that direction, it was rushed by the crowd. A regiment of cavalry was dispersed through the city to

round up anything on wheels that it might be loaded with supplies and sent to the front. Subsequently there appeared among the Virginia hills a weird procession made up of hacks (their drivers shouting imprecations at being thus shanghaied), teams taken from streetcars, hucksters' carts and private carriages.

Somewhere in that fantasia (or perhaps on a previous day, for the date is questionable) there was an ambulance carrying two people, assorted medical supplies and 400 loaves of freshly baked bread. One of the occupants was a philanthropically-minded young man named John Fowle, the other, his fiancée, was a girl of about eighteen who had spaniel eyes, somewhat too prominent teeth and an unconventional hairdo. Her name was Elida Rumsey. One or both of them had money to spend, and they seem to have bought the ambulance some time before for use in their various charitable projects in and around Washington. There was nothing particularly unusual in that, for about this time a number of well-to-do people invested in ambulances to be used in free-lance work among the troops.

Elida had a good singing voice, and she and John organized concerts for the soldiers at which she sang patriotic ballads with a great deal of feeling while standing on a Confederate flag. The songs were sentimental favorites of the day, "The Battle Cry of Freedom," "The Young Recruit" or "The Dying Soldier Boy," and when she reached the chorus she stamped on the flag.

There are various versions of the events which followed after these two left Washington, and perhaps Elida, who loved to tell her adventures, is herself responsible for the discrepancies. Somewhere along the road, most probably at the Long Bridge, they were stopped by a guard and told they could go no further. This was the kind of situation Elida thoroughly enjoyed, for she loved drama and she loved being conspicuous. She climbed out of the ambulance, threw herself on her knees in the mud before the sentry and begged him to let her go to the wounded boys. Probably a crowd gathered—in any event this touching scene was too much for the sentry, who let her pass.

They drove all night, and in the morning they found a small building which was being used as a field hospital. The story (and it sounds like one of Elida's) states that the wounded were being stacked one on top of another, like logs of wood. Elida stayed outside, standing in the back of the ambulance, handing out loaves of bread until they were all gone. Then she decided to go inside. Elida was a high-strung young lady who could not stand the sight of blood, and the rear of a battle-

field was the last place she should have been. Considering her temperament, she did not behave too badly. The floor was slippery with blood. She averted her eyes and bent over a soldier with a bandaged arm. The bandage was tight and he was in considerable pain and, never stopping to think that the tight bandage might have a purpose, Elida took it off. At first everything was all right. A shot had gone completely through the arm and a scab had formed, but Elida decided the scab should be washed off. She found some water and went to work. The scab loosened. Then she saw little spurts of bright red arterial blood coming out of the wound. In a second the whole artery opened and she was drenched by a pulsing jet of blood.

History does not record what happened to her patient, but Elida fainted and had to be carried out to the ambulance. After a while she revived, and it is to her credit that she went back to the hospital and worked for the rest of the day.

The rest of the story has nothing to do with her adventures that day except in so far as it shows what a trial a girl like Elida could be. Shortly after her return to Washington a boil appeared on her face, which she attributed to blood poisoning caused by washing wounds. The boil had to be lanced, but Elida's courage failed her. The doctor insisted, and finally she said she thought she could face the frightful ordeal if she could look at some soldiers who had lost their arms or legs.

She was taken to a surgical ward in Judiciary Hospital and a chair was placed for her at one end of the room. The surgeon stood ready beside her. She gazed with her great spaniel eyes at the mutilated men on the cots for a while, then she raised her face to the waiting surgeon and told him, one imagines in what dramatic tones, that she was ready to face her suffering.

Elida's nursing adventures are good illustration of why medical men were becoming more and more determined to eliminate unregulated, volunteer service. Subsequently Elida and John, whom she married the next year in a manner quite in keeping with her character, established a reading room in Washington for soldiers. They had hit on a good and useful undertaking, and one which had the incidental advantage of keeping Elida away from wounded men.

The final evacuation of Fairfax took place on the second of September and the full-scale withdrawal of the army was under way everywhere. Most of the volunteers had been sent back or had managed to struggle home, but there were still enough of them in the neighborhood of Fairfax to cause Haupt considerable concern. He sent instructions to

the officer in command at Fairfax Court House not to inform them of the approach of the enemy for fear it would bring on the panic which Haupt had dreaded all along, but first to evacuate all the wounded.

The Union losses from Cedar Mountain to this time, including wounded and men who had seen enough of war and had slipped away never to return, were in the neighborhood of 30,000. Pope, a much-discredited man, withdrew his army into the fortifications which protected Washington along the south bank of the Potomac. The army was close to demoralization, and McClellan, who had once so effectively restored its morale, was sulking in Alexandria. McClellan no longer had an army, for it had been taken from him piecemeal. He had not been removed from command, but his command had been removed from him.

These were some of the darkest days of the war. The country was deeply dissatisfied, and the Emancipation Proclamation, gathering dust in the President's desk, had to wait for a brighter day. Three generals had been tried in the vital Eastern theatre, McDowell, Pope, and McClellan, and all had failed, nor did there seem to be another promising candidate. To Lincoln it seemed that McClellan might do again what he had done once before, and restore the defeated army. Neither the Cabinet nor the War Department agreed with the President, but in spite of this, on September 2nd, he gave McClellan back his command.

NOTES

[1] Once more the Nightingale pattern is evident in Miss Dix' attitude, for her advice in this instance recalls Miss Nightingale's policy of passive persistence in the early days of Scutari.

[2] Lincoln replied to Greeley in a telegram on August 22, 1862, which was published in part on August 23rd in the *Washington National Intelligencer*.

15

REBELS IN THE CORN

★

CHRONOLOGY

1862

September 5–6   Lee crossed the Potomac into Maryland.

September 7   Lee established his headquarters two miles from Frederick, Maryland.

September 10   "Stonewall" Jackson began his march to a rendezvous with other parts of Lee's army around Harper's Ferry. Confederate headquarters near Harper's Ferry evacuated.

September 13   McClellan entered Frederick. Special Order 191, giving Lee's plans for dividing his army and capturing Harper's Ferry, was picked up in Frederick by Private Mitchell of the 27th Indiana, and put in McClellan's hands the next day.

September 14   Battle of South Mountain.

September 15   Lee, with part of his army, took a position on the hill above Antietam Creek, near Sharpsburg. Union garrison at Harper's Ferry surrendered. McClellan's forces began to arrive at Antietam.

September 16   First day of the battle of Antietam. McClellan maneuvered his forces into position and made contact with the enemy.

September 17   A day of heavy fighting resulting in a Federal victory.

September 22   Lincoln finished the second draft of the Emancipation Proclamation and called the Cabinet.

September 23   Emancipation Proclamation appeared in the newspapers.

October 1   Lincoln inspected McClellan's army.

October 6   Lincoln ordered McClellan to pursue Lee.

November 1   McClellan crossed the Potomac to pursue Lee, who placed himself between McClellan and Richmond.

November 7   Lincoln relieved McClellan of command.

November 9   General Burnside took command of the Army of the Potomac.

★

> *Yet there the victory lies, if ye but knew.*
> —James Russell Lowell

ONCE MORE McClellan performed a miracle and transformed a mass of beaten, dispirited men into a self-respecting army. It was the work for which he was most fitted, but when he had completed that task, the old faults which had caused the President to feel misgivings about re-appointing him began to manifest themselves once more. The Army, according to the General, was not strong enough to meet an enemy who, he was convinced, was greatly superior in numbers. He complained of a lack of equipment and felt that he must have time to give the men the high polish of soldierly discipline he believed essential to a campaign. It would, he thought, be some months before the army would be in any condition to risk a fight. When at length the weary President persuaded McClellan to move, the General began a procrastinating, cautious march through Maryland in the general direction of Lee's Army of Northern Virginia, which was camped on the western side of the wall-like South Mountain.

Lee's headquarters were near the town of Frederick, only forty miles from Washington, and the presence of the Confederate army was terrify-ing the people of Baltimore, Philadelphia and the capital city. Lee's

immediate objective, however, was not any of these places, but the town of Harper's Ferry, which was garrisoned by a small Union force and where there were large stores of arms and ammunition. He gave his officers his plan for the attack on Harper's Ferry in Special Order Number 191 which was soon to become famous as "The Lost Order." In it, Lee directed the division of his army for the purpose of attacking Harper's Ferry from different sides, placing each division under a different commander and designating separate routes for each to follow. Lee's plan was a bold one, for in dividing his army he risked piece-meal destruction, but he expected to gain his object and unite his forces before the slow-moving McClellan could know what was happening.

When one copy of Special Order Number 191 had been given to each of the officers who were to command the divided parts of the army, there was one copy left over. Some unknown person used it to wrap some cigars but what happened then will probably be a mystery forever.

Lee's officers and their commands departed for the rendezvous at Harper's Ferry and on the eleventh of September Lee himself went to Hagerstown to await the outcome of the attack.

On the thirteenth, units of McClellan's Army of the Potomac entered Frederick, and Private Mitchell from Indiana, walking along a street in the town, found the packet of cigars, read the writing on the wrapping and had the intelligence to take it to an officer. Not long thereafter, it was in McClellan's hands. No greater piece of luck ever befell a commanding general, for there was, or should have been, time to save Harper's Ferry and, more important, to destroy Lee's army piece by vulnerable piece.

One of the commanders whom Lee sent on the Harper's Ferry expedition was "Stonewall" Jackson, who was to attack the garrison there from the Virginia side. The day he began his march was fine, the sun shone and the fall air was cool and bracing.

> Up from the meadows rich with corn,
> Clear in the cool September morn,
>
> The clustered spires of Frederick stand
> Green-walled by the hills of Maryland.

Jackson had with him as a member of his staff a young man of romantic appearance named Henry Kyd Douglas, who kept a diary and who was with Jackson continuously all of the day which was made famous by

Whittier's poem.[1] As Jackson's column went through the town of
Frederick:

> Up rose old Barbara Frietchie then,
> Bowed by her fourscore years and ten;
>
> Bravest of all in Frederick town,
> She took up the flag the men hauled down;
>
> In her attic-window the staff she set,
> To show that one heart was loyal yet.
>
> Up the street came the rebel tread,
> Stonewall Jackson riding ahead.
>
> Under his slouch hat left and right
> He glanced: the old flag met his sight.
>
> "Halt!"—the dust-brown ranks stood fast;
> "Fire!"—out blazed the rifle-blast.
>
> It shivered the window, pane and sash;
> It rent the banner with seam and gash.
>
> Quick, as it fell, from the broken staff
> Dame Barbara snatched the silken scarf;
>
> She leaned far out on the window-sill,
> And shook it forth with a royal will.
>
> "Shoot, if you must, this old gray head,
> But spare your country's flag," she said.
>
> A shade of sadness, a blush of shame,
> Over the face of the leader came;
>
> The nobler nature within him stirred
> To life at that woman's deed and word:
>
> "Who touches a hair of yon gray head
> Dies like a dog! March on!" he said.

Whittier believed to the end of his days the legend he immortalized.
He had heard the story from the novelist Mrs. E.D.E.N. Southworth, who
was living in Georgetown at the time and who sent him a newspaper
clipping about it. The story was subsequently confirmed, or partly confirmed, he said, by "various responsible persons," among them Dorothea
Dix, but Douglas asserted that Jackson was not even there. Jackson and

Douglas had left the marching men to call on a minister whom they found to be sleeping and, being unwilling to disturb him, rode back to the head of the column by the shortest way, through Mill Street, which did not take them past the house where Barbara Frietchie lived.

And so a literary controversy was born.[2] There was a woman named Barbara Frietchie and she is buried at Frederick. She was ninety-six year old and bedridden. One version of the story says a Mrs. Mary Quantrell waved the flag, another that old Barbara waved it, but on the twelfth, when Burnside was riding through. A flag said to be Barbara's flag survives. It has a tear in it but it was not rent and tattered as it would have been by a volley of shot.

There seems to have been a veritable orgy of Union flag-waving on that day and on other occasions when Lee's troops rode through. Some young ladies with the Stars and Stripes tied over their bosoms were routed from their place on the curb when the soldiers made the obvious remark. Others waved flags in their hands, and these goings-on seemed to amuse the Rebel officers and men. Two or three months later Anna Holstein ran across another version of the story of the old lady with the flag. Mrs. Holstein, who had been nursing the wounded from Antietam, stayed in Frederick with an elderly friend identified as Mrs. J. This old lady took Mrs. Holstein up to the attic and showed her a flag she had waved while some Union prisoners were being marched through the street below. Long afterward, when Mrs. Holstein read Whittier's poem, she thought perhaps the Frietchie legend might have grown out of this incident.[3]

"Stonewall" Jackson was most certainly not the kind of man to order his men to fire on an old lady in an attic window. That same day Jackson and his staff (of which Douglas was the youngest member) rode into Middletown where two pretty young girls with red, white and blue ribbons tied in their hair and little Union flags in their hands, ran out of a house and waved their flags almost in the General's face. Jackson smiled, bowed and lifted his battered old hat to them. That was all, and the girls ran away giggling.

Jackson, shabby, dour, preoccupied, was a great favorite with young Southern ladies, and on this march they treated him as modern girls would a movie hero. Douglas recalled that the closed shutters of the General's headquarter's window were pried open and "little maiden noses and cherry lips were pressed against the clouded panes of glass, and little twinkling stars of eyes tried to pierce the gloom of that forbidden room in search of their hero." They forced the window up and threw

roses at him until finally he relented and let them come in. They swarmed around him begging for his autograph, and when one of them asked for a lock of hair (he had a full beard, but not much to spare from his head), he firmly ushered them out, but by that time there was not a button left on his coat.

McClellan, meanwhile, with the rarest of opportunities within his reach, failed to seize it. He notified the commander at Harper's Ferry to hold out, that he was on the way, and then, with deliberation, he started to move forward. On the fourteenth there was fighting of considerable severity at two of the passes across South Mountain which caused further delay, and on the fifteenth, while McClellan was some distance away, Harper's Ferry, with all its valuable stores, fell into the hands of the enemy.

That day Lee, with the part of his army not engaged at Harper's Ferry, took up a position on the hills above the winding creek of Antietam near the village of Sharpsburg. The valley below was filled with fields of corn which in that rich soil had grown taller than a man's head. On the other side of the creek the ground rose again into rolling hills and here during the course of the day the first scattered advance of McClellan's army appeared. The rest of McClellan's army wheeled into position on the sixteenth.

Now was the time for McClellan to strike—now, while Lee was understrength and in a vulnerable position with only a narrow strip of land between the rear of his army and the Potomac river. Some fighting developed, but McClellan spent most of the day in maneuvering, placing his artillery and studying the terrain. It was a day wasted and it gave Lee time to put the pieces of his army together again.

Three days earlier Clara Barton had been instructed by someone whose name she was never willing to disclose, to go to Harper's Ferry where she would find work to do. This is more than a little mysterious, since on that date the "Lost Order" had not yet been handed to McClellan and probably proves nothing but the fallibility of memory as a basis for history, but in any event she left Washington on Sunday, September 14th, to follow the army in a white-topped "prairie schooner" drawn by a six-mule team, which had been lent to her by the Quartermaster Department. The wagon was loaded with supplies and she had "remembered at the last moment" to tie up a few things for her own use in a handkerchief. On this occasion she was not permitted to take any other women with her, but she was accompanied by three men to act as field workers.

The extraordinary looking wagon caught up with the army on the

fifteenth and, unable to pass, plodded along in the rear. That night she and her party ate an early supper, slept a while, and again took to the road. They drove for hours past the sleeping camps and by daylight, when bugles roused the men and the army slowly began to move, the white wagon merged into the column well up in the advance. That day was Tuesday the sixteenth, and when Clara arrived on the hills above Antietam Creek she had the wagon drawn up in a field near some units of artillery.

Night came and the two armies were facing each other in long lines on the heights above the winding stream and Clara watched the smoke from the campfires rising in the still air. Her heart was heavy and she felt an oppressive "sense of impending doom." "I was faint, but could not eat; weary, but could not sleep; depressed, but could not weep." She sought a dark corner in the vast recesses of the wagon, dropped on her knees and prayed that God might impart "somewhat of wisdom and strength to my heart—nerve to my arm—speed to my feet, and fill my hands for the terrible duties of the coming day—and heavy and sad I awaited its approach."

This Clara whom we see alone on her knees in the dark recesses of the wagon on the eve of the bloodiest day of the war, had changed more in a year and a half than most people change in a lifetime. In the days when she had relieved the pressure of her emotions by firing at targets in the Monument grounds, she had been high-strung, nervous, given to violent feelings and nameless longings which filled her with constant unrest. That Clara was gone forever, and in her place there was now a well-rounded, mature woman, secure in her life work, calm, selfless, tender. Intelligence and purpose had come to replace the uncertainty which once looked out of her dark eyes. The lines of her broad mouth were shaped by kindliness and control.

Clara was up at dawn on that fateful day, watching the start of the battle with field glasses. Below her, in the valley, the mists were melting away. She listened to the bugles calling the armies to battle and the sound echoed for her through all the years which followed. Then she set out in the wagon to find a place where she and her supplies were needed. She found it in the rear of Hooker's command where the dead and wounded already lay thick in the trampled corn. The fighting here had stopped earlier, and the stretcher-bearers were plunging into the corn forest, hunting for the men by the sound of their cries. That Antietam corn, on which the spent musket balls pattered like rain, filled many a soldier seeking escape with a false sense of security. The corn hid everything from

Clara's view, but she saw a path going through it and the path led to a house which was being used as a hospital.

And there she met Dr. Dunn, who had seen her appear out of the night at Cedar Mountain. There was a moment of pleased recognition and the warmth of friendship between these two who had only met once; then Clara went to work. Hospital supplies had not yet arrived and the surgeons were dressing wounds with corn husks. Clara's arms were filled with lint and bandages. "With what joy," she said, "I laid my precious burden down among them."

She worked all that day cooking, dressing wounds, doing anything she could. At the end of it, there was a bullet hole in her sleeve, her eyes smarted, her mouth was dry from the dense, drifting smoke of battle and her ears rang with the crash of artillery fire. That night, the surgeons worked by the light of candle-lanterns which Clara, remembering her fear of setting the hay on fire at Fairfax, had brought with her. On the third day Clara had a fever, and she and her helpers returned to Washington, Clara so exhausted that she slept on the wagon bed all the way.

One other woman—at least one other—Amanda Farnham of St. Johnsbury, Vermont, knew about the movements of the Union army in advance. She arrived in Washington on the fourteenth, tried that day to get a pass to the front and failed. The next morning she went to see Secretary Stanton, who by this time was beginning to have misgivings about volunteer workers on battlefields, and it is startling to find that he not only gave her a pass but assigned her an ambulance as well. Amanda arrived at Antietam in the thick of the fighting, on the afternoon of the bloody seventeenth and established herself among the wounded of French's Division. During the course of that day, Clara had performed a small operation with a penknife but Amanda removed a bullet with a far more feminine instrument, a pair of buttonhole scissors, though why she happened to be carrying them on a battlefield is hard to imagine.

Some strange scenes took place behind the lines that day. Mrs. John Harris and Helen Gilson arrived at a hospital near a cornfield in the evening. Probably it was the same hospital where Clara was working, and the candle-lanterns were winking like stars. The wounded lay everywhere, groaning and crying out in agony, and stretcher-bearers were constantly arriving with more. Mrs. Harris knelt by the side of a dying boy to help him say his prayers. He put his hand in hers, and years later it seemed to her that she could still feel his touch. She began to pray and some of the wounded moved themselves near and joined in the prayer. Then Helen Gilson sang, standing with clasped hands, looking off into the

darkness, with the star-like lights all around her. She sang in her rich, deep voice, "There is rest for the weary," and some of the wounded men joined in, and all grew quieter.

On this day of battle and for several days thereafter, there were many women on the field. John Adams, kneeling by his dying brother, looked up to see Mary Lee standing beside him. Mary had followed her son to battle, like many another whose names are lost, and like many another, she cared for the wounded when the fighting had ended. There were women with most of the regiments. During the heavy fighting, someone saw a "nurse or a laundress" (how that term "laundress" persisted) from one of the Irish regiments, standing in the thick of it, yelling and wildly swinging her bonnet around by its strings.[4]

The roster of the women contains many names which became famous in volunteer nursing—Mrs. M. M. Husband of Philadelphia, Mrs. M. M. C. Hall, the Mary Lee already mentioned, who was also from Philadelphia, Miss Tyson, Alice Smith, who was only eighteen, Mary Holland, Mrs. Holstein and many others. Some worked on the field, some at the general hospital which Dr. Letterman had set up at nearby Smoketown. All day and all night these women (slim figures without their hoops) moved about among the wounded, nursing, cooking, writing letters for those who could not hold a pen. Many of them stayed for weeks and left only to begin their work all over again at the battle of Fredericksburg.

Antietam was the first real test of Dr. Letterman's system of handling the wounded with an ambulance corps directly responsible to the Medical Department. The casualties were unexpectedly heavy, but all of the 9,500[5] Union wounded were collected and given shelter within twenty-four hours. The buildings in the vicinity of the battlefield made poor and inadequate hospitals—a situation Letterman corrected before the next major engagement by having a supply of hospital tents available. The medical supplies were insufficient, though not seriously so for any length of time. The fault here lay beyond Letterman's control, the transportation of medical supplies not being in the hands of the Medical Department. By tradition, in a line of march the wagons containing these supplies brought up the rear, and as a result they were apt to be in fairly inaccessible places when they were needed. When the troops had to travel light, non-medical officers not infrequently abandoned the medical supplies altogether and when this happened, the medical officers were helpless. Though in time the Medical Department was able to improve this situation, the problem was never really solved to anyone's satisfaction.

Washington, Baltimore, and Philadelphia all received their share of

Major Belle Reynolds

Miss Mary J. Safford

the wounded from Antietam. But instead of the old plan to move all the seriously wounded directly from the field to distant general hospitals —a plan which had failed whenever it was tried—Letterman established two camp hospitals near the field. They went into operation a few days after the battle, with facilities for about a thousand men each, and were staffed and equipped in the manner of general hospitals. These camp hospitals were the first of their kind and proved to be so successful that they became the pattern for others.

Whatever present day strategists may think of McClellan's tactics in the battle of Antietam, his detractors at the time that it was fought felt that it was a battle without glory for its commanding general. Though his strength was greatly superior to Lee's, he threw away his advantage by making a series of wasteful attacks instead of one concerted effort. Overcome by caution, he did not use his reserves, and never, at any time, employed anything like the strength he might safely have used. He had it in his power to destroy Lee's army, open his way to Richmond and win the war. Instead, he contented himself with partial and fragmentary success.

McClellan was far from agreeing with this opinion. He wrote to his wife after the battle, "Our victory was complete and the disorganized Rebel army has rapidly returned to Virginia. . . . I feel some little pride in having, with a beaten and demoralized army, defeated Lee so utterly and saved the North so completely. Well, one of these days history will, I trust, do me justice. . . ."

It seems almost incredible that he could so have deluded himself, or so misinterpreted Lincoln's instructions as to believe the North safe so long as Lee's army was not destroyed. "I believe," he wrote, "that I have done all that can be asked of me in twice saving the country." There followed then one of the self-pitying and oft-repeated threats to resign. He did not know that the handwriting was already on the wall and that Lincoln had made a promise to himself to remove McClellan if he permitted Lee to place his army between Richmond and the Army of the Potomac.

The battle of Antietam, indecisive though it was, nevertheless gave Lincoln the victory for which he had been waiting. On the twenty-second of September he finished the second draft of the Emancipation Proclamation, called the Cabinet and presented it to them. It was to be given to the newspapers the next day, though the final ratification would have to await the convening of Congress. The Proclamation as finally issued on the following New Year's Day, decreed that all slaves in the rebellious

states should be free. Exempted from the provisions of the Proclamation were the state of Tennessee, where civil government had been restored, certain parishes (counties) of Louisiana which had elected Congressmen, though they were not seated, some counties of Virginia in Union control and those counties which were to become the State of West Virginia, as well as slaves in the Union slave-holding states.

With the Proclamation temporarily out of the way, the President was free to turn his attention to McClellan and the army, and early in October he went to McClellan's camp to see for himself whether the General's complaints of the lack of equipment had any foundation in fact. He spent many hours riding through the encampment, talking with the men and examining the condition of their arms. Among the military men he made a strange, half ludicrous figure, sitting in the saddle with his stovepipe hat on his head, and his long, black trousered legs reaching almost to the ground. He looked to one who saw him on a similar occasion, like nothing so much as "a pair of tongs on a chair back." His face was worn and tired, and in a picture taken of him on that inspection trip, he has a sad, remote look, as though he felt the loneliness of the responsibilities he bore.

The President returned to Washington satisfied that the army was in condition to pursue Lee and an order to that effect was sent to McClellan. "The President directs that you cross the Potomac and give battle to the enemy or drive him South." Words could not be plainer, but McClellan continued to do nothing at all, giving Lee time to recover from the shock of battle. And a week after the order, Lincoln wrote McClellan a long, patient letter, setting out once more the arguments for an immediate advance. The General was in a complicated emotional state in these days, compounded of self-pity and his conviction that he had already saved the nation. He replied to the President that he was unable to advance for the reason that his cavalry horses had sore tongues.

At this point Lincoln lost all patience and telegraphed to McClellan, "I have just read your despatch about sore-tongued and fatigued horses. Will you pardon me for asking what the horses of your army have done since the battle of Antietam that fatigues anything?"

Finally, on the first of November, McClellan moved sluggishly across the Potomac in pursuit of Lee. A few days later Lee did precisely that which Lincoln had been striving to prevent, placing himself between McClellan and Richmond. Once more McClellan was too late.

It was the last time. On November 7th, General Burnside, accompanied by General Buckingham, entered McClellan's tent and presented

an order to him which relieved him of command and installed General Burnside in his place. Late that night, McClellan wrote to his wife, "Of course I was much surprised; but as I read the order in the presence of General Buckingham, I am sure that not the slightest expression of feeling was visible in my face . . ." On several occasions McClellan had written to Mrs. McClellan of his longing to retire. Now that retirement was an actuality, he found that he did not relish it. "They have made a great mistake," he wrote. "Alas for my poor country!"

There are those who believe with Lincoln that McClellan's slowness to move and failure to take advantage of the enemy's weakness was blameworthy; the scale of blame extending from incompetent to traitor. There are others who assert that when he refrained from action, it was for sound reasons and that he was one of the great generals of the war. The nature of the controversy insures that it can never be resolved, for the disputants are armed, not with proof, but with opinion.

McClellan was maladroit in his dealings with Lincoln and certain members of the Administration, and in consequence he was disliked, but the rank-and-file of the army trusted him and gave him a devotion such as few commanders have inspired. It was one of his misfortunes that most of his enemies were influential and most of his friends were not. The difficulty with Lincoln, moreover, was obviously based on the antipathy of two hopelessly incompatible personalities magnified by the wartime relationship. But out of the acrimony which seems to be inseparable from any discussion of this man, there emerges the clear facts that he was never really defeated by Lee and that he was the only general in 1861 and 1862 who had any success against the Army of Northern Virginia—when it was at the height of its power.

NOTES

[1] Henry Kyd Douglas, *I Rode with Stonewall* (University of North Carolina Press, Chapel Hill, 1940).

[2] George O. Seilheimer, *Battles and Leaders of the Civil War,* "The Historical Basis of Barbara Frietchie." (The Century Company, New York, 1884-1889) pp. 618-619.

[3] Mrs. William H. Holstein, *Three Years in Field Hospitals of the Army of the Potomac* (J. B. Lippincott and Company, 1867) p. 25.

[4] Thomas Livermore, *Days and Events,* quoted in Henry Steele Commager's *The Blue and the Gray* (The Bobbs-Merrill Co., Inc., Indianapolis and New York, 1950).

[5] Thomas Livermore, *Numbers and Losses in the Civil War* (Indiana University Press, Bloomingdale, Indiana, 1957) p. 92.

16

BURNSIDE'S BLUNDER

---- ★ ----

CHRONOLOGY

1862

December 12   Laying of the pontoon bridge across the Rappahannock was begun.

December 13   The battle of Fredericksburg opened in the morning. By nightfall the Union forces had suffered a crushing defeat.

December 14   The battle of Fredericksburg was over but the troops remained on the field.

December 31   Battle of Stone's River. West Virginia admitted as the thirty-fifth state of the Union.

---- ★ ----

Farewell, bristling heights!
Farewell, sad Fredericksburg!
Farewell, river of sorrows;
Farewell, soldiers death-determined
Upon whose mournful sacrifice
We must shut unwilling eyes.
—Julia Ward Howe

GENERAL BURNSIDE was well aware that the chief complaint against McClellan concerned his tortoise-like pursuit of the enemy, and after assuming command of the army, Burnside moved very rapidly indeed as far as the town of Falmouth on the Rappahannock River. The lovely,

218

quiet town of Fredericksburg lay on the opposite bank a little way up-stream, and Burnside's plan was to base his army there, compelling Lee to come out of his impregnable position in the mountains into terrain where he could be fought more easily.

The plan might have worked if the army could have occupied Fred-ericksburg at once, before Lee arrived, but there were no pontoons with which to build bridges for the heavy supply wagons, and by the time they were procured, about two weeks later, Lee was safely intrenched on the heights behind the town. Burnside was not a limber-minded man, and having conceived a plan, it was hard for him to discard it in favor of another. He was determined to make Fredericksburg his base though the river crossing would have to be made in the face of enemy fire from the shelter of the town and, once across, Lee's artillery on the heights could pour a murderous fire into the advancing Union troops. Almost all of Burnside's officers thought that the risks were too great, but he ordered the crossing to be made, and on the twelfth of December the laying of the pontoon bridge began. The work had to be carried on under heavy fire from the Confederates in Fredericksburg, but by the middle of the after-noon the bridge was finished, at a high cost in killed and wounded, and the troops began to cross. On the cold and foggy morning of the thirteenth, Burnside began his attack.

On the bank of the river opposite Fredericksburg there stood a large house with spreading wings and two tiers of galleries, in the Southern style, known as the Lacy House. When the Union forces arrived they found it deserted, for the owner had long since left to join the Con-federates. The location of the house made it ideal for a hospital and the work of converting it began before the attack opened. On the morning of the twelfth Clara Barton stood on one of the galleries and watched the engineers struggling to build the pontoon bridge across the Rappa-hannock. "The high bluffs narrow the river at this point," she wrote, "until I think a strong man might throw a stone across it." Stray shots from the rifles of the sharpshooters across the river, who were trying to prevent the building of the bridge, struck the Lacy House from time to time, but Clara had a veteran's indifference to them.

The next day the battle commenced and at ten in the morning Clara was sent for by a surgeon in charge of a hospital in Fredericksburg. "Come to me," his note read. "Your place is here." So Clara herself crossed the flimsy bridge. She recalled the experience afterward as a dramatic one, and she told it that way to enthralled lecture audiences

after the war. ". . . we were rocking across the swaying bridge, the water hissing with shot on either side.

"Over into that city of death, its roofs riddled by shell, its very church a crowded hospital, every street a battle line—every hill a rampart, every rock a fortress, and every stone wall a blazing line of forts! . . . An officer stepped to my side to assist me over the debris at the end of the bridge. While our hands were raised in the act of stepping down, a piece of an exploded shell hissed through between us, just below our arms, carrying away a portion of both the skirts of his coat and my dress, rolling along the ground a few rods from us like a harmless pebble in the water."

The battle of Fredericksburg became one of the bloodiest and most disastrous of the Union defeats. The Union loss in wounded, killed and missing was 12,000; the Confederate loss was less than half that number. All day on the fourteenth the armies remained stationary, then, under cover of darkness on the fifteenth, the Union forces slipped away across the river, abandoning the little territory they had fought so hard to win. Burnside was in despair, and at one time, still clinging to his plan to occupy Fredericksburg, he seriously talked of renewing the attack, a course of action which would have added suicide to murder. Fortunately he was dissuaded from sacrificing the remnants of his army, and in his report he took on himself the blame for the defeat, exonerating the men who were with him. "For the failure in the attack I am responsible . . ." He pleaded to be relieved of his command and on January 25, 1863 he was replaced by General Joseph Hooker, who had commanded one of the three divisions in the recent battle. (Reserve)

The wounded in those days, even under the most favorable conditions, suffered terribly. The difficulties of collecting them, the slow, crude means of transportation, the lack of adequate pain killers, and the general ignorance of first aid methods all played their part, so that when one speaks of the care of the wounded as being "adequate," it was not, by modern standards, even remotely satisfactory. Some of the field hospitals at Fredericksburg might have been more efficiently run. Some of the wounded lay all night on the frozen ground, and there were horrors beyond anyone's control, as when the dry grass in which some of the wounded lay was set on fire by cannon balls. In spite of these disasters, however, the care of the Fredericksburg wounded was a distinct advance, an advance which is astonishing in view of the red tape, prejudice, tradition and divided authority which bedeviled Surgeon Letterman.

Like the good executive that he was, Letterman had not confined

himself to trying to cure the obvious and surface ills, but had attacked the blocks and weaknesses in the organization itself, and by so doing opened the way for continuing improvement. Letterman had seen clearly that the root of the evils of field medicine was in the organization of medical supply and relief on a regimental basis. Disregarding lesser flaws for the time, he had recreated the medical structure on a division and brigade foundation, a change which, during the battle of Fredericksburg, did away with much of the time-honored medical chaos.

He appointed a staff of medical inspectors and defined the duties of the surgeons, assigning some to the handling of supplies, others to the operation of front line first aid stations and others to surgical work in the division and brigade hospitals. One surgeon in each hospital was given the heretofore neglected task of keeping records, a work which made possible a statistically factual view of the problems of field medicine. During the battle, ambulances crossed the pontoon bridge with the troops instead of following on in the rear of the supply wagons. The stretcher-bearers were up with the front line when it went into action, and this group of men, who had once shown so great a talent for invisibility, now displayed the morale of combat soldiers.

Before these reforms, any surgeon was permitted to operate with little or no supervision, with the result that many surgeons who had gone to the front principally to gain experience, attempted operations of a character and intricacy that should never have taken place under field conditions. Such men regarded the masses of wounded as a license to experiment. Others were untrained and incompetent. Still others were temperamentally unfit for their work. Letterman put a stop to this surgical jamboree by designating in each division hospital, teams of competent men, who alone were entrusted with the operating.

These changes added up to so great an improvement that the Sanitary Commission, which was warm in its praise, found itself, for the first time, in a merely supplementary role. The medical work at Fredericksburg did not please everyone, however. Clara Barton was critical, and so was Walt Whitman, who thought there were not enough cots and objected to a pile of severed arms and legs he saw outside the Lacy House. Barton was a perfectionist in such matters, and Whitman, who had only begun his work as a hospital visitor, had no means of knowing that the conditions he deplored were in reality an improvement over what had gone before. Neither one knew that Letterman was attacking the source of the trouble.

The division hospital was usually under canvas during a campaign,

when it became a more or less mobile unit, the seriously disabled being sent on to a general hospital. The tent hospital was by no means a hardship, except in winter. They had wood floors, a stove for heat and the free circulation of air reduced the dreadful hospital smell which, in more substantial buildings, seemed to permeate everything. When the troops were in winter quarters, however, huts made of logs were built to house the sick, if no permanent buildings were available. The huts had floors and fireplaces and the patients lay on crude cots, fitted with ropes to support mattresses made of sacks of straw. There might be eight or ten of these log huts on either side of a duck-board "street" with a cookhouse and laundry at one end, the whole having rather the look of a pioneer village. In theory, there were no women attached to these division hospitals, for Secretary Stanton continued to be opposed to their playing a part in field nursing, but he was never able to weed them all out, and some of the "division women" remained to the end.

The semi-open hospital, with its free circulation of air, had the additional advantage of reducing the danger from the unregulated doses of anesthesia. These were usually administered by an inexperienced person under the casual supervision of an harassed surgeon whose idea it was to put the patient under as quickly as possible. Before the war, the popular anesthesia in the North had been ether, for the reason, it would appear, that ether was first introduced in the North, but the South, where the medical traditions were French, preferred to use chloroform which was the popular anesthetic in the Paris hospitals of the day.[1] With the outbreak of war, however, the field surgeons almost universally took up the use of chloroform because its action was rapid and the quantity needed was small, though it was generally understood that chloroform was a more dangerous drug than ether.

It is difficult now to estimate the proportion of major operations performed in these division hospitals with the aid of an anesthetic, but it may have been sixty or eighty percent. If the supply of chloroform gave out, as in emergencies it not infrequently did, the patient was often prepared for the operation with a large drink of whiskey—if there were any on hand, and that seemed to be a commodity which was seldom in short supply. If all else failed, and the patient had to be fully conscious, the surgeon relied on speed, and the best of them could cut off a leg at the thigh in forty seconds, not counting the relatively painless tying off of the blood vessels.

Disinfectants, as we know them, were not used, but sometimes a wound was cleaned with whiskey, or a mixture of whiskey and chloro-

form, a treatment which was particularly effective in maggot-infected wounds, for it brought the worms out, as one soldier noted with satisfaction, "on the run." Fresh wounds were treated with water dressings, until they began the inevitable suppuration, when an ointment made of two parts fresh lard and one part white wax was applied—which would seem to be as efficient a way to handicap nature in the process of healing as man could devise.

The existence of microorganisms was known, but their connection with disease was not, and the pus which appeared in every wound was regarded as a necessary and beneficial development. There was a feeling, especially among the women, that sick and wounded men were better off in clean surroundings than in dirty ones, and some doctors believed that cleanliness was a positive factor in promoting recovery, but "cleanliness" merely meant swept floors and fresh bed linen, and cleanliness in the surgical meaning of the word was unknown. The operating surgeon held his scalpel, when not in use, between his teeth and the suture needles he kept threaded and ready in the lapel of his uniform. Water was often scarce in field hospitals and wounds were washed with a sponge in a basinful of water which was made to last for as many patients as possible. It has been said of that sponge that it killed more men than the bullets of the enemy, but somehow a surprisingly large proportion of the wounded managed to survive the unwise treatment of their wounds.

Sometimes nature lent a hand in odd ways. Much has been written of the maggots which often appeared in the wounds of those who were left for some time on the battlefield. Most of the battles were fought in agricultural country, where flies abounded. They settled on the open wounds and shortly the little white worms appeared. There also exists in farm country a bacillus, which causes a particularly virulent type of infection, known as "bacillus welchii" or more commonly, "b-welchii." A wound may carry b-welchii deep into the body, where it thrives on damaged tissues and finds its way into the blood stream.

B-welchii, however, does not like exposure to oxygen. It was discovered in the First World War—when b-welchii constituted a serious problem—that the danger of infection was greatest from deeply penetrating wounds, or wounds in which the damage was partly concealed from the air. At that time a surgical technique called *débridement* was found to be effective. This consisted of removing every particle of damaged tissue from the wound and exposing the wound surface to the air.

The wounds of the Civil War were not typically as deep as those caused by modern shrapnel, and so the damage done by b-welchii was not so extensive, but the danger was there, though the surgeons did not understand the problem with which they were dealing. And the maggots, repulsive though they might be, helped to reduce the danger by accomplishing the cleaning of the wound, much as the surgeon did when he employed the technique of *débridement*.

In addition to field, brigade and division hospitals, there were, by the end of 1862, one hundred and fifty-one general hospitals with a capacity of 58,700 beds.[2] It was a remarkable development, for at the start of the war there had been post hospitals, but no general hospitals at all. Some were good, some bad, but the majority belonged in the first category. They all had women nurses (numbering over 3,000 before the end of the war) or a staff of nuns acting as nurses.

Some of the general hospitals occupied buildings not constructed for the purpose. Others were built after the most approved European plan and consisted of a number of separate buildings, or "pavilions," a word which is still familiar in hospital nomenclature. The greatest of these was, perhaps, the Jeffersonville, Indiana General Hospital which consisted of numerous elongated pavilions (called "wards") radiating from a hub. The reason for this type of construction was the prevalence among surgical patients in those days, of three infectious diseases, erysipelas, pyemia and hospital gangrene. They were spread largely by that dread sponge, and once one of these diseases appeared, it seemed to infect the very walls, so that it was impossible to eradicate. For this reason, the pavilion type of hospital construction, which had been developed in Europe, was adopted in this country, since a small unit building, if infected, could be abandoned temporarily or even torn down.

Hospital diseases had become such a scourge in England that anyone with an injury which caused a break in the skin had a far better chance of recovery if he remained in his own home, however dirty that home might be, instead of going to a hospital. In this country, the hospital diseases also reached epidemic proportions in some places, though they were not the serious menace that they were abroad. They appeared in the war, but for some reason which the pavilion construction does not seem wholly to explain, they were not a major problem. Probably the fact that these hospitals were staffed by women who insisted on cleanliness, had a good deal to do with keeping the hospital diseases in check. Perhaps it was in part that troops on the move are always more able to

resist disease than troops in camp and the health standards of the army had greatly improved, the proportion of sick having dropped from thirty percent in May of 1861 to the astonishing low of eight percent in these winter months.

The general hospitals were regularly inspected by women agents of both the Sanitary Commission and the Christian Commission, the best known of the former being Mary Livermore and her friend Mrs. Hoge, and of the latter a cold-eyed executive of great ability named Annie Wittenmyer. It was Mrs. Wittenmyer who developed the special diet kitchen for general hospitals which has ever since been a part of hospital management. These women inspectors were constantly on the lookout for ways of improving the care of the sick, and they became the doom of many a dishonest hospital steward or surgeon who was cheating the patients in the quality of the food or diluting the coffee with sawdust, and pocketing the profit. These women walked many miles of hospital wards, stopping to speak to the boys, interviewing nurses and doctors, examining kitchens and laundries.

Most of these wards were as cheerful as the women could make them with flowers and pictures and special decorations at Christmas time. Over the beds of those who had fresh wounds, cans of water were so arranged as to release drops onto the bandages, and Mrs. Wittenmyer speaks of the sound of the slow drip, drip, drip as getting unbearably on her nerves.

Usually each bed had a table beside it and a box in which the patient might keep such little objects as he might possess. The men often pasted pictures inside the lids of these boxes, the equivalent of the "pin-up girl," or scenes distinctly not of a religious nature. Some of the nurses were shocked by such levity and one of them was very proud of having removed all the boxes in her ward to paste tracts over the offending pictures.

Some of the hospital wards were kept as rigidly uniform as a barracks, but usually the nurses managed to create a semblance of home atmosphere. There were books, but never enough of them, and entertainments and concerts in which the men joined. Gifts were shared, and if a particularly pretty patchwork quilt arrived, each man was allowed to have it on his bed for a little while. The convalescents made innumerable articles of wood and bone and metal, taking great pride in their various skills. All this was not very scientific compared to modern occupational therapy, psychiatry and scientific nursing care, but neither

was it as coldly impersonal, and the best of the general hospitals must have been fairly pleasant places for homesick young men.

One of the nurses in the Columbia College Hospital in Washington, Rebecca Pomroy, has left an account of a typical day in the life of a general hospital nurse, and considering the nurse was on duty from five in the morning until after nine at night, for at least six days a week, the life was a strenuous one:

"The reveille is played at five, and all who are able to get up, must make their beds, wash, and be ready at the drum-call, at six o'clock, for breakfast. The nurses have theirs at seven. Making of beds, sweeping and dusting done, the attendant brings up the breakfast for those who are not able to get up. After this, two boys wash the dishes, two sweep the rooms, two wash the spittoons, while two contrabands empty the slops. Then commences the dressing of wounds, making the boys comfortable, some sitting in bed reading, others playing checkers, while quite a number are getting ready to go to their regiments. Several are being shaved, others having their hair cut, while another is watering my flowers.

"At eight, the surgeon's call with drum and fife, when everything must be in order. Then come the orders for medicines, soap, crackers, etc., for not a thing is allowed without an order from the surgeon of the ward.

"After wounds are dressed, blisters, plasters and medicines attended to, the Bible is read; and here a boy takes his from his pocket, and tells how it saved his life when shot through the lungs, and it parried the force of the blow.

"At eleven o'clock the medicines come up from the dispensary, and while administering them, a number of invalids came up four flights of stairs to see a bead bag from Chelsea, made by a widow lady, whose only son fell a sacrifice in this cruel war.

"At twelve o'clock the drum beats, and all go to the mess-room for dinner. Company almost always at noon, and unless we go at the time, we either lose our dinner, or it is cold. But there is a carriage, and the lady calls for the nurse on the upper floor. She knows the ward well, for her feet were the first to bring the little luxuries that my sickest boys had.

"It is Mrs. Secretary Wells, with her large tin pails; one with pickles and onions, and the other with baked apples. We can afford to go without our dinner, as our boys will enjoy so much; it is such a comfort to go through the hospital, and give to the desponding and sickest, those delicacies. How kindly she speaks to the boys, cheering them by her smile, and giving them books and papers.

"After the dinner is through, our sewing circle meets; then all my boys get round a bed, and the socks are mended. It is amusing to see the pain as well as pleasure they manifest, as each tugs to outdo the other. There are sometimes twenty-five pairs to mend, and that helps the nurse.

"At five o'clock the drum calls for supper. After that the wounds are dressed, then at seven the surgeons call, when sleeping powders, poultices, etc., are administered.

"At half-past eight the drum beats for all to be in bed, at nine the bells ring (or taps), then lights are extinguished, and all conversation ceases, while the nurse arranges the medicine for the watchers."[3]

Each hospital had volunteer workers, both men and women, who were called "visitors." They came, not to work, but to cheer the wounded and to help them with personal problems. Hospital visiting was, on the whole, a less successful form of volunteer war work than that contributed by the nurses. This was especially true in the early days of the war, when the visitors worked without any real supervision or control. The lady visitors, considered the hospitals as much their territory as the public parks. Visiting had a romantic, sentimental appeal and there was no labor involved. As a result, women went to the wards in numbers often sufficient to impede the work of the doctors and nurses. Some of the visitors brought tracts and sat by the sick boys, exhorting them to a better life. These were lugubrious ladies, who longed to prepare the dying for the hereafter and succeeded admirably in spoiling their enjoyment of the present.

One of them, who became a nurse (though always retaining the psychology of a visitor), because of "an intense desire to preach a living, loving Savior to dying men," records a conversation with a sick boy.

"What, my boy, playing checkers on Sunday?" . . .

"Why, is it Sunday? . . . The fact is, I have been so long in the army I have lost the run of Sabbaths.". . .

"If you shut up your checkerboard and promise me not to open it again on Sunday . . . I will provide you with a Testament and some nice little hymn books. Then," she writes, "I passed with a heavy heart to find other work to do. . . ."[4]

Most of the hospital visitors fortunately had a less gloomy outlook and concentrated on bringing the boys food. They did not always consult the doctors, but distributed their cakes, pies and jellies as the spirit moved them. Sometimes this sort of benevolence was detrimental, but some-

times the delicacies brought by the ladies were the only eatable food the patients received. "Think of sick men," one of the visitors wrote, "with fever, pneumonia or chronic diarrhea, eating raw pork and lying upon the cold, damp ground . . ."[5] Wherever conditions such as these were found, the hospital visitors and their work belong wholly on the credit side of the ledger.

Some of the visitors made pets of the boys, invariably the younger, better looking ones. "May I comb your hair, my boy?" a lady asks. "Yes, mam, I suppose so—but it will be the thirteenth time today." Variations on that story were told on both sides of the lines throughout the war. Walt Whitman, who spent much time visiting the men in hospitals, thought that "a large number of the visitors . . . do no good at all, while some do harm."[6]

Whitman brought to his self-appointed duties of hospital visiting a sensitivity and understanding, not merely of the physical needs of the patients, but of their spiritual wants as well. He knew that sick men needed cheerfulness and that they seemed to draw strength from the presence of a strong, healthy person in the wards. He understood that suffering men sometimes needed to be left alone and should not be forced to talk to strangers. He also knew that a crowded ward was no guarantee against loneliness and that a man in weakened condition may be jealous of attention given others. He was aware that the men frequently needed a little money with which to make small purchases, but that it must be given them with tact. "He who goes among soldiers with gifts, etc.," Whitman wrote, "must beware how he proceeds. It is much more of an art than one would imagine. They are not charity patients, but American young men, of pride and independence. The spirit in which you treat them, and bestow your donations, is just as important as the gifts themselves."[7]

Louisa Alcott, still restive because she had no part to play in the war, had applied for a position in the Army Nursing Corps to which she was now eligible, having reached the required age of thirty years. Two days before the battle of Fredericksburg she was notified by Miss Dix' representative in Boston to report at once for duty at the Union Hospital in Georgetown. Three days after she arrived there, she and her two roommates were awakened by a banging on the door and a voice shouting, "They've come! they've come! hurry up, ladies—you're wanted." Louisa rushed to the window and saw what she took to be a whole fleet of market carts but which were, in reality, forty ambulances bringing wounded men from the battle of Fredericksburg.

Louisa dressed with hurried, trembling fingers, dreading the day which confronted her, and ran downstairs.

"The first thing I met," she wrote later, "was a regiment of the vilest odors that ever assaulted the human nose . . . and the worst of this affliction was, everyone had assured me that it was a chronic weakness of all hospitals, and I must bear it. I did, armed with lavender water, with which I so besprinkled myself and premises, that, like my friend, Sairy, I was soon known among my patients as 'the nurse with the bottle.' Having been run over by three excited surgeons, bumped against by migratory coal-hods, water-pails, and small boys; nearly scalded by an avalanche of newly-filled teapots, and hopelessly entangled in a knot of colored sisters coming to wash, I progressed by slow stages up stairs and down, till the main hall was reached, and I paused to take breath and a survey. There they were! 'our brave boys,' as the papers justly call them, for cowards could hardly have been so riddled with shot and shell, so torn and shattered, nor have borne suffering for which we have no name, with an uncomplaining fortitude, which made one glad to cherish each as a brother. In they came, some on stretchers, some in men's arms, some feebly staggering along propped on rude crutches, and one lay stark and still with covered face, as a comrade gave his name to be recorded before they carried him away to the dead-house. All was hurry and confusion; the hall was full of these wrecks of humanity, for the most exhausted could not reach a bed till duly ticketed and registered; the walls were lined with rows of such as could sit, the floor covered with the more disabled, the steps and doorways filled with helpers and lookers on; the sound of many feet and voices made that usually quiet hour as noisy as noon; and, in the midst of it all, the matron's motherly face brought more comfort to many a poor soul, than the cordial draughts she administered, or the cheery words that welcomed all, making of the hospital a home.

"The sight of several stretchers, each with its legless, armless, or desperately wounded occupant, entering my ward, admonished me that I was there to work, not to wonder or weep; so I corked up my feelings, and returned to the path of duty, which was rather 'a hard road to travel' just then. The house had been a hotel before hospitals were needed, and many of the doors still bore their old names; some not so inappropriate as might be imagined, for my ward was in truth a *ball-room,* if gunshot wounds could christen it. Forty beds were prepared, many already tenanted by tired men

who fell down anywhere, and drowsed till the smell of food roused them. Round the great stove was gathered the dreariest group I ever saw—ragged, gaunt and pale, mud to the knees, with bloody bandages untouched since put on days before; many bundled up in blankets, coats being lost or useless; and all wearing that disheartened look which proclaimed defeat, more plainly than any telegram of the Burnside blunder. I pitied them so much, I dared not speak to them, though, remembering all they had been through since the rout at Fredericksburg, I yearned to serve the dreariest of them all. Presently, Miss Blank tore me from my refuge behind piles of one-sleeved shirts, odd socks, bandages and lint; put basin, sponge, towels, and a block of brown soap into my hands, with these appalling directions:

" 'Come, my dear, begin to wash as fast as you can. Tell them to take off socks, coats and shirts, scrub them well, put on clean shirts, and the attendants will finish them off, and lay them in bed.'

"If she had requested me to shave them all, or dance a hornpipe on the stove funnel, I should have been less staggered; but to scrub some dozen lords of creation at a moment's notice, was really—really—. However, there was no time for nonsense, and, having resolved when I came to do everything I was bid, I drowned my scruples in my wash-bowl, clutched my soap manfully, and, assuming a business-like air, made a dab at the first dirty specimen I saw, bent on performing my task *vi et armis* if necessary. I chanced to light on a withered old Irishman, wounded in the head, which caused that portion of his frame to be tastefully laid out like a garden, the bandages being the walks, his hair the shrubbery. He was so overpowered by the honor of having a lady wash him, as he expressed it, that he did nothing but roll up his eyes, and bless me, in an irresistible style which was too much for my sense of the ludicrous; so we laughed together, and when I knelt down to take off his shoes, he 'flopped' over and wouldn't hear of my touching 'them dirty craters. May your bed above be aisy, darlin', for the day's work ye are doon!—Whoosh! there ye are, and bedad, it's hard tellin' which is the dirtiest, the fut or the shoe.' It was; and if he hadn't been to the fore, I should have gone on pulling, under the impression that the 'fut' was a boot, for trousers, socks, shoes and legs were a mass of mud. This comical tableau produced a general grin, at which propitious beginning I took heart and scrubbed away like any tidy parent on a Saturday night. Some of them took the performance like sleepy children, leaning their tired heads against me as I worked, others looked grimly scandalized, and several of the roughest colored like bashful girls."[8]

Louisa labored all that long day, fighting a battle against her own weakness when the horrors came close to being too much for her:

"By eleven, the last labor of love was done; the last 'good night' spoken; and, if any needed a reward for that day's work, they surely received it, in the silent eloquence of those long lines of faces, showing pale and peaceful in the shaded rooms, as we quitted them, followed by grateful glances that lighted us to bed, where rest, the sweetest, made our pillows soft, while Night and Nature took our places, filling that great house of pain with the healing miracles of Sleep, and his diviner brother, Death."[9]

Louisa was too sensitive and too imaginative for the role of hospital nurse. She wrote of her experiences later with the determined cheeriness with which her mother had taught her and her sisters to meet poverty and adversity, but she was not able to free her mind of the impressions of suffering. Before six weeks of service were ended, hard work and strain had weakened her so that she fell an easy victim to what may have been pneumonia or typhoid. During her illness, Miss Dix brought Louisa wine and food and little gifts to make her comfortable and Louisa thought her "a kind old soul, but very queer and arbitrary."

Bronson Alcott arrived at the hospital one day, having been summoned when it seemed likely that Louisa could not live, and a few days later, sick as she was, she suddenly wanted passionately to be taken home:

"Had a strange, excited journey of a day and night—half asleep, half wandering, just conscious that I was going home; and when I got to Boston, of being taken out of the car, with people looking on as if I was a sight. I daresay I was all blowzed, crazy, and weak. Was too sick to reach Concord that night, though we tried to do so. Spent it at Mr. Sewall's; had a sort of fit; they sent for Dr. H., and I had a dreadful time of it.

"Next morning felt better, and at four went home. Just remember seeing May's shocked face at the depot, Mother's bewildered one at home, and getting to bed in the firm belief that the house was roofless, and no one wanted to see me."[10]

The war was over for Louisa, and she who "was never ill before this time" was "never well afterward."

Sometime during her war days Louisa wrote a poem-parody—perhaps to keep her spirits up, for it is in the vein of bright cheerfulness which was her armor against the world:

"Beds to the front of them,
Beds to the right of them,
Beds to the left of them,
    Nobody blundered.
Beamed at by hungry souls,
Screamed at with brimming bowls.
Steamed at by army rolls,
    Buttered and sundered.
With coffee not cannon plied,
    Each must be satisfied,
Whether they lived or died;
    All the men wondered."

Her hospital experiences she wrote into a little book which she called *Hospital Sketches,* in which that anxious cheerfulness wears threadbare, and a desperate realization of life's realities shows through, for the war left its mark on her permanently. It had broadened and deepened her understanding of life, so that, from that time on, she wrote from a richer maturity. She continued to spend much of her time in the elm-shaded town of her childhood, where she had returned childlike with illness, but life for her was never the same again.

NOTES

[1] R. Villeneuve, *L'Anesthesie Usuel op. cit.* Barbara M. Duncan, *The Development of Inhalation Anaesthesia* (Oxford University Press, 1947).

[2] P. M. Ashburn, *A History of the Medical Department of the United States Army* (Houghton, Mifflin Company, Boston and New York, 1929).

[3] Anna L. Boyden, *Echoes from Hospital and White House* (D. Lothrop and Company, Boston, 1884), pp. 164–166.

[4] *The Bugle Call, or a Summons to Work in Christ's Army* by "A Volunteer Nurse." (The American Tract Society, New York, 1871).

[5] Julia S. Wheelock, *The Boys in White* (Lange & Hillman, 1870). Julia Wheelock was employed as a hospital visitor by a Michigan society. The quotation refers to "Camp Misery" outside Washington.

[6] Walt Whitman, *The Wound Dresser* (The Bodley Press, New York, 1949).

[7] *Ibid.*

[8] Louisa May Alcott, *Hospital Sketches* (Hurst & Co., New York), pp. 50–54.

[9] *Ibid:* p. 70.

[10] Louisa May Alcott, *Life, Letters, and Journals* (Roberts Brothers, Boston, 1892), p. 146.

17

THE PERILS OF A REAL PAULINE

———————————— ★ ————————————

CHRONOLOGY*

1863

January 1   Final issuance of the Emancipation Proclamation. A cessation of hostilities.

January 2   General Bragg renewed his attack on Rosecrans. This failed and Bragg withdrew, leaving Stone's River battlefield to the Union forces.
For the next six months military activities in this sector were confined to raids and skirmishes.

January 25   General Burnside's resignation accepted and General Joseph Hooker appointed to command the Army of the Potomac.

March 3   Congress passed the Enrollment Act, making all male citizens between twenty and forty-five years of age liable for military service.

May 1–4   Battle of Chancellorsville, a Union defeat. Stonewall Jackson mortally wounded.

May 8   Lincoln issued a Conscription Proclamation activating a Congressional law passed on March 3rd.

June 23   Start of General Rosecrans' Tullahoma campaign in which
                 General Bragg was flanked out of his position and forced
                 out of middle Tennessee, to fall back on Chattanooga.

* The chronologies of the Vicksburg and the Gettysburg campaigns have
  been separated, to avoid confusion, from the operations of the Army of
  the Cumberland.

———————————————— ★ ————————————————

> *O the hempen cravat is an elegant thing!*
> *For once on your neck, it gives you full swing.*
> —R. H. Stoddard

THE LIST OF UNSATISFACTORY GENERALS was lengthening. McDowell,
Pope, McClellan, Burnside. And now, at the beginning of the new year,
Joe Hooker was in command of the Army of the Potomac, and the work
of restoring a shattered army had to be done all over again. Nothing
more could be expected of the defeated soldiers until that work was
done. But in the West, the war was active in spite of winter cold and
mud. On December 30th General Rosecrans, in command of the Army
of the Cumberland, met General Bragg's army at Stone's River. The
first day of fighting took fearful toll of the Union troops, but the next
day, with all the advantages on his side, General Bragg failed to attack.
On January 2nd he struck at the Union lines once more, but the charge
was repulsed, and that night, to the complete astonishment of the Union
commanders, he withdrew his army to a position some distance away,
leaving Rosecrans in possession of the field. It was not a victory for
the Union army, but neither was it a defeat.

After Stone's River, Rosecrans went into camp at Murfreesboro
to rest his men, with his main base at Nashville. Bragg also went into
camp with most of his force at Tullahoma, and a smaller force at
Shelbyville, sixteen miles to the northwest. The two armies were not
twenty-five miles apart, and there they stayed, facing each other, for
six long months, a rest period which both Halleck and Grant, who was
beginning his Vicksburg campaign, considered far too long. Rosecrans'
housekeeping was excellent. His camp was clean and comfortable and
he kept his men from growing soft with occasional skirmishes and

raiding expeditions to tear up sections of Confederate railroad track. During one of these skirmishes, in the month of March, while the Confederates were in panic retreat, the color-bearer of the Third Arkansas Confederate Cavalry was shot down. A seventeen year old girl, Alice Thompson, who had been watching the fight from a farm house, saw him fall, ran out, seized the colors and rallied the regiment.

All these long months, Rosecrans watched Bragg carefully to prevent Bragg from making a move which would take him by surprise, and the only way of doing this was by sending spies into enemy country. The espionage work done for the various armies makes up some of the most picturesque passages of the war. In the early days there was no central organization, and spying was anybody's business. There were spies working for the State Department, the War Department, the Navy Department, and the various armies in the field. In addition, there was a considerable amount of spontaneous, undirected volunteer spying engaged in by patriotic citizens, many of them women. In February of 1862, espionage activities were more or less concentrated under the army, but the adventures of the spies continued to be intensely dramatic, as when a group of them stole a train deep in Confederate territory.

There were both "spies" and "scouts," the difference in their functions being roughly what their names imply, but they were somewhat overlapping categories, one group not infrequently performing the duties of the other. There were women in both groups, for espionage had a strong attraction for adventuresome, intensely patriotic women on both sides of the lines.

One of them, Pauline Cushman, was so much the perfect woman spy of melodrama that some of her doings seem amusingly improbable. But if all the doubtful incidents of her great adventure are discarded, her story is still a startling one. A good deal of the melodrama Pauline herself contributed, for she loved to heighten any situation in which she found herself, and she never ceased to play a part until the shadow of the noose fell over her, and life became too real for acting. She saw herself objectively always, as the central figure on a stage, and the little touches which she added when life was not exciting enough or romantic enough to suit her, lacked in artistic subtlety but in drama never.

Pauline even looked the part of the siren-spy. She was Creole, with a French mother and a Spanish father who had bequeathed her a dark and brilliant coloring and a murky, seductive type of beauty, which burnt out rapidly in the fire of her own emotions, for though she was

lovely to look at when the war began, a picture taken afterward shows her face hard and bold, without any of its one-time allure.

She was probably about twenty-eight when the war broke out and she had been married to an actor called Charles Dickinson, a tie which, like subsequent ones, she did not find uncomfortably binding. Dickinson became a musician in the Union army, caught a fever and died, which does not seem to have overwhelmed her with grief, but it may have been because of him that her sympathies were, secretly, with the North.

Pauline was an actress—she could not have been anything else and have been true to her own nature. In March of 1863, while Grant was headquartered at Milliken's Bend and Rosecrans was still in camp preparing for the next move, and about the time a woman orator, Anna Dickinson, was making the opening speech of the Republican campaign, Pauline was playing in the *Seven Sisters* at Woods Theatre in Louisville, a town which was irrepressibly boiling with Southern sympathy. Pauline was not an actress in the great tradition of the other Cushman, and she made no attempt to be. She liked a noisy, show-off part, or a chance to sing a good, rousing song, with the footlights shining up into her face, where her figure could be seen to advantage and where she could receive the applause with an arrogant toss of her head. In the Louisville production, she wore a tight-fitting man's costume which made her well-rounded contours all the more blatantly feminine.

There were two paroled Southern officers idling around Louisville at the time whom Pauline had, as someone has gracefully expressed it, "admitted to a certain degree of friendship." These two, assuming her heart was with the South, dared her to drink a toast during the performance to Jeff Davis and the Confederacy. They offered her money for the deed, a figure which has been reported as 3,000 dollars, but as, with the passage of time, there is a strong tendency for an extra zero or two to add itself to such sums, the probability is that the amount was nothing like so large.

Pauline saw in their dare the chance of making a sensation, and there was nothing she loved more dearly. But she had an idea of her own, and she went to see Colonel Moore, the Federal Provost Marshal Moore, a dour-looking man with a cold, suspicious eye and a big, drooping mustache which looked as though he had glued it on as a disguise. Probably he already knew Pauline, and she was quite possibly already engaged in pointing out dangerous Southern sympathizers to the Federal authorities. Moore approved of Pauline's accepting the dare, because it would establish her publicly and firmly as a Confederate and conceal her

espionage activities. He promised to be in the theatre, with a guard, to protect her in case the audience got out of hand.

Word flew around Louisville, probably spread by Moore's agents, of the excitement which was likely to take place at Wood's Theatre that night, and at curtain time the house was packed, with not even standing room, by Southern sympathizers who had gone there to cheer. The play began. Then, at the appointed moment, Pauline in her tight trousers, with a champagne glass in her hand, walked away from the other actors and came directly to the footlights. The actors fell silent and stared in astonishment. A rustle of excitement swept like a breeze through the house. Pauline raised her glass. In a loud, clear voice she said, "Here's to Jeff Davis and the Southern Confederacy. May the South always maintain her honor and her rights."

Then she drank quickly whatever it was that was in her glass, and pandemonium broke out. Everybody rose to cheer, yell, hiss and stamp. In a moment a fair-sized riot was in progress, and one imagines Colonel Moore and his guards were busy, not only trying to restore order, but noting who was yelling for and who against the Union. Some one got Pauline off the stage into the wings where an apoplectic manager fired her; at which, no doubt, she laughed with characteristic bold bravado. She was through with stage acting for the present.

Pauline had become a Southern heroine in a night, and all sorts of people who favored the Southern cause came to her boardinghouse, some surreptitiously, some boldly. They confided in her, sure of her loyalty, and she sent to the Provost Marshal's office a steady flow of information about blockade running, counterespionage, and the various operations of the enemy behind the Union lines.

Her fame spread, and a manager of a theatre in Nashville offered her a job, probably counting on her being a box-office attraction whatever the color of her politics. So, with the approval of the Provost Marshal's office, Pauline went to new and somewhat richer pastures, for Nashville, close to the Confederate lines, was even more teeming with enemy undercover activity than Louisville had been.

Pauline opened, with an ovation, in a play called *The Married Rake* and queened it around Nashville. She was having a glorious time. It was espionage at its palmiest. Meanwhile Rosecrans was still in his fine, well-policed camp at Murfreesboro, still resting his men, and arguing with Grant and Halleck that his presence there was preventing Bragg from adding to Grant's problems in the Vicksburg campaign. Rosecrans did not actually move until the twenty-third of June, but it was now May

and he was anxious to learn as much as he could about the disposition of the forces in the shadowland of the enemy he was about to enter.

Rosecrans' chief of scouts and espionage was a Colonel Truesdail, an able intelligent man, and one, obviously, of some imagination, for he saw in Pauline a spy who could be used for truly important work behind the rebel lines. He sought her out and told her that the objective he had selected for her was Bragg's army and that he wanted all the information she could get relating to troop movements, armed strength and fortifications. Her excuse for visiting the camps would be that she was searching for a brother (she actually had one somewhere in the Confederate army). She was to accept any invitations from staff officers, but Truesdail warned her not to ask questions or to seem the least curious. She must always tell the same story about searching for her brother, and she must never, for any reason, put anything but a record of her expenses on paper.

On May 26th she took the oath of allegiance to the United States, rather solemnly, it is to be imagined. Then Truesdail presented her with a six-shooter, and her service in the Army of the Cumberland began. Getting her out of Nashville in a way not to arouse suspicion presented no problem.

Nashville was a war-torn town with many wrecked buildings and the better ones used as hospitals and store houses. The pride had gone out of Nashville, the streets were filthy and littered with debris, the houses were shabby, and every alley, every courtyard stank. The inhabitants were violently secessionist, who made trouble on every opportunity, and there was a floating population of thieves, prostitutes and other underworld characters. Periodically, the Army cleaned up the town, rounding up the prostitutes and shipping them out of the district, but they came back again, like vermin crawling out from under the rubbish. Periodically, too, the Confederate women who were suspected of aiding the enemy or who were so vociferous as to be a nuisance to the occupation force, were escorted toward the Rebel lines and left to find their own way southward. Nothing was more convincingly natural than that Pauline should be sent out of the city with one of these sweepings.

In the country, at a prearranged meeting place, a fine bay horse was waiting for her. There were goodbyes, and she rode away, alone. The first night she made contact with a Confederate smuggler in a lonely shack on the Big Harpeth River. He was one of those disreputable, war-spawned characters who played both sides for what he could gain, working with a partner, a Unionist one day, a Rebel the next.

Probably Truesdail had directed Pauline to this man, for shifty and unreliable as he was, he could get her safely into the Confederate lines. But he drove a hard bargain. She was forced to sell him her fine horse and saddle for a hundred dollars in Confederate money, a fraction of their real value. One of his men drove her in a buggy over bumpy, muddy roads to Columbia, and left her there. And there she learned something about war inflation prices. At the hotel a breakfast of hoe cakes without butter, coffee made of rye and a little fat bacon cost her eight dollars. We hear of her buying a chicken for $4.50 (a dollar to the slave who went for it, two dollars for the chicken, one dollar for cooking it and fifty cents for the butter), prices which show how badly she was cheated when she sold the horse.

The railroad out of Columbia had been torn up by a Federal raiding party and Pauline had to wait for three days before she could go on to Shelbyville, about thirty-five miles, as the crow flies, south and east of Columbia. But she did not waste her time. She made the acquaintance of a quartermaster Captain named Blackman, who had just come from Vicksburg. Pauline was in the service of the Army of the Cumberland, which had nothing directly to do with the Vicksburg campaign, but what she learned from Captain Blackman would almost certainly be forwarded on to Grant.

She hoped to find Bragg's headquarters at Shelbyville, but he was not there. The district, however, was a rich one for a spy as it was full of young officers eager to make friends with a young woman who did not have the look of a prude. She picked out a Captain of engineers, made friends and told him the story about her search for her brother. He was eager to help, gave her a letter to General Bragg and told her where his headquarters might be found. Somehow, in the course of this, she found herself alone in a room with some of the engineer's plans and drawings. Probably she did not have time to study them and could not have understood them, but they seemed to her important and, violating the solemn warning Truesdail had given her, she stole some of them.

When Pauline arrived at Shelbyville, Bragg was not there, but it was plain to her that there was much military information to be gained in the neighborhood. And she was enjoying herself. She began moving around the country on horseback, sometimes, one account says,[1] in a man's dress, though that would have been a risky disguise for a figure like Pauline's. There is a tale, possibly false, of a wild ride with the Rebels after her when she was trying to deliver her report to a small Union force, a capture, an escape. If it ever happened, it did not scare her out of the

country, for back she went to Columbia and the amorous Captain Blackman.

The realities of a spy's life caught up with Pauline in time, but there in Columbia she was still living in a dream world of romantic adventure. She was actress to the heart—one of those to whom make-believe is reality and reality the purest make-believe. She was still play-acting the part of a spy in the manner (a trifle too theatrical) in which she believed it should be played. It has been said of her that she resisted the temptations of the camp. Captain Blackman, however, conceived the idea of dressing her up in a Confederate uniform and taking her along with him as his aide, which would seem to throw some doubt on that pompous statement. The uniform was made—but just there the story grows vague again.

Pauline went to Tullahoma and back to Shelbyville again, at each place coquetting with handsome officers, walking with them over fortifications with the train of her riding skirt thrown over her arm, gazing in wide-eyed innocence at guns and earthworks. Having once successfully disregarded Truesdail's warning about carrying written material, it no longer had any meaning for her. She made drawings wherever she went, and presumably she had some way of sending them back to the Union lines.

It was dangerous work and she was becoming, perhaps, too well known. She decided the time had come to return to Nashville, so she went back to that dilapidated smuggler's shanty north of Columbia on the Big Harpeth River and asked to be taken through the Confederate outposts to the Union lines. She carried the Confederate uniform which the gallant Captain had ordered for her, in her carpet bag—just why it is hard to imagine. Her secret papers she put in the exact place where any experienced searcher would be most likely to look for them—under the lining of her extra pair of shoes. The shoes she then packed safely away with the pretty Confederate uniform.

Pauline was to learn, this late, a primary lesson in espionage, which is that men who live by their dishonest wits are full of treachery. Perhaps she knew too much about their shady dealings with the Confederates. More likely they merely saw a chance to collect two sums of money instead of one, the first from her as her price of escape, the second from the Confederates as a reward for informing against her. However it was, before she reached safety, a Confederate agent appeared and took her and her precious carpet bag into custody.

He put her on a horse. He did not search her and so he did not find

the gun in her pocket. He was contemptuous of a woman spy, perhaps, and he rode ahead of her down a leafy forest trail. Now was her chance, and at the same time the test of whether she was only an actress playing at espionage, or a true spy, ready to do a spy's duty and kill to save the papers which she carried. The gun was in her hand. She was all actress and nothing more. She could not pull the trigger. And the change in her must date from this moment, for the actress was at last face to face with reality.

Pauline's story sometimes totters on the brink of farce, and the next incident is one of those times. She was taken to Anderson's Mills, the local headquarters of the Confederate scouts where, after a wait of some hours, she was turned over to John Hunt Morgan, who had recently been made a Brigadier General. Morgan was another story-book character. He rode a horse like a madman and designed his own uniform, which is still the privilege of an officer of general rank. His sleeve had gold braid halfway to the shoulder, his hat was broadbrimmed like a Dumas musketeer, with a long black plume. His beard was sharp-pointed and the ends of his thin, upturned mustache were long enough to blow in the wind.

He looked Pauline over with his bold, amused stare and began at once to pay her compliments. Pauline's hope revived and she flirted with him, giving it her best effort. He called her "Pauline," she called him "Johnny." He pressed his attentions boldly and she was greatly flattered and played the role of *femme fatale* up to the hilt, though possibly with some overtones of desperation.

No doubt she thought she had fascinated him and that he would help her to escape. Morgan, however, had been married not many days before to a young woman he was really in love with, and the admiration Pauline thought he had for her was not of the quality she supposed. He turned her over to the authorities at Hillsboro, and rode away.

And here the story goes in two directions. One account states that she bribed a Negro to shout, "The Yanks are coming," and that in the ensuing panic she jumped on a horse and fled. The other tale, and the more likely, though we have nothing but common sense to guide us in choosing between them, is that someone else gave the alarm, and that in the confusion she stole a horse and rode away. If there was a Union raiding party in the neighborhood, she failed to find it. She rode for a long time, until she came to the pickets on the outer Confederate line. She talked her way past five of them (later it was said she knew the password, and perhaps she did) but the sixth picket would not let her

go on because she did not have the pass from headquarters required of everyone who went through the lines.

She turned back again and rode on, frightened and desperate. Night came, and she knocked on the door of one of the dreary farmhouses of the district. A child had just died in the house, but the farmer and his wife took her in and she spent an apprehensive night, for she must have known that she had left a well-marked trail behind her, a trail easy for mountain scouts to follow. And they followed her. The next day four of them captured her.

No badinage with the handsome Morgan this time. She was taken to the headquarters not of Morgan but of General Nathan Bedford Forrest, who was an altogether different sort of person, and Pauline must have known the minute she saw him that play-acting the *femme fatale* would get her nowhere. Forrest was a rough, hard-bitten character who had been a slave trader and a planter. He had none of the romantic, chivalric ideals of other cavalry commanders, and his men were as rough and ready as himself. Most cavalry men would not condescend to do anything that could not be done on the back of a horse, but Forrest's men would turn themselves into infantry or even into day laborers at their leader's command. Forrest had no military training, he hated style and tradition, he fought in any manner which seemed likely to succeed, and he was one of the true military geniuses of the war. He was ungrammatical, crude and impatient, and when Pauline was brought to stand before him, he had a pile of papers relating to her on his desk. He made an acid comment or two and ordered her taken on to Shelbyville.

That night there was a guard set in front of her tent but she tried to escape by crawling on all fours under the tent bottom. She was in the midst of this maneuver when she found herself confronted by General Forrest, who was on a night prowl around the camp. He drove her back, with his usual verbal forcefulness, presumably, and set a guard all the way around her tent. The guards amused themselves by telling horrible stories about how captured Yanks were treated, while Pauline listened, lying on her cot, frightened, trapped, exhausted mentally and physically by the strain.

From here on, half the story is sheer nonsense, created, one suspects, by Pauline's own not very first-rate imagination. Under this heading should go such improbabilities as that, when she saw Morgan once more, he gave her a gold watch, his diamond ring and a silver mounted pistol. How trust the tales of a woman who, for over six years[2] deceived her husband into thinking a child she had "adopted" was his own? In

the same category should go the story that her guards took the most tender care of her and that as she lay sick in the intolerable heat one of them came to fan her. There is also the story that the Confederate provost marshal, Captain Pedden, fell in love with her and proposed to her, though it was he who brought her the news that she had been sentenced to be hanged. Also it is difficult to imagine that during her imprisonment the three Generals—Bragg, Cheatham and Forrest (of all people, Forrest)—paid her frequent visits.

But there are events which have the texture of truth. One of them is that when she was arraigned before General Bragg and a military court, questions, searching, prolonged and relentless, were fired at her. She was placed under close guard, and the fear, the anxiety, the hostility which surrounded her, and the terrible heat broke her down completely so that she was ill, truly ill, with no play-acting involved. And while she waited, in an agony of suspense, for the verdict of the military court, women of the town came to jeer at her until she broke down and wept in utter misery.

These things have the sound of truth. Then at last Captain Pedden brought her the verdict of the court: guilty and to be hanged by the neck until dead.

Did Pauline know that the Confederates had never executed a woman spy? And they never did. That remained to be accomplished by our own generation, when Edith Cavell was shot by the Germans, and Ethel Rosenberg was electrocuted, though not in time of war, by ourselves. No sentence of death would have been carried out on Pauline, though she may not have realized this.

The end of the story came shortly after she was sentenced. On the twenty-third of June, Rosecrans broke up the fine camp where he had stayed so long, and sent his army rolling toward Bragg. He began the movement with a feint to the right, around the left flank of the forces based on Shelbyville. On the night of the twenty-fourth, General Stanley, in command of the Union flanking movement, ordered many campfires built, to deceive the Confederates into thinking that Shelbyville was about to be attacked by the whole of Rosecrans' army. Meanwhile the main force moved toward the left, and on the twenty-seventh occupied Manchester, on Bragg's right flank. It was a brilliant move. Bragg, who had retired to Tullahoma, fearing that Rosecrans would attack him in the rear, pulled out all his forces and retreated all the way southward to Chattanooga.

The evacuation of Shelbyville was a wild confusion of shouting, the

pound of horses hooves, the lurch and sway of supply wagons. In the confusion, Pauline was left behind, and the Union forces found her in the house where she had been held a prisoner, weakly joyful at her deliverance and through with the life of a spy forever.

A story like Pauline's is a research worker's nightmare, for the whole story is bestrewn with falsehoods, errors and half truths. Each teller has added, although perhaps unconsciously, a little fiction, a little heightening of the drama. Added to this is the difficulty of recapturing a personality and the almost impossible task of pinning anything so elusive down on a printed page. And when that personality has been dead for years, giving it a semblance of life and truth is like trying to capture a wisp of mist or the momentary darkness of a passing shadow. Not any of her photographs seems to jibe with the woman herself as the facts—those precarious or vague facts—portray her. Perhaps the photographs are bad. Perhaps she was not a good subject. Perhaps. Perhaps. And yet she was real—very real, and the main facts of her story are true.

NOTES

[1] Sarmiento, Ferdinand L., *Life of Pauline Cushman, the Celebrated Union Spy and Scout* (United States Book Co., New York, 186?), pp. 151–155.

[2] Horan, James D., *Desperate Women* (G. P. Putnam's Sons, New York, 1952), pp. 118–119.

18

UNCLE SAM'S WEBB-FEET

---------------------★---------------------

CHRONOLOGY*

1862

November 2   Start of the Vicksburg Campaign.

November 13   Grant's force arrived at Holly Springs.

December 19   General Forrest raided the railroad at Jackson, Tennessee, the beginning of a week of raids on Grant's supply line for the first attempt at Vicksburg.

December 20   General Van Dorn attacked Holly Springs, Grant's supply base.

December 26   General Sherman started up the Yazoo River.

1863

January 10   Grant moved his headquarters to Memphis.

January 30   Beginning of intensive work on the canal and on a waterway through Lake Providence.

February 2   The levee at Yazoo Pass cut.

February 24   Expedition moved into the new waterway at Yazoo Pass.

March 11   Attack on Fort Pemberton.

March 13   Second attack on Fort Pemberton failed. Admiral Farragut brought the Gulf fleet up the river to run the batteries at Port Hudson. Only two ships got by.

March 15   Admiral Porter started via Steel's Bayou, in fourth attempt at Vicksburg.

March 24   Expedition returned to the Mississippi. Troops concentrated at Milliken's Bend.

March 27   Canal scheme abandoned. The attempt to make a waterway through Lake Providence given up about the same time.

April 16   Admiral Porter's fleet ran past the batteries at Vicksburg. Beginning of final attempt to capture the city.

*Note: For the sake of clarity, the events of the Vicksburg campaign have been separated from those which were taking place at the same time in the Eastern theatre.

★

> *"Nor must Uncle Sam's webb-feet be forgotten. At all the watery margins they have been present. Not only on the deep sea, the broad bay, and the rapid river, but also up the narrow muddy bayou, and wherever the ground was a little damp, they have been, and made their tracks."*
>
> —Abraham Lincoln

WHILE BURNSIDE, newly come to his command, was still looking across the river toward Fredericksburg, before Rosecrans had fought his indecisive battle at Stone's River, one of the great campaigns of the war was having an inconspicuous beginning in the West. This was the campaign against Vicksburg, Southern citadel high on the bluffs above the Mississippi. The whole of the great river, since the capture of New Orleans, was in Union hands, except for a stretch of about two hundred miles between Vicksburg on the north and Port Hudson on the south, and until that stretch could be cleared the Confederacy would continue to draw on the rich agricultural resources which the water and rail facilities in that region laid open to them. Vicksburg was the key city, and until it was in Union hands the Confederacy would remain united.

Mrs. A. H. Hoge

Mrs. Fanny Ricketts

Kady Brownell

With the dismal series of failures in the East, the hopes of the Administration had turned to the West. The old desire to free the Mississippi from enemy control took on new meaning. Vicksburg became almost a symbol. In July of 1862, the Western commander, General Halleck, had been called to Washington and made General-in-Chief of all the Armies. Halleck's promotion left Grant in unofficial command of the army in Mississippi and in western Tennessee. In October, his command was made official and he was given the special assignment of clearing the Mississippi River.

He was faced with a difficult strategical problem. Vicksburg, high on a steep bluff, with fifteen miles of batteries mounted on the bluff and along the shore line, was impregnable to an attack from the river. To the south of the city was a stretch of swampy forest country laced by streams and bayous. To the north there were more swamps and streams and a more or less navigable river known as the Yazoo. Only at the back of the city was the ground high and open, and here the railroad ran to Jackson where it connected with the line running north to Holly Springs and Memphis. An attack from this direction would not be impeded by swamps, but the supply line from a Northern base would be long and vulnerable to enemy raids. This, however, was the route to Vicksburg which Grant chose. Grant himself dates the start of the Vicksburg campaign from November 2nd when he began the preliminary troop movements, and by the thirteenth he was at Holly Springs, where he established a large base of supply.

Grant's plan included another attack, to be launched by General Sherman, up the Yazoo River against Chickasaw Bluffs, the intention being to divide the forces of the Vicksburg commander, General Pemberton. On the twenty-sixth of December Sherman started up the Yazoo, but Grant's plans had failed to develop. Unknown to Sherman, General Forrest staged a series of raids on Grant's rail communications, raids which were so effective that they put the railroad out of commission for the rest of the war. While these raids were in progress, the Confederate cavalry commander, General Van Dorn, destroyed Grant's base of supply at Holly Springs. Grant was forced to withdraw without being able to communicate with Sherman and as a result when Sherman attacked Chickasaw Bluffs on the twenty-ninth he was repulsed. The first attempt to attack Vicksburg had failed, but it was not all loss, for Grant learned a military lesson not in the textbooks, which was that, under certain conditions, an army could live and live well off the country without

any base of supply. It was a lesson which both Grant and Sherman were to make good use of later.

The second attempt to find a route to Vicksburg involved a most extraordinary engineering project. The Mississippi, in the Vicksburg area, turned on itself and flowed for a time in a northeasterly direction, then made a loop and flowed southwest, returning to its old course at a point not far from its departure. Vicksburg was at the upper end of the loop, and at the lower end the two sections of the river were separated only by a narrow strip of land. In 1862 the bold scheme had been conceived of cutting through this land strip so that the river would no longer loop northward, and Vicksburg would become an inland city.

The attempt to cut the canal had been a failure, largely for engineering reasons, but Lincoln liked the project, and in January of 1863 Grant ordered the work resumed, though he himself had no great faith in the value of the plan, for the canal was well within range of the Vicksburg guns for its entire length. Four thousand men were set to work altering and enlarging the ditch, aided by two dredges equipped with locomotive lights for night work. At the same time, Grant ordered the levee at Lake Providence cut in the hope of opening a channel through the lake to the Red River and so to the Mississippi below the blockade at Vicksburg.

Of the two schemes for by-passing the fortress city, the canal seemed rather the more promising, and the distance to be traveled would be infinitely less. It had been supposed that if a sizable ditch were dug and the river let in, that the action of the water would sweep out a wide, deep channel. There were difficulties from the start. The season had been unusually rainy and digging the ditch was like trying to shovel pea soup. The river rose and washed out a barricade before the ditch was ready, then it fell and could not be diverted into the new channel. The gunners at Vicksburg soon had the exact range of the canal and the bombardment was continuous. Hundreds of men were killed or wounded, and hundreds more sickened from swamp fever and typhoid.

Some of the sick and wounded were taken to a little hospital upstream, a hospital made of tents which had been pitched close to the levee. There were no bluffs on this side of the river, and the levee was the only protection there was in that barren, muddy territory against the shells from the Vicksburg batteries. Behind the hospital there was a Union battery and all day and all night the shells of both armies went screaming overhead. There was little danger that the hospital would be hit, but the noise was nerve-wracking, so that there was no sleep for the sick men but the sleep of exhaustion. Most of the men had been there a long time, and

they had lost all hope of ever being moved to a better place. Morale was, understandably, at a low ebb.

The surgeon in charge seems to have been really concerned for the welfare of his men and anxious to do anything he could to lighten the listless depression of his patients. He remembered having heard that Annie Wittenmyer was on a Sanitary Commission boat not far away, and he thought that if she could be persuaded to visit the hospital that the presence of a woman might cheer the disheartened men. Annie was state agent for Iowa, and she frequently acted for both the Sanitary Commission and the Christian Commission. Though her chief responsibility was supposed to be toward the boys of her own state, she was one of those who helped to break down the narrow conception of state aid, and she considered the field of her duties to be wherever she and her supplies could do the most good.

The trip to the hospital was not a safe one, for the road was under shellfire most of the way, and the canal ditch, which was partly filled with water, had to be crossed. A party of four set out for the hospital on horseback, the surgeon, General Cyrus Bussey, Mrs. Bussey and Annie. Mrs. Bussey, who was little and lovely to look at, rode sidesaddle on her own horse. Annie had no horse of her own, but the surgeon found her a cavalry mount, a big, rawboned, disillusioned veteran, whom nothing could surprise. Her saddle was a heavy regulation cavalry saddle which must have been exceedingly uncomfortable. Of how Annie was dressed for this extraordinary ride there is, unfortunately, no record.

The surgeon had crossed the ditch that morning and knew a safe place, if any place under constant bombardment could be called safe. The party drew rein on the bank and looked down at the steep, muddy sides and the muddy water in the bottom. One look was enough for General Bussey, who refused to let his wife try to cross. The water was not deep, the surgeon said, though there did seem to be more than when he had crossed earlier and there was a swift current. He said he would go first to prove it was safe and he set his horse sliding down the bank. He did not know that a river barrier had given way and that the water was rising rapidly. He plunged in and found himself instantly over his horse's depth and struggling in the strong current. He reached the opposite bank and shouted to the others that he must have missed the crossing, but that upstream it was "perfectly safe."

They rode up a little way and it did not look in the least safe, but Annie was Kentucky bred and a fine horsewoman. She was also as intrepid as any of the women who worked under the guns. She set her big

horse to the bank and they slid down and into the water. This crossing was worse than the other. They were out of their depth and her horse was struggling hard. General Bussey plunged down the bank to rescue her, but there would have been small chance for that in the strong current. Annie needed no rescuer. She kept her seat, swam her horse like an expert, and reached the opposite bank safely, though soaked to the skin.

Annie, the surgeon, and the General rode the rest of the way to the hospital single file, at a gallop. Shells were coming over and the Confederate gunners had the range of the road. Union mortar boats were sending their wobbly, snub-nosed missiles into Vicksburg and the noise was deafening. "It was a wild ride," Annie thought.

The plight of the men in the hospital shocked her deeply. "They longed for quiet and sleep, but the guns of the two armies were thundering over their heads night and day." The whole incident was characteristic of Annie Wittenmyer—the intrepidity, the anger at needless suffering and the determination to find a remedy. Grant was in the neighborhood at that time, and the next day Annie saw him and told him that the hospital must be broken up and the men moved at once to a better place. Grant never failed to take heed when Mrs. Wittenmyer made a request of him, for he trusted her and behaved toward her almost as though she were one of his own officers. That night, under cover of darkness, the hospital was evacuated and the wounded men sent to good hospitals at Milliken's Bend, twenty-five miles away.

Grant's next attempt to attack Vicksburg from the rear was based on another grandiose engineering project. About 200 river miles above Vicksburg, and a little way south of Helena, Arkansas, there was a tangled district of swamps, bayous and waterways known as the Yazoo Pass. The Pass led through swamp jungle into the Coldwater River, which joined the Tallahatchie River, and together they flowed southward to join the Yalobusha River and the northernmost reaches of the Yazoo. This intricate system of waterways was believed to be more or less navigable and it led to high ground from which an army might be marched to the rear of Vicksburg.

The difficulty lay in the Pass itself, where the water channels were shallow and meandering. The Pass, an old inlet of the Mississippi, had been walled off by a levee, and the great river rolled by higher than a man's head above the swampy Pass. The scheme was to cut the levee at this point, letting the waters of the Mississippi pour through until the

water level in the pass had risen enough to permit the shallow-draught river boats to steam through.

The plan was an ingenious one, and it presented no great engineering difficulties. The levee was cut and the rushing waters did most of the work. For days the Mississippi boiled through the gap in a cataract, down to the swamps eight or ten feet below.

On the twenty-fourth of February the gunboats moved into the Yazoo Pass and Sherman followed along with his troops, on what dry land he could find, to protect the boats from land attack. The expedition encountered fantastic difficulties from the start. The waterways were narrow and full of submerged snags. Trees had to be cut to widen the passage and overhanging branches wreaked havoc with smokestacks and pilot-houses. In the still, watery forest ahead the enemy could be heard chopping trees to block the channel and sharpshooters hidden along the banks harassed the boat crews. Progress was often inch by inch, but after days of incessant toil the expedition reached Fort Pemberton, the first Confederate stronghold at the juncture of the Yalobusha and the Yazoo. Fort Pemberton was no more than some breastworks built of cotton bales with earth tossed over them and there was a sunken hull in the channel. This war, more filled with strange turns of fate than most wars, produced one of the strangest here. The sunken hull which blocked the progress of the Union boats was all that remained of a famous ship, the *Star of the West,* which had attempted to relieve Fort Sumter in 1861. She had been captured by the Confederates, used as a river boat and at last lay here in her desolate fresh-water grave.

The cotton fort and the dead hull made further progress impossible, and the expedition ignominiously retraced its course through the network of waterways. Admiral Porter made another attempt, by another water route, to penetrate this desolate country. This too failed, and unable to turn his fleet around, he backed out, and on March 24th he regained the Mississippi, his boats battered by snags and overhanging branches— a strange plight and a strange adventure for a salt-water sailor.

The great river, all this while, teemed with traffic. There were supply ships and hospital ships and transports. There were iron sides—gunboats and mortar boats, rams, "tin-sides" and barges. Some were equipped with thick armor plate, others had no armor other than barricades of cotton bales around the decks. Most of these steamers were strange-looking craft, misshapen, light of draft. They went swiftly downstream with the current, but on the upstream run they labored hard, their thick, black smoke visible for miles above the cottonwood trees.

The river was broad and yellow with mud, desolate, the banks lined with trees from which moss trailed like mourning veils. There were no high bluffs on the western shore of the river like those on the Vicksburg side. For a long distance from Young's Point, opposite Vicksburg, the land was level, with a good road just behind the levee. But here and there the levees had been cut, and the river, pushing through, had flooded the country, ruining whole counties, stretching out into a vast, shallow sea. As a result, the road was impassable when the water was high and it was unusually high all that long winter.

After the failure of the fourth attempt to flank Vicksburg, most of Grant's army was on the western side of the river, concentrated in two main bases at Milliken's Bend and Young's Point and in lesser encampments, where there was enough dry ground, in various spots along the seventy miles between. Some of the men lived in camps which were always soggy. Some, preferring to be dry, lived on overcrowded boats in the river.

There was little for the men to do while Grant was planning his next move, waiting for the rains to stop and the river to fall. Inevitably there was a great deal of sickness. Thirty-three and a third percent of Grant's army was incapacitated that spring, and in addition to the ever present swamp fever, there were outbreaks of measles and smallpox. At the end of March, Grant adopted Letterman's medical reforms, creating an ambulance corps under the direction of the Medical Department and a system of field hospitals, but the regimental hospitals remained active, largely because the distribution of the troops over so long a stretch of territory made larger units impractical. The hospital boats moved up and down the river all the time, collecting the sick and wounded from the expeditions up the waterways and the more serious cases from the camps along the western shore, and transporting them to base hospitals at Helena. All these hospital ships had women workers on board, but there were few Dix nurses, for Miss Dix still clung to her original idea that female nurses belonged in base hospitals and seldom elsewhere. The pressure of war, however, had made her slightly less rigid-minded about handling organization problems herself, and though she never gladly delegated authority, it became necessary for her to accept the help of agents in staffing the great base hospitals in the west.

In addition to the hospital boats, the supply boats of the Sanitary Commission were constantly waddling like busy ducks up and down the river, and on occasion, when they were not loaded to the guard rails with crates and boxes, they too transported sick and wounded. These boats

were staffed by both men and women, regular field workers and special representatives of the Sanitary Commission, and as the Sanitary Commission staffs worked in almost complete harmony with other organizations, there was often a pooling of labor and supplies. These people were executives. They had charge of distributing supplies worth many thousands of dollars, and their reports formed the basis for guiding the output of the aid societies. They had considerable status in the army (both Mrs. Wittenmyer and Mary Livermore carried passes signed by the Secretary of War) and they had ready access to division and corps commanders, and even to General Grant. Nevertheless, there was not one of these women in any theatre who would not set this dignity aside and nurse and cook whenever necessary.

Mary Livermore, who ran the central office of the Western Sanitary Commission at Chicago, went down the river in March, as an inspector for the Commission. She was instructed to visit every hospital, however small or inaccessible, between Cairo and Young's Point, and of these there were hundreds. Her reports were to be published in the Chicago press and in the bulletins of the Sanitary Commission. She took with her, in addition to the usual hospital supplies, such anti-scorbutics as barrels of potatoes, onions, turnips and sauerkraut. There were cases of tea, sugar, condensed milk, canned fruit, jellies, beef extract, codfish, and brandy. Also she undertook to deliver about 500 boxes sent by individuals to the soldiers at the front. Few women have ever traveled with so much baggage, but for herself, Mary had learned to travel light and the main items of her own were a teapot, an alcohol heater, tea, condensed milk, sugar, crackers and a pair of knee-length rubber boots.

She set out down the river in a "little, rickety, wheezy, crowded, unsafe craft," with several army wives on board who were going as far as Memphis, which was the farthest south civilians were permitted. One of these women, the newly-married wife of the Colonel of the Twelfth Michigan Regiment, went with Mary to visit a small hospital. There a young lad, dying of consumption, said to her, "Can you sing something for a dying man?" She had a fine, well-trained voice. She sat on a camp-stool beside his bed, took his hand in hers and sang "Nearer My God to Thee." She sang very movingly, the men in the ward were weak from long illness, and some of them began to weep. The dying boy gazed at the singer with eyes made luminous by fever. "Can you sing 'The Sweet By and By?' "

She sang, and this time all the sick men joined in. Then she sang "Sweet Home," very feelingly, but this was too much for everybody.

"The scene that followed," Mary said, "was alarming. Men buried their faces in the pillows and wept aloud; and others who were sitting up, . . . threw themselves face downward. . . ." "This," Mary thought, "would not do." To change the atmosphere, she called for rousing songs —"Rally Round the Flag, Boys," "America" and others. Then they heard the boat whistling for them, and the women left, singing as they went,

> "There's a good time coming, boys,
> Wait a little longer. . . ."

There were eleven hospitals in Memphis, with nearly 8000 patients in them, and more arriving all the time. Mary went to all of them and visited every ward, and talked with every patient. In one of these hospitals, the "Gayoso," Mother Bickerdyke was matron, and it was known the whole length of the river as "Mother Bickerdyke's Hospital." There she ran a stupendous laundry project for all the hospitals, in addition to her work as matron.

Livermore found her quarreling, as usual, with the head surgeon. A fine row broke out. Bickerdyke triumphed, and she was ever one to enjoy her triumphs. "And, doctor," she said, "I guess you hadn't better get into a row with me (she meant another row) for whenever anybody does one of us always goes to the wall. And 'tain't never me!"

After a stay of two weeks in Memphis, where she shared an unpeaceful room with the dynamic Bickerdyke, Mary sailed down the river with her stores on a shot-battered boat named the *Tigress*. She was often on shore, jouncing over the levee road in an ambulance, or if the mud was too deep for wheels, pulling on the rubber boots and trudging along on foot. Much of the country had been under water all winter long, and the levee, being the only ground in which it was possible to dig, was full of graves. The action of the rains and floods had washed many of them out, so that as she went along she often passed half disinterred, decaying bodies. And so far had she come along the hard road of experience, that though she had come near to fainting on her first visit to a hospital, the gruesome sights of the levee did not disturb her.

She went from hospital to hospital and if she did not have time to talk to each patient, she made a speech, telling them that all the women of the North were working for them, sacrificing for them and thinking of them with loving pride. She may have been a trifle irritating sometimes, a little too much the brisk social worker. She may have been a little too prone to say, "Come, come, boys, we must all cheer up," and to lose

sight of individuality in a composite picture of her own creating. Unquestionably, Walt Whitman was the more understanding hospital visitor, but Mary Livermore had a way of leaving a wake of organization and efficiency behind her, to say nothing of the supplies she distributed, and in this sense she was important to every hospital she visited.

There were many regimental hospitals, most of them without any women nurses, and the quality of the hospital depended in the main on the quality of the surgeon in charge. One of them held about 200 men, "all of them very sick, all lying in their uniforms on the bare board floor, with their knapsacks for pillows, with no food but army rations, no nurses but convalescent soldiers, themselves too sick to move except on compulsion, the sick men covered with vermin, tormented by flies during the day, and devoured by mosquitoes at night—and their surgeon dead-drunk in bed.

"I went through the four large wards of the hospital, each one as horrible as the other. In all the wards men were dying, and in all they seemed hopeless and despairing. There was no complaint, no lamentation—only now and then some delirious fever patient would clamor for 'ice water,' or 'cold water right from the well.' I stooped down and took one man by the hand, who was regarding me with most beseeching looks. 'My poor boy,' I said, 'I am very sad to see you in this dreadful condition.' He pressed my hand on his eyes with both his own, and wept aloud.

"Weeping is contagious, and in a few moments one half the men in the hospital were sobbing convulsively. I was afraid it would kill them, they were so excessively weak, but it was some time before they could be calmed. I had taken along in the ambulance, tea, sugar, condensed milk, and crackers. After I had made tea and distributed it with the crackers, I went back to medical headquarters to report the disgraceful condition of the hospital."[1]

When she arrived at Young's Point, Mary and some friends had an interview with General Grant, which decided two points for her—first, that he was not a talkative man, and second, that he was not intemperate. All the way from Chicago she had heard tales of his drunkenness, as, indeed, had everyone, and when she left his tent, she looked at her friends and said, "Thank God!"

The question of whether Grant drank to excess or not has never been settled, and probably never will be, but rumors of his drunkenness were persistent enough to reach Lincoln, who liked Grant because he was a fighter. It was in July of 1862, when Halleck had been called to Washington as General-in-Chief and Grant was being considered for the command

of the armies in the West, that Lincoln made his famous remark about Grant's drinking. "Can you tell me the kind of whiskey?", Lincoln enquired, "I should like to send a barrel to some of my other generals."

There has been a good deal of speculation ever since as to what Grant's favorite brand of whiskey really was. There was one man who knew, Colonel Isaac Stewart, Grant's adjutant who was with him from before Vicksburg until the fall of Richmond. Stewart told about it in an interview in 1885.[2] He said that during all that time he only knew of Grant's taking one drink, but that then it was a whopper. It was on February 23, 1863, the night before the departure of the Yazoo Pass expedition, and Grant was harassed. Stewart, McPherson and some others, all very tired, were sitting in the cabin of the *Magnolia,* waiting for the morning. Grant called for a drink, and when the whiskey was brought to him, he filled his tumbler to the brim. The brand he asked for was "Old Crow."

At Young's Point Mary visited a large hospital made of tents put together in such a way that they opened one into another. The dirt floor, Mary said, was "dropsical," and sank at every step, the footprints immediately filling with water. The legs of the cots had pieces of board under them to keep them from sinking. The food was army rations, and the cooking was done in an iron cauldron slung over a fire of cottonwood logs outdoors. The place buzzed "like a bee-hive" with flies and a particularly virulent kind of gnat. The men were so weak that their weakness itself had become a disease, and they lay listless with despair.

Mary Livermore walked briskly into this scene. "Now, boys, . . . I have lots of good things for you. The folks at home have sent me down here and given me everything that you need: eggs, tea, crackers, white sugar, condensed milk, lemons, ale, everything—and your surgeon wants you to have them." Then she went to the man in the first cot—a man of her own age, but so weak that he was like a child. "Now my boy," she said, "if you could have just what you wanted, what would you ask for?"

Even that decision was an effort for him, but he told her he thought he would like a poached egg, toast and tea. Mary unpacked her teapot and spirit lamp and set them up near him. Some of the men brushed the flies off their faces and dragged themselves up a little way to watch, and she told them that she would fix for each one in turn whatever he wanted to have. When the tea and toast were ready, Mary propped up the forty-five year old "boy" with his knapsack and pillow and put the plate of food into his hands. He tried to smile and it was a ghastly grimace on his emaciated face, and then he began to cry. He clutched the food to him and wept.

Mary stayed with these poor men for three days, her three-pint teapot constantly in use. Then the *City of Memphis* arrived to take them to large, comfortable hospitals in the North. Not long after this, Mary herself went home, her long, hard inspection trip ended. Wherever the boat stopped on the way north, it seemed to her that she could see signs of coming action. Troops were gathering, the sick and wounded were all being moved north, the river was more crowded with boats than it had been a little while before. Mary was right in believing that these things indicated that the Army would shortly be on the move, for Grant was about to launch his final attack on Vicksburg.

This time his plan, about which he kept his own counsel, to prevent interference from Washington, was to launch his attack from the south. He had not much confidence in the operations at Yazoo Pass, but though the country below Vicksburg was also swampy and laced with waterways, there was dry land in the direction of Jackson and once there, Vicksburg could be approached from the rear. His troops, however, would have to be ferried across the river and before that could be done, transports, armored craft, and supply ships would have to be run past the fifteen miles of shore batteries at Vicksburg.

The blockade was to be run by seven ironclad gunboats (one of them being Admiral Porter's flagship, the *Benton*), three transports without troops but loaded with campaign supplies, some rams and wooden gunboats. The night of the sixteenth of April was chosen and because the ships could carry no lights, the decks were painted white to help the gunners to see to load their guns. Pilot-houses and smoke-stacks, that would silhouette against the night sky, were taken down, and all exposed machinery was protected with cotton-bale barricades.

Grant was to watch the running of the blockade from the deck of a ship anchored at the northern end of the blockaded stretch of river. Mrs. Grant, who often came to visit her husband in camp, bringing one of the children with her, was to go with him to watch the exciting scene, and she invited Annie Wittenmyer to join her. Because of the great secrecy of the attempt, Mrs. Grant did not send her note inviting Mrs. Wittenmyer until nine o'clock that night. Mrs. Wittenmyer went with the orderly who had brought the note, to meet the General and his wife, and together the party went out to the ship.

The night was very dark, and rain was falling. When they reached the ship, they found most of Grant's generals there waiting for them. There were no other ladies in the party, though Belle Reynolds, a distinguished lady since Shiloh, and General McClernand's recent bride were on an-

other ship. Grant's ship left Milliken's Bend for Young's Point as soon as the party was on board, for the running of the blockade was to begin at ten o'clock.

When they arrived, they found the river full of looming black shapes—the ships of the fleet with all lights out and boiler fires hidden from view. Everyone stood on deck, peering with intense interest into the blackness, knowing well that they were about to see one of the great spectacles of the war. Presently Grant and the other officers went up on the hurricane deck and Annie and Mrs. Grant found a place far out on the guards of the ship.

After a time they saw a gunboat, "blacker than that starless night," Annie said, creeping silently past. "Then another and another, down under the guns." Admiral Porter, on the *Benton,* led the way, the others following swiftly. They passed the first of the Vicksburg batteries without being seen. Then there was a vivid flash and an explosion like a clap of thunder. The alarm had been given and in an instant the shoreline was a blaze of fire. The ironclads, in a long procession, their great guns swung out, replied with broadsides. The artillery duel was at its height, and the ship the ladies were on swayed with the concussions.

The alarm had been given by the Confederate river patrol who then crossed the river and set fire to houses on the Union side. The plan had been well thought out, for the ships were silhouetted against the blazing houses, making them perfect targets. Many were hit, but miraculously, gunboats, transports with coal and hay barges lashed to their sides, rams, one after another, sailed through into safe water beyond reach of the guns, and the women on the command boat, clutching each other and tearful with excitement, saw each send up its signal rocket. Only one, the wooden ship, *Henry Clay,* failed to reach safety. She was struck and set on fire, and as the flames mounted, Annie and Mrs. Grant saw for an instant the flag in a blaze of light. Then the smoke hid it and the *Henry Clay,* drifting helplessly, burned to the water's edge.

Ten boats reached safety that night. Six nights later, six more river steamers ran the blockade with barges in tow. On this night, one ship was sunk, all were damaged and about half the barges were lost. Grant now had a transport and supply fleet south of Vicksburg. He was ready to take his army across the river.

NOTES

1 Mary Ashton Rice Livermore, *My Story of the War* (A. D. Worthington & Company, Hartford, Conn., 1887), p. 302.
2 New York *World.* August 7, 1885.

19

WOMEN OF VICKSBURG

★

CHRONOLOGY

1863

April 17   Col. Benjamin H. Grierson started a cavalry raid near Memphis, arriving at Baton Rouge sixteen days later.

April 29   Admiral Porter attacked Grand Gulf, and, abandoning the attack, ran the fleet past the batteries there that night. Sherman moved troops up the Yazoo, making a feint at Haynes' Bluff which caused consternation in Vicksburg.

April 30   Grant's troops began to land on the east bank of the Mississippi.

May 1   Port Gibson was captured. Sherman withdrew from the Yazoo.

May 3   Admiral Porter took possession of Grand Gulf.

May 7   Grant's army left Grand Gulf and began to live off the country.

May 12   Battle of Raymond.

May 14   Jackson captured.

May 16   Battle of Champion's Hill.

May 17   Action at Big Black River.

May 18   Grant's army arrived before Vicksburg.

May 19   An assault on Vicksburg failed.

May 22   A second assault failed. Beginning of the siege.

July 3   General Pemberton requested terms of surrender.

July 4   Vicksburg surrendered.

★

> *Calm as the second summer which precedes*
> *The first fall of the snow,*
> *In the broad sunlight of heroic deeds,*
> *The city bides the foe.*
>
> —Henry Timrod

EVENTS NOW BEGAN to move rapidly. On April 29th Admiral Porter attacked Grand Gulf with all the fire power he had brought past the Vicksburg batteries. At the same time Sherman set out to make a feint at Haynes' Bluff, which was never intended to be a real attack, but which caused consternation in Vicksburg. Porter's attack on Grand Gulf failed, and he ran his fleet southward, past the batteries there, that night. On the thirtieth, Grant's army began to cross the river. Once there he was, as he himself expressed it, "in the enemy's country, with a vast river and the stronghold of Vicksburg" between him and his base of supply. He was, in fact, in so perilous a position that he carefully neglected to notify General Halleck of his plans until too late for the General-in-Chief to order him back.

One after another, Port Gibson, Grand Gulf, Raymond and then Jackson, the capital of Mississippi, fell as Grant moved rapidly inland, north and east, applying the lesson he had learned and living off the country through which he passed. Sherman, back from the Yazoo, was appalled at the thought of an army without supply lines moving deep into enemy country, though he himself later brought this technique of war to its perfection. The country through which Grant moved was well stocked, however, and the troops helped themselves with a will. There were sharp, staccato encounters with the enemy from May 12th to 17th when Pemberton, in command of the enemy forces, retreated behind the fortifications of Vicksburg.

There was a Union woman in Vicksburg during these anxious days.

We do not know her name, but only the initials—"Mrs. H— L—."
But we know her thoughts, her hope, and the anxiety that grew into fear
and finally into terror, for she left a record of the days which followed.[1]
On the morning of the day Pemberton returned, defeated, to Vicksburg,
Mrs. L and her husband were eating a scanty breakfast (food was even
then scarce in Vicksburg) when one of the people from L's office appeared, saying, "They are upon us, the Yankees will be here by this
evening."

Strange as it may seem, the L's were relieved that the long suspense of
threatened attack would at last yield to action. For months past there
had been a slow but steady bombardment of the city from the gunboats
on the river, which made the streets and houses sufficiently unsafe to
constitute an unremitting nervous strain. In addition to the food shortage,
all sorts of merchandise was in short supply, for all available transportation was in use by the army. The people of Vicksburg were exhausted
before the siege had begun.

By the middle of March the bombardment had done enough damage so
that people were having caves dug in which to take shelter—those famous
caves of Vicksburg, row on row, cut into the face of the clay bluffs. The
digging of them had become an industry. Two cave diggers worked for a
week on one for Mr. and Mrs. L, hollowed out of the hill back of their
house, charging thirty dollars for their work. It was a modest cave, well
supported on wooden props, but when Mrs. L went into it she felt
suffocated by the smell of damp earth and it seemed to her like being shut
in a tomb. Then, after all the trouble, the owner of their house returned
and possessed himself of both house and cave.

On the eighteenth of May, the citizens of Vicksburg saw Grant's army
arrive and begin to deploy into position around the city. A strange sight
it was, for as the army had come through the country, they had brought
with them every sort of conveyance they could find. There was a long
procession of them, wagons, buggies, carts, traps and the gleaming, silver-
mounted open carriages in which the planters' families took the air. They
were all piled high with barrels of flour, corn meal, sides of bacon, hams
and other provender garnered on the route—and the 3,400 men who had
been wounded since the crossing of the river.

Grant hoped to take Vicksburg without a siege, and to this end he attacked the city on the nineteenth of April. The attackers failed to storm
the fortifications, and a second attempt was made on the twenty-second.
The second attack, which also failed, added 2,500 more wounded and the
yellow hospital flags began to fly from tents all around the city. Now the

siege began. Parrot guns, rifle guns and mortars fired into the city day and night. It seemed to give the soldiers pleasure to identify the different kinds of shells as they came over, but to Mrs. L they were all equally terrible. The noise was incessant and nerve-wracking and often punctuated with the rattling crackle of musketry. In mounting terror, Mrs. L wrote in her journal, we are "surrounded by a ring of fire."

Lacking a cave, they spent their nights in the cellar, re-reading Dickens by the faint light of a candle to keep from thinking about the shells bursting above them. The cellar was damp, and all the bedding had to be carried up into the open air each day. There were three silent intervals in every twelve hours during which the shelling stopped—while the gunners were eating their meals, Mrs. L supposed. During these brief periods of safety, the Negro cook prepared the L's meals, which had to be eaten in haste. "I am so tired of corn bread . . . that I eat it with tears in my eyes," Mrs. L wrote. Each day she sent the terrified cook to market with five dollars to buy mule meat, but Mrs. L, who, like everyone else was hungry all the time, could not bring herself to eat it. For supper they ate cold rice, and milk from a neighbor's cow, thankful each day the cow remained alive. Sick soldiers, who had nothing to eat but pea-flour bread and spoiled, greasy bacon, came often to the door begging for the bowl the corn bread had been mixed in. To the leavings in the bowl they would add water and some of the revolting bacon, and cook a sort of soup.

Clothing had grown scarce and precious even before the siege began. One day L bought his wife a pair of tattered shoes for which he had paid ten dollars, but the tops disintegrated at the first wearing. Necessity taught her invention. She made new tops from some old coat sleeves, soaked the soles and stitched them to the cloth tops, and she felt a little pride and a little pleasure in her achievement. Sewing materials were valuable and she had but six pins which she wrapped carefully after each using to keep them from rust.

May became June, the days and nights were hot, and the air in the caves was stifling. The streets were full of rubble from the shattered buildings, but no half-starved animals any longer prowled the ruins for they had all been eaten. Everyone was in tatters, everyone looked exhausted and strained. During the lulls in the bombardment, people came out of the caves to sit in the sunlight and sometimes there was band music and the beating of drums. But when the first shell screamed overhead, everyone dove into the stifling darkness of the caves and the city lay silent under its doom. L's office had long since closed, and in the lulls he sometimes went out to buy newspapers, which were printed on wall-

paper, but there never was any news, though no lack of brave, defiant editorials. Grant, in his headquarters outside the city, received copies of those papers as regularly as though he were on the subscription list.

On the twenty-first of June Mrs. L wrote:

"I had gone upstairs today during the interregnum to enjoy a rest on my bed, and read the reliable items in the 'Citizen,' when a shell burst right outside the window in front of me. Pieces flew in, striking all around me, tearing down masses of plaster that came tumbling over me. When H rushed in I was crawling out of the plaster, digging it out of my eyes and hair. When he picked up a piece as big as a saucer beside my pillow, I realized my narrow escape. The window-frame began to smoke, and we saw the house was on fire. He ran for a hatchet, and I for water, and we put it out. Another shell came crashing near, and I snatched up my comb and brush and ran down here. It has taken all the afternoon to get the plaster out of my hair, for my hands were very shaky."

The 25th was worse:

"A horrible day. The most horrible yet for me, because I've lost my nerve. We were all in the cellar, when a shell came tearing through the roof, burst upstairs, tore up that room, and the pieces coming through both floors down into the cellar, one of them tore open the leg of H's pantaloons. This was tangible proof the cellar was no place of protection from them. On the heels of this came Mr. J to tell us that young Mrs. P had had her thigh-bone crushed. When Martha went for the milk she came back horror-stricken to tell us the black girl there had her arm taken off by a shell. For the first time I quailed. I do not think people who are physically brave deserve much credit for it; it is a matter of nerves. In this way I am constitutionally brave, and seldom think of danger until it is over; and death has not the terrors for me it has for some others. Every night I had lain down expecting death, and every morning rose to the same prospect, without being unnerved. It was for H I trembled. But now I first seemed to realize that something worse than death might come: I might be crippled and not killed. Life, without all one's powers and limbs, was a thought that broke my courage. I said to H, 'You must get me out of this horrible place; I cannot stay; I know I shall be crippled.' Now the regret comes that I lost control, because H is worried, and has lost his composure, because my coolness has broken down."

The army outside the city had settled down to the siege, the soldiers making themselves comfortable in their quarters as troops always will when left in one place for any length of time. There was constant firing

from the Confederate guns, both musketry and heavy artillery, but not enough to be seriously disturbing. Everyone was busy and, in the main, happy, for every man knew that the days of the city were numbered and that it was only necessary to wait.

When the news reached the North that Grant had taken up his position before Vicksburg, visitors flocked to the scene, many women among them, so that the camp had something of a holiday air. The women from the Sanitary and Christian Commissions were there early, among them, Mrs. Hoge, friend of Mary Livermore and, jointly with her, manager of the busy Chicago offices of the Sanitary Commission. Mrs. Hoge was a heavy set woman with a grim face. She was possessed of undoubted executive ability, but she lacked the saving grace of Mary's humor. She had many of the faults to which Walt Whitman objected, including the social worker's tendency to lose sight of individuality in human suffering, never doubting that the garment of good works must be a universal fit. Furthermore, she was overly fond of making sententious speeches to the soldiers, full of noble sentiments, convinced that her words struck chords of deep feeling, in which, it is to be feared, the lady often deceived herself.

She had courage—a fact which she never let anyone overlook—and when she arrived at Vicksburg she went right out to visit the men in the rifle pits. "I found the heat stifling," she said, "and as I bent to avoid the whizzing minnies, and the falling branches of the trees, cut off by an occasional shell, I felt that war was a terrible reality." At about the same time, inside the city, Mrs. L's pen was leaving a record of her terror. "Get me out of this horrible place"—words for the lecture platform and a cry from the heart—the spurious and the real.

In the rifle pits, dodging branches and Minié balls, Mrs. Hoge made her customary speech. "Why boys, the women at home don't think of much else but the soldiers. If they meet to sew, 'tis for you; if they have a good time, 'tis to gather money for the Sanitary Commission; if they meet to pray, 'tis for the soldiers; and even the little children, as they kneel at their mother's knees to lisp their good-night prayers, say, God bless the soldiers." Sentiment was common currency in her day, but one wonders whether the reaction of Grant's tough veterans was quite as she describes it. "Instead of cheers as usual, I could only hear an occasional sob and feel solemn silence."

It is interesting to see the different ways in which the women of the war faced danger. Clara Barton found an exhilaration in it, as though only then she felt herself fully alive. Livermore was calm and ladylike,

and only a little interested in discussing her feelings afterward. Bicker-dyke was always too busy coping with whatever the crisis might be to pay any attention to shells and bullets. Annie Wittenmyer prayed, and it brought her strength.

Annie came to Vicksburg at the beginning of the siege, in charge of hospital supplies, and it was necessary for her to go every day to visit the hospitals around the city. She discovered at once that all of them were within range of the Vicksburg guns and that her whole day's work would have to be under fire. She had been in danger a number of times before, but not for long. The work at Vicksburg was another matter, and in addition to the shells, there were the sharpshooters who would not, it is true, shoot a woman, but as Annie discovered, it was not always possible for them to distinguish—at a distance. This state of affairs did have the advantage of weeding out of the service the curiosity seekers and what Annie calls the "bombastic dress-parade workers," leaving the field to the capable and the serious.

When Annie found that she was afraid, and had spent a night in prayer, she was convinced that no harm could come to her. But she immediately asked the obvious question—why it was that the hospitals were located in the danger zone, and that the danger was real she knew, for shortly after she arrived, one of them received a direct hit. She was told that General Johnston's army was near and that it had been necessary to draw in the lines. She requisitioned an ambulance for use in going from hospital to hospital, but she was sent instead a very fine, silver mounted carriage which had been captured in Jackson. That carriage seemed to draw the enemy fire. The road was just far enough away, so that most of the shots were low in their trajectory and only chipped the wheels. It was not until after the siege, however, that she discovered that the carriage was a special target because the story had gone around Vicksburg that it belonged to an old and infirm general who was using it to inspect his troops.

Her driver, who was terrified, used to drive from place to place at full gallop, and one day, when she went to visit a hospital on the bluff, the trip proved to be so dangerous that the surgeon in charge persuaded her to wait until night before returning. She passed the day helping with the work of the hospital, and then she sat down in a camp chair to rest. There was a patch of weeds growing outside and their tops were moving constantly, as though, she thought, partridges were running through them. She mentioned this to the surgeon who smiled and said, "Why those are bullets."

"Do bullets come as near as that?"

"Oh yes, they are flying around here quite thick."

"Do you consider yourself safe while in this tent?"

"It is considered very safe. The bullets fall a little short, you see."

Nevertheless, three days later a man was killed sitting in the chair where she had sat.

Often, in her drives around Vicksburg, she saw Grant on his little black horse with his thirteen year old son Fred, who acted as his orderly, and they were always much nearer the lines than she. There was a stretch of road Annie liked because there were some trees which hid the carriage from the enemy batteries, giving her a brief sense of security. It was here, however, that a shell struck. Annie heard the scream as it approached, and then, for some time, she knew nothing more.

But if she managed to control her fear of shot and shell, Annie could not conquer her hatred of the little lizards which were everywhere in great numbers. The soldiers had grown used to them though they crawled over their blankets while they slept, and Bickerdyke did not mind them, though they darted across her path at night when she was on her way to some hospital, lantern in one hand and big brown pitcher of lemonade in the other. The lizards were harmless, but to guard against them, Annie and most of the other ladies[2] had the legs of their cot beds set in jars of water and tucked the covers in with care.

Bickerdyke in her shabby boots and her clean, worn calico dress was everywhere, pursuing her self-appointed duties, tongue-lashing everyone who opposed her, spending all day and half the night in the hospital tents. She continued to be a great trial to some of the surgeons, but Sherman liked her and Grant liked her for they recognized in her vigorous motherliness a tonic for the wounded men, and they were beginning to have more than a little respect for her executive ability. She took orders from no one, found work which, in her opinion, needed to be done and attended to it, no matter whose routine she disrupted. One day someone went to General Sherman, burning with indignation about some act of hers. The General said he was sorry but there was nothing he could do. "She ranks me. You must apply to President Lincoln."

As the month of June came to its close, it became evident that Vicksburg could not hold out much longer, and that General Johnston did not have the strength to break through Grant's lines and rescue the city. On the third of July, Mrs. L wrote in her journal, "Today we are down in the cellar again, shells flying as thick as ever; provisions so nearly gone, except a hogshead of sugar, that a few more days will bring us to

starvation indeed. Martha says rats are hanging dressed in the market for sale with mule meat: there is nothing else. The officer at the battery told me he had eaten one yesterday. We have tried to leave this Tophet and failed, and if the siege continues I must summon that higher kind of courage—moral bravery—to subdue my fears of possible mutilation."

That day, Annie Wittenmyer was making her accustomed rounds when abruptly all firing ceased. Silence, and then the small, everyday sounds beginning to re-assert themselves. At first the stillness was almost overwhelming. Then the news swept through the encampment, like the crest of a tidal wave, that white flags had appeared on the fortifications of Vicksburg.

That afternoon Grant and Pemberton met outside of the fortifications, and, walking away from their staffs, they stood talking together in the shade of an oak tree. (Subsequently, the entire tree was carried away in small pieces by the souvenir hunters.) The negotiations for the surrender lasted far into the night, and the surrender ceremonies took place, with some appropriateness, from the Northern point of view, on the next day which was the Fourth of July. Annie and General Stone's wife, both carrying field glasses, went to a height of ground known as Fort Hill from which there would be a good view of all that was taking place. They saw the Union army drawn up in long lines outside the fortifications and presently Pemberton's defeated force marched out of the city and began to stack their arms. There were no cheers. The men of the one army instinctively paid to the men of the other the tribute of silence. Grant, followed by the officers of his staff, rode by the place where the ladies were standing, and the officers gave the two ladies a salute which Annie described as "that peculiar and graceful lifting of the right hand, open, to the full length of the arm, with a graceful wave and touching the cap—a salute never seen in civil life, unless some old soldier forgets himself." With their glasses, the two ladies saw the meeting of Grant and Pemberton. Then the officers of both sides moved forward and there were flashes of sunlight from the swords as they were presented and immediately handed back.

Mrs. L's journal entry for that day reads:

"It is evening. All is still. Silence and night are once more united. I can sit at the table in the parlor and write. Two candles are lighted. I would like a dozen. We have had wheat supper and wheat bread once more. H is leaning back in the rocking chair; he says:
    'G, it seems to me I can hear the silence, and feel it, too. It wraps me like a soft garment; how else can I express this peace?'

"But I must write the history of the last twenty-four hours. About five yesterday afternoon, Mr. J, H's assistant, who, having no wife to keep him in, dodges about at every chance and brings us the news, came to H and said:

'Mr. L, you must both come to our cave tonight. I hear that tonight the shelling is to surpass everything yet. An assault will be made in front and rear. You know we have a double cave; there is room for you in mine, and mother and sister will make a place for Mrs. L. Come right up; the ball will open about seven.'

"We got ready, shut the house, told Martha to go to the church again if she preferred it to the cellar, and walked up to Mr. J's. When supper was eaten, all secure, and the ladies in their cave night toilet, it was just six, and we crossed the street to the cave opposite. As I crossed, a mighty shell flew screaming right over my head. It was the last thrown into Vicksburg. We lay on our pallets waiting for the expected roar, but no sound came except the chatter from neighboring caves, and at last we dropped asleep. I woke at dawn stiff. A draft from the funnel-shaped opening had been blowing on me all night. Every one was expressing surprise at the quiet. We started for home and met the editor of the "Daily Citizen." H said: 'This is strangely quiet, Mr. L.'

'Ah, sir,' shaking his head gloomily, 'I'm afraid the last shell has been thrown into Vicksburg.'

'Why do you fear so?'

'It is surrender. At six last evening a man went down to the river and blew a truce signal; the shelling stopped at once.' "

The next day, July 5th, Annie Wittenmyer went into the damaged city and at once to the hospitals, though it seemed to her that the whole city might be called one vast hospital. She had received from Mr. Yeatman, President of the Western Sanitary Commission, a large shipment of hospital supplies, in anticipation of the surrender, to be used for the relief of the Confederate hospitals of Vicksburg. These she immediately dispensed while the Army issued rations to the starving citizens.

Grant assigned a house to Annie, and one day, shortly after the surrender, when she was at headquarters, he asked her if she was comfortable there. She said that she was exceedingly comfortable, for though the house had been badly battered by shells and the stairs to the dining room had been shot away, it was a vast improvement on a tent. The slaves of the former owner were still there, and Annie went on to say what good servants they were, especially the cook, who prepared really

excellent meals. General McPherson had been listening to this and he said, "Why don't you ask us up to test her cooking?"

When Annie went home with the news that Generals Grant and Mc-Pherson would be there to dine next day at one, Mrs. Stone, who shared the house, was filled with consternation. There was not, she said, one decent tablecloth, or two dishes that matched. "And how," she wanted to know, "are they to walk up that inclined plane on the boards?"

Annie replied that since they themselves managed it three times a day, she thought the Generals could make out, and went off to interview Aunt Dinah, the cook. The whole household exploded into activity, a grin on every Negro face, and Aunt Dinah announced that, "I'll hab de tablecloth so slick a gnat's heel would fly up on it." At the prospect of a party, Mrs. Stone and Annie felt light-hearted and gay, and a little surprised at feeling so.

The Generals, in their best uniforms, arrived, and there were eager black faces peering out from every corner. The ladies and their guests went up to dinner, Annie on General Grant's arm and Mrs. Stone on the arm of tall, handsome General McPherson. General Stone who had gone ahead, helped them up the steeply-sloping planks. Before sitting down, the men spent some time examining the damage to the room, trying to decide from what battery the shell had come and finally concluding that it must have been fired by one of Admiral Porter's gunboats. Everyone laughed a great deal and ate a great deal, and Aunt Dinah kept the pantry door ajar so that she could hear them praise her food. Afterwards, she summed it all up. "Oh, Laws a massa, didn't dey praise my cooken! I never felt so big in mah life. Seems to me I'se one of the biggest cooks in the world."

General McPherson was killed by a sharpshooter's bullet near Atlanta, and long years later Annie dined with Grant in the White House.

NOTES

A Woman's Diary of the Siege of Vicksburg. Under Fire from the Gun-boats. (Century Illustrated Magazine, VIII, 1885.)
Some other women present at the siege of Vicksburg or working on the hospital boats in the river were, Mrs. Henrietta L. Colt, Anna Clapp, Mrs. O. E. Hosmer, Hattie Wiswall, Ruth Sinnotte and Lucy L. C. Kaiser. Lucy had received a new commission from Miss Dix to replace the one lost in the trunk she took to the battle of Shiloh. At Vicksburg, she emerged briefly from obscurity when she "sassed" a party of high officers which included General Grant. Afterward, this scrawny little parrot of a woman preened herself in pride over this occurrence.

20

WHERE THE GRAPES OF WRATH ARE STORED

★

CHRONOLOGY

1863

June 3   General Lee left his position on the Rappahannock and started north.

June 9   Defeat of J. E. B. Stuart's cavalry at Brandy Station, Virginia.

June 11   Confederate forces began to cross the Potomac.

June 13   General Ewell reached Winchester.

June 14   The Army of the Potomac left the vicinity of Fredericksburg. Major General Early attacked Winchester, forcing Union General Milroy to retreat.

June 15   Lincoln called on Pennsylvania and contiguous states to supply 120,000 men. About 50,000 responded.

June 17   Federal garrison at Harper's Ferry removed to Maryland Heights, leaving the Shenandoah without Union troops.

June 24   Chambersburg, Pennsylvania, occupied by General Ewell. Hooker's army began to cross the Potomac at Edward's Ferry.

June 26   General Early reached Gettysburg. Rear guard of Hooker's army crossed the Potomac.

June 27   General Hooker resigned. York, Pennsylvania, surrendered to General Early.

June 28   Lincoln appointed George Gordon Meade commander of the
Army of the Potomac. J. E. B. Stuart captured a Federal
wagon train at Rockville, delaying his advance. General Early was
in Wrightsville, Pennsylvania. Jenkin's cavalry reached Mechanicsburg. The advance of Ewell's corps reached the heights
across the river from Harrisburg.

★

> *Mine eyes have seen the glory of the coming of the Lord;*
> *He is trampling out the vintage where the grapes of*
> *wrath are stored;*
> *He hath loosed the fateful lightning of His terrible*
> *swift sword;*
> *His truth is marching on.*
>   —Julia Ward Howe

WHILE GENERAL ROSECRANS was still biding his time in his spotless
camp at Murfreesboro, and Grant was waiting for Vicksburg to fall into
his hands, Lee started on a spectacular second invasion of the North.
He left his position on the Rappahannock on June 3rd, shifting some of
his forces northward to the Shenandoah Valley, which was like a broad
highway, sheltered by mountain walls on either side. Jeb Stuart, Lee's
famous cavalry commander, whose duty it was to keep Lee informed of
the movements of the enemy, was sent out by another route. At Brandy
Station he had a sharp clash with the Union forces (which toned down
some of the cocksureness the Confederate cavalry had acquired) and
rode off to a series of storybook adventures.

Ewell, the commander of Lee's Second Corps, reached the Shenandoah Valley on June 13th, and the rapidity of his advance threw Pennsylvania into a state of panic alarm. His troops continued to roll along,
sweeping everything before them, until, on the seventeenth, when the
Federals evacuated Harper's Ferry, the Valley was cleared of Union
troops.

On June 24th, Chambersburg fell to the Confederate advance. Lee
was now far into Northern territory, with attenuated supply lines, living
largely off the country. This was a rich land, well stocked with fat
cattle, geese and chickens. Smoke houses were filled with hams, corn

cribs were bursting with last year's golden grain. There was everything, in fact, that foraging soldiers could desire, but one of the inexorable conditions attached to living off the country is that the army cannot tarry, but must move constantly to renew its supplies. The next objective was Harrisburg, the capital city, on the far bank of the broad Susquehanna River. Meanwhile, Stuart and his men were riding around, enjoying themselves, tiring their horses, but not keeping Lee informed of the whereabouts of the Union army.

The Union army, still under the command of Hooker, who was mistrusted by his own officers and the War Department, had started to move from the vicinity of Fredericksburg. The abandonment of a base by a great army cannot be carried out without infinite complications, and in the neighborhood of Fredericksburg there were 9,000 wounded who could not be left behind. Letterman began to evacuate the hospitals, the tents and all the supplies on the twelfth of June. The wounded were to be sent by train to Washington and Alexandria, and those who were seriously ill had to be carried on their cots to the station, a distance of over a mile. By the evening of the fourteenth, the evacuation was complete.

While Lee's forces were sweeping through Maryland and Pennsylvania without any serious opposition, Hooker moved slowly, like a rheumatic old dog-of-war, in spite of repeated appeals from Lincoln to strike at Lee's army, which was stretched out thinly for a distance of more than seventy miles. Hooker was thinking only of falling back to form a line of defense in front of Washington. Then, as though awaking suddenly from sleep, he jerked his army into motion on the night of the twenty-fifth, got it across the Potomac, and on the twenty-sixth, made one of the most rapid marches of the war to Fairfax. He was harboring notions of harassing Lee's rear, though Lincoln and Halleck had left him in no doubt of their desire for direct and positive action, and when this scheme of his was vetoed, he lost his temper and resigned.

That happened on the twenty-seventh, when the Confederate cavalry was nearing Harrisburg. About four in the morning of June 28th, General Hardie, chief of staff to Secretary of War Stanton, appeared at the headquarters of General Meade and woke the General from a sound sleep. Meade, trying to shake himself awake, thought he was being put under arrest, but he was not at all pleased to discover that the real purpose of Hardie's nocturnal visit was to break the news to him that he had been chosen to supersede Hooker in the command of the Army of the Potomac.

There is little wonder that Meade was not anxious to accept the honor being thrust upon him. He had scant knowledge of Lee's movements or intentions, or even of the disposition of the forces he was to command. There was no coherent plan for him to follow, and he was being asked to take command at one of the most crucial times of the war. Hardie, after much argument, persuaded him, however, and as dawn was breaking, the two Generals mounted and rode away to notify Hooker that he had been relieved.

On that same day, Lee learned for the first time both the whereabouts of the Union Army and that it was under a new command. One of Longstreet's scouts had come in with the news, for Stuart, who was supposed to be "the eyes and ears" of the Army, was far away at Rockville, twelve miles from Washington. He had been ordered to go to Gettysburg with all haste, but at Rockville he met a Federal train of 150 wagons, a juicy prize for the cavalry, which he could not resist. A brief skirmish resulted in the capture of 125 of them, which he took along with him. He headed for his rendezvous, men and horses fatigued, slowed to the pace of the heavily-loaded wagons, so hampered by these and other encumbrances that he arrived at Gettysburg after the battle had begun. There are many who believe that Stuart lost the battle of Gettysburg that day at Rockville, and that had he arrived on time, with his command unwearied, he could have turned the tide of battle. ✓

Events were crowding fast toward the climax. While the cavalry was chasing the wildly swaying wagons at Rockville, other Confederate cavalry had ridden into Mechanicsburg and elements of Ewell's corps were gazing at Harrisburg from across the broad Susquehanna. On the thirtieth Lee rode out of Chambersburg on his famous horse, Traveller, and headed for Gettysburg on which all the elements of the Confederate Army were now converging.

A Union cavalry division, under General John Buford, was already there. Buford knew the Confederates were in the neighborhood, and on the thirtieth he had driven away a detachment of troops that had been sent to Gettysburg to capture shoes, of which the Confederate Army was always in need. The next morning, Buford's pickets, stationed on the Chambersburg Turnpike, about a mile and a half west of Gettysburg, saw the head of a Confederate infantry column approaching.

Buford, like General Nathan Bedford Forrest, was a commander with some original ideas about the use of cavalry which had brought him fame. He dismounted his men, every fourth man being detailed to hold the horses, brought up his artillery and prepared to meet the infantry on its

own terms, while couriers, riding hard, went off to notify Meade. The engagement opened with long-range firing by the artillery, and the battle of Gettysburg, which has been called one of the truly decisive battles of history, had begun.

For some time after the first encounter, Lee's forces were not sure that they were confronted by anything more formidable than some detached units of Meade's army, or local home guards, and then out of the past comes the voice of an excited Confederate soldier, so clear, so human, that it must have been real: "Hell, that ain't no milishy—that's the Army of the Potomac!"

A short distance west of the village of Gettysburg, on the Chambersburg Pike, there was a school for girls, known as the Oakridge Seminary, in charge of a Miss Carrie Sheads. The school, which still stands, was in session and there was great excitement among the girls when some of Buford's cavalry came to camp close by. Miss Sheads was not alarmed by the arrival of the troops. Confederates had been in the neighborhood, but no one was really afraid of them and when the Union cavalry arrived, little girls in their best dresses stood on the street corners singing patriotic songs to the passing cavalry, or tossed them little bouquets of garden flowers to wear in the bands of their hats.

Miss Sheads had heard rumors of the advance of Lee's army, but the presence of Union troops made everyone feel secure. The village seems not to have realized what was happening elsewhere. A woman had attempted to go through the advancing Rebel army to warn the village, but she was detained for a time by the invaders.[1] Miss Sheads thought it would be foolish to close the school, but she planned a holiday for the girls the next day so that they could go to see the cavalry camp. She and her school would, in a matter of hours, be in the midst of some of the fiercest fighting of the war.

She awoke to the sound of firing. At first the shots were distant and infrequent, but before she could have formed any clear idea of what was happening, she heard the sharp crack of guns nearby. Perhaps, if there were any girls in the school that morning, Miss Carrie Sheads stood guard over them against a danger she was powerless to avert. Perhaps she peered cautiously from a window and saw the moving lines of blue and gray. She had little time to be afraid, however, for soon the house was full of wounded men, and the schoolteacher found herself matron of a field hospital in the front line of battle.

There was hand-to-hand fighting through the grounds of the school— bitter, desperate fighting of the sort which left no doubt in the mind of

anyone who saw it, that no compromise between the two contestants was possible, and that killing and hatred would only stop when one side had been fought to a finish. The troops which had come to Buford's relief were driven back, and the retreat trapped Colonel John Wheelock of the 97th New York Infantry in the dooryard of the school. When he saw that he and some others were surrounded by the Confederate advance, he ran up the school steps and waved his handkerchief as a sign of surrender. The white handkerchief was not seen, or for some reason not understood, and the Confederates continued to fire on the trapped Union soldiers.

The Colonel opened the door and shouted for someone to bring him a white tablecloth and it was Miss Carrie herself who came with one in her hands. The Colonel waved it frantically and the firing ceased. Then the Colonel went inside and down into the cellar, for shells and round-shot were striking the house. A number of people were already there— Miss Carrie, her father, and some Union soldiers.

Presently a Confederate officer appeared and told them they were all prisoners, demanding the Colonel's sword as a token of surrender. Rather than give up his sword to the enemy the Colonel said he would break it in two, and he exerted all his strength on it, but the sword would not break. The Confederate officer pointed his revolver at the Colonel and told him to hand over the sword or he would be shot.

The scene that followed rings false to modern ears, but this was an age in which men held romantic ideals dear, and were touchingly willing to die for them. The Colonel, then, drew himself up proudly, tore open the front of his uniform, baring his breast, and told the Rebel officer to shoot, for he would rather die than surrender his sword to a traitor. At that, Miss Carrie's father stepped between the two men and begged them both to be sensible. The Confederate officer pushed him roughly aside and leveled his revolver at the Colonel. Miss Carrie took her father's place, making a shield of herself in front of the Colonel, and pleaded with the Rebel officer not to shoot down a defenseless man. Then she asked the Colonel to give up his sword peaceably, but he replied: "This sword was given me by my friends for meritorious conduct, and I promised to guard it sacredly, and never surrender or disgrace it; and I never will while I live."

The next move came with perfect theatrical timing. That moment, some other prisoners came into the cellar and this drew the Confederate officer's attention away from the Colonel. Miss Carrie at once took the sword, belt and all, and hid it in the folds of her dress (which she could

have done easily for the regulation infantry sword was only a little more than thirty-five inches long). With the sword in safekeeping, the Colonel had no objection to being made a prisoner, and when the Confederate officer returned, he surrendered himself, explaining that one of his men had taken the sword and escaped. The story has an appropriate ending, for five days later the Colonel escaped and returned to retrieve his sword from Carrie.[2]

The Oakridge Seminary was struck by artillery fire more than sixty times during the battle and two shells went completely through the building. Miss Carrie continued to nurse the wounded who had been carried into the school until the three days of battle had ended, and with the silencing of the guns she is lost to sight.

During the first day of battle, Meade, not yet wholly convinced that the inevitable clash of the two armies should take place at this time or in this location was, nevertheless, moving up his troops. They were no longer the green, undisciplined, fantastically garbed troops of former days, but uniformed veterans, tough, self-confident, capable of surviving forced marches which would have been impossible for the three-months volunteers, able to look after themselves in battle. There were women with the army, officers' wives for the most part, but some wives of enlisted men also, and, in a sense, some of them were veterans too, having traveled with the army through many vicissitudes.

Arabella Barlow was one of these veteran Army wives. Arabella was young, pretty, and when the war broke out, very much in love with a young lawyer named Francis C. Barlow. He was a dark-eyed, thin, intensely serious young man for whom life had no lighter side. He enlisted as a private four days after Lincoln's first call for troops and he married the pretty Arabella the next day. Young Mrs. Barlow stayed as close to the army as she could, not minding the hardships because she was happy.

By the time Lee and McClellan fought at Antietam, Barlow was a Colonel. He distinguished himself for bravery on the field, and Arabella nursed him for long weeks until he was well again. In recognition of his gallantry, he was made a Brigadier General—the "boy general," he was called by those who resented both his youth and his capability. As the General's lady, Arabella was charming and always busy with good works, for it was part of the pattern for an army wife in camp to occupy herself with social service activities of one sort or another. In this Arabella, who liked people and thinking up new projects, was something of a leader.

Barlow was in command of a division which wore the crescent moon insignia of the Eleventh Corps on its sleeves, and when the two armies collided at Gettysburg, he and his men were bivouacked at Marsh Creek, about eight miles from the village. Arabella was with him there. For reasons which are not clear, the Eleventh Corps was not sent into the fight until after one P.M., when it came swinging up the famous Emmitsburg Pike, over boot tops in mud, but making good time of it nevertheless. Fighting was in progress in the west, and the people of Gettysburg had, for the most part, taken to their cellars, though others had fled the village in search of a place out of reach of the artillery fire. Somewhere near the village, the men of Barlow's division must have seen a woman and two little girls, and the little girls were having a hard time in the deep mud. They were going to a house owned by some people named Weikert, at the foot of a hill called Little Round Top, which was very nearly the worst place for them to go, but what happened to them there belongs to the story of the next day's battle.

Barlow and his men were involved in heavy fighting and forced to retreat toward Cemetery Ridge. Through the dust and smoke of the battle, Confederate General John B. Gordon saw Barlow, sword in hand, trying to rally his men. Later, in the Confederate advance, Gordon came to the place where he had seen Barlow and found him there wounded, lying on the ground with the dead around him. Gordon reined in his horse and dismounted. He lifted Barlow's head and gave him water from his canteen, asking the young man his name and if he thought he was badly wounded.

Barlow had been shot by a Minié[3] ball which had gone through his chest and come out near his spine, paralyzing his arms and legs, and he told Gordon he was certain he had received a mortal wound. Gordon felt sure this was true. He called some soldiers, ordered Barlow put on a litter and himself followed to the rear, where he had the litter set down in the shade of some trees. Barlow asked Gordon to take out of his pocket a package of letters from his wife, which he always carried with him, and to destroy them. One version of the story is that Barlow asked Gordon to read the last of the letters aloud to him, and this the General did. Then Barlow asked Gordon if he should live to the end of the war and should ever meet his wife, to tell her that he thought of her as he was dying, to assure her that he had died doing his duty, and that he was willing to give his life for his country. The speech was, in a way, a formula which every dying man, from private to general, tried to make if death gave him time but the words were not the less sincere

because of that. And having spoken them, the dying Barlow added one more thing. Tell her, he said to Gordon, that his deepest regret was not to see her face once more. The two Generals talked a little longer. Barlow told Gordon that his wife was not far away, and Gordon was touched, because his own wife had also followed him to war. Then Gordon went away, reluctantly, for he had liked the enemy stranger.

The memory of young Barlow stayed with him all that day and when, at evening, the fighting ended, Gordon sent out a flag-of-truce with a message for Arabella and a safe conduct through the lines. The picture must have had the dramatic story-quality beloved of painters of the day—twilight, the big white flag fluttering from its short pole, the battle-soiled soldiers, and Arabella in her wide skirt, crossing the open fields. She brought her husband back to the Union lines, though with some difficulty, and he recovered.

Some time later, Barlow read in the newspaper of the death in battle of John Gordon, not knowing that it was a relative with the same name as the man who had rescued him at Gettysburg. So it was that each thought the other dead until they met by chance at a Washington dinner party fifteen years later. The friendship which had begun in the liking each had taken for the other during the battle, lasted the rest of their lives.[4]

One of the little girls whom Barlow's men had met on their way to join the battle was named Tillie Pierce.[5] When the shells began to fall in Gettysburg, Tillie's mother had sent her away from the village in the care of a neighbor woman who was taking her own little girl to a place of safety. Until some of the houses were struck by shells, Tillie had enjoyed herself. She loved the excitement of cavalry riding through the town, and she made many little bouquets to give to the men, but she forgot all about them in her eagerness to run out of doors and join the other little girls who were singing patriotic songs on the street corners.

That had been in the early morning of the first day of battle, but by mid-afternoon she was well on her way out of town, nearly up to her knees in mud and tired out by the struggle of walking. The neighbor woman, whose skirt was heavy with mud and water, decided they all must rest and she led them to a farmhouse on the Taneytown Road— the only house nearby. It was a small white building, a story-and-a-half high, with low beamed ceilings and a large fireplace where the cooking was done. The little house now has a sign beside the picket fence identifying it as General Meade's headquarters, but when Tillie was there,

Meade had not yet arrived, though there were many soldiers on the roads nearby.

One of the soldiers, who was driving an empty wagon to the rear, offered the three refugees a ride and they were glad to accept. The Weikert house, where they were going, was no more than two miles or a little more away, but Tillie remembered the discomfort of that ride to the end of her days, for the wagon had no springs and there were large stones under the mud of the road. Soldiers on foot, mounted officers, teams of horses drawing guns, all the paraphernalia of battle, went past them as they jolted along. They were near the Weikert house when a gun caisson not far from them which was filled with ammunition blew up, wounding and blinding the driver. Soldiers carried him into the Weikert house, to an upstairs room, wrapped his burned body in cotton and left him there.

The Weikert house looks today much as it did then. It is a pleasant two-story house of gray stone with white trim, standing at an angle to the road. There is a small white barn, a well with a pump and a picket fence running down to the road. At the bottom of the field in front of the house is a grove of trees and a spring with a ribbon of bright green winding away into the underbrush, and across the road rises the steep wooded slope of Little Round Top.

Tillie had no time to be frightened by the blowing up of the caisson. Someone put a pail in her hand and sent her to the spring to carry water to the troops passing by on the road. She carried so many pails full that after a time the spring ran dry and she had to pump water out of the well. That would be hard work for a little girl, but the farmhouse yard must have been filled with soldiers most of the time, and no doubt they helped her and were kind to her, teased her and made much of her, in the way soldiers treat children in every war everywhere.

Some of the events of these days may not have remained in Tillie's memory in the precise order in which they happened. Indeed, it would be surprising if they had, for time is strangely distorted during battle, and that would be as true for the little girl carrying the pail as for the soldier firing his gun. At some time, soldiers bringing wounded men began coming into the yard and leaving their burdens in the barn. Tillie went to look at them (that day or the next) and from them she learned what may have been her first lesson in maturity, for though she had looked at the soldier blinded in the explosion of the caisson with the uncomprehending curiosity of childhood, the sight of the men in the barn suddenly made suffering real to her, and she wept.

It must have been on the second day of the fighting, while Tillie was

going back and forth with her pail, that a wagon stopped by the fence and unloaded a pile of crude, unpainted coffins, which is astonishing, for all wagons carrying supplies not essential to the fighting had been ordered far to the rear. What the coffins did signify was that someone somewhere had designated the farmhouse as a field hospital and it was already being operated as one before anybody in the house quite knew what was happening.

On one of her trips to the road—which must still have been closely packed with moving troops—Tillie saw a soldier crawling on hands and knees in the mud and an officer, yelling at him to stand up and march, struck him again and again with the flat side of his sword. After a little of this, it became evident to the officer that the man he was beating could not rise, and he went away, leaving the soldier in the mud. When the officer had gone, some soldiers who had been standing by picked up the beaten man and carried him into the house. Tillie, watching this scene, heard them say that the sick soldier had sunstroke. She could see how angry the others were and she heard them say that they would "mark" the officer for what he had done. No one needed to tell her that they meant that when they went into battle, they would shoot the officer. And she knew, without anyone telling her, that it would not be the first time in the war that such a thing had happened.

Later on, three officers rode up on fine horses and one of them asked Tillie for a drink of water. She filled a tin cup and reached it up to him, and taking it, he smiled down at her. He had a serious expression even when he smiled, and he seemed preoccupied, as though only the shell of him was there, sitting on a fine horse while in his mind he was active at some other place. Then Tillie realized that the troops in the road were standing still and cheering, and presently someone told her that the officer to whom she had given the cup of water was General Meade.

The sound of firing had been coming closer and more wounded men were brought in. The Weikert farm had become a hub of activity and Tillie was feeling the way men do in battle, that things occurred without her being aware that they were happening, and she was too busy to expend thought or emotion on them. There were dead men in the yard and in the field beyond, and she did not know when they had fallen. The road was empty and little puffs of dust arose now and then, seemingly without cause. She scarcely gave thought to them even when she heard the sharp *ping* the bullets made when they struck something hard. Tillie went into the house and found that it was filled with the warm smell of baking bread. There were many women in the kitchen, making the bread

in batches for the wounded soldiers. The wood in the big black stove was crackling and the kitchen was stifling hot.

The cannonading had been growing louder, shaking the house with each heavy boom, and the women were shouting to make themselves heard. Then, suddenly, everyone in the kitchen was seized by fright, much as chickens in a yard are sometimes all frightened at once, in an instant. The women and children, all of them, ran out of the house and away across the fields, leaving the bread in the oven. Tillie ran too, slipping and stumbling over the hummocks in the grass. They were all running toward a house a half mile away, but when they got there, the house seemed strange and unsafe and, compelled by their common fear, they all ran back again, across the fields into the kitchen. Then they began to think like individuals again and someone remembered the bread, which should have been burned black. The soldiers, it seemed, had taken it out of the oven, and the women shouted at each other about how thankful they were. Then they set about baking more bread, while the little house trembled to the guns.

After a while the cannonading seemed to come closer and the women took fright again, leaving their work and going into the front room, Tillie with them. They stood in a group, close together, listening, and there came a terrific crash which seemed to be close outside the house. In the thick silence which followed, there was another sound, a thud, on the other side of the closed door to the hall. After a minute or two, someone got up the courage to go and see what it was, and found the blinded soldier lying on the hall floor. He had been forgotten and left alone upstairs. The shell striking outside had terrified him, he had groped his way to the steep stairs, and fallen. Everyone was filled with pity for him. He was carried upstairs and put to bed again, but after that someone stayed with him.

By evening, when the fighting slackened, the house and yard, as well as the barn, were filled with wounded men. Surgeons had appeared, and had taken charge of the premises as a field hospital. As darkness came, the guns fell silent, and Tillie and everyone else helped with the wounded. Outside, the night was still, but there must have been a sense of hordes of men filling the countryside, a feeling of the woods and fields being populous. In the house there were sounds of women's quick steps on the board floors, and the groans of the wounded. Tillie wandered into a room and found a soldier, with a burning candle in his hand sitting on the floor beside a wounded officer. When the soldier saw the little girl,

he asked her if she would take his place and hold the candle for a while, so she took it from him and sat down.

She asked the officer if he were badly wounded and he said, "Yes, pretty badly." The scene is somehow a moving one. The silence of the guns, and summer insects singing in the night. The still, stifling heat, heavy with impending rain, the thick, sweetish smell of blood, and the little girl sitting beside the prostrate officer with the candle in her hand. She asked him if he suffered much, and he said, "Yes, I do now, but I hope I will be better in the morning." He asked her if she would come to see him then and made her promise him. Presently the soldier returned, and Tillie got up and gave him the candle. Then she went away, and as she left the room, it seemed to her that the wounded officer was looking after her.

The next morning she went back to keep her promise. She found the officer, but there was no one with him. She went up to him and bent over him and saw that he was dead. That is the story of the death of General Weed as Tillie remembered it years later.[6]

This day, the battle did not threaten the house, or did not seem to do so quite so much, and the wounded kept everyone busy. The yard was full of them, waiting their turns at the operating tables. These tables were benches and the surgeons were working with a kind of desperate intentness, but here, as in every other field hospital, they could not begin to look after all who needed their care. (Five days later, wounded men still waited their turn at those bloody tables and many surgeons had broken down under the strain.)

Tillie went to a window and looked out on the scene in the yard. She never forgot a detail of that scene. There was a pile of arms and legs by the roadway, higher than the fence. Men lay, or sat slumped over with their backs against the fence, or crawled on all fours like weak animals. There were the surgeons' bent backs and the women kneeling to give a drink of water, their calico skirts puffing out around them. One of the operating benches was close to Tillie's window and Tillie watched a surgeon holding a sawed-off cattle horn over the wounded man's face. She was too exhausted to be curious, but after a while it came to her that the horn had a piece of rag or sponge inside and that the surgeon was using it to chloroform the wounded man.

When the battle was over, Tillie and the neighbor woman and her daughter set out for home, but the country was changed and nothing in it was familiar. The strangeness frightened her. There were the dead men lying in the fields, and they had the look of those who have newly died

in battle, of having grown too big for the clothes they were wearing. The smell of these men and of their dead horses was like a fog over the fields.

The town seemed unfamiliar also, the houses damaged by shellfire and branches of the trees shot away. Tillie's own house did not seem like the same house she had left. Tillie rushed in, calling for her mother, running toward her, and then it appeared that Tillie too had changed, for during a long moment her mother did not know who she was.

NOTES

[1] Sophronia E. Bucklin, *In Hospital and Camp* (John E. Potter & Co., Philadelphia, 1869).

[2] This incident is told by J. Warren Gilbert in a publication called *The Blue and the Gray*.

[3] The Minié ball derived its name from a French Captain Minié who invented it.

[4] Brigadier General John B. Gordon, *Reminiscences of the Civil War* (Chas. Scribner's Sons, New York, 1903).

[5] Tillie Pierce Alleman, *At Gettysburg* (W. Lake Bozland, New York, 1889).

[6] General Weed, Commander of the 3rd Brigade, 2nd Division, 5th Corps, was wounded on Little Round Top. He lived only about an hour or two after reaching the Weikert house. His body was carried to the porch and placed with the bodies of Colonel O'Rourke and Lieutenant Hazlitt, who were killed in the fighting for Little Round Top and it was probably here that Tillie found him in the morning.

21

THE LAST FULL MEASURE

★

CHRONOLOGY

1863

July 1   The battle of Gettysburg began in the early morning with an engagement of Buford's and Pettigrew's forces. General Reynolds killed. Heavy fighting. Union forces retired to Cemetery Hill. The town was in Confederate hands. Lee in control of all roads but the Emmitsburg, Taneytown and Baltimore Turnpikes.

July 2   Fighting in the Peach Orchard and the Wheat Field. Culp's Hill and the Round Tops occupied by Union forces.

July 3   Artillery duel. Pickett's charge repulsed.

July 4   Confederates remained in the neighborhood.

July 5   Union forces alone on the field.

July 7   Lee's army reached the Hagerstown, Williamsport area.

July 13   Lee's army retreated across the Potomac to safety.

July 13–16 New York draft riots.

★

It is for us the living, rather, to be dedicated
here to the unfinished work for which they who
fought here have thus far so nobly advanced.
—Abraham Lincoln

No one knows with any certainty how many women were killed in the battle of Gettysburg. There are tales of women in the ranks, on both sides, who lost their lives fighting, but the probability is they are not true. The one woman known beyond doubt to have been killed did not die with a gun in her hands. Her name was Jennie Wade, and she lived in the village with her mother and a married sister. When the fighting swept through the village, the three women could not escape because the married daughter, Mrs. McClelland, had just given birth to a baby.

The house was small, as were most of the houses in the neighborhood. The bed where the young mother lay with her baby was in the kitchen where Jennie was baking bread to give to the soldiers. The house was struck by a shell which came through the wall of the kitchen and broke off one of the posts of the bed. Jennie and her mother, more afraid, it seems, for the sick girl than for themselves, carried a large rocking chair down to the cellar, then they carried Mrs. McClelland and her baby down and put her into the chair with the baby in her arms.

A great many other people had gone down into their cellars when the shelling began, and some of them were hiding Union soldiers. Some of the cellars had a foot or two of water in them and the people sat on the tops of barrels, not daring to light a candle for fear they would be discovered. Mrs. Wade stayed with her older daughter, but Jennie went back to the kitchen to see about the bread, which had risen and was ready to knead.

Jennie's hands were plunged in the spongy mess of dough when a shot came into the kitchen. Down in the cellar, Mrs. Wade heard a noise which alarmed her, and she ran upstairs to see what had happened. She found Jennie on the floor by the kneading tray, dead.

Shock, lifelong habit, bravery perhaps, and a mass of unidentifiable memories and instincts are the ingredients of people's actions in times of danger, and no one can predict what sort of behavior the mixture will produce. Jennie's mother went on with Jennie's work and finished the breadbaking with Jennie lying dead on the floor beside her. That night some soldiers buried Jennie, in her dirty calico dress, with the dough still clinging to her fingers, her body wrapped in a flag. They felt the dough was honorable, no doubt, like the black smudges of gunpowder

on the face of a soldier dead in battle. Jennie lies on Cemetery Hill, and an anonymous poet wrote a long poem about her, which begins:

> Oh, Jenny Wade! are you still here?
> The rebel troops are pressing near,
> And our brave soldiers wait the din
> That their assault will usher in.
> 'Tis said our ranks already thin,
> For sleeping on those heights are men
> No bugle call will wake again.[1]

The battle ended on the third day in an undisputed victory for the Union troops. There were, taking both sides together, over 43,000 killed, wounded and missing out of an approximate 170,000 officers and men engaged. The Federal wounded amounted to nearly 14,500, and in addition many Confederate wounded were left on the field to tax still further the Union hospital facilities. Surgeon Letterman had been seriously handicapped in his preparation for the battle by two orders of June 19th and July 1st which required wagons transporting medical supplies to resume their traditional place at the rear of the advancing columns. As a consequence supplies were not on the field when they were needed, and that situation, added to the unprecedented number of wounded, meant that some were left on the field longer than should have been necessary.

News of the battle went to Washington, Philadelphia, and Baltimore promptly, so that preparations were begun in those places to receive the wounded while the fighting was still in progress. It then appeared that the single track railroad to Gettysburg was a serious bottleneck. Stations along the route were swamped with more freight and impatient passengers than the road could possibly cope with. There was a shortage of every kind of rolling stock. In fact, all the classic troubles of a railroad in wartime beset this one. Most of the time, only two unscheduled trains a day pulled into Gettysburg, and the same weary trains, at some unspecified time, rattled back again, and the trip to Baltimore which normally was made in eight hours, now took twenty-four.

As soon as news of the battle reached the big cities, hundreds of people tried to go to the battlefield. There were pathetic groups going to search for their dead or wounded, surgeons, volunteer and otherwise, Sisters of Charity (who did excellent work there), and a mass of women who were field workers for the Army Nursing Corps, Sanitary or Christian Commissions, the Germantown Field Hospital Association, or some

other organization. In addition, there were many women who went in groups, or singly, or in the company of some doctor, with no plan but to find useful work when they arrived on the field.

The day had long since passed when women tried to take trunks to battle, but all the organizations and even the volunteers attempted to bring along crates of food and hospital supplies, and as most of the people refused to let their property out of their sight, emotional scenes were constantly occurring. As long after the battle as July 14th, Mrs. Edmund Souder and her husband, volunteer workers, had to wait at Hanover Junction, about twenty-five miles from the battlefield, for eight hours in the steaming heat. Four of those hours were spent sitting in a railroad car, like an oven, which they did not dare to leave. Their companions, some sisters and a priest, were near to fainting from the heat of their heavy robes. Even so, the Souders counted themselves lucky, for up to that time most of the women taking the overnight trip to Gettysburg had been forced to sleep in open boxcars, which were literally boxes on wheels open to the sky on top.

In Gettysburg, the travelers slept wherever they could. Most of the villagers were making a good thing out of renting rooms and some, like Mrs. Souder, camped out on the parlor floor of the inn, a carpet bag for a pillow, in company with as many prostrate forms as the room would hold.

Meanwhile, Secretary Stanton and Miss Dix were doing everything they could to keep volunteer women out of the battle area. An exception had to be made for the ladies of the two Commissions, and Stanton was always glad to issue passes to the Sisters of Charity, whose work he admired. It was the unauthorized volunteers, who crowded the hospital tents, got in the surgeons' way but did no real work, whom he determined to exclude. An order was issued to honor no passes not issued by himself, but the field commanders continued to do pretty much as they chose, and it seems likely that more women broke through than were stopped by Stanton's decree.

On July 5th, Cornelia Hancock, a young Quaker girl from New Jersey, set out in company of her brother-in-law, Dr. Henry Child, and a group of older women, to work in the hospitals at Gettysburg. All of them had passes from somewhere, but at the station in Baltimore they met Miss Dix. That lady, still struggling with the intricacies of her job like someone caught in the meshes of a fish net, had gone herself to the railroad station to intercept unauthorized women going to the front, for in the midst of the crisis, that seemed to her the most important thing

to do. Harassed, hot, angry, she was challenging everyone as though she were a private in the provost marshal's guard.

She pounced on the group of which Cornelia Hancock was a member and looked each woman over with her severe judgematic stare. Their passes were in order, they were all elderly and plain—in short, just what she was looking for—with the exception of Cornelia. Miss Hancock was told she was far too young, and that she must go home at once. But Miss Hancock slipped away, and when Miss Dix's back was turned, she climbed quickly into the Gettysburg train and hid there. When she reached Gettysburg, on July 6th, she found that nurses were so badly needed that no one questioned her age, not even Miss Dix when, later, she put her head inside a hospital tent and saw Cornelia working there.

Cornelia's first duties were in a church where hundreds of wounded lay on boards which had been covered with hay and laid across the backs of the pews. When these men were sent to field hospitals, Cornelia left to work with the Second Corps wounded who had been gathered together about five miles from Gettysburg. Her walk there across the battlefield was one long horror. The dead had not been buried and the dreadful stench seemed to her worse than the sight of death or the shrieks of the wounded. When she reached the Second Corps field hospital, she found an operating table had been set up under the trees and the wounded still waiting their turn three days after the last shot was fired. Food and supplies were scarce and would have been critically so but for the Sanitary Commission.

There was no one at this open-air hospital to tell Cornelia what to do, but it seemed to her obvious that the men, who were in a state of utter exhaustion from the battle and the pain of their wounds, were in great need of food. There had been nothing but hardtack in most of the hospitals, but supply wagons were even then arriving. Cornelia helped herself to bread and jam, but there were no knives, no spoons, no plates. She sat on the ground and tore the bread into pieces, spreading jam on them with a stick, while all around her the wounded men turned their heads to watch. Then she found a shingle for a tray and went among the men, stooping to give each one a piece.

Two weeks later, it was the same story—the battlefield stench, which could be smelled miles away as the train drew near, the women who worked on the field using clothes soaked in camphor, cologne or smelling salts, and burying their heads under their pillows at night to shut out the moans and anguished cries of the wounded. In the town,

broken windows, battered houses and the streets sprinkled with chloride of lime to fight the smell which nothing but time would mitigate.

The shortage of surgeons was still acute, and both Cornelia Hancock and Mrs. Souder thought that the need for women nurses was also desperate. In the early days, some of the hospitals had none at all; then, when the restrictions were finally relaxed, as many worthless workers as good ones came on the scene. Cornelia was particularly irritated by the dressy ones who drifted around cheering the boys but doing no useful work. Cornelia, in boots and a torn calico dress, worked hard from daylight until after dark and she thought that even Miss Dix (who had regained her poise and equanimity) should do more than peer around her when she came into a tent. A number of ladies with secessionist sympathies had come out from Baltimore to work among the Rebel wounded, and for the most part the other women did not object to them, but Mrs. Souder and some of the other Northern nurses were never able to conquer their hatred of the Rebels, and though the care they took of the Rebel wounded was conscientious, they found the work distasteful and were glad to relinquish it.

The hospitals were organized by corps, at first, but only in a general way, for every church and available building was filled with wounded who had been carried there during the fighting and could not be moved. Days after the battle ended, many of the wounded were still without shelter, or with no more over them than blankets propped on sticks. The weather continued hot, and until the sixteenth there were heavy showers every day. One observer saw seriously wounded men lying under the eaves of a building, with the water from the roof pouring on them in a heavy stream.

A general hospital, known as Letterman Hospital, was established to care for those who were too seriously wounded to be moved to one of the big, nearby cities, and it became an efficient, well-run place, like a village of tents. There was another hospital called the Lodge, close to the railroad tracks where the wounded who were to be shipped out were cared for until room could be found for them on the crowded cars. This was, in theory, little more than a way station, but it had tents, cooking facilities and a surgeon. Trainloads of wounded left twice a day, but often the loaded ambulances arrived too late, and the wounded men had to be cared for overnight. The station was run by the Sanitary Commission whose members were here, as in every other hospital in Gettysburg, making up the deficiencies and correcting the errors of government.

And here also was an old friend, Georgeanna Woolsey—the irrepress-

ible "Georgy" of the Transport Service. Georgy and her mother, Mrs. Jane Newton Woolsey, had received word that Georgy's brother, Charles, had been wounded and they had hurried to the battlefield, arriving shortly after the fighting had stopped. There they found that the news about Charlie was false, but Olmstead would not let two such able women escape him, and he put them in charge of the station where, in the days that followed, they fed and cared for 16,000 men.

Olmstead had no such scruples as Miss Dix about exposing the wounded men to the sight of a pretty young girl, and on a good many occasions young women whom Miss Dix had refused went to the front with the Sanitary Commission and proved their worth. Georgy, with her charm, her exuberant youth and her unfailing good humor, must have been like a tonic to the wounded men. But Georgy had changed a little since the days with Katharine Wormeley on the Peninsula. Reading the letters she wrote from Gettysburg, it seems that her unfailing cheerfulness is no longer based on the high spirits of youth so much as on a faith in and love for people. Her charm is no longer the reckless, lavish, laughing energy of a boarding-school girl let loose on the world. The charm is still there, and the energy, and the laughter, but it seems now to come from tenderness, and comprehension. Gay little Georgy had matured, as why should she not in the midst of war, since she had the intelligence, the courage and the heart to cope with war's demands. Let her speak for herself.

"No man of the sixteen thousand went away without a good hot meal, and none from our tents without the fresh clothes he needed. Mother put great spirit into it all, listened to their stories, petted them, fed them, and distributed clothes, including handkerchieves with cologne, and got herself called 'Mother'—'This way, Mother,' 'Here's the bucket, Mother,' and 'Isn't she a glorious old woman?'— while the most I ever heard was, 'She knows how; why, it would have taken our steward two hours to get round; but then she's used to it, you see;' which, when you consider that I was distributing hot grog, and must have been taken for a barmaid, was not so complimentary! Then those Rebels too, miserable fellows; we hated them so much when they were away from us, and couldn't help being so good to them when they were in our hands. I am, or should be, angry with myself in that I felt worse when Lieutenant Rhout of the 14th South Carolina died on my hands, singing the Lutheran chants he had sung in his father's church before they made a soldier of him, than when E. C. writes me that Amos was their oldest

son, and that she and his father were over sixty . . . I am glad
we helped those Rebels. They had just as much good soup,
when our procession of cans and cups and soft bread and general
refreshment went round from car to car, as they wanted; and I
even filled the silver pap-cup that a pretty boy from North Carolina
had around his neck, though he was an officer and showed no intention to become a Unionist. Yes, it was his baby cup, and his
mother gave it to him; and he lay on the floor of the baggage car,
wounded, with this most domestic and peaceful of all little relics
tied round his neck . . ."

While Georgy and her mother were still at Gettysburg, their house
in Brevoort Place in New York was threatened by mobs rioting against
the draft. Hatty and Carolina Woolsey, who were alone in the house,
were forced to leave. Another daughter, Abby, left a charming picture of
the socialite Mrs. Woolsey at Gettysburg.

"Just imagine Mother in a straw hat and heavy Gettysburg boots,
standing cooking soup for two hundred men at a time, and distributing it in tin cups; or giving clean shirts to ragged Rebels; or sitting on a pile of grocer's boxes, under the shadow of a string of
codfish, scribbling her notes to us."

It remained for another member of this able family, Jane Woolsey,
Superintendent of the Fairfax Seminary Hospital, to make an evaluation
of volunteer nursing:

"Was the system of women nurses in hospitals a failure? There
never was a system. That the presence of hundreds of individual
women as nurses in hospitals was neither an intrusion nor a
blunder, let the multitude of their unsystematized labors and
achievements testify. So far as I know, the experiment of a compact,
general organization was never tried. Hospital nurses were of all
sorts and came from various sources of supply; volunteers paid or
unpaid; soldiers' wives and sisters who had come to see their
friends, and remained without any clear commission or duties;
women sent by state agencies and aid societies; women assigned by
the General Superintendent of Nurses; [Miss Dix] sometimes, as in
a case I know of, the wife or daughter of a medical officer drawing
the rations but certainly not doing the work of a 'laundress.' These
women were set adrift in a hospital, eight to twenty of them, for the
most part slightly educated, without training or discipline, without
company organization or officers, so to speak, of their own, 'reporting' to surgeons, or in the case of persons assigned to her, to the

General Superintendent, which is very much, in a way, as if
Private Robinson should 'report' to General Grant.

". . . let a nurse be ever so obstinate, ignorant and flabby-
minded, she will eagerly, even gaily, starve herself to feed a sick
soldier. She may be totally impervious to ideas of order; she may
love 'hugger-mugger' and roundabout ways of getting at direct objects, she may hopelessly muddle the ward returns . . . but she
will cheerfully sacrifice time, ease and health to the wants and
whims of a wounded man."[2]

While the overworked surgeons and nurses toiled in the mud and
rain on the Gettysburg battlefield, Lee was winding his painful way,
burdened by thousands of wounded, toward the Potomac, and when he
arrived, the river was in flood. He might have been trapped there, with
his back to the river and that, in conjunction with the capture of Vicksburg in the West, must certainly have brought the war to an end. But if
Lee was slow to escape, Meade was even slower to pursue, and in the
end the Confederate army was able to cross the river in safety without
having to stand and fight. Lincoln expressed his disappointment in a
letter which he was too kind to send, but sentences in it reveal the depth
of his heartbreak.

"I do not believe you appreciate the magnitude of the misfortune
involved in Lee's escape. He was within your easy grasp, and to
have closed upon him would, in connection with our other late
successes, have ended the war. As it is, the war will be prolonged
indefinitely. If you could not safely attack Lee last Monday, how
can you possibly do so south of the river, when you can take with
you very few more than two-thirds of the force you then had in
hand? It would be unreasonable to expect, and I do not expect you
can now effect much. Your golden opportunity is gone, and I am
distressed immeasurably because of it.

"I beg you will not consider this a prosecution or persecution of
yourself. As you had learned that I was dissatisfied, I have thought
best to kindly tell you why."[3]

By little and by little, order was brought out of the chaos at the
battlefield, until only the well-run general hospital remained. Many of
the women stayed on and nursed there, until, about the middle of
November, that too was evacuated.

One more great event was to take place there, however, before the
battlefield became a silent shrine to memory. On the nineteenth of
November, 1863, ceremonies were held there to dedicate the cemetery.

The principal speaker was to be the famous Edward Everett, and almost at the last moment, the President was invited to attend and to say a few words.

Emily Souder went to this ceremony. She had given up her nursing some time before, but something—perhaps the feeling that most war workers have, that the war may well prove the high point in their lives—drew her back to Gettysburg. The trip was an arduous one, involving the crossing of the Susquehanna in an open boat. The day she arrived she hired a carriage to drive over the battlefield, for when she nursed there, she had only seen that part of it where she worked. The field was pock-marked with patches of freshly turned earth, for the dead had recently been disinterred and moved to Cemetery Hill. And for the first time she saw the shocking, pathetic litter with which every foot of a battlefield is strewn, a litter beyond the imaginings of those who have not seen it. She stopped the carriage and hunted among it for souvenirs taking away as much as she could carry.

Though Everett was to be the guest of honor at the ceremonies, Emily Souder's interest was not in him but in the President, and when she returned to town she found everyone there shared her feeling. The President was expected to arrive shortly, and the excitement was intense. She did not see his train come in, but that evening she stood in the crowd which filled the little square in front of the Wills House, where he was staying. The crowd shouted for him, and presently he appeared, standing tall and dark against the white building. He acknowledged their greetings and he promised to say a few words to them on the following day.

He had written out the "few words" before he left the White House (the story that he wrote them on the train is one of the numerous legends which surround the Gettysburg episode). They were written in a hand that bears witness to his weariness, on two pieces of White House stationery, one page scribbled in pencil, one in ink. This original draft is now in the Library of Congress. That night at the Wills house, he copied his words onto a single sheet of paper. This copy, which is also in the Library of Congress (both copies having been presented to the Library by the children of John Hay) was the one he took with him to the ceremony.

The procession, including townspeople, visitors and some soldiers, started for Cemetery Hill in the morning. The progress was solemn and slow. The President was on horseback, bands played funeral music and heavy guns boomed at long-spaced intervals. Lincoln seemed to Emily like the chief mourner, and in this she had more insight than she knew.

Emily found the scene at the cemetery impressive. A wooden speakers' platform had been built on the crest of the hill, outside the cemetery wall, and from it there was a view over the village and the battlefield. Below the platform and just before the ground dropped sharply, were the soldiers' graves. They had been placed in long, graceful curves, radiating outward from the central point where the speakers' platform stood. The headstones, which were level with the ground, bore such American names as Hawes, Bennett, Wagner. Interspersed among them were the graves of the unknown dead, so many of them that the reading of their inscriptions is like the tolling of a bell—"Unknown, Unknown, Unknown." Before each group of graves was the State marker—New Jersey 78, Massachusetts 154, Vermont 81, Pennsylvania 534. The sight of these graves moved Emily deeply, as it must those who see them today.

The crowd gathered around the speakers' stand, and Emily thought it a vast multitude, though by present day standards it would seem small. A flag floated over the stand; sun glinted from the slanting bayonets. Emily, feeling a trifle annoyed that no special place had been provided for the ladies, listened to the preliminaries for a time, then it occurred to her that she could just as well read the speeches in the newspapers, and she wandered off to pick sprigs of green to send as mementos to her friends.

Edward Everett spoke for two hours in ornate and finely rounded sentences. Emily did not hear him. Then the President rose and came to the front of the platform, and Emily was far away. He held in his hand the piece of paper on which he had copied his address, and he spoke it without alteration except that he added the words "under God" toward the close, so that this sentence became: "It is rather for us to be here dedicated to the great task remaining before us—that from these honored dead we take increased devotion to that cause for which they gave the last full measure of devotion—that we here highly resolve that these dead shall not have died in vain—that this nation, under God, shall have a new birth of freedom—and that government of the people, by the people, for the people, shall not perish from the earth."

Some who heard Lincoln that day thought his voice was unpleasantly high and flat in tone. Some disliked his middle-western accent and thought his simple phrases uncouth compared to Everett's practiced oratory. But there were some, and Everett was among them, who felt the sincerity and were aware of the vision which made the voice echoing over the quiet November hills the voice of the nation.

NOTES

[1] Anonymous, *Jenny Wade of Gettysburg* (J. B. Lippincott & Company, 1864).

[2] Jane Stuart Woolsey, (privately printed, D. Van Nostrand, New York, 1868).

[3] From draft of letter to General G. G. Meade, July 14, 1864. Never sent or signed.

Ref: Roy P. Basler *Abraham Lincoln: His Speeches and Writings* (World Publishing Company, Cleveland and New York, 1946).

22

THE LASH AND THE SWORD

---------------------------------- ★ ----------------------------------

CHRONOLOGY *

March 20, 1850   Publication of *Uncle Tom's Cabin* by Harriet Beecher Stowe.

September 18, 1850   The Fugitive Slave Act passed by Congress.

August 6, 1861   The Confiscation Act approved by Congress, permitting the President to receive enlistments of fugitive slaves.

March 10, 1862   The House of Representatives passed a law prohibiting the return of fugitive slaves by army officers. The law was subsequently passed by the Senate.

March 31, 1862   General Hunter relieved General T. W. Sherman of command of the Union forces at Port Royal, South Carolina, and began using Negroes as soldiers.

May 2, 1862   The First Regiment of Kansas Colored Volunteers was ready to take the field. This was the first regiment of Northern colored troops.

May 7, 1862   General David Hunter ordered recruiting of Negroes in the Department of the South. Within a few months the First South Carolina Volunteer Regiment was

ready to serve. This was the first fully armed Negro regiment.

June 20, 1862   Slavery prohibited in the territories by act of Congress.

July 17, 1862   Congress passed an act empowering the President to accept Negroes for military and naval duty whether slave or free.

August 4, 1862   Governor Sprague of Rhode Island appealed to the Negroes of his state to enlist. This was the first call in the North for Negro troops.

August 22, 1862   General Butler appealed to the Negroes of New Orleans to enlist. Four regiments were mustered in during the next three months.

September 22, 1862 President Lincoln issued a preliminary Emancipation Proclamation.

January 1, 1863   The Emancipation Proclamation.

January 13, 1863   General Daniel Ullman was authorized by Lincoln to raise four Negro regiments.

February 21, 1863   Massachusetts began to recruit Negro troops.

October 13, 1863   Recruiting stations for Negroes established in Maryland, Tennessee and Missouri. After this, recruiting of Negroes was general.

June 28, 1864   Congress repealed the Fugitive Slave Law.

January 31, 1865   Passage of the Thirteenth Amendment to the Constitution abolishing slavery.

March 3, 1865   Freedmen's Bureau established by Congress.

*Note: This is a special chronology of the Negro and the War.

———————————————————————— ★ ————————————————————————

Say, darkeys, hab you seen de massa,
Wid de muffstash on he face,
Go long de road some time dis mornin',
Like he gwine leabe de place?
He see de smoke way up de ribber
Whar de Lincum gunboats lay;
He took his hat and leff berry sudden,
And I spose he's runned away.
De massa run, ha, ha!
De darkey stay, ho, ho!
It mus be now de kingdum comin'
An' de yar ob jubilo.

—Henry Clay Work

N₀ WAR OF ANY SIZE is ever fought without taking to itself some aspects of a revolution, either while the war is still in progress, or as a part of the readjustment. The Civil War, having begun as a rebellion, assumed its revolutionary characteristics openly with the issuing of the Emancipation Proclamation. But since, on the rough road to freedom, there is no place in logic to cry "halt," it became clear that the freeing of slaves by word of law still left unsolved a part of the problem. A further step would have to be taken, though it might be with reluctance by many, for having given the black men the title of freedom, a beginning would have to be made in granting the substance of freedom.

With a shortage of fighting manpower developing, the discussion of what to do with the slave who had been freed centered, to a large extent on whether or not he should be employed as a soldier. Aside from the other questions involved, it is difficult to grant a man freedom and then deny him the right to fight for it, and so it came about that a strong belief developed that guns should be put into the hands of the Negroes. With some, the reasons for doing so were idealistic, with others, a simple matter of expediency, and, as with every imaginable aspect of the war, both points of view found expression in verse. On the side of the rights of man:

"Freedom!" their battle-cry,—
"Freedom! or leave to die!"
Ah, and they meant the word!
Not as with us 'tis heard,—
Not a mere party shout;
They gave their spirits out,
Trusting the end to God.[1]

There were others in plenty whose reasons for wanting to arm the Negro were far less abstract:

> In battle's wild commotion
> I shouldn't at all object
> If Sambo's body should stop a ball
> That was coming for me direct.[2]

Whichever form the sentiment in favor of arming "Sambo" assumed, there were many who were opposed. Not a few believed, in spite of the demands of logic, that "the trade of being kilt, belongs but to the white."[3] There were others, and among them President Lincoln, who recognized the worth of the contraband as a laborer for the armed forces, but doubted that he would prove to be a good soldier.[4]

The Confederate States began the enlistment of manumitted Negroes before Negroes in any category were enlisted in the North, though the President had been empowered to accept fugitive slaves as soldiers by the Confiscation Act of August, 1861. When, in the spring of 1862, the Union military commander in South Carolina began to use freed slaves as soldiers, the War Department was seriously disturbed, and an acrimonious correspondence ensued, with the removal of the officer in command. From this troubled and somewhat undignified beginning, the acceptance of the Negro as a soldier spread rapidly, though at first his pay was not equal to that of a white man in uniform. In the end, approximately 179,000 Negroes carried arms in the service of the North.

The enlistment of Negroes helped materially to solve one of the great and growing problems of the war, which was what to do with the slaves who were seeking refuge with the Union forces in ever greater numbers as the armies moved southward. At first they were confined, more or less as prisoners, in concentration camps, and the men used to some extent as laborers. After the enlistment of Negroes was begun, the handling of the liberated slaves became fairly well systematized in most places. The men were at once taken into one or another of the colored regiments, or employed as laborers for a small wage. The women, the children and the aged were established in settlements where they were allotted land to raise food, provided with clothing, churches and schools. A large part of the resettlement work, especially in the early days, was carried on by private organizations and supported by private funds, though a government bureau was established for the purpose, and government bore an increasing amount of the burden.

In the spring and summer of 1863 the work was just beginning.

Cornelia Hancock, after Gettysburg, went to work among the Negroes in Washington. Helen Gibson eventually dedicated herself to this work, and there were many others. Some colored people took part in the rehabilitation of the slaves, and among them Harriet Tubman, who was one of the most remarkable women, black or white, that the times produced.

Harriet had escaped from slavery sometime in the Forties when she was about twenty-five years old. From that time on she had but one idea: to rescue from slavery as many of her people as she could. She would work for a while to earn money, and then she would disappear, to return sometime later, shepherding a small and frightened group of slaves. These forays into slave country were dangerous in the extreme. Harriet would arrive secretly in the slave quarters of some plantation and hide herself there until she had made her preparations. Then some night she and a small band of fugitives would slip away into the darkness, and disappear into the woods and swamps. They traveled at night, lying hidden in the swamps all day, and the babies lay sleeping in baskets, drugged to prevent them from crying.

When night came, the little party would silently rise and resume the journey, Harriet setting the course by the North Star. The way was often rough and hard, but Harriet, who had been a field hand, was equal to the hardships of the journey. Sometimes the fatigue, the hunger and the fear would be too much for one or another of the slaves to bear, but Harriet would let no one turn back for fear the rest would be discovered. She carried a revolver and if one of them, exhausted, refused to go further, Harriet took it out and aimed it at him, saying, "Dead niggers tell no tales. You go on or die."[5]

Harriet learned to know most of the prominent people of the abolition movement: Emerson, with whom she lectured on one occasion, the Alcotts, the Howes, Wendell Phillips and Frank Sanborn, friend of John Brown. She had known John Brown also and might well have been with him on the Harper's Ferry raid had she not been ill on that fateful day. Sanborn, who came near to being imprisoned for befriending John Brown, brought Harriet to call on the Hermon Chapins, who had returned for a brief stay in Concord, where they had once lived. They remembered—and passed the memory on to other generations—a large, powerfully-built woman in her middle years, sad-eyed, grave, unsmiling. There was something strongly of the earth about her. She was reserved in manner but not anti-social in attitude except toward the slave-owning

society of the South—but the result of having lived in primitive hardship, at war with a segment of society.

The little gathering at the Chapins drank tea. Tubman was polite and attentive, but it could be sensed that her mind and her emotions were dwelling in a place no ordinary person could enter but in imagination. She had a habit of bowing a little when she spoke, but there was nothing of servility in it, for her dignity was real, and she did not consider the question of racial equality in terms of herself. As with John Brown, no one who had any contact with Tubman ever forgot her. The big, tired face crossed with scars from her mistresses' lash, the head with the dent in it where she had been hit with a scales-weight thrown by an angry overseer, the sense of implacable hatred under the outward calm, were evidence of terrible and deeply disturbing things.

When war came, Harriet went with Butler's Massachusetts troops to the defense of Washington. From that time on we find passes issued to her in various places, Beaufort, Hilton Head, and others. She worked unofficially for the government, and for a time she was attached to the Sanitary Commission. Now and again she went on scouting trips alone into enemy country, though there was a price on her head, and once she rode on a train in which notices were posted offering a reward for her capture.

She was entitled to draw Army rations, but she seldom did so after she discovered that this aroused the jealousy of other Negroes, and if she needed money, she baked pies which she sold to the soldiers. She nursed soldiers and contrabands, and there is an account purporting to be in her own words, of her nursing work. It is easy to suppose the words are, in truth, her own for they have a metrical quality which is the particular and lovely talent of her race: "I'd go to de hospital, I would, early eb'ry mornin'. I'd get a big chunk of ice, I would, and put it in a basin, and fill it with water; den I'd take a sponge and begin. Fust man I'd come to, I'd thrash away de flies, and dey'd rise, dey would, like bees roun' a hive. Den I'd begin to bathe der wounds, and by de time I'd bathed off three or four, de fire and heat would have melted de ice and made de water warm, an' it would be red as clar blood."[6]

Toward the end of 1861, a large area around Hilton Head, South Carolina, was occupied by the Union troops. When the troops arrived, they found that the owners of the rice plantations had fled inland, driving as many of their slaves as they could ahead of them. Many were left behind, on the mainland and on the sea islands. The town of Beaufort, which the Union troops entered on December 8, 1861, had been aban-

doned, and a number of the slaves, who refused to go with their masters, had been shot. The Union soldiers found the Negroes looting the town, drinking, eating the supplies left in the storerooms, dressing up in their masters' clothing.

That had happened on all the plantations in the district, but when the abundance of the larders and cellars had been consumed, the Negroes were in a desperate plight, for they did not know even the rudiments of how to care for themselves. By the time the Union troops arrived, most of the former slaves were living in an indescribable state of squalor and demoralization, many of them close to starvation.

It was to this blighted region of empty plantation houses and abandoned rice fields that Tubman was sent, and for some time she worked among her people, both there and in Florida. The Negroes of the rice plantations seemed strange, almost foreign, to the Maryland-bred Negro woman, for they spoke a tongue so different from her own that she could only with difficulty understand what they were saying. They trusted her, nevertheless, and the military authorities soon discovered that she could get information which they could not. And so it came about naturally that scouting became part of her work.

It may have been in this connection that she first met Colonel James Montgomery, who commanded the regiment of Negro troops. Montgomery was as extraordinary a character as the war produced. He hailed from Kansas, where he had associated himself with John Brown in the bloody fracas there before the war. He was black-bearded, soft-spoken, and polite, but underneath a somewhat cultured surface, he was a ruthless guerilla fighter, a border chieftain of the classic type.

In Kansas, he lived in perpetual turmoil and danger. His wife once said, "I do get plumb tired of being shot at, but I won't be druv out," a sentiment which exactly matched his own. He had an honest and deep hatred of slavery, of the thing itself for its human evils and not alone for its political aspects in the Kansas war. He was committed to slaughter and destruction. Blood was his argument and he blighted the land through which he passed.

A certain vein of determined hatred in Harriet's nature matched in intensity his own ruthlessness. They became allies, trusting one another, although it would seem they were not friends in the accepted sense. They found themselves walking the same path and so, for a little distance, they trod it together.

In the first part of 1863, the Union forces were making raids into the interior to dismantle the torpedoes which the rebels had planted in the

river. Harriet knew the country from her scouting expeditions, and when, in June of 1863, a raid was organized to strike inland, up the Combahee River, Tubman was chosen to go in company with Montgomery. He was to be in charge of the gunboats and the military operations, and Tubman (whom he called "Moses" because she was the deliverer of her people) was to manage the hundreds of slaves on the river plantations along the way.

The raiding party set out at night on June 2nd, with 150 Negro troops in three gunboats. They met little rebel resistance anywhere, and the owners of most of the plantations fled when they saw the smoke of the gunboats down the stream. The colored soldiers were put ashore in row-boats, and they ran from one plantation to another, burning, hacking, pillaging, and dragging out anything of value. It had more of the aspects of a saturnalian orgy than of a raid.

News traveled in the mysterious manner of the South, from one Negro settlement to another, that the "Lincum gumboats" were coming to set free the slaves and when the overseers attempted, with lashes and guns, to drive the slaves inland, they refused to be driven and rushed in crowds to the river banks. The sight must have been an extraordinary one. Every road, every field, every pathway, filled with slaves, men, women and children, rushing toward the river. This is what it looked like to Harriet, in words purported to be her own:

"I nebber see such a sight, we laughed, an' laughed, an' laughed. Here you'd see a woman wid a pail on her head, rice a smokin' in it jus' as she'd taken it from de fire, young one hangin' on behind, one han' roun' her forehead to hold on, 'tother han' digin' into de rice-pot, eatin' wid all its might; hold of her dress two or three more; down her back a bag wid a pig in it. One woman brought two pigs, a white one an' a black one; we took 'em all on board; named de white pig Beauregard, and de black pig Jeff Davis. Sometimes de women would come wid twins hangin' roun' der necks; 'pears like I never see so many twins in my life; bags on der shoulders, baskets on der heads, and young ones taggin' behin', all loaded; pigs squealin', chickens screamin', young ones squallin'."[7]

They waded into the water screaming and praying to be taken to the gunboats out in the stream. They seized the rowboats and tried to clamber aboard in such numbers that there was danger of the boats cap-sizing. The soldiers beat their grasping hands with oars, and still they clung. Then Colonel Montgomery shouted from the deck of his gun-

boat: "Moses—sing!" She lifted up her strong, deep voice over the shouting and the tumult:

> Of all the whole creation in the East or in the West,
> The glorious Yankee nation is the greatest and the best.
> Come along! Come along! don't be alarmed,
> Uncle Sam is rich enough to give you all a farm.

At least, that is what she said she sang when she told the story in her old age, sitting at peace in her own little house in Auburn, New York. There was a chorus shout of "Glory" and, as was the negro custom when that word was shouted, they all raised their arms high in the air. In that instant, the soldiers poled the boats to safety.

In the end, all of the Negroes were taken on board the gunboats, and the expedition steamed back down the river. In the melee, Harriet's skirt had been all but torn off. She had gone on shore with the soldiers and had picked up two young pigs belonging to a sick woman and was carrying them, one under each arm, when the order to "double quick" was shouted. Harriet started to run, stepped on her skirt and fell. Looking over the damage later and finding that the dress was in tatters, she made up her mind that a skirt was a poor sort of costume to wear on a raid. So she found someone to write a letter for her to a Soldiers' Aid Society of Boston, telling about her experience and asking them to please send her what she called a "bloomer." It is pleasant to know that the ladies of the Society, setting aside any prejudice they may have had against bloomers, promptly made and sent her a pair.

Between 750 and 800 Negroes were taken away—rescued is perhaps the better word, considering the plight of abandoned slaves—from the plantations up the river. The men were asked to enlist, and most of them entered the army as soldiers under Montgomery. A settlement was established for the rest at an abandoned plantation known as the Smith Plantation because of its recent owners, or the Old Fort Plantation because of the ruins of a Spanish fort which had been built there in 1562, when the Combahee was known, appropriately enough, as the River Jordan. The Negroes were proud of their freedom and proud of their settlement, which they named Montgomery Hill in honor of their deliverer, though the land occupied was as flat as the top of a table.

In the North, there was a growing enthusiasm for the work of educating the former slaves. The Freedman's Aid Society was established in Boston, the National Freedman's Relief Committee in New York, and there were similar organizations in other cities. The Boston Society sent

to the Old Fort Plantation a woman named Elizabeth Botume, one of those intrepid young New England schoolteachers who, from the late Forties onward, were to be found in the most unlikely, remote places, coping alone with problems which might well appall a government bureau.

Elizabeth Botume was gay, charming, intelligent, fearless, and she had need of all these qualities. She lived and taught in the windowless, desolate old house, and after a time another young teacher was sent down from Boston to join her. Together they labored there, creating their little oasis, all but cut off from the world for all the rest of the war.

NOTES

[1] George Henry Boker, *The Black Regiment*. From *Poems of the War* by same author—published in Boston, 1864.

[2] Charles Graham Halpine (Private Miles O'Reilly), *Sambo's Right to be Kilt*.

[3] *Ibid.*

[4] For President Lincoln's views on emancipation and the use of colored troops, see his letter to James C. Conkling of August 26, 1863.

[5] Lillie B. Chase Wyman, *Harriet Tubman* (New England Magazine, March 1896, vol. 14 [new series]).

[6] Sarah H. Bradford, *Harriet the Moses of Her People* (Geo. R. Lockwood & Son, New York, 1886).

[7] *Ibid.*

23

THE BRAVE AND THE FAIR

---------------------- ★ ----------------------

CHRONOLOGY

1863

July 14	Dissatisfaction at Washington because of Lee's escape.
July 18	Union forces repulsed at Fort Wagner outside Charleston.
September 2	Knoxville, Tennessee, occupied by Union forces.
September 7–8	Federals took Fort Wagner.
September 9	Rosecrans occupied Chattanooga.
September 15	Lincoln suspended writ of habeas corpus throughout the Union.
September 19–20	Battle of Chickamauga resulting in a defeat of Rosecran's forces.
October 16	Grant given command of the Military Division of the Mississippi.
October 23	Grant arrived at Chattanooga.
October 23–25	Battle of Chattanooga.
October 26– November 10	Bombardment of Fort Sumter.
October 27	The Chicago Sanitary Commission Fair.

306

November 14   Sherman joined Grant at Chattanooga.

November 23–25   Battle of Chattanooga, a Union victory.

November 24   Union assault on Lookout Mountain by General Hooker.

November 25   Union assault on Missionary Ridge by General Thomas.

November 26   The first national observance of Thanksgiving Day.

December 7   Opening of the 38th Congress.

December 8   Proclamation of Amnesty to Confederates taking the oath of allegiance.

December 14–21   Boston Sanitary Fair.

─────────────── ★ ───────────────

> *The sun is a-shining to welcome the day*
> *So heigh-ho, come to the Fair*
> —Anonymous

BY MIDSUMMER OF 1863, after the shock of the Vicksburg campaign and the battle of Gettysburg, the army of women was functioning smoothly. Strong links bound the home workers to the workers in the hospitals and at the front. Huge quantities of supplies flowed in a steady stream. Individual women had learned to understand the nature of their own abilities and most of those whom we met in the early days, coping desperately with the unfamiliar, had found the work for which they were best adapted, and were doing it as though war would have no end.

"Major" Belle Reynolds was with her husband near Vicksburg, where she stayed for some time, helping in the hospitals. Cornelia Hancock was teaching contraband children and across the years we hear her soft-spoken words, "Thee must not think me too young for the work." After her work on the battlefield of Gettysburg Georgy Woolsey was asked to write a little book about her experiences to be sold for the benefit of the Sanitary Commission. She dashed it off with her usual exuberance,

calling it "Three Weeks at Gettysburg," and to her surprise, it became popular, not only here, but in England.

Mrs. Holstein had become matron of the United States General Hospital on the York Turnpike near Gettysburg. Annie Wittenmyer and her secretary, Mary Shelton, with headquarters on the *Van Phul,* were traveling up and down the river, inspecting hospitals. Sister Adeline Tyler, who had rescued the wounded soldiers after the riots in Baltimore, was Superintendent of nurses at the Naval School Hospital, Annapolis. Ellen Sherman had taken the children to visit the General in the camp at Vicksburg which had become as bright as a flower garden with the ladies' summer frocks. In August, Louisa Alcott's *Hospital Sketches* was published. It was a little book which she tried to make amusing and gay. Bickerdyke was continuing her incredible career of good works. The Sanitary Commission, deciding to accept that which it could not hope to control, had made her one of its field workers and had not yet quite abandoned hope of persuading her to keep her accounts at least approximately straight. Clara Barton still labored wonderfully to maintain the touch between hundreds of boys and their homes, so that her name was beloved in many, many households.

Katharine Wormeley was working in a hospital at Portsmouth Grove, Rhode Island. Kate Chase had recently married the gallant Governor Sprague and was heading toward unhappiness. And Kady Brownell. We see her briefly, at night, after the hard march to Newbern, wet to the skin, her feet blistered and sore, a very human Kady, sitting under a tree in the darkness, her head on her husband's shoulder, weeping. She fought well in the battle and was wounded. Now, in 1863, both she and her husband had returned home. She treasured for the rest of her life her discharge signed by General Burnside, her sword and the flag she had carried at Newbern. Miss Dix had come to look like an old woman, but her iron determination still conquered her exhaustion. We see her now and again, at a railroad station, in a hospital ward, still concerning herself with little kindnesses and with petty quarrels which made her tremble, while out in the West, Mr. Yeatman and the Sanitary Commission were quietly doing her work for her, and in the East she had all but lost control. She was still the Lady Superintendent of Army Nurses in name, and her somber clothing still rustled with the majesty of her pretended power, but no one except very young girls like Cornelia Hancock feared her any longer, and her pretending fooled no one, least of all, perhaps, herself. She was a tragic figure, but she never gave up, and a year later Georgy was to write from the Beverly Hospital, "We had a

good-natured laugh over a visit from Miss Dix, who, poor old lady, kept up the fiction of appointing all the army nurses."

"Poor old lady" in truth. In 1863, much of her power vanished in War Department Order number 351 which, in thoroughly bureaucratic fashion, while confirming in one clause her sole authority in appointing nurses, wiped it out in the next by providing that nurses could also receive special appointments from the Surgeon General. Many surgeons, for a wide variety of reasons, not all of them worthy, applied for these special appointments for their chosen nurses and when this happened, Miss Dix frequently saved face by hastily presenting them with an appointment from herself as well.

Mrs. Livermore and Mrs. Hoge were in Chicago in the late summer of 1863, facing a serious problem. The long Vicksburg campaign, with its attenuated lines of transportation, its costly hospital ships, and above all the increased numbers of sick and wounded, put a great strain on the resources of the Sanitary Commission. What no one realized at the time was that this campaign was only the forerunner of Grant's bloody, ruthless brand of warfare, which would make necessary an ever larger flow of supplies and greatly augment hospital facilities all over the North. After Lee's escape from Meade, following Gettysburg, it was clear that the war would not be soon ended, and to carry on its work the Sanitary Commission would have to have considerable sums of money.

How that money was to be raised for their section of the country, puzzled and troubled the two able ladies, until together they hit on the idea of having a fair, to be held in Chicago but to involve as much of the country as could be persuaded to help. Their thought turned out to be one of the important ideas of the war. They hoped to raise $25,000, an ambition which made the men of the Commission laugh.

A council of the women of the Northwest was called in Chicago on the first of September, and afterward the ladies went to work with such a will that on a single day, seventeen bushels of mail were sent from the rooms of the Sanitary Commission.

Contributions to be sold at the fair began to arrive from all over the country, among them some pieces of machinery that were so large that Mrs. Hoge and Mrs. Livermore decided to build a temporary structure near the main hall in which to house them. The two ladies interviewed a builder, who agreed to do the work and then they discovered to their shocked amazement that the builder would not accept their signatures on a contract. Under provisions of the common law, as married women,

they did not have the power to make contracts, and their husbands would have to sign for them. Mary Livermore who had, since the beginning of the war, handled thousands of dollars, did not know that such a provision existed. She began to make inquiries and discovered that under common law she did not own the money she earned, or have control of her children, and she said crisply that now she knew what her work after the war was going to be.

That as intelligent and experienced a woman as Mary Livermore did not know about these provisions of the common law is a fairly good indication that they did not, in reality, cause hardship in the society with which she was familiar. Apparently no one explained to her how the common law could, under certain circumstances, be modified under equity, and she seems not to have known about the crusade of the Woman's Rights Movement, though its members had been vociferating for a decade.

The fair opened on October 27th with a parade, and schools and businesses were closed for the occasion. As Mrs. Livermore pointed out, though men eventually helped in the enterprise, the original fair was at the start wholly the work of women. The donations which poured in on the astonished ladies ranged from socks to sheet iron, and they came from all parts of the North. Pigs, cows, horses, lace, harvesters, fans and carrots went on sale. A Chicago jeweler offered a gold watch as a prize to be given to the largest contributor.

There were lotteries, raffles, entertainments and even a restaurant. Anna Dickinson made a speech, standing precariously on a chair, and another speech from a platform, at a charge of three hundred dollars each. Anna, the "girl orator," was just twenty-one years old, plump and famous. She had spoken in the same lecture series with Emerson and Wendell Phillips and had recently had one of her glossy black curls shot off by some one in the audience who did not like her politics.

Most of the prominent ladies of Chicago had charge of tables filled with merchandise for sale, and out-of-town aid societies sent delegations of helpers. Some of the men did not like the idea of their wives acting as salesladies, among them General Sherman, who wrote to Ellen, "I don't approve of ladies selling things at a table. So far as superintending the management of such things, I don't object, but it merely looks unbecoming for a lady to stand behind a table to sell things. Still, do as you please."

The great sensation of the Fair was President Lincoln's gift of the original draft of the Emancipation Proclamation. With it came a letter:

"Executive Mansion
Washington, October 26, 1863

To the Ladies having charge the North-Western Fair
for the Sanitary Commission, Chicago, Illinois:

According to the request made in your behalf, the original draft
of the Emancipation Proclamation is herewith enclosed. The formal
words at the top, and the conclusion, except the signature, you
perceive are not in my hand-writing. They were written at the State
Department, by whom I know not. The printed part was cut from a
copy of the preliminary proclamation, and pasted on merely to save
writing. I had some desire to retain the paper, but if it shall con-
tribute to the relief and comfort of the soldiers, that will be better.
Your obedient servant,

A. Lincoln."

The draft of the Proclamation was purchased by Thomas B. Bryan and
given to the Chicago Soldiers' Home. Eventually it was sent to the
Chicago Historical Society for safekeeping and was destroyed in the
great fire of 1871. The price Mr. Bryan paid for the document was
$3,000, which was the largest sum brought in by a donation from an
individual, and so it was the President who won the prize of the gold
watch. It was sent to him along with a letter of some charm signed by
Mrs. Hoge and Mrs. Livermore on behalf of the "Ladies of the North-
Western Fair."

The Fair remained open for many days, and when the last of the
crowd departed, when the trimmings were swept away and the exhausted
ladies counted their gains, it was discovered that the Fair had earned
close to a hundred thousand dollars.

"Sanitary" fairs became the rage. Boston held a fair in December
which brought in $140,000 dollars from merchandise which included a
washing machine sold for $300. There were some old friends present.
Julia Ward Howe, her copper-colored hair hidden under one of her de-
mure bonnets, gathered information for her husband's paper, the "Commonwealth," Katharine Wormeley wrote a book especially for the Fair
called "The United States Sanitary Commission" which brought in several thousand dollars. Louisa Alcott dramatized some scenes from Dickens and went to Boston to act, a thing she dearly loved to do, but she was
disappointed. "Our night was not at all satisfactory to us, owing to the
falling through of several scenes for want of actors. People seemed to
like what there was of it, and after a wearisome week I very gladly came
home again. Our six entertainments made twenty five hundred dollars for
the Fair."

To the New York Fair, which took place on April 14, 1864, Lincoln sent a copy of his Gettysburg address to be sold for the benefit of the sick and wounded soldiers.[1] This he did at the request of Edward Everett who had informed Lincoln that he was going to donate the manuscript of his own address at Gettysburg and asked Lincoln to write a copy of his remarks for the same purpose. Both manuscripts were sold and that of Lincoln became known as the Everett copy.[2] Later, for the Baltimore Fair, Lincoln donated another copy of the Gettysburg address, known as the Bliss copy.[3]

The sum earned by all the big fairs reached the amazing total of nearly three million dollars. This was big business, the result of executive ability of the first order. The pretty ladies of 1861, sitting in their parlors stitching the ridiculous havelocks and scraping lint, had ended by startling the world.

While the fairs were a-brewing, the battles of Chickamauga and Chattanooga were fought. The first, commanded by Rosecrans, resulted in a Union defeat, and afterward Lincoln said to John Hay that he thought Rosecrans seemed "stunned, like a duck hit on the head." The General retreated to Chattanooga, where he was replaced in command by General George Thomas.

Grant, over-all commander of the newly created Military Division of the Mississippi, arrived on the scene on October 23rd and the fighting began that day. On the twenty-fifth, at ten o'clock at night, Grant wired Lincoln: ". . . I believe I am not premature in announcing a complete victory over Bragg. Lookout Mountain Top, all the rifle pits in the Chattanooga Valley, and Missionary Ridge entire, have been carried and are now held by us. I have no idea of finding Bragg here tomorrow."

Mother Bickerdyke had been at Chickamauga and was now with the troops at Chattanooga. The weather was bitterly cold. The wounded were sheltered in tents through which the wind blew icy blasts. Each group of tents was pitched around a central bonfire of huge logs and a minimum of heat along with much smoke came through the open tent flaps. Mother Bickerdyke, her heavy dress full of holes where sparks had burned it, heated bricks and carried them to the wounded men. She was profligate with wood for the fire she tended, and one late afternoon she discovered that the wood pile would not last the night. She sought out an officer and asked him to send a detail to cut more wood, but he refused, saying that it was too nearly dark. Mother Bickerdyke could not let the matter rest there, for with no heat in the bitter wind, she feared some of her "boys" would be dead before the morning came.

Somewhere, she found a sergeant and some men, and she, who never gave a man a drink of whiskey unless he was about to undergo an operation without chloroform, offered them hot toddy if they would help her find wood. Nearby, there were some minor fortifications, no longer in use, built of logs and earth. She and the men dismantled them and dragged the wood back to camp, and all night long she kept the bonfire blazing.

But destroying military installations is a serious offense in the Army Regulations. The next day Mother Bickerdyke, with more to do than any one woman could manage, was rushing from tent to tent with hot bricks, stirring great caldrons of soup, dragging huge logs onto the fire, when an officer arrived and told her she was under arrest. He was right in principle if wrong in the laws of humanity, and Mother Bickerdyke turned on him. The reply she is supposed to have made was, "All right, I'm arrested. Now don't bother me—I got work to do."

The newspaper correspondents had long since discovered that Mother Bickerdyke was good copy, and they printed the story, adding the picturesque detail of some days spent in the guardhouse. There was an investigation in which she defended what she had done, speaking with her customary vigorous tartness, and the authorities, probably with those newspapers in mind, let the whole matter rest there.

It may well be that these two battles were the hardest tour of duty in the war for Mother Bickerdyke. The cold, the need to be awake much of the night, and the heavy burden of work with no woman to help her, must have told on her dreadfully. She was no longer young and many of the wrinkles which covered her face like a fine mesh, must have lodged there during these days. Then news came that Mrs. Porter and Annie Wittenmyer were on their way to join her and would arrive on New Year's Day. Mother Bickerdyke went to the station to meet them and when she saw these two capable and famous women step off the train, for the first and only time in her long years of toil, Mother Bickerdyke wept.

And so 1863 came to an end. For the Negroes it was "The Year of Jubilo." For Lincoln, it was a year of dissatisfaction, bordering on despair, because of the way all his top generals, with the exception of Grant, had prosecuted the war. But it was also the year in which the Confederates lost the war, though this was not realized as yet on either side of the lines. The tide of the Confederacy had begun to recede after Gettysburg, and another tide was rising, strong and clear, the sweeping progress of Grant's invincible army that would shortly inundate the South.

NOTES

[1] There are five known copies of the Gettysburg address in Lincoln's handwriting. The first copy was written in Washington sometime before the delivery of the address, and the second copy was written either the night before or the day of the Gettysburg ceremonies. Both of these copies were presented to the Library of Congress by the children of John Hay, one of Lincoln's private secretaries.

[2] The Everett copy was the third copy. Some time after the New York Sanitary Fair, it passed into the hands of the family of Senator Henry W. Keyes of New Hampshire, from whom it was purchased by Thomas F. Madigan, New York autograph dealer, in 1930. (This copy is sometimes referred to as the Keyes copy because of its long association with the Keyes family.) Madigan sold it to James C. Ames, Chicago investment banker. After his death, it was purchased from his widow for $60,000. The purchase price was raised by contributions from the Illinois school children and a donation from Marshall Field of Chicago. In March, 1944, this copy was presented to the Illinois State Historical Library, its present owners.

[3] The Bliss copy of the Gettysburg Address is the fifth copy. The fourth copy, known as the Bancroft copy, was that first written by Lincoln for the Baltimore Fair at the request of George Bancroft, historian and biographer, who planned to reproduce it in a publication, "Autograph Leaves of Our Country's Authors." For this purpose, a heading and signature were necessary and, since the copy Lincoln made did not have either of these, it was necessary that another be made. Bancroft was allowed to keep this fourth copy and it was later purchased by Mrs. Nicholas Noyes of Indianapolis and presented to Cornell University.

The Bliss copy—the fifth—is the one Lincoln sent Bancroft to replace the fourth copy. It was owned by Professor William J. A. Bliss at the time of his death in 1943, and was sold at auction for $54,000 by his heirs in April, 1949. The purchaser was Oscar B. Clintas of Havana, former Cuban Ambassador to the United States, who died in 1957. In July, 1959, this fifth and final copy of the Gettysburg Address was turned over to the Federal government by the Clintas heirs, to be placed in the Lincoln Room of the White House.

24

NORTHERN FLAGS IN SOUTHERN BREEZES

★

1864

February 14	Sherman captured Meridian, Mississippi, destroying quantities of supplies.
February 20	Federal expedition defeated at Olustee, Florida.
February 22	The House passed a bill authorizing the President, with the consent of the Senate, to appoint Grant a Lieutenant General.
February 29	Lincoln nominated Grant to the rank of Lieutenant General, a rank which was revived by Congress for Grant's benefit.
March 11	Act of Congress of this date gave legal sanction to Letterman's army medical reforms.
March 12	Grant made General-in-Chief. General Halleck became Chief of Staff.
March 17	Grant and Sherman met at Nashville, Tennessee, and arranged for the double, concerted drive against the Confederacy.
March 18	Sherman assumed command of Military Division of the Mississippi.
April 8	Union defeat at Sabine Cross Roads, Louisiana.

May 4	Army of the Potomac crossed the Rapidan. Sherman's forces advanced into Georgia.
May 5	Butler took City Point, Virginia, in a surprise attack.
May 5–6	Battle of the Wilderness.
May 8–17	Battle of Spotsylvania. Little fighting on the 11th, but heavy fighting on the 12th.
May 13–16	Battle of Rosaca, Georgia.
May 15	Union forces defeated at New Market in the Shenandoah Valley.
May 16	General Butler held the Army of the James at Bermuda Hundred.
May 23–24	Battle of North Anna.
May 24	Sheridan rejoined the army on the march from North Anna to Cold Harbor, his cavalry having gone entirely around Lee's army.
May 26	Grant directed that the base of supplies be moved to White House from Port Royal.
June 1–3	Battle of Cold Harbor, Virginia.
June 7	Lincoln renominated for President and Andrew Johnson for Vice-President.
June 11	General Early arrived before Washington. General Wright (Union) arrived at Washington the same day. The 19th corps under Major-General Emory also arrived at Washington.
June 12	Early began his retreat, Wright following.
June 12–16	Army of the Potomac moved south of the James River, making necessary the evacuation of White House.
June 16–18	Union assault on Petersburg, Virginia, unsuccessful. The siege began.
June 25	General Burnside commenced running the mine at Petersburg.
June 26	Evacuation of White House base complete.

June 27	Battle of Kenesaw Mountain.
June 30	Explosion of mine under Petersburg fortifications.
July 4	Congress adjourned.
July 9	Battle of Monocacy, Maryland, delayed Early.
July 11	Early arrived before Washington.
July 12	Battle of Fort Stevens. Early started to retire.
July 13	Early escaped across the Potomac into Virginia.
July 22	The Battle of Atlanta. (Atlanta did not fall, however, until September 2nd.)
July 30	Chambersburg, Pennsylvania, burned by General Early's orders.
August 5	Union victory in Mobile Bay.
August 22	Joseph K. Barnes commissioned Surgeon General.
August 29	Democratic Convention nominated General McClellan for President.
August 30	Surgeon General William A. Hammond dismissed from service.
September 2	Fall of Atlanta.
September 19–22	Defeat of Early by Sheridan at Winchester and Fisher's Hill.
October 19	Battle of Cedar Creek—a decisive victory of Sheridan over Early.
October 27	Battle for possession of Hatcher's Run.
November 8	Lincoln reelected.
November 15	Atlanta set on fire. Most of the army left this day to begin the second part of the march to the sea.

———————————————— ★ ————————————————

εντευθεν εξελαυνει
(*And the next day he marched onward*)
—Xenophon

GℰNERAL GRANT'S POPULARITY throughout the country was now very great, and Lincoln recognized in him the long-sought commander of the armies. On the appropriate date of February 22nd, the House passed a bill authorizing the President, with the consent of the Senate, to appoint Grant a Lieutenant General—a rank last held by Washington. In handing Grant his commission on March 9th, Lincoln said, "With this high honor devolves upon you also a corresponding responsibility. As the country herein trusts you, so, under God, it will sustain you." On March 12th Grant received his appointment as General-in-Chief, and Halleck became Chief of Staff. Sherman inherited Grant's former command of the Military Division of the Mississippi and Meade remained in command of the Army of the Potomac, over which Grant was to exercise special supervision. At the beginning of 1864, the Federal troops were in control of the entire Mississippi Valley, though the Confederates held the territory west of the river as far north as the Arkansas River. Pensacola, St. Augustine, Key West and Port Royal were in Northern hands, but Savannah, Charleston and Mobile were still held by the Confederates. The Army of the Potomac was watching Lee along the Rapidan and the Rappahannock Rivers.

Following the ceremonies surrounding Grant's promotion (which caused him acute embarrassment) he made a hurried trip to the West to confer with Sherman. The two generals met at Nashville, the rail head for Chattanooga, on the seventeenth of March and made plans for a double thrust into the heart of the Confederacy. The two attacks were to be launched simultaneously against the two great Southern armies. Grant was to strike at General Lee and the Army of Northern Virginia, which was in camp below the Rapidan, and Sherman at General Johnston and the Army of Tennessee in northern Georgia. Grant's objective would be the James River, and Sherman was to push through to Atlanta.

After their conference, Grant returned to the East, and Sherman remained where he was to gather supplies for nearly 100,000 men and to wait for Grant's signal. With only a single-track railroad running from Nashville to Chattanooga, and an acute shortage of rolling stock, Sherman's task was not easy, though he planned to begin his march with supplies reduced to a minimum. All the headquarters paraphernalia for himself and his staff would go in one wagon, the men would have no tents

and very little, except ammunition and some food staples, which they could not carry on their backs.

Sherman was vigorously in control of his command. He was nervous, irritable, high-strung. Every red hair bristled, there was an aggressive stubble on his chin, and his head turned on his scrawny neck with quick jerks like a bird's.

One of the first acts of his command was to forbid the use of the railroad to private persons, with no exceptions whatsoever, and to deny railroad car space for the shipment of Sanitary Commission and Christian Commission supplies. But in giving his order he had reckoned without Mother Bickerdyke, who appeared, angry as usual, demanding medical equipment for her Chattanooga hospital. Sherman made an exception for her, but about this time he wrote to Charles A. Dana at the War Department, "To make war we must harden our hearts. Therefore, when preachers clamor and sanitaries wail, don't join in, but know that war, like the thunderbolt, follows its laws and turns not aside even if the beautiful, the virtuous and charitable stand in its path." To some members of the Christian Commission, who wanted permission to ship a consignment of Bibles, he snapped, "Rations and ammunition are much better."

Stanton, who had long tried vainly to get women out of the front lines, issued yet one more order that no woman, whoever she might be, was to be allowed to stay with the army, and Sherman, who thoroughly detested women in the midst of war, except possibly Bickerdyke, issued his own orders that no women were to be allowed inside the lines. There was little he could do about Bickerdyke, in any event, since she carried a pass from Grant to travel where she chose. On April 15th, Grant gave out an order expelling "all females" from the front line areas, though without cancelling Bickerdyke's pass, which he had probably forgotten. In spite of this paper barrage, the women continued to come. They filtered in, silted in, drifted in softly and unobtrusively like thistledown, and wherever there were wounded men, there were also the women.

One day, a small woman dressed like a man, with the insignia of a medical officer on her uniform, appeared before Sherman. She was Dr. Mary Walker, who had been at Gettysburg, but Sherman looked at her trousers, her mannish face, her short, black hair parted in the middle, and did not like what he saw. She had a complaint to make concerning the things the men said about her costume.

"Well," Sherman said, "if you want them to stop, why don't you take off those clothes?"

"What's the matter with these clothes? Aren't they strictly physiological?"

"Yes, but damned unfeminine."

Dr. Walker, dress reformer and woman's rightist, went away from there to be captured not long afterward and sent, as a prisoner of war, to Libby Prison. Later, when Sherman told about his encounter with the belligerent little doctor, he said, "Would you believe it, that damn fellow Stanton sent that woman out just to bother me."[1]

The harassed General made hordes of benevolent women cackle with indignation like righteous hens. The more intelligent members of the two great Commissions realized, however, that Grant and Sherman represented a new type of general officer, and that these two would accept help only if the charitable organizations lived up to the same standards of Spartan efficiency set for the army. Thereafter, there occurred a general tightening up which, beginning at the top, ran like vibrations of an electric current, all the way back to the aid societies.

In April, Sherman moved twenty miles south of Chattanooga to Ringgold. The spearheads were nearing the time of their launching and he waitec tensely for the signal. Grant moved first. At midnight of May 3rd, the Army of the Potomac began the crossing of the Rapidan and all the next day the troops, with bands playing and flags flying, occupied the country on the farther bank. Here was a tract of tangled forest, known as the Wilderness and here, hidden by pale green spring foliage, Lee was waiting.

The two armies met on the fifth of May and fought a two-day battle with results that would have caused any of the generals who had previously commanded the Army of the Potomac to retire across the Rapidan and lick his wounds. 2,200 Union men lay dead, 12,000 wounded and 3,300 were missing.[2] Some were burned to death when the thickets caught fire, some, lost in the fog of smoke from the guns and from the burning woods, blundered into the enemy lines. Grant scarcely paused. By nightfall of May 7th the Army of the Potomac was moving south once more.

Sherman also had begun to march. He met the enemy at Resaca in Georgia on May 13th in a type of warfare utterly different from Grant's. Deliberately, Grant met the enemy head-on and full force with terrific impact. Sherman, fighting a running fight much of the time, side-stepped the enemy like a dancer, in a series of brilliant flanking movements. His progress was as he had planned, swift and light. In his rear, Bickerdyke and Porter jounced along in an ambulance, and, with one of the wings of

his army rode handsome, big, Madame Turchin who had been born and reared with the Russian army. She rode side-saddle on a horse which was also handsome and big and, with her well-cut trailing skirt, she made a striking picture.

Grant's next head-on encounter with Lee came at Spotsylvania Court House in Virginia on May 8th and lasted ten days. In the course of it there took place the desperate hand-to-hand struggle for a stretch of breastworks known forever after as the Bloody Angle, where there was some of the fiercest fighting of the war. The casualties were once more appalling but the people of the North believed that the end of the war was in sight. To the crowd gathered around the White House, Lincoln read Grant's telegram of May 13th, which contained the famous words, "I propose to fight it out on this line if it takes all summer," and the crowd went wild with enthusiasm.

On June 1st, Grant met the enemy at Cold Harbor, north of the Chickahominy River, not far from the scenes of the Peninsula Campaign of 1862. Cold Harbor was a Union defeat which strewed five acres of ground with 10,000 dead. There was great suffering, but throughout the battle the supply wagons of the Sanitary Commission were well up toward the front lines.

Both parts of the double offensive were moving more slowly than had been anticipated. Though Grant had thrown his army headlong at the Confederate positions without counting the cost in casualties, he had not been able to destroy Lee's army. Sherman had been on the march for two months and had not yet reached Atlanta. Grant's plans for support from other commanders had gone awry. As the people of the North saw more and more plainly that the war would not end soon, depression replaced enthusiasm. Day after day the newspapers carried long lists of casualties, many hundreds of women were in mourning, and the news from Grant's army was received with shocked horror.

Spotsylvania had added 6,000 killed and wounded to the 14,000 of the Wilderness, and Cold Harbor had reduced Grant's army by another 12,-000. Some of the wounded were sent to Belle Plain and to Fredericksburg, where the Lacy house was once more serving as a hospital. Clara Barton who, like other women, had been having trouble getting a pass, was granted one when the authorities realized in how desperate a plight the wounded were. There was not enough food, and few medical supplies. Barton ". . . saw crowded into one old sunken hotel, lying helpless upon its bare, wet, bloody floors, 500 fainting men hold up their cold, bloodless, dingy hands as I passed, and beg me in Heaven's name

for crackers to keep them from starving (and I had none); or to give them a cup that they might have something to drink water from, if they could get it (and I had no cup and could get none); . . . I saw 200 six-mule army wagons in a line . . . reaching so far out . . . that I never saw the end of it," bringing more wounded.

That experienced campaigner, Cornelia Hancock, was in Fredericks-burg, building fires where it did not seem possible to build them and hanging above them on poles, long rows of kettles. Cornelia was the first Union woman in the city, but some Dix nurses and volunteers soon ar-rived, for the War Department interdiction against women could not be maintained in the face of the crisis.

Eventually, most of the wounded were sent to Washington where some from the early fighting were being cared for. The women who went to the wharves to meet them, wept when they saw how many there were. For three days an unbroken procession of ambulances moved into the city, but Washington was ready to receive them. At the start of the cam-paign, all convalescents had been sent away, and for once in the long, dark history of suffering, there were enough beds, enough surgeons, enough nurses.

Cornelia, who had thought that the wounded in Fredericksburg were better off than those of Gettysburg only because they were housed in buildings instead of tents, had gone south with the Army. She had gone in an open wagon with Mary Lee and Georgy Willets to White House from which Katharine Wormeley had made so dramatic a departure. White House was again full of wounded. Annie Etheridge was there looking, after three years in the field, as sunburned as any soldier. Annie had been in the recent battles, but because of the haze of later-day adulation and a confusion of dates, it is impossible to see her clearly. The base at White House was broken up on June 26th, and Cornelia left there under circumstances as thrilling as Katharine's adventures had been.

After Cold Harbor, Grant moved south of the James River, around Richmond, to Petersburg, Virginia, where he arrived on June 16th. Petersburg, twenty-one miles from Richmond, was the point at which three railroads, which formed a part of Lee's communication lines, con-verged from the south. If Richmond was to be captured, Petersburg must first be taken and here the two great armies once more came face to face. From June 15th to 18th, there was heavy fighting in front of Petersburg, but the city did not fall, and Grant's army settled down for a siege.

On the fifth of July, a year and a day after the surrender of Vicksburg, Sherman, on a hill top, saw Atlanta in the distance. On the twenty-

second, a fierce battle was fought for the possession of the city, and he too prepared for a siege. On the second of September, in the small hours of the night, a courier arrived at Sherman's headquarters to tell him that the breakthrough had occurred and that the Union troops were entering the city. Sherman sent the civilian population away, moved his headquarters into the city, and immediately began to prepare for the final sweep southeast to the sea.

And there too were the women—gentle, persistent, adamant. Mother Bickerdyke, Sherman was willing to tolerate, for between Sherman and this woman there had grown up "an unintimate but powerful understanding."[3] The General cherished her, scolded her, laughed at her and brushed aside all complaints against her, and she regarded him with a mixture of emotions which might be described as affectionate exasperation.

Bickerdyke was privileged, but Sherman had issued orders forbidding anyone not a soldier to go beyond Chattanooga. One day he caught sight of Annie Wittenmyer and shouted at her, "Stop madam, who are you? How did you get here?"

"I am Mrs. Wittenmyer, State Agent for Iowa and agent of the Christian Commission."

"How dare you come, how *dare* they *let you come* after such positive orders as I have issued? Go *home,* madam. Take the first train back and don't stop this side of Chattanooga. *Go.*" And Elvira Powers who was watching and told the story with enjoyment, said that Mrs. Wittenmyer never walked faster in her life.[4]

Sherman renewed his orders but it was hard, sometimes, for his subordinates to refuse a pass to a woman who had powerful political connections. One day in October, one of the officers stationed at Chattanooga, wrote to Sherman that a woman had arrived there with a large quantity of supplies demanding a pass to Atlanta and what should he do about it? Sherman replied, "Always send a barrel of pork in place of a woman."

Bickerdyke pleaded with the General to be allowed to go with him on his march from Atlanta, but he was adamant in his refusal. He suggested, however, that she go around by sea and meet him at the point on the coast where he would come out, though it seems unlikely that he confided his destination to her, for only his wing commanders were given that information in advance. On the twelfth of November Sherman sent his last telegram from Atlanta and gave orders to cut the wires. Demolition squads had already begun to wreck factories and buildings in the city. On the fifteenth, the city was set on fire and the troops began to march.

Mother Bickerdyke was on the last train to leave. On the sixteenth, Sherman himself rode out of Atlanta, and the North heard no more from him for five long, anxious weeks.

NOTES

[1] Lloyd Lewis, *Sherman, Fighting Prophet* (Harcourt, Brace & Company, 1932).

[2] Figures based on *Numbers and Losses in the Civil War* by Thomas L. Livermore (Indiana University Press, Bloomingdale, 1957).

[3] L. P. Brockett, M.D. and Mary C. Vaughan, *Woman's Work in the Civil War* (Zeigler, McCurdy & Co., R. H. Curran, Boston, 1867).

[4] Elvira J. Powers, *Hospital Pencillings* (Edward L. Mitchell, Boston, 1866), p. 92.

25

WITH CHARITY FOR ALL

───────────────── ★ ─────────────────

CHRONOLOGY

1864

December 5   Second session of the 38th Congress assembled.

December 16   Sherman arrived before Savannah and commenced the siege.

December 15–16 Confederates routed at Nashville, in Tennessee.

December 20   General Hardee evacuated Savannah.

December 21   Sherman took possession of Savannah.

December 25   Lincoln gave the news of the capture of Savannah to the country.

───────────────── ★ ─────────────────

> *And Husband and Etheridge and Harlan and Case,*
> *Livermore, Alcott, Hancock and Chase*
> *And Turner and Hawley and Potter and Hall,*
> *Ah! the list grows apace as they come at the call.*
> —Clara Barton

IN THE SUMMER OF 1864, City Point, Virginia, became the most important place in the country. The army had settled down for a siege of Petersburg, and City Point, ten miles away at the confluence of the James and the Appomattox Rivers, became Grant's base of supplies. At

the beginning of the siege, City Point was a sleepy river landing consisting mainly of some mud flats, tumbled-down wharves, a few small dwellings and pine groves, overlooked by a fine old house on a bluff called the Eppes mansion. In wet weather the mud was a foot deep and of a consistency to pull off a boot. In dry weather the mud turned to dust, so that the air was thick, like that of a flour mill.

As soon as the army arrived, this forlorn spot began to change. New wharves stretched out along the river, but they could not keep pace with the growing river traffic. Boats towing long strings of barges crowded the river, waiting their turns to add to the huge piles of supplies on the shore. Some of the mountains of supplies belonged to the Sanitary Commission, for the field officers of that enterprising organization arrived on June 18th, while the first assault on Petersburg was still in progress.

The first soldiers to be wounded at Petersburg were brought to City Point and housed in a tent hospital that grew, in the following months, until it covered many acres. The hospital was divided by numbered streets, with a broad central avenue at the end of which was the supply headquarters of the Sanitary Commission, and to facilitate the unloading of the wounded, the railroad from Petersburg was run into the hospital grounds. The first wounded to arrive had been loaded like logwood onto flatcars, but in time hospital coaches were installed, fitted with cots hung on broad bands of elastic. The hospital trains, and the promptness with which the wounded were taken from the field, saved many lives.

At one side of the hospital, near the headquarters of the Sanitary Commission, was a street of state relief agency tents and the large supply tents of the Christian Commission. Most of the state agents were women and there were women workers in both the Commissions. Supplies were abundant because of the success of the great sanitary fairs. The Sanitary Commission issued all sorts of articles to supplement those issued by the Army, and the Christian Commission had a cookhouse where the workers prepared food which they distributed in the hospital more or less indiscriminately and at odd hours, much to the annoyance of the surgeons and the ladies who ran the huge kitchens.

Water for this vast undertaking was brought from the river by steam engine pumps operated, surprisingly, by the Christian Commission. As the hospital grew, the dust increased until, as one of the nurses remembered, it was impossible to see the river through the fog, or even a tent not many feet away. Eventually Grant, who often visited the hospital, ordered the water supply increased sufficiently to water the hospital

streets and to cool the tents by wetting the canvas. The mud, however, was never conquered.

City Point had a hotel, built hurriedly by an enterprising Northerner, a church, a chapel, sutlers' stores and barber shops, but ladies-of-joy who tried to locate there were promptly run out of town. Corps headquarters were located there, and Grant and his staff occupied a log building and several tents on the grounds of the Eppes house where there was shade and a fine view of the rivers.

City Point, which far surpassed White House, was the first of the great bases, American style, the forerunner of the base at Brest in the First World War. It was the gigantic stage set on which was played the grand finale, with the boom of cannon, the dress parades, great explosions that shook the earth, and at the end, flames from Petersburg lighting the backdrop and the Stars and Stripes flying over the captured city.

And for the grand finale, in traditional manner, most of the cast came on the stage. Lincoln, Grant, Sheridan, Sherman briefly, and Custer of Indian fighting fame, all made their entrances. The women came—Dix, Hancock, Annie Etheridge, Wittenmyer, Gilson, Mary Husband, Mrs. Holstein (like Cornelia Hancock, an old friend from Gettysburg), Mrs. John Harris, indefatigable lady from Philadelphia, Mary Lee, Charlotte McKay, and many, many more. Some of the Woolseys came, but not until the curtain was going down. Barton was there briefly. Mary Todd Lincoln and Mrs. Grant came, and numerous wives of generals, including Arabella Barlow, who died of a fever contracted while working there.

Most of the nurses and women who ran the diet kitchens worked without pay, leading busy, humdrum lives. A few of them had adventures to relate, some fell sick and some died there. When an ammunition barge exploded in the river not far from the hospital, a Mrs. Spencer was struck by a shell fragment, but saved from serious injury by the resilient wires of the crinoline which, contrary to local custom, she happened to be wearing.

Bridget Divers (or Deavers) was there—"Michigan Bridget" as she was called by the troops. She had attached herself to the First Michigan Cavalry, in which her husband served as a private, rode a government horse, carried arms, and on several occasions took the place of a fallen man in the ranks. At Petersburg, she was ordered away from the front and became for a time, Cornelia Hancock's tent mate. Cornelia thought her "a splendid hand to work," and in one of those vignettes which have survived the passage of time, at a surprise inspection of the hospital kitchen, we see her delighted because the floor had just been scrubbed.

There is a weird story about this Irish girl, told by the reliable Mrs. Husband, about her rescue of the body of the captain who commanded the company of which she considered herself a member. She and an orderly rode out at night to the place where the captain had been killed, found his body, strapped it to Bridget's horse and carried it to an undertaker in City Point. The embalmed body was again strapped to Bridget's horse and she rode off in search of a coffin in which to ship him to his friends in Michigan. Bridget was a rough-and-tumble character, common, vigorous and kind-hearted.

The women of the hospital had to learn the technique of tent life, like any soldier. The tents were hot in summer and rain beat on the canvas, inches from their beds, with the sound of drums. They were waterproof until something, a pillow perhaps, touched the material and then the contact caused a leak which could not be stopped. Many a newcomer had to learn that the candle must be blown out before she began to undress, for if it were not, a perfect silhouette was visible from outside. Thieves could reach in between the tent pegs at the bottom to abstract a purse from under a pillow or, quite as serious, a pair of shoes, and not infrequently the peace of night was shattered by the screeches of a frightened lady in a nightcap.

It was inevitable that Wittenmyer should visit City Point, as inevitable as that Miss Dix should do so likewise. The two great ladies who, it may be supposed, had no special liking for each other, met on the steamer going south. Wittenmyer thought Miss Dix the stateliest woman she had ever seen, "very dignified in manner and conversation." She was wearing the customary plain dress with neat linen collar and cuffs and no ornaments, not even a breast pin, for Miss Dix practiced that which she preached.

It was night before these two formidable women arrived at City Point. No one was expecting them and both town and hospital were overcrowded, but Miss Dix said, "I have no concern, there are always plenty of cots and I'll find room in some of the nurses' tents." With that they parted. Mrs. Wittenmyer, after some trouble, found a place to sleep on a pile of boxes in a storeroom of the Christian Commission. Some one brought her a candle and a bundle of straw and shavings for a mattress and, using her carpet bag for a pillow, she arranged herself for sleep.

There was a knock on the door and when Mrs. Wittenmyer opened it, "that stately woman, with all her dignity upon her," walked in and asked if she could share the storeroom for the night. "As Miss Dix was old enough to be my mother," Mrs. Wittenmyer said, "of course there was

but one thing to do, and that was to give up my bed of shavings and straw to her, and with the stub of an old broom, try to clear a place on another part of the floor for myself."

Cornelia Hancock was running a "low diet" kitchen where the food for two or three hundred men was prepared. After the first hard days were over she lived comfortably in a tent with a floor, and was writing home for a piece of carpet and a tablecloth to make her quarters pretty. Her letters, filled with the graceful Quaker "thees" and "thous," ask again and again to have clothing sent to her, for like all the other women she was forever short of dresses and shoes. Cornelia was in love, but sensibly, without coquettishness, as became a Quaker girl. The man was Dr. Dudley, a surgeon, but the love affair did not have a happy ending. When Cornelia died in her eighties, a packet of old letters was found which were marked, "to be burned after my death." Perhaps they were from Dr. Dudley, but we will never know, for her instructions were carried out.

Adelaide Smith arrived on the scene early, and found life in the great hospital exactly to her liking. She was fond of managing, and she had plenty of energy when the hard day's work was done, for such activities as singing in the choir or going on long horseback rides. She was a plain girl, with pulled back hair which she wore in a waterfall behind, but she seems to have made up for her plainness by the vigor of her personality. She liked men and wanted to be popular, but she liked her own opinions better and defended them so pugnaciously that she was embroiled in a good many quarrels. Those which she won were still giving her satisfaction when she recorded them forty-seven years later.[1]

Adelaide was not an Army Corps nurse, though Miss Dix tried to enlist her, for she preferred, as she said "to do independent work." It was very independent, and in the course of it she had some sort of brush with Cornelia Hancock. What the trouble was about, we do not know, but the situation was saved when Adelaide was invited to assist in the New Jersey and Pennsylvania agencies.

The transfer was probably engineered by Dr. Hettie K. Painter, who directed the work of those Agencies. Dr. Painter was a petite, calm-faced Quaker woman with a kind smile and the confidence inspiring manner of the true physician. She was good to the bumptious Adelaide, as she must have been to everyone she met. On Christmas day she invited Adelaide to go on a pleasure drive with her to Hatcher's Run. As they went in a springless ambulance, the pleasure part of it would seem to be prob-

lematical, but Dr. Painter's son was the telegrapher of the encampment, and she was anxious to see him.

They found the lad in a Negro cabin, bent over his instruments. In the course of the visit young Painter (he was barely seventeen) said to Adelaide, "Miss Smith, you are always looking up some souvenir of the war, here is something that you may appreciate. This is a telegram from General Sherman, received here this morning en route, and I immediately forwarded a copy to President Lincoln in Washington. It is therefore a copy of the message before it was dispatched to the President." The telegram read:

"The United States Military Telegraph
    Savannah, Ga., 23, 1864
    Via Fortress Monroe, 25
To his Excellency, President Lincoln:
    I beg to present you as a Christmas gift the city of Savannah, 150 heavy guns and plenty of ammunition; also about twenty-five thousand bales of cotton.

                                        W. T. Sherman
                                        Major General"

After thirty-two days of utter silence, during which Sherman had been cut off from the outside world, he had completed the three-hundred mile march through enemy territory and entered Savannah almost without a struggle.

Mother Bickerdyke did not meet him there. True to his word, he had sent her an order for a ship, and she had set out from Philadelphia with the ship loaded with supplies, but at Wilmington, North Carolina, she found the recently released prisoners from Andersonville, and as they were in pitiable condition, Sherman's supplies traveled no further.

Sherman, leaving Savannah, marched northward through the Carolinas. Bickerdyke rejoined him at Beaufort, and remained there until after Lee's surrender.

Many people from the surrounding countryside had taken refuge in City Point and had been trapped there by the siege, so that all the houses were filled and food grew scarce.

One of the refugees was Mrs. Roger Pryor, but she was no longer the gay, self-confident, snobbish young woman of pre-war Washington. Her husband, now a General, was at the front. Some of her children were at a house in the country which she could not reach through the Union lines. Her two young boys were with her and another child was on the

way. Her money was almost gone, and she walked the streets of Petersburg for days hunting a place to live.

Finally she was lent an overseer's house in some slave quarters on the outskirts of Petersburg. The place was full of wasp nests and black with the greasy smoke of many meals. Some of the floor boards were loose and the furnishings consisted of three chairs, a table, and a pine bed with a trundle. There were no curtains or rugs and no china. The attic bedroom where she and the children slept was so small that when the trundle bed was pulled out, it filled all the space.

The day after Christmas her child was born with the aid of a Petersburg doctor and a fieldhand slave woman named Anarchy. Three weeks later, she was still in bed and ill. One of her boys ran upstairs to her room crying in a frightened voice, "Oh, mamma, an old gray soldier is coming in."

"He stood—this old gray soldier—and looked at me, leaning on his saber.

" 'Is this the reward my country gives me?' he said; and not until he spoke did I recognize my husband."[2]

One day at City Point one of the nurses in her customary hurry, ran out of a hospital tent with a slop jar in her arms—and stopped in her tracks, staring open mouthed at a tall figure in a black frock coat and tall stovepipe hat. It was the President, who with Mrs. Lincoln, came to City Point in the last days of March. He spent much time going from bed to bed, talking with great sympathy to the wounded boys, his eyes unutterably sad. Mary Blackmar Brusen, a medical student in charge of a ward of wounded Confederate soldiers, told of one of those visits. The orderly came running into the ward crying:

"President Lincoln's coming!" "I was at the extreme end of the hospital tent," the young doctor wrote, "but girl-like, started forward that I might see him. At that instant, oh, such a puny, helpless wail, as of sick and dying infants, issued from every throat: 'Oh, don't leave us, Miss! He is a beast! He will kill us!"

"I replied: 'Oh, no! He is a grand good man!' Again and again came forth that puny wail, 'Don't leave us, Miss!' till I finally said, 'Well, I'll not leave you, don't fear!' but by that time I had got to the front of the tent and the orderly had pulled back a flap on my request so that I peered out. Within about fifteen or twenty feet were General Grant, with the inevitable cigar, and President Lincoln, so tall, so lank, giving evidence of much sorrow, looming over him. I heard General Grant say distinctly, 'These are Confederate

quarters.' President Lincoln immediately said, 'I wish to go in here alone!'

"I drew myself up into the corner as close as possible, and he bent under the flap and came in. He went at once to a bedside, and reverently leaned over almost double, so low were the cots, and stroked the soldier's head, and with tears streaming down his face he said in a sort of sweet anguish, 'Oh, my man, why did you do it?' The boy in gray said, or rather stammered weakly, almost in a whisper, 'I went because my State went.' On that ground floor, so quiet was the whole ward, a pin could almost have been heard to fall. President Lincoln went from one bed to another and touched each forehead gently, and with tears streaming asked again the question, and again heard the same reply. When he finally passed out from these boys, some gray and grizzled, but many of them children, there came as from one voice, 'Oh, we didn't know he was such a good man! We thought he was a beast!' "[3]

Mary Todd Lincoln was a tragic figure in these days, for she had never recovered, either physically or mentally, from the shock of Willie's death and from the effect of an accident when she had been thrown from her carriage and had struck her head. Her beauty, if she had ever possessed any, had long since vanished. Her eyes were hard and resentful, her stubborn mouth was dragged down at the corners by sorrow. She was consumed by a burning fire of jealousy both for her prerogatives as the wife of the President, and of any woman who made even the slightest claim to her husband's attention. Lincoln, saddened by her state and patient under the frequent lashings of her tongue, called her "Mother" and showed her unfailing gentleness, but her tempers and the public scenes she made were a severe trial to him.

Gossip about Mrs. Lincoln's eccentric behavior was rife in Washington, and it seems certain that the insanity for which her son Robert had her committed for some months in 1875, had already commenced. One day a party, consisting of the President, Adam Badeau, Mrs. Lincoln, Mrs. Grant and some others, was on the way to Fort Stedman. For part of the journey over the rough roads, the men, except Badeau, rode on horseback, and the two ladies, with Badeau as escort, rode in an ambulance.

"I chanced to mention," Badeau recalled, "that all the wives of officers at the army front had been ordered to the rear—a sure sign that active operations were in contemplation. I said not a lady had been allowed to remain, except Mrs. Griffin, the wife of General Charles Griffin, who had obtained a special permit from the Presi-

dent. At this Mrs. Lincoln was up in arms, 'What you mean by that, sir?' she exclaimed. 'Do you mean to say that she saw the President alone? Do you know that I never allow the President to see any woman alone?' She was absolutely jealous of poor, ugly Abraham Lincoln.

"I tried to pacify her and to palliate my remark, but she was fairly boiling with rage. 'That's a very equivocal smile, sir,' she exclaimed, 'Let me out of this carriage at once. I will ask the President if he saw that woman alone.' Mrs. Griffin, afterward the Countess Esterhazy, was one of the best known and most elegant women in Washington, a Carroll, and a personal acquaintance of Mrs. Grant, who strove to mollify the excited spouse, but all in vain. Mrs. Lincoln again bade me stop the driver, and when I hesitated to obey, she thrust her arms past me to the front of the carriage and held the driver fast. But Mrs. Grant finally prevailed upon her to wait till the whole party alighted, and then General Meade came up to pay his respects to the wife of the President. I had intended to offer Mrs. Lincoln my arm, and endeavor to prevent a scene, but Meade, of course, as my superior, had the right to escort her, and I had no chance to warn him. I saw them go off together, and remained in fear . . . for what might occur. . . . But General Meade was very adroit, and when they returned Mrs. Lincoln looked at me significantly and said: 'General Meade is a gentleman, sir. He says it was not the President who gave Mrs. Griffin a permit, but the Secretary of War.' Meade was the son of a diplomatist, and had evidently inherited some of his father's skill.

"At night, when we were back in camp, Mrs. Grant talked the matter over with me, and said the whole affair was so distressing and mortifying that neither of us must ever mention it; at least, I was to be absolutely silent, and she would disclose it only to the General."[4]

There was worse to come. At a review of the troops the President was to appear on horseback accompanied by the Generals Grant and Ord. Mrs. Lincoln and Mrs. Grant were to go in the ambulance, accompanied by Badeau, but Badeau, not caring to have the sole responsibility if another scene should occur, had arranged for General Horace Porter to accompany them.

The ladies were late and the President directed that the review was to begin without them. Mrs. Ord, on horseback, had meanwhile, asked if it would be proper for her to accompany the reviewing party and one of the officers present told her, "Of course! Come along!"

They had ridden halfway down the line, bands playing, soldiers at

"present arms" when the ambulance came in sight. Mrs. Ord at once left the reviewing party and, accompanied by the officer whom she had questioned, galloped across the field to join Mrs. Lincoln and Mrs. Grant. It was evident that something unpleasant had occurred. They were received coldly by Mrs. Lincoln, Mrs. Grant was silent and obviously embarrassed and the two men appeared to be unhappy. There seemed to be no course open to Mrs. Ord and her companion but to retire. Moreover, the ambulance was full, and Mrs. Ord, remaining on horseback, rode for a time beside the President.

Badeau recalled that:

"As soon as Mrs. Lincoln discovered this her rage was beyond all bounds. 'What does the woman mean,' she exclaimed, 'by riding by the side of the President? and ahead of me? Does she suppose that *he* wants *her* by the side of *him?*' She was in a frenzy of excitement, and language and action both became more extravagant every moment. Mrs. Grant again endeavored to pacify her, but then Mrs. Lincoln got angry with Mrs. Grant; and all that Porter and I could do was to see nothing worse than words occurred. We feared she might jump out of the vehicle and shout to the cavalcade. Once she said to Mrs. Grant in her transports: 'I suppose you think you'll get to the White House yourself, don't you?' Mrs. Grant was very calm and dignified, and merely replied that she was quite satisfied with her present position; it was far greater than she had ever expected to attain. But Mrs. Lincoln exclaimed: 'Oh! you had better take it if you can get it. 'Tis very nice.' Then she reverted to Mrs. Ord, while Mrs. Grant defended her friend at the risk of arousing greater vehemence.

"When there was a halt, Major Seward, a nephew of the Secretary of State, and an officer of General Ord's staff, rode up, and tried to say something jocular. 'The President's horse is very gallant, Mrs. Lincoln,' he remarked; 'he insists on riding by the side of Mrs. Ord.' This of course added fuel to the flame. 'What do you mean by that, sir?' she cried. Seward discovered that he had made a huge mistake, and his horse at once developed a peculiarity that compelled him to ride behind, to get out of the way of the storm.

"Finally the party arrived at its destination and Mrs. Ord came up to the ambulance. Then Mrs. Lincoln positively insulted her, called her vile names in the presence of a crowd of officers, and asked her what she meant by following up the President. The poor woman burst into tears and inquired what she had done, but Mrs. Lincoln refused to be appeased, and stormed till she was tired. Mrs. Grant still tried to stand by her friend, and everybody was shocked and

horrified. But all things come to an end, and after a while we returned to City Point."[5]

Scenes such as these were bitterly hard for the President to bear, and
someone noted at this time that when he talked his face was often alight
with animation, but when he was silent, it fell once more into the deeply
graven lines of sadness. But in the midst of grief and care he never lost
his humor and seemed always to be ready for one of his gentle jokes.

General Collis who, with his pretty, fashionable wife Septima, was
quartered in a little farmhouse at City Point, recalled such an occasion.
Prisoners were coming into City Point that spring in such numbers that
they overflowed the famous prison stockade called the Bull Pen, and
they were allowed to stay outside since, discouraged and half-starved as
they were, there was no danger that they would try to escape. The Bull
Pen was for men in the ranks, but there were some high officers among
the prisoners and they received quite different treatment.

One of them was General Barringer of North Carolina. Collis recalled:

> "Mr. Lincoln was at City Point, [and] the General one day
> begged me to give him an opportunity to see him as he walked or
> rode through the camp, and happening to spend that evening with
> the President in the tent of Colonel Bowers, Grant's Adjutant-
> General, who had remained behind to keep up communication with
> the armies operating across the James River, I incidentally referred
> to the request of General Barringer. Mr. Lincoln immediately asked
> me to present his compliments to the General, and to say he would
> like very much to see him, whispering to me in his quaint and jocose
> way: 'Do you know I have never seen a live Rebel general in full
> uniform.'
>
> "At once communicating the President's wish to General Bar-
> ringer, I found that officer much embarrassed. He feared I had over-
> stepped the bounds of propriety in mentioning his curiosity to see
> the Northern President, and that Mr. Lincoln would think him a
> very impertinent fellow, besides which he was muddy, and tattered,
> and torn, and not at all presentable.
>
> "Reassuring him as best I could, he at last sought out those em-
> bellishments which a whisk, a blacking brush, and a comb provided,
> and we walked over to headquarters, where we found the President
> in high feather, listening to the cheerful messages from Grant at the
> front.
>
> "I formally presented General Barringer, of North Carolina, to
> the President of the United States, and Mr. Lincoln extended his

hand, warmly welcomed him, and bade him be seated. There was, however, only one chair vacant when the President arose, and this the Southerner very politely declined to take.

"This left the two men facing each other in the center of the tent, the tall form of Mr. Lincoln almost reaching the ridge-pole. He slowly removed his eyeglasses, looked the General over from head to foot, and then in a slow, meditative and puzzled manner inquired:

" 'Barringer? Barringer? from North Carolina? Barringer of North Carolina: General, were you ever in Congress?'

" 'No, Mr. Lincoln, I never was,' replied the General.

" 'Well, I thought not; I thought my memory couldn't be so much at fault. But there was a Barringer in Congress with me, and from your State too!'

" 'That was my brother, sir,' said Barringer.

"Up to this moment the hard face of the President had that thoughtful, troubled expression with which those of us who knew him were only too familiar, but now the lines melted away, and the eyes and tongue both laughed. I cannot describe the change, though I still see it and shall never forget it. It was like a great sudden burst of sunshine in a rain storm.

" 'Well! well!' exclaimed the great and good man, burying for the moment all thought of war, its cares, its asperities, and the frightful labor it had imposed upon him; his heart welling up only to the joyous reminiscence which the meeting brought him.

" 'Well! well!' said he; 'do you know that that brother of yours was my chum in Congress. Yes, sir, we sat at the same desk and ate at the same table. He was a Whig and so was I. He was my chum, and I was very fond of him. And you are his brother, eh? Well! well! shake again.' And once more in the pressure of his great big hand, his heart went out to this man in arms against the government, simply because his brother had been his chum and was a good fellow.

"A couple more chairs by this time had been added to the scant furniture of the Adjutant-General's tent, and the conversation drifted from Mr. Lincoln's anecdotes of the pleasant hours he and Barringer had spent together, to the war, thence to the merits of military and civil leaders, North and South, illustrated here and there by some appropriate story, entirely new, full of humor and sometimes pathos.

"Several times the General made a movement to depart, fearing he was availing himself too lavishly of Mr. Lincoln's affability, but each time was ordered to keep his seat, the President remarking that they were both prisoners, and he hoped the General would

take some pity upon him and help him to talk about the times when they were both their own masters, and hadn't everybody criticising and abusing them.

"Finally however, General Barringer arose, and was bowing himself out, when Mr. Lincoln once more took him by the hand almost affectionately, placed another hand upon his shoulder, and inquired quite seriously:

" 'Do you think I can be of any service to you?'

"Not until we had all finished a hearty laugh at this quaint remark did the President realize the innocent simplicity of his inquiry, and when General Barringer was able to reply that 'If anybody can be of service to a poor devil in my situation, I presume you are the man,' Mr. Lincoln drew a blank card from his vest pocket, adjusted his glasses, turned up the wick of the lamp, and sat down at General Barringer's desk with all the serious earnestness with which you would suppose he had attached his name to the Emancipation Proclamation.

"This was, however, all assumed. He was equipping himself and preparing us for one of his little jokes. While writing he kept up a running conversation with General Barringer (who was still standing and wondering) to this effect:

" 'I suppose they will send you to Washington, and there no doubt they will put you in the old Capitol prison. I am told it isn't a nice sort of place, and I am afraid you won't find it a very comfortable tavern; but I have a powerful friend in Washington— he's the biggest man in the country—and I believe I have some influence with him when I don't ask too much. Now I want you to send this card of introduction to him, and if he takes the notion he may put you on your parole, or let up on you that way or some other way. Anyhow, it's worth while trying.'

"And then very deliberately drying the card with the blotter, he held it up to the light and read it to us in about the following words:

" 'This is General Barringer, of the Southern army. He is the brother of a very dear friend of mine. Can you do anything to make his detention in Washington as comfortable as possible under the circumstances?

A. Lincoln.

To Hon. Edwin M. Stanton,
Secretary of War.'

"Barringer never uttered a word. I think he made an effort to say 'Thank you' or 'God bless you,' or something of that kind, but he was speechless. We both wheeled about and left the tent.

"After walking a few yards, not hearing any footsteps near me, and fearing Barringer had lost his way, I turned back and found this gallant leader of brave men, who had won his stars in a score of battles, 'like Niobe, all tears,' audibly sobbing and terribly overcome.

"He took my arm, and as we walked slowly home he gave voice to as hearty expressions of love for the great Lincoln as have been since uttered by his most devoted and life-long friends.

"A few years afterwards I met the General socially in Philadelphia, and we went over this episode in his life, as I have narrated it, and then, for the third time, his eyes filled as he told me how he had wept and wept at 'the deep damnation of his taking off.' "6

Mrs. Lincoln, stricken, perhaps, with remorse as she often was after one of her tirades, and almost broken under the lash of her own emotions, left City Point on April 1st. No reason for her sudden departure was given, but it is easy to believe that it was in reality a flight. Two telegrams to her husband, recently discovered, came from her at this time, the telegraphic form disguising the characteristic misuse of the comma which gave to her style an illusion of breathlessness. One telegram complains of her discomfort on the boat on which she was traveling. The other saying in part, " . . . cannot you return on some other vessel. We are most uncomfortable on this and would like your boat . . ."7

Before Mrs. Lincoln left, Grant departed for the beginning of the Appomattox campaign, and Lincoln resumed his old habit of haunting the place where the telegraph operators were receiving news from the front. In these days he was gaunt, anxious and pale from restless nights. During his troubled slumber he had a dream which he told to his friend, Ward Hill Lamon:

"There seemed to be a deathlike stillness about me. Then I heard subdued sobs, as if a number of people were weeping. I thought I left my bed and wandered downstairs. There the silence was broken by the same pitiful sobbing, but the mourners were invisible. I went from room to room; no living person was in sight, but the same mournful sounds of distress met me as I passed along. It was light in all the rooms; every object was familiar to me; but where were all the people who were grieving as if their hearts would break? . . . Before me was a catafalque, on which rested a corpse wrapped in funeral vestments. Around it were stationed soldiers who were acting as guards; and there was a throng of people, some gazing mournfully upon the corpse, whose face was covered, others weeping pitifully. 'Who is dead in the White House?' I demanded

of one of the soldiers. 'The President' was his answer; 'he was killed by an assassin!' Then came a loud burst of grief from the crowd, which awoke me from my dream. . . ."[8]

NOTES

[1] Adelaide W. Smith, *Reminiscences of an Army Nurse in the Civil War* (Greaves Publishing Co., New York, 1911).

[2] Mrs. Roger Pryor, *Reminiscences in Peace and War* (The Macmillan Co., New York, 1904).

[3] Sylvia G. L. Dannett, *Noble Women of the North* (Thomas Yoseloff, New York, 1959), pp. 344-345.

[4] Philip Van Doren Stern, *An End To Valor* (Houghton Mifflin Company, Boston, 1958), pp. 87-88.

[5] *Ibid.*, pp. 94-95.

[6] Septima M. Collis, *A Woman's War Record* (G. P. Putnam's Sons, New York, 1889), pp. 62-70.

[7] From National Archives.

[8] Stern, *op. cit.*, p. 149.

26

THE END CAME SWIFTLY

---------------------------------- ★ ----------------------------------

CHRONOLOGY
1865

January 15   Fort Fisher, North Carolina, captured by the Union forces.

February 1   General Sherman started on his campaign in the Carolinas.

February 3   Peace conference held at Hampton Roads, Virginia.

February 17   Surrender of Columbia, South Carolina.

February 18   Charleston, South Carolina, abandoned.

February 22   Wilmington, North Carolina, captured.

February 27   Sheridan's cavalry began the clearing of the Shenandoah Valley.

March 4   Lincoln's second inauguration.

March 21–23   Troops from Fort Fisher and Wilmington joined Sherman's forces at Goldsboro, North Carolina.

March 25   Lincoln left for City Point to confer with Grant.

March 26   Sheridan joined Grant at City Point, Virginia.

March 29   The opening of Grant's spring campaign. Battle of White Oak Road began.

March 29–April 2   Grant's final assault on Petersburg.

March 31   Action at Dinwiddie Court House.

340

April 1	Battle of Five Forks.
April 2	Fall of Petersburg.
April 3	Fall of Richmond.
April 4	Lincoln in Richmond for a stay of two days.
April 6	Fighting at Sayler's Creek.
April 7	Lee, in a note to Grant, asked terms of surrender.
April 9	Lee surrendered the Army of Northern Virginia to Grant at Appomattox Court House.
April 11	Mobile, Alabama, evacuated.
April 12	Capture of Montgomery, Alabama.
April 14	President Lincoln shot. Seward and his son attacked and wounded seriously.
April 15	The death of President Lincoln. Andrew Johnson inaugurated.
April 19	Funeral services for President Lincoln in Washington.
April 26	Surrender of General Johnston to Sherman in North Carolina. Booth shot.
May 10	Jefferson Davis taken prisoner in Georgia.
May 10–June 30	Trial of the Lincoln conspirators
May 23–24	Grand Review of the Armies in Washington.

———————————————— ★ ————————————————

O withered is the garland of the war
—William Shakespeare

AT THE CLOSE OF 1864, the disintegration of the Confederacy was far advanced. Sherman had swept through Georgia to Savannah and turned northward to leave a trail of ruin through South Carolina. Sheridan had cleared the Shenandoah Valley and shattered Early's army.

Thomas had defeated Hood at Nashville, and the great days of the Army of the Tennessee were over. Mobile was in Union hands and Fort Fisher, North Carolina, which guarded the last Confederate seaport, was lost early in January of 1865. Only two great Confederate armies remained in the field as effective fighting forces: Johnston's in the Carolinas and Lee's once mighty Army of Northern Virginia which, for nine months, had faced Grant at Petersburg.

Grant's spring campaign for the capture of Petersburg and Richmond opened on the twenty-ninth of March. On that day, the troops, with bands playing and colors flying, began to move out of City Point like sands from an hourglass. Grant was abandoning his log house on the bluff for new headquarters in a muddy field, and there would be little left at City Point but the hospital and the Bull Pen.

There was a brief scene of farewell beside the railroad tracks while the horses and gear belonging to Grant and his staff were loaded into boxcars. Lincoln, towering above the little General, shook hands all around, a whistle blew, Grant climbed aboard. The train pulled out, gathered momentum in the open country, but a large part of the track had been laid hastily, without grading, and the motion of the train over the hummocks of ground, gave this historic departure the ludicrous appearance of a roller-coaster.

Fighting outside Petersburg began almost at once, and from then until the end, though it varied in intensity, it only ceased for brief intervals. On April 1st a battle was fought at Five Forks as the Union Army moved north and east. On April 2nd a messenger came into the church in Richmond where President Davis was attending the service and handed him a telegram which he read and quickly left the church. There were murmurs and a rustling throughout the congregation as men and women, certain that the President had received grave news, turned to gaze questioningly after him. The telegram was from Lee stating that the government must leave Richmond that night.

Mrs. Davis had departed on March 31st and Davis had presented her with some money in gold, saying, "If I live you can come to me when the struggle is ended, but I do not expect to survive the destruction of constitutional liberty." Then he put a pistol into her hands, saying, "I charge you solemnly to leave when you hear the enemy approaching . . ."

By two o'clock of April 2nd the Confederate Government evacuated Richmond and the archives of the defeated nation were burning in the streets. That same day, the Union troops entered Petersburg, which Lee had abandoned the previous day. Grant arrived about nine o'clock and

set up his headquarters in a brick house, and there Lincoln joined him, bringing with him his son Tad. The President's tired face was lit with pleasure as he shook Grant's hand, and then, for a time, the two men earnestly discussed the future of the South.

As soon as the city, which for so long had bristled with guns, lay open and helpless, the sight-seers began to arrive. Women from the hospital at City Point wandered through the streets gazing with curiosity at the Confederate ladies in their fashions of four years earlier while the Petersburg ladies gazed in astonishment at the nurses' ankle-length, hoopless skirts.

Away to the south and west, fierce fighting was still going on, but the Confederate army had begun to crumble. Many soldiers, knowing full well that the end was near and not wanting to be killed in the last days of a war which was already lost, laid down their arms and accoutrement and slipped away to their homes, never to return. So many Confederate muskets were thrown away that the Union soldiers used them to corduroy a road. Hundreds of prisoners were marched back to the stockades at City Point, and on the field the Confederate dead lay with none to bury them.

Richmond fell into Federal hands on April 3rd. The Union army was now below the city, facing north and east, and most of the leaders of the Confederacy had reached the bitter conclusion that the days of their long, brave fight for existence as a separate state were numbered. President Davis was not among them. The day after the fall of Richmond, in an address to the people of the Confederacy, he said nothing was needed "to render our triumph certain but the exhibition of unquenchable resolve." He was a tragic figure, receding into obscurity.

Lincoln arrived in Richmond on April 4th. Part of the city was burning still, and debris littered the streets. Ruined chimneys and tottering walls stood out against the skyline. The sun was darkened by smoke, and the air was heavy with the stench of smoldering cotton. Lincoln, in company with Admiral Porter, young Tad, and a small guard, began the two-mile walk to the house formerly occupied by President Davis. Hostile people gazed at him from windows and doorways, but as he moved slowly forward he was surrounded by deep silence.

News of his arrival flew ahead of him, however, and it was not long before the Negroes began to gather around him and to move with him up the streets, a laughing, praying mob that turned the progress of the gaunt President into a strange and moving triumphal procession. One of them was heard to cry in a loud voice, "Bres de Lord, dere is de great

Messiah," and kneeling in the roadway, he tried to kiss the President's feet.

Lincoln remained in Richmond for two days and after his departure came the tourists. Cornelia Hancock (who had already sent home most of her possessions and those of Annie Etheridge) went with a party of nurses, taking horses with them on the boat. They visited Libby Prison and the ruins and Cornelia thought that "beauty was apparent even in the desolate, dejected city." Georgy and her mother hastened to Richmond and somehow managed to be gay in the setting of devastation. One can understand the nurses wanting to see the city near which they had worked for so long, but there is something unpleasant about the fashionable ladies who came out of curiosity and nothing more, though the point of view of those who have lived through years of war is not always clear a generation or two later.

When Lincoln returned to City Point, he was cheered by a crowd of Confederate prisoners and, turning to Admiral Porter he said, ". . . if Grant is wise he will leave them their guns to shoot crows with and their horses to plough with; it would do no harm." At City Point he received word that Seward had been thrown from his carriage, and he left for Washington at once. It was there, on the ninth of April, that he received word of Lee's surrender at Appomattox Court House.

The formalities of the surrender were businesslike, courteous, and restrained, though there were emotional moments both before and after the surrender when the soldiers caught sight of the defeated General. No doubt as in all wars, most of the rank and file were thinking about returning to their homes to resume lives that war had interrupted. But there were a few among those multitudes at Appomattox Court House who understood that with the closing of the surrender conference an era had come to an end, and when they walked away from the historic scene they would be facing an America in which nothing of importance would ever again be the same.

The meeting of the two Generals took place in the parlor of a red brick house belonging to Wilmer McLean. In 1861, this unfortunate man had been living on a farm through which ran the stream called Bull Run and during the battle, his house was taken over as a field hospital, his crops were trampled and the lives of his household were in danger. Having had enough of war forever, he decided to move to so remote a district that he would never again be in the path of the contending armies. The place he selected was Appomattox Court House.[1]

After the signing had been concluded and the Generals had departed,

souvenir hunters attacked the McLean house, Sheridan bought the table at which Grant had signed the surrender for twenty dollars in gold. The table Lee had used was bought by General Ord for forty dollars. He intended to make a present of it to Mrs. Grant, but she gracefully declined. McLean, it appears, did not want to sell his possessions but he was given no choice in the matter, and he had to stand by and watch his now historic furniture going through the front door on the shoulders of stalwart orderlies. The rank and file attacked the garden for flowers to press and in a few minutes the grounds looked as though a swarm of locusts had passed that way.[2]

At the City Point hospital that night there was a great bonfire in celebration of victory, which Charlotte McKay and the other nurses attended. Not many days later, the news reached City Point that President Lincoln, whom all at the hospital had learned to love, had been shot by the actor, John Wilkes Booth, and had died of his wounds. Here as everywhere in the country, no one believed at first that it could be true. That afternoon, Charlotte, still in doubt, went to the headquarters of the Quartermaster Department, where the talk was of nothing else. Meanwhile, confirmation was received elsewhere in the base and while Charlotte and some officers were looking out the window, they saw all the flags on the ships in the river being simultaneously lowered to half mast.[3]

The soldiers convalescing in the hospital were stricken with grief at the death of the great and good man who had taken their hands in his. Many a nurse and soldier wept. The women made mourning badges to wear and the men begged for them, but there was not enough black material in camp to supply the demand. All who found the means hung mourning symbols over the doors of their quarters. Adelaide Smith donated a "full train black skirt" which she could "illy spare," and in a short time it had become ribbons of black floating over the entrances of the tents.

The great days of the hospital at City Point were over. Most of the nurses and many of the wounded had gone North. The armies too were moving North. There were some badly wounded men who could not be sent away, and some women remained to care for them. Charlotte McKay and Bridget Divers remained. Mrs. Collis was there, nursing a sick child, and there were others. Work was easier and the women began to rest and to wonder about the future. Many of them were anxious to go north for the Grand Review of the Armies to be held in Washington on May 23rd and 24th. When the time came, Cornelia Hancock would be in the reviewing stand and others in the crowds along the Avenue. Mother Bick-

erdyke would ride in the parade, wearing her clean, worn calico dress and a sunbonnet, sitting sidewise, like a great lady, on a cavalry horse— a figure of fun, majestic, substitute mother for ten thousand boys.

Charlotte McKay went to Petersburg to take charge of a low diet kitchen at the Fair Grounds Hospital, which was still filled with wounded Confederate soldiers. One morning she was awakened early by the notes of a bugle sounding reveille close at hand. She was startled, for some weeks had passed since those notes had been heard and she seems to have felt a pang of nostalgia, which many a war nurse would feel in days to come. She arose and went to the window and there, spread out before her was a camp with rows and rows of white tents. An army had come there during the night. It was Sherman's army on its way to Washington where it would march on the second day of the Grand Review. That review would mark the end, for when it was over, their duties would be over and they would shortly be mustered out.

Hermon Chapin, Cleveland businessman and a person of some political influence in his state, went to Washington to see the Grand Review.[4] His acquaintanceship among the military included both Grant and Sherman, but he was more especially interested in the latter, and in the ragged veterans who would march the second day. That morning, Hermon left the Ebbitt House early and found the city alive with anticipation. The air sparkled with spring sunshine. All over the city, bands exploded into music. A fresh breeze fluttered the red, white and blue bunting, and the long streamers of black, mourning for the dead President. People were already moving toward Pennsylvania Avenue, but Hermon made his way toward the open space behind the Capitol where he knew the troops would pause before beginning the march and where he hoped to see without being jostled by the crowds.

All night long the troops had been moving into the city from Alexandria, their feet like the sound of muffled drums, and when Hermon arrived at the Capitol they had begun to assemble there. They were big men from the west country, taller than the men in the Army of the Potomac, bronzed, hardy, confident, dressed in the soiled uniforms of the campaign. Some were tattered, some were barefoot, and Sherman, he knew, had wanted it that way, for this was not to be a dress parade, but a review of a conquering army fresh from its victories.

The men were standing at ease, laughing and talking, and pretty young girls with flowers in their hands ran here and there among them, their swaying hoopskirts, like bright balloons. They were giving the flowers to the soldiers to wear in their caps and tuck into their gun barrels. Hermon

stared at them, his thoughts transported to those days when laughing girls like these had thrust their little bunches of flowers on the green youth of a nation going off to war. Where were they now, those girls so bright with life? Tear-streaked, many of them, care-worn. Dim figures draped in black. These girls belonged to a new generation and to an America at peace.

Brooding over that future, Hermon moved away, and found himself near some big guns, formidable black monsters that had been mounted here for the defense of Washington. He wandered toward the nearest of them and laid his hand on the long, black barrel. Would they be melted down now? Iron. Iron for a nation at peace, iron for ploughs and rails and harvesters, a nation rich in iron lying under the sod of Michigan.

When Hermon came out of his dream and turned to face the scene once more, he saw that fresh troops had arrived and that something had happened to draw them all together, to focus them. Sherman. There he was on his horse, a fine roan, sitting a little sidewise in his saddle talking to some officers, and the electric quality in him was strongly apparent.

Watching him, Hermon was aware of a new intensity in his own feelings, as though life had an increased meaning. It was not the first time the thin man with the bristling red hair had made him feel so. There were soldiers now in every direction as far as the eye could see and the air was tense with expectancy. All their eyes were turned toward Sherman, who was sitting easily, relaxed, but Hermon saw a pulse beating on the side of the scrawny neck, making the skin jump rhythmically.

There had been trouble over the terms of surrender Sherman had tried to make with Johnston. Sherman had wanted to be merciful, believing that this was Lincoln's wish. Stanton and the radicals held different views. The controversy grew acrimonious, boiled over into the newspapers, and in these last weeks the country had taken sides. The General was smarting under criticism, and to what extent it had tarnished his glory, no one knew. And it came to Hermon that this very thing was in Sherman's mind, that he knew when he faced the throngs on Pennsylvania Avenue that he would have the answer.

Sherman was looking ahead now, in the direction they would move, and the muscles in his face had hardened. Then everyone was looking ahead. The forest of bayonets was shifting, catching the light. Then suddenly they were all slanting backward in even rows and the men were in even rows, swaying as they marked time. The pretty girls had gone. There was a moment of tense stillness. Then Sherman moved out, walking his horse slowly, his eyes straight ahead. It was as though he were

alone, riding toward the people who lined the Avenue and crowded the windows and the rooftops, facing the verdict of history.

Hermon saw him go out of sight around the Capitol, and then he heard a sound like the roar of the sea, a roar of acclaim. And he too wanted to shout, to let the pressure of admiration and pity and joy burst out of him.

Sherman rode on, erect, not turning his head, and a solid wall of sound moved ahead of him. The air was filled with flowers. Wreaths of them hung around his horse's neck and the marching men behind him trod on a carpet of them. Now the General began to think about those men and to worry about how they were marching. His ragged veterans cared nothing for style and on the campaigns their drill had grown rusty. How would they compare in the eyes of the world with the better dressed, better regimented men of the Army of the Potomac who yesterday had ridden the same route? He wanted to know. He wanted desperately to see this fighting machine he had created, marching in triumph. Only once he looked back. As he reached the rise of ground at the Treasury, he rose in his saddle and looked behind.

The men were marching with a rhythmic unity which drill can paraphrase but never create since it comes in its perfection only from shared experience. His veterans were an army in the deepest sense. Bayonets, perfectly aligned, flashed as they swung in the sun. Legs made strong on long marches through Southern swampland, swung forward and back like swaying fringe. That look backward was a summit of experience in Sherman's life.

He did not prolong it. A few moments later the sun glinted as he drew his sword and held it upright before his face. He was nearing the reviewing stand, near the President, his wife, his enemy Stanton, personalities who peopled his individual life and narrowed his horizons. A moment more, and he was past them, and his men were passing also, file on file, marching into history.

NOTES

[1] Philip Van Doren Stern, *An End to Valor* (Houghton Mifflin Company, Boston, 1958), pp. 243-244.

[2] *Ibid.*, pp. 275-76.

[3] In 1944, the author was standing at a window in Washington when the flags all over the city began to go down to commemorate the death of Secretary Frank Knox. The sight was deeply moving.

[4] Hermon Chapin was the author's grandfather. This account is based largely on his journal.

27

THEIR LEGACY

---- ★ ----

> *What is there that abides*
> *to make the next age better than the last?*
> —James Russell Lowell

A CROSS THE LONG PERSPECTIVE of the years the women of the Civil War
appear a little larger than life. They were sometimes weak, sometimes
faltering, not infrequently mistaken and ill-advised, but at long last their
work had a profound effect, not only on the status of women in a peacetime society, but on the attitude of civilized nations toward the human
wreckage of war.

For themselves, their greatest gain was freedom. Before the war, the
attitude of the male part of society toward a woman was not one of
trust. It was thought that she must be protected, chaperoned, shielded
and that if she were not, something would occur which would be detrimental to herself and to the prestige of the husband or father whose name
she bore. She must not be alone with a man other than her husband. She
was not to appear in public places. Law courts, the lecture platform, the
theatre, or any place where her talents or abilities were called into play
were closed to those women who would remain respected in their
communities.

The concept that women could not be trusted has an ancient and forgotten lineage stemming from man's rights respecting paternity and
property and his desire to protect them. And long ago the idea that it
was wrong for a woman to deal with the world on her own initiative because it was dangerous to man's interests, became shortened to the simple

proposition that it was wrong—thereby transforming what was a pure matter of expediency into a moral issue. In the mid-Eighteenth Century, the world had long since lost sight of the expediency and retained only the taboos.

And having determined that it was wrong, in the sense that it was not respectable for a woman to take unrestricted part in the activities of the world, men rationalized the restrictions they had placed on her by the dogma that she lacked the proper abilities. Most men and some women believed that woman had "not the type of mind" and was "not fitted by nature" for a long list of activities which included nearly every occupation which might take her out of the home.

The ancient beliefs in woman's moral and intellectual frailties had begun to weaken before the Civil War, like frayed rope with some strands broken and some still holding firm. During the war, several thousand women demonstrated in a manner which could not be disputed that it was possible for them to live and work in most unconventional conditions and emerge with dignity and reputation undamaged. Furthermore, women displayed abilities of a high order in such masculine preserves as executive work, organization and the handling of money, and on a scale which was, to say the least, impressive. With such a record to her credit a woman could not again be put in bondage, and the ancient beliefs concerning her need for protection and her lack of aptitudes began to look like the nonsense they were. Obviously, she did not gain complete emancipation. Some few strands of the rope still held firm, but in the war years she made great progress toward freedom. Nor was it merely a few gifted women who emerged from the war with increased stature and greater freedom, for the benefits accrued to the whole generation whether or not they were capable as individuals of making use of them.

In the process of winning the confidence of others, women gained confidence in themselves and there is a new and impressive sureness discernible in their approach to postwar problems. The woman's rights movement flared up again, but the character of the crusade had changed, and the emphasis was less on the reform of laws affecting property ownership and children and more on laws relating to working conditions, the vote and other aspects of woman's place as an active member of society. She took more part in the management of her community, she entered business and she concerned herself with the betterment of educational facilities for her sex, and it became evident that she had learned how to subordinate her private advantage to the public good.

Much gain to others as well as to herself grew out of woman's achievements in the war. Dr. Henry W. Bellows, true to his knack for seeing the horizon over the heads of the crowd, thought that the steadfastness of women during the war had an important influence on the morale of the country, and that their work created a sense of nearness of the people to the government. Certain it is that they changed civilized governments everywhere in respect to the humanitarian treatment of soldiers and that out of the change came the International Red Cross.

Not all the gains made by the women for themselves and others have proved permanent, and the most serious loss is, perhaps, the moral good arising from voluntary participation in the war effort. The work of the volunteer has many faults. It is erratic, unskilled, and largely beyond the reach of discipline. It is difficult to mechanize and organize. Voluntary work can be highly productive, but the productivity tends to depend on special stimuli and to come in spurts. It is equally prone to lag, and both these tendencies create major problems. And in so far as it does create problems, it is incompatible with efficient war.

But there are values in volunteer participation beyond the usefulness of the product. The enlistment of unpaid civilian workers creates a sense of participation in and identification with the cause of the war, which is the very dynamo of democracy. It is not the sock knitted by some old lady which is important in modern war. A single knitting machine can reduce her labors to ludicrous insignificance. It is the fact that she is taking active part in the trials and triumphs of her country that is important—not so much to her but to the country—and the usefulness of the sock is beside the point.

The incompatibility between volunteer work and the efficient pursuit of war was apparent during the Civil War, but the repeated failure of the government to make adequate provision for the sick and wounded made the work of volunteers literally indispensable. The character of modern warfare has italicized the incompatibility, and the part played by voluntary participation has been progressively assumed by a bureaucracy created to produce efficiency. (Efficiency is the goal of a wartime bureaucracy. Whether a bureaucracy does or does not achieve efficiency is not part of this argument.) As a consequence, the scope and variety of volunteer participation is on the wane. Perhaps no compromise to save any of its values is possible and before long the total mobilization of a population for total war may end voluntary participation altogether.

That is probably inevitable, but when that time comes something rich and virtuous and uplifting will have been lost from the world.

BIBLIOGRAPHY

Adams, George Worthington. *Doctors in Blue.* Henry Schuman, New York, 1952.

Adams, James Truslow. *The March of Democracy: The Rise of the Union* and *From Civil War to World Power.* (2 vols.) Charles Scribner's Sons, New York and London, 1932, 1933.

Alcott, Louisa May. *Hospital Sketches.* Hurst & Company, New York.

Alcott, Louisa May. *Life, Letters and Journals.* Roberts Brothers, Boston, 1892.

Alcott, Louisa May. *Little Women.* Grosset & Dunlap, New York, 1947.

Aldrich, Thomas. *Battery A, 1st Rhode Island Light Artillery.*

Alleman, Tillie (Pierce). *At Gettysburg.* W. Lake Bozland, New York, 1889.

Andrews, Matthew Page. *The Women of the South in War Times.* The Norman, Remington Co., Baltimore, 1920.

Ashburn, P. M. *A History of the Medical Department of the United States Army.* Houghton, Mifflin Co., Boston and New York, 1929.

Bacon, Georgeanne Woolsey. *Three Weeks at Gettysburg.* Anson D. F. Randolph, New York, 1863.

Baker, Nina Brown. *Cyclone in Calico: The Story of Mary Ann Bickerdyke.* Little, Brown & Co., Boston, 1952.

Barrett, Joseph H. *Life of Abraham Lincoln.* Moore, Wilstach & Baldwin, New York, 1865.

Barrett, O. S. *Reminiscences of the Old 4th Michigan Infantry.*

Barton, William E. *The Life of Clara Barton.* (2 vols.) Houghton, Mifflin Co., Boston and New York, 1922.

Basler, Roy P. *Abraham Lincoln: His Speeches and Writings.* World Publishing Co., Cleveland and New York, 1946.

Beard, Charles A., and Beard, Mary R. *The Rise of American Civilization.* The Macmillan Co., New York, 1930.

Beard, Mary R. *America Through Women's Eyes.* The Macmillan Company, New York, 1933.

Beard, Mary R. *Woman As Force in History: A Study in Traditions and Realities.* The Macmillan Co., New York, 1946.

Belden, B. L. *United States War Medals.* New York, 1916.

Benjamin, Israel Joseph. *Drei Jahre in Amerika, 1859-1862.* J. J. Benjamin II, Hannover, 1862.

Biddle, Gertrude Bosler, and Lowrie, Sarah Dickinson, Eds. *Notable Women of Pennsylvania.* University of Pennsylvania Press, 1942.

Billings, John Shaw. *Report on Barracks and Hospitals with Descriptions of Military Posts.* Government Printing Office, Washington, D.C., 1870.

Blackstone, Sir William. *Commentaries on the Laws of England* (7th Edition), 1775.

Boker, George Henry. *Poems of the War*. Boston, 1864.

Botume, Elizabeth Hyde. *First Days amongst The Contrabands*. Lee and Shepard, Boston, 1893.

Boyden, Anna L. *Echoes from Hospital and White House: A Record of Mrs. Rebecca R. Pomroy's Experience in War-Times*. D. Lothrop & Co., Boston, 1884.

Bradford, Sarah H. (Eliza Hopkins). *Harriet the Moses of Her People*. George R. Lockwood and Son, New York, 1886.

Bradford, Sarah H. *Scenes in the Life of Harriet Tubman*. W. J. Moses, Printer, Auburn, N. Y., 1869.

Branch, E. Douglas. *The Sentimental Years*. D. Appleton-Century Co., New York, 1934.

Bremer, Fredrika. *The Homes of the New World: Impressions of America*. (3 vols.) Arthur Hall, Virtue and Company, London, 1853.

Brockett, L. P., M.D. and Vaughan, Mary C. *Woman's Work in the Civil War: A Record of Heroism, Patriotism and Patience*. Zeigler, McCurdy & Co., R. H. Curran, Boston, 1867.

Brooks, Van Wyck. *The Flowering of New England*. E. P. Dutton & Co., New York, 1936.

Brown, George William. *Baltimore and the Nineteeth of April*. Johns Hopkins University Studies, Baltimore, 1887.

Brown, Harvey E. *The Medical Department of the United States Army from 1775-1873*. Surgeon General's Office, Washington, D.C., 1873.

Brown, Herbert Ross. *The Sentimental Novel in America, 1789-1860*. Duke University Press, Durham, N.C., 1940.

Bruce, H. Addington. *Women in the Making of America*. Little, Brown & Co., 1929.

Bucklin, Sophronia E. *In Hospital and Camp*. John E. Potter & Co., Philadelphia, 1869.

The Bugle Call or A Summons to Work in Christ's Army by "A Volunteer Nurse." The American Tract Society, New York, 1871.

Burnett, Constance Buel. *Five for Freedom*. Abelard Press, New York, 1953.

Butterfield, Roger. *The American Past*. Simon and Schuster, New York, 1947.

Campbell, R. W. *History of the 17th Regiment, Illinois Volunteers*. Public Library.

Castleman, Alfred L. (Surgeon of the 5th Regiment of Wisconsin Volunteers) *The Army of the Potomac*. Strickland and Co., Milwaukee, 1863.

Catton, Bruce. *Glory Road: The Bloody Route from Fredericksburg to Gettysburg*. Doubleday & Co., Inc., Garden City, N.Y., 1952.

Catton, Bruce. *This Hallowed Ground*. Doubleday & Co., Garden City, N.Y., 1956.

Charnwood Lord. *Abraham Lincoln*. Garden City Publishing Co., Inc., N.Y., 1917.

Cheney, Ednah D. *Louisa May Alcott, Her Life, Letters and Journals.* Roberts Brothers, Boston, 1892.

Chester, Giraud. *Embattled Maiden: The Life of Anna Dickinson.* G. P. Putnam's Sons, New York, 1951.

Clarke, Edward H. "Practice of Medicine" in *A Century of American Medicine 1776-1876.* Henry C. Lea, Philadelphia, 1876.

Collis, Septima M. (Mrs. Genl. Charles H. T. Collis) *A Woman's War Record: 1861-1865.* G. P. Putnam's Sons, New York and London, 1889.

Commager, Henry Steele, Ed. *The Blue and the Gray.* (2 vols.) The Bobbs-Merrill Co., Inc., Indianapolis and New York, 1950.

Conrad, Earl. *Harriet Tubman.* The Associated Publishers, Inc., Washington, D.C., 1943.

Cook, Sir Edward. *The Life of Florence Nightingale.* (2 vols.) Macmillan and Co., London, 1913.

Cowie, Alexander. *The Rise of the American Novel.* American Book Co., New York, 1948.

Cunnington, Dr. C. Willett. *Feminine Attitudes in the Nineteenth Century.* The Macmillan Company, New York, 1936.

Dahl, Caroline H., L.L.D. *The College, the Market, and the Court; or, Woman's Relation to Education, Labor, and Law. 1866-1914.* The Rumford Press, Concord, N.H., 1914. (Memorial Edition.)

Dannett, Sylvia G. L., Ed. *Noble Women of the North.* Thomas Yoseloff, New York, London, 1959.

Davis, Margaret B. *Mother Bickerdyke.* A. T. Dewey, San Francisco, 1886.

Dexter, Elias. *Portraits of the Civil War Period.* New York.

Dexter, Elisabeth Williams (Anthony). *Career Women of America, 1776-1840.* Marshall Jones Co., Francestown, N.H., 1950.

Dickens, Charles. *American Notes for General Circulation.* Wilson & Co., New York, 1842.

Ditzion, Sidney. *Marriage Morals and Sex in America—A History of Ideas.* Bookman Associates, New York, 1953.

Dock, Lavinia L., R.N. and Stewart, Isabel Maitland, A.M., R.N. *A Short History of Nursing.* G. P. Putnam's Sons, New York, London, 1931.

Dodge, Bertha S. *The Story of Nursing.* Little, Brown & Co., Boston, 1954.

Douglas, Henry Kyd. *I Rode with Stonewall.* University of North Carolina Press, Chapel Hill, 1940.

Dowdey, Clifford. *Death of a Nation.* Alfred Knopf, New York, 1958.

Duncan, Louis C. *The Medical Department of the United States Army in the Civil War.* Washington, D.C., 1914.

Eberle, Irmengarde. *Nurse! The Story of a Great Profession.* Thomas Y. Crowell, New York, 1944.

Edmonds, S. Emma E. *Nurse and Spy in the Union Army.* W. S. Williams & Co., Hartford, Conn., 1865.

Ellis, Thomas T., M.D. *Leaves from the Diary of an Army Surgeon.* John Bradburn, New York, 1863. ·

Emerson, Edwin, Jr. *History of the Nineteenth Century Year by Year.* Vol. III, P. F. Collier & Son, New York, 1902.

Epler, Percy H. *The Life of Clara Barton.* The Macmillan Company, New York, 1946.

Faulkner, Harold Underwood. *American Economic History.* Harper and Brothers, New York, 1931.

Finley, Ruth E. *The Lady of Godey's: Sarah Josepha Hale.* J. B. Lippincott Co., Philadelphia and London, 1931.

Fischel, Dr. Oskar, and Von Boehm, Max. *Modes and Manners of the Nineteenth Century represented in the Pictures and Engravings of the Time.* Translated by M. Edwardes. (Vol. III, 1843-1878) J. M. Dent and Co., London; E. P. Dutton & Co., New York, 1909.

Foner, Philip S. *History of the Labor Movement in the United States.* International Publishers, New York, 1947.

Frank, Sister Charles Marie, C.C.V.I., R.N., M.S. *The Historical Development of Nursing.* W. B. Saunders Co., Philadelphia, 1953.

Freeman, Douglas Southall. *R. E. Lee: A Biography.* (4 vols.) Charles Scribner's Sons, New York, 1934.

Gilmore, Inez Hayes. *Angels and Amazons.* Doubleday, Doran, New York, 1953.

Gordon, Brigadier General John B. *Reminiscences of the Civil War.* Charles Scribner's Sons, New York, 1903.

Gordon, Seth C., M.C. *The Attitude of Women of the North and South During and Since the War of the Rebellion. In Military Order of the Loyal Legion of the United States. Maine Commandery War Papers.* (Vol. IV.) Lefavor-Tower Co., Portland, 1915.

Gould, Major John M. *History of the First, Tenth, Twenty-ninth Maine Regiment.* Stephen Berry, Portland, Me., 1871.

Grant, U. S. *Personal Memoirs of* (2 vols.) Charles L. Webster & Co., New York, 1885.

Greeley, Horace. *The American Conflict.* O. D. Case & Co., Hartford, Conn., 1866.

Greenbie, Sydney and Marjorie Barstow. *Anna Ella Carroll and Abraham Lincoln.* University of Tampa Press and Falmouth Publishing House, Inc., Manchester, Me., 1952.

Greenbie, Marjorie Barstow. *Lincoln's Daughters of Mercy.* G. P. Putnam's Sons, New York, 1944.

Greenhow, Rose O'N. *My Imprisonment.* Richard Bentley, London, 1863.

Handlin, Oscar. *This Was America.* Harvard University Press, 1949.

Hanson, John W., Chaplain. *Historical Sketch of the Old Sixth Regiment of Massachusetts Volunteers.* Lee and Shepard, Boston, 1866.

Harris, Elisha. *United States Sanitary Commission.* Crosby and Nichols, Boston, 1864.

Harris, Seale, J. Marion Sims. *Woman's Surgeon.* The Macmillan Co., 1950.

Haupt, General Herman. *Reminiscences.* Wright & Joys Co., Milwaukee, 1901.

Hayward, J. Henry. *Poetical Pen-Pictures of the War.* New York, 1864.

Hazen, General W. B. *A Narrative of Military Service.* Ticknor and Company, Boston, 1885.

Henry, Robert Selph. *The Story of the Confederacy.* Garden City Publishing Co., Inc., Garden City, N.Y., 1931.

Higginson, T. W. *Woman's Rights Almanac, 1850.* Z. Baker & Co., Worcester, Mass.; R. F. Walcott, Boston, 1850.

Higginson, Rev. Thomas Wentworth. *Woman and Her Wishes.* Curtis & Butts, Rochester, 1851.

History of Nursing and Sociology. Compiled by A Sister of Charity of Emmitsburg, Maryland. The Brewer-Colgan Co., Bridgeport, Conn., 1929.

Hoge, Mrs. A. H. *The Boys in Blue.* E. B. Treat & Co., New York; C. W. Lilley, Chicago, 1867.

Holland, Mary A. Gardner. *Our Army Nurses.* B. Wilkins & Co., Boston, 1895.

Holstein, Mrs. William H. (Anna). *Three Years in Field Hospitals of the Army of the Potomac.* J. B. Lippincott & Co., Philadelphia, 1867.

Home, Edgar Erskine. *Victories of Army Medicine.* J. B. Lippincott Co., Philadelphia, London, Montreal, 1943.

Horan, James D. *Desperate Women.* G. P. Putnam's Sons, New York, 1952.

Howe, Julia Ward. *Reminiscences.* Houghton, Mifflin & Co., Boston and New York, 1899.

Humphreys, Charles A. *Field, Camp, Hospital and Prison in the Civil War, 1863-1865.* Press of George H. Ellis Co., Boston, 1918.

Hurn, Ethel Alice, B.A. *Wisconsin Women in the War Between the States.* Wisconsin History Commission, May 1911.

Jacquette, Henrietta Stratton, Ed. *The South After Gettysburg: Letter of Cornelia Hancock from the Army of the Potomac.* University of Pennsylvania Press, Philadelphia, 1937.

Jenny Wade of Gettysburg. Anonymous poem. J. B. Lippincott & Co., 1864.

Johnson, Charles B., M.D. *Muskets and Medicine.* F. A. Davis, Philadelphia, 1917.

Johnson, Robert Underwood, and Buel, Clarence Clough, Eds. *Battles and Leaders of the Civil War.* The Century Company, New York, c. 1884-1889.

Jones, Katharine M. *Heroines of Dixie.* The Bobbs-Merrill Co., Inc., Indianapolis-New York, 1955.

Josephine, Hannah. *The Golden Threads. New England's Mill Girls and Magnates.* Duell, Sloan and Pearce, New York, 1949.

Kane, Harnett T. *Spies for the Blue and Gray.* Hanover House, Garden City, N.Y., 1954.

King, William C. *Camp-fire Sketches and Battlefield Echoes.* Springfield, Mass., 1889.

Kirkland, Frazer. *Anecdotes of the Rebellion.* J. H. Mason, St. Louis, 1889.

Langdon-Davis, John. *A Short History of Women*. Literary Guild of America, 1927.

Lanman, Charles. *The Red Book of Michigan, a Civil, Military and Biographical History*. E. B. Smith & Co., Detroit, 1871.

Leech, Margaret. *Reveille in Washington 1860-1865*. Harper and Brothers, New York and London, 1941.

Letterman, Jonathan. *Medical Recollections of the Army of the Potomac*. D. Appleton and Company, New York, 1866.

Lewis, Lloyd. *Sherman, Fighting Prophet*. Harcourt, Brace & Co., New York, 1932.

Livermore, Mary Ashton Rice. *My Story of the War*. A. D. Worthington & Co., Hartford, Conn., 1887.

Livermore, Mary A. *The Story of My Life*. A. D. Worthington & Co., Hartford, Conn., 1897.

Livermore, Thomas L. *Numbers & Losses in the Civil War in America: 1861-65*. Civil War Centennial Series, Indiana University Press, Bloomington, Ill., 1957.

MacKay, Mrs. C. E. *Stories of Hospital and Camp*. Claxton, Remsen & Haffelfinger, Philadelphia, 1876.

Marshall, Helen. *Dorothea Dix Forgotten Samaritan*. University of North Carolina Press, Chapel Hill, 1937.

Maxwell, William Quentin. *Lincoln's Fifth Wheel—The Political History of the United States Sanitary Commission*. Longmans, Green & Co., New York, London, Toronto, 1956.

Mearns, David C. *The Lincoln Papers*. (2 vols.) Doubleday & Co., Inc., Garden City, N.Y., 1948.

The Medical and Surgical History of the War of the Rebellion. Government Printing Office, Washington, D.C., 1870-1888.

Mill, John Stuart. *The Subjection of Women*. Longmans, Green, Reader and Dyer, London, 1883.

Miller, Francis Trevelyan, (Ed.). *The Photograph History of the Civil War*. (10 vols.) The Review of Reviews Co., New York, 1911.

Milton, George Fort. *Conflict, The American Civil War*. Coward-McCann, Inc., New York, 1941.

Monaghan, Jay. *Civil War on the Western Border 1854-1865*. Little, Brown & Co., Boston, 1855.

Mooney, Thomas. *Nine Years in America*. J. McGlashan, Dublin, 1850.

Moore, Frank (Ed.). *Personal and Political Ballads*. George P. Putnam, New York, 1864.

Moore, Frank (Ed.). *The Rebellion Record*. (12 vols.) G. P. Putnam, New York, 1861-1866.

Moore, Frank. *Women of the War; Their Heroism and Self-Sacrifice*. S. S. Scranton & Co., Hartford, Conn., 1866.

Morris, Lloyd. *Incredible New York*. Random House, New York, 1951.

Morton, S. G. *Illustrations of Pulmonary Tuberculosis*. Key and Biddle, Philadelphia, 1834.

Mott, Frank Luther. *Golden Multitudes, The Story of Best Sellers in the United States.* The Macmillan Co., New York, 1947.

Mug, Sister Mary Theodosia. *Lest We Forget. The Sisters of Providence of St. Mary-of-the-Woods in Civil War Service.* Providence Press, St. Mary-of-the-Woods, Indiana, 1937.

Nason, George W. *History and Complete Roster of the Massachusetts Regiments, Minute Men of '61 who responded to the First Call of President Abraham Lincoln, April 15, 1861, to defend the Flag and Constitution of the United States.* Smith and McCance, Boston, 1910.

Nightingale, Florence. *Notes on Nursing, What It Is and What It Is Not.* William Carter, Boston, 1860.

Olnhausen, Mary Phinney. *Adventures of an Army Nurse.* Little, Brown and Company, Boston, 1903.

Ossoli, S. Margaret Fuller. *Woman of the Nineteenth Century.* H. G. Clarke Co., London, 1845.

Packard, Francis R., M.D. *History of Medicine in the United States.* Paul B. Hoeber, Inc., New York, 1931.

Papashvily, Helen Waite. *All the Happy Endings.* Harper and Brothers, New York, 1956.

Parsons, Emily Elizabeth. *Memoir of,* Little, Brown & Co., Boston, 1880.

Powers, Elvira J. *Hospital Pencillings, being a diary while in Jefferson General Hospital, Jeffersonville, Indiana, and others at Nashville, Tennessee, as Matron and Visitor.* Edward L. Mitchell, Boston, 1866.

Pratt, Edwin A. *Pioneer Women in Victoria's Reign.* George Newnes, Ltd., London, 1897.

Prinzing, Friedrich. *Epidemics Resulting from Wars.* Clarendon Press, Toronto, 1916.

Pryor, Mrs. Roger A. *Reminiscences of Peace and War.* The Macmillan Co., New York, 1904.

Reed, William Howell. *Hospital Life in the Army of the Potomac.* William V. Spencer, Boston, 1866.

Rice, Allen Thorndike. *Reminiscences of Abraham Lincoln by Distinguished Men of His Time.* The North American Review, New York, 1888.

Richards, Laura E., and Elliott, Maud Howe, assisted by Hall, Florence Howe. *Julia Ward Howe.* (2 vols.) Houghton, Mifflin Co., Boston & New York, 1915.

Robertson, John. *Michigan in the War.* W. S. George & Co., Lansing, 1882.

Robinson, Victor, M.D. *White Caps.* Philadelphia and New York, 1946.

Rogers, Agnes and Allen, Frederick Lewis. *The American Procession.* Harper and Bros., New York and London, 1933.

Ross, Ishbel. *Angel of the Battlefield. The Life of Clara Barton.* Harper & Bros., New York, 1956.

Ross, Ishbel. *Child of Destiny The Life Story of the First Woman Doctor.* Harper & Bros., New York, 1949.

Russell, William Howard. *My Diary North and South.* Harper & Bros., New York, 1863.

Sandburg, Carl. *Mary Lincoln, Wife and Widow.* Part I by Sandburg; Part II by Paul M. Angle. Harcourt, Brace & Co., New York, 1932.

Sarmiento, Ferdinand L. *Life of Pauline Cushman.* United States Book Co., New York.

Seilheimer, George O. *Battles and Leaders of The Civil War.* "The Historical Basis of Barbara Frietchie." The Century Company, New York, 1884-1889.

Sheridan, P. H. (General) *Personal Memoirs.* (2 vols.) Charles L. Webster & Co., New York, 1888.

Slaughter, Rosalie. *Woman Surgeon.* Frederick A. Stokes, 1937.

Smith, Adelaide W. *Reminiscences of An Army Nurse During the Civil War.* Greaves Publishing Co., New York, 1911.

Souder, Mrs. Edmund A. *Leaves from the Battle-field of Gettysburg.* Caxton Press of C. Sherman, Son & Co., 1864.

Southworth, Mrs. E.D.E.N. *Capitola's Peril.* M. A. Donohue & Co., Chicago.

Southworth, Mrs. E.D.E.N. *The Hidden Hand.* Hurst & Co., New York.

Southworth, Mrs. E.D.E.N. *The Deserted Wife.* T. B. Peterson & Bros., Philadelphia, 1855.

Stackpole, Edward J. *They Met at Gettysburg.* Eagle Books, Harrisburg, Pa., 1956.

Stedman, Edmund C. *The Battle of Bull Run.* Rood and Carleton, New York, 1861.

Stern, Madeleine B. *Louisa May Alcott.* University of Oklahoma Press, Norman, 1950.

Stern, Philip Van Doren. *An End to Valor, Last Days of the Civil War.* Houghton Mifflin Co., Boston, 1958.

Stillé, J. B. *History of the United States Sanitary Commission.* J. B. Lippincott, Philadelphia, 1866.

Story, Joseph. *Commentaries on Equity Jurisprudence as Administered in England and America.* Charles C. Little and James Brown, Boston, 1849.

Stowe, Harriet Beecher, and Beecher, Catharine. *The American Woman's Home.* J. B. Ford, New York, 1869.

Strong, George Templeton. *The Diary of.* The Macmillan Co., New York, 1952.

Sweetser, Kate Dickinson. *Ten Girls from History.* Duffield & Co., New York, 1912.

Swift, Hildegarde Hoyt. *The Railroad to Freedom; a story of the Civil War.* Harcourt Brace & Co., New York, 1932.

Tarbell, Ida M. *The Life of Abraham Lincoln.* (2 vols.) Doubleday Page & Co., New York, 1919.

Tharp, Louise Hall. *Three Saints and a Sinner—Julia Ward Howe, Louisa, Annie and Sam Ward.* Little, Brown & Co., Boston, 1956.

Thomas, Benjamin P. *Abraham Lincoln.* Alfred A. Knopf, New York, 1952.

Tooley, Sarah A. *The Life of Florence Nightingale.* S. H. Bousfield & Co., Ltd., London, 1905.

Trollope, Anthony. *Miss Ravenel's Conversion.* Rinehart & Co., Inc., New York, 1955.

Trollope, Anthony. *North America.* J. B. Lippincott, Philadelphia, 1862.

Trollope, Frances. *Domestic Manners of the Americans.* Harpers, New York, 1938.

Twain, Mark. *Life on the Mississippi.* Harper & Bros., 1904.

Twain, Mark. *Autobiography.* Harper & Bros., 1924.

Valentine, D. T. *Manual of the Corporation of the City of New York, 1861.* Edmund Jones & Co., New York.

Villard, Oswald Garrison. *John Brown. A Biography Fifty Years After.* Alfred A. Knopf, New York, 1943.

Villeneuve, R. *L'Anesthesie Usuel.* Oxford University Press, 1947.

War Songs of The Blue and The Gray. Hurst & Co., New York.

Ware, Norman. *The Industrial Worker 1840-1860.* Houghton Mifflin Co., Boston, New York, 1924.

Watson, B. F., (Colonel) *An Oration . . . in Commemoration of the Sixth Regiment of Massachusetts Volunteers, April 19, 1861.* (Delivered April 19, 1886, at Lowell, Mass.) Livingston Middleditch, New York.

Wheelock, Julia S. *The Boys in White; The Experience of a Hospital Agent.* Lange & Hillman, New York, 1870.

Whitman, Walt. *The Wound Dresser.* The Bodley Press, New York, 1949.

Whitton, Mary Ormsbee. *These Were The Women.* Hastings House, New York, 1954.

Williams, Blanche C. *Clara Barton, Daughter of Destiny.* J. B. Lippincott Co., New York, 1941.

Williams, George W. *A History of the Negro Troops in the War of the Rebellion.* Harper & Bros., New York, 1888.

Wittenmyer, Mrs. Annie. *Under the Guns.* (Introduction by Mrs. General U. S. Grant). E. B. Stillings & Co., Boston, 1895.

Woodbury, Augustus. *A Narrative of the Campaign of the First Rhode Island Regiment.* Sidney S. Rider, Providence, 1862.

Woodward, Joseph Janvier. *Outlines of the Chief Camp Diseases of the United States Armies.* J. B. Lippincott & Co., Philadelphia, 1863.

Woolsey, Jane Stuart. *Hospital Days.* D. Van Nostrand, New York, 1868.

Wormeley, Katharine Prescott. *The Other Side of War with the Army of the Potomac.* Ticknor and Co., Boston, 1889.

Worth, Jean Philippe. *A Century of Fashion.* (Translated by Ruth Scott Miller.) Little Brown & Co., Boston, 1928.

Young, Agnes Brooks. *Recurring Cycles of Fashion.* Harper & Bros., New York and London, 1937.

2. General Reference Works

American Women—Fifteen Hundred Biographies. (2 vols.) Mast, Crowell and Kirkpatrick, New York, 1897.

Appleton's Cyclopaedia of American Biography. Appleton & Company, New York, 1887.

Dictionary of American Biography. Charles Scribner's Sons, New York, 1936.
Encyclopedia of American Biography. American Historical Society, Inc., New York, 1934.
The Iconography of Manhattan Island 1498-1909. Robert H. Dodd, New York, 1926.
The Official Atlas of the Civil War. Thomas Yoseloff, New York, 1958.

3. GOVERNMENT DOCUMENTS, ORDERS, REPORTS

Statistics of the United States in 1860. Eighth Census, Washington, 1866.
The War of the Rebellion, Official Records. Government Printing Office, Washington, D.C., 1902.
War Department General Orders, No. 43. Adjutant-General's Office, Washington, April 19, 1862.

4. NEWSPAPERS

Bangor (Maine) Whig and Courier. January 20, 1876.
Boston Daily Journal. May 18, 21, 23, 25, 1861.
Boston Daily Evening Transcript. April 18, 26, 29, 1861.
Gettysburg Times. Human Interest Stories of the Battle of Gettysburg, 1927.
New York Daily Tribune. July 26, 28, 1861.
New York Times. July 19-25, 1861.
New York Times. McLaughlin, Kathleen. "Co-Education Era Thrills Oberlin." October 7, 1937.
Portland, Maine Transcript. July 27 and August 3, 1861.
Providence, R.I. Journal. July 29, 30, 31, 1861 and January 2, 1910.
True Flag, Boston. May 18, 1861.
Daily National Intelligence. Washington, D.C. April 19 through May 15, 1861; July 16, 1861; August 23, 1862.
World Courier and New York Enquirer. July 23-25, 1861.

5. PAMPHLETS

Anderson, Hardin L. *The Story of the Illinois Central Lines During the Civil War.* Illinois State Historical Society.
Bellows, Henry W. *The United States Sanitary Commission.* Reprinted from Johnson's Universal Encyclopedia, G. P. Putnam's Sons, New York.
A Brief Outline of What the Sanitary Commission Has Done and Is Doing. 1861.
Carroll, Anna Ella. *Claim before Congress Asking for Compensation for Military and Other Services in Connection with Civil War.* Government Printing Office, Washington, March 28, 1874.
Carroll, Anna Ella. *Miss Carroll's Claim before Congress in Connection with the Tennessee Campaign of 1862.* Government Printing Office, Washington, 1873.

Carroll, Anna Ella. *Memorial of Anna Ella Carroll, asking Compensation for service rendered the United States in the war of rebellion*. Government Printing Office, Washington, June 1872.

Carroll, Anna Ella. *Reply to the speech of Honorable J. C. Breckinridge, delivered in the United States Senate, July 16th, 1861*. H. Polkinson, Washington, 1861.

Carroll, Anna Ella. *The Relation of the National Government to the Revolted Citizens Defined*. H. Polkinson, Washington, 1861.

Circular Letter. *To the Loyal Women of America*. United States Sanitary Commission, Washington, 1861.

Fleming, Thomas P. *Dr. Elizabeth Blackwell on Florence Nightingale*. Blackwell Collection, Rare Book Room, Academy of Medicine, Columbia University, New York City, 1956.

Proceedings of the Woman's Rights Convention Held at Worcester, October 15 and 16, 1851. Fowler and Wells, New York, 1852.

Proceedings of the Woman's Rights Convention Held at Worcester, October 23rd and 24th, 1850. Prentiss Sawyer, Boston, 1851.

A Record of the Metropolitan Fair in Aid of the United States Sanitary Commission. Hurd and Houghton, 1867. (New York Historical Society Library.)

Report of the Woman's Rights Convention Held at Seneca Falls, New York, July 19th and 20th, 1848. John Dick, Rochester, 1848.

The Transactions of the American Medical Association. (VIII) Philadelphia, 1855 through 1860.

What They Have to Do Who Stay at Home. Sanitary Commission, November, 1862.

6. PERIODICALS

Heaton, Claude Edwin. "Control of Puerperal Infection in the United States During the Last Century." *American Journal of Obstetrics and Gynecology*, XLVI, No. 4, October 1943.

The American Journal of the Medical Sciences. Philadelphia, 1855-1860.

Krause, A. K. "Tuberculosis and Public Health." *American Review of Tuberculosis*, XVIII, 271-322, 1928.

"Mrs. Annie Wittenmyer." *The Annals of Iowa*, IV, Series 3, April 1899-January 1901.

Dodge, Mary Abigail. "A Call to My Countrywomen." *Atlantic Monthly*, March, 1863.

Woman's Diary of the Siege of Vicksburg by "Mrs. L." *Century Illustrated Magazine*, VIII, 1885.

Holt, Rosa Belle. "A Heroine in Ebony." *The Chautauquan*, XXIII, No. 4, 459-462, July 1896.

Stevenson, Isobel. "Nursing in the Civil War." *Ciba Symposia*, Vol. 3-4, July 1941.

Stevenson, Isobel. "Medical Literature of the Civil War Era." *Ciba Symposia*, Vol. 3, July, 1941.

Godey's Lady's Book, September, 1860.

Harper's Weekly, VIII, 1864. Metropolitan Sanitary Fair.

Gallaher, Ruth A. "Annie Turner Wittenmyer." *Iowa Journal of History and Politics,* XXIX, 518-569. State Historical Society of Iowa, Iowa City, 1931.

"Women in Dentistry." *The Journal of the American Dental Association.* Chicago, September, 1928.

Sigaud, Louis A. "Mrs. Greenhow and the Rebel Spy Ring." *Maryland Historical Magazine,* 173-198, Baltimore, September 1946.

Milton, Nerissa Long. "Freedom Train" by Dorothy Sterling. *The Negro History Bulletin,* 139, March 1954.

The Negro History Bulletin, March 1954. Washington, D.C.

Wyman, Lillie B. Chace. "Harriet Tubman." *New England Magazine,* 110-118, March, 1896.

Phillips, Bessie. *First Woman Doctor with the Army. New York Times Magazine,* July 11, 1943.

Benedict, Frank Lee. "The Orphan's New Year." *Peterson's Magazine,* January 1864.

Spirit of the Fair. John F. Trow, New York, April 5-23, 1864. (Library, New York Historical Society)

Nevins, Allan. *The United States Sanitary Commission and Secretary Stanton.* (LXVII) Proceedings of the Massachusetts Historical Society, 1945.

BIOGRAPHICAL NOTES

These notes contain events in the lives of notable women war workers before and after the Civil War. About some of these women little is known outside of the war years, and parts of their histories are necessarily blank.

LIST OF BIOGRAPHIES

ALCOTT, Louisa May
BARTON, Clara
BICKERDYKE, Mary Ann (Mother)
BLACKWELL, Dr. Elizabeth
BOTUME, Elizabeth Hyde
BROWNELL, Kady
CARROLL, Anna Ella
CUSHMAN, Pauline
DICKINSON, Anna Elizabeth
DIX, Dorothea Lynde
ETHERIDGE, Annie
GILSON, Helen Louise
HANCOCK, Cornelia
HOGE, MRS. A. H.
HOLSTEIN, Anna

HOWE, Julia Ward
LIVERMORE, Mary
OLNHAUSEN, Mary Phinney
REYNOLDS, Belle
RICKETTS, Mrs. Fanny
SAFFORD, Mary J.
SMITH, Adelaide W.
TUBMAN, Harriet Ross
TURCHIN, Madame Nadine
TYLER, Sister Adeline
WALKER, Dr. Mary E.
WITTENMYER, Annie
WOOLSEY, (The Woolsey Family)
WORMELEY, Katharine Prescott

LOUISA MAY ALCOTT

1832-1888. Louisa Alcott was born in Germantown, Pennsylvania, on November 29th. She was the second of the four daughters of Amos Bronson and Abigail May Alcott. Much of her life was spent in Concord, Massachusetts. Louisa received most of her education from her father, a distinguished lecturer and teacher, whose ideas were too advanced and impractical to earn him an adequate income. Perhaps equally important in Louisa's education was her contact with the great men of Concord who were interested in the intelligent, tomboyish young girl. At sixteen, Louisa herself became a teacher, a not unusual age in those days to begin a teaching career.

Louisa accepted a position as a companion and she left home with a wardrobe of three dresses (all she owned), some stout aprons, and a five-dollar bill. The "companion" had to sweep, chop wood, shovel snow and rake ashes. She left at the end of seven weeks, receiving four dollars for her pay, which she returned.

Louisa's first novel was begun in 1860 and published in 1864, under the title of *Moods*. When war broke out, she planned war stories, and worked for the soldiers' aid society. John Brown's daughters came to board with the Alcotts, and Louisa's thoughts continued to be with the war. In November of 1862, she applied for a place as a nurse in Washington and was accepted.

The letters Louisa had written to her family from Georgetown were published in the *Commonwealth* in 1863 under the title *Hospital Sketches*, and in book form a year later. She became editor of *Merry's Museum*, a magazine for children, in 1867, and in 1868, the first volume of *Little Women* was published, followed in 1869 by the second volume. These were followed by *Old Fashioned Girl* and *Aunt Jo's Scrap Bag* in 1870, *Little Men* in 1871, *Work* in 1873, *A Modern Mephistopheles* (a novel published anonymously) in 1877. Louisa died in Boston on March 6th, 1888, and in her Will she directed that all her unfinished manuscripts and letters be burned unread.

CLARA BARTON

1821-1912. Clara Barton was born in North Oxford, Massachusetts, on Christmas Day. She was the fifth and last child of Captain Stephen Barton and Sarah Stone, and was baptized Clarissa. She began her schooling at the age of four, and was sent away to school when she was eight. When she was eleven, her brother David was injured and Clara became his nurse. For two years she did little else.

Clara returned to school for a time. In 1850, she entered the Liberal Institute of Clinton, New York, as a student. In 1852, she went to Hightstown, New Jersey, to teach, and later opened a free school in Bordentown, teaching without pay until she was granted a certificate on July 1, 1852. The school grew, but she resigned when a male superintendent was placed over her. In February, 1854, she went to Washington where she became a clerk in the Patent Office.

At the end of the war, Clara set up a register of missing men at Annapolis, and on July 8, 1865, she and others went South to identify the graves at Andersonville. Congress eventually reimbursed her for her work on the register.

In 1869, while in Switzerland, Clara became interested in the Red Cross. She took up the cause of the Red Cross in America, and after a long struggle, the Treaty of Geneva was ratified by the United States in March of 1882. This accomplishment, which was predominantly hers, earned her the title of the Founder of the Red Cross in the United States. She directed the relief work of the American Red Cross for many years.

Clara wrote much, but her main works were *An Official History of the Red Cross, The Red Cross in Peace and War, A Story of the Red Cross,* and *Story of my Childhood*. She died at her home in Glen Echo, Maryland, on April 12, 1912.

MOTHER BICKERDYKE

1817-1901. Mary Ann Ball was born on a farm in Knox County, Ohio, on July 17th. She was the daughter of Hiram Ball and Annie Rodgers. Her mother died when Mary was seventeen months old, and from that time until her sixteenth year, Mary was raised mainly by her grandparents. She attended a one-room log schoolhouse but there was probably no more formal education.

At sixteen a girl was considered old enough to "hire out," and it may have been for that purpose that Mary went to Oberlin, Ohio. Later, she went to live with an uncle near Cincinnati, and it was there she met a Cincinnati widower with children, named Robert Bickerdyke, whom she married on April 17, 1847. There were three children by this marriage.

In 1856, the Bickerdykes moved to Galesburg, Illinois, where Robert died in 1859, and for some years Mary supported the children by practicing as a "botanic physician."

After the war, Mother Bickerdyke became Assistant Director of the Protestant Home for the Friendless in Chicago. She resigned after a year to work for needy veterans. Hearing of good land to be had free in Kansas, she secured free transportation for fifty veterans' families to resettle there. Mother Bickerdyke went with them, and for two years ran a boardinghouse —the Galina Dining Hall—for them.

In 1870, she answered a call from her friend, Mary Safford, in New York, to help clean up the slums of that city. For four years she worked for the Protestant Board of City Missions, then returned to Kansas. In 1876, Mother Bickerdyke went to California, remaining there until 1887. The previous year, she had been granted a pension of twenty-five dollars a month by Act of Congress, and decided to return home to Kansas to join a son who was Superintendent of Schools in Russell County. While there, a home for ex-nurses and soldiers' widows and children was founded in Ellsworth, Kansas, and named the Mother Bickerdyke Home.

After a last visit to her native state of Ohio, she returned to her home with her son at Bunker Hill, Kansas, where she died on November 8, 1901.

DR. ELIZABETH BLACKWELL

1821-1910. Elizabeth Blackwell was born on February 3rd in Bristol, England. Her father was Samuel Blackwell, poet, philosopher, reformer and ardent abolitionist. Her mother was Hannah Lane, daughter of a wealthy Bristol merchant. Elizabeth, the third daughter, shared with the other children excellent tutoring in a wide variety of subjects. The family fortune was lost in the political troubles of 1830-31, and in August of 1832, the Blackwells emigrated to America, settling in New York. In 1838, they moved to Cincinnati, Ohio, where Mr. Blackwell died, leaving nine children and heavy indebtedness.

Elizabeth applied to all the leading medical schools for admittance and

was rejected because of her sex. Eventually, she was accepted by the Geneva Medical College in New York State, where she was granted a degree, the first given to a woman.

After her graduation in 1849, Elizabeth entered La Maternité, a lying-in hospital in Paris, for the equivalent of an internship. There, an infection caused the loss of sight of one eye. She studied for a time at St. Bartholomew's Hospital in London. She returned to New York in 1850 and began to practice the next year.

With her sister Emily, who had also received a medical degree, Elizabeth started the New York Infirmary for Women and Children. The Infirmary, which is still in existence, was opened on May 12, 1859.

In 1865, the Infirmary was expanded into a college, and Elizabeth took the Chair of Hygiene. In 1869, she returned to England where she practiced in London, and helped to found the London School of Medicine for Women in which she taught gynecology. She was the first qualified woman medical practitioner in Great Britain.

Elizabeth was the author of *Pioneer Work in Opening the Medical Profession to Women: Autobiographical Sketches,* published in 1895. She died at Hastings, England, on May 31, 1910.

ELIZABETH HYDE BOTUME

When Harriet Beecher Stowe's book, *Uncle Tom's Cabin,* was published, Elizabeth Botume was in central Georgia, and a copy was sent to her there. It was unwrapped at the Post Office, read by the postmaster and his clerk, and passed on to all the young men in town. Then the book was thrown in the fire and word was sent to Elizabeth that this "would be the fate of all other incendiary documents."

On October 25, 1864, Elizabeth was selected by the New England Freedmen's Aid Society to teach the freed Negroes at Beaufort, South Carolina. She sailed on October 29th on the government steamer, *Arago.*

Elizabeth established a school for the freed slaves at Old Fort Plantation, and remained at her post for many years.

 ## KADY BROWNELL

1842-19-? What records exist of Kady's early life, state that Kady McKensie was born in Caffaria, South Africa, in December of 1842, the daughter of Angus and Alice McKensie. Her father was a Scottish-born soldier in the British Army.

In 1861, Kady was living in Providence, Rhode Island, in which year, according to local tradition, she married Robert S. Brownell, a mechanic, who, but a few days later (April 17th) enlisted as a private in Company H of the First Rhode Island Detached Militia. Kady went with him to war, taking active part in the battles of Newbern and Bull Run.

became Superintendent of nurses at the training school for nurses which was affiliated with the Massachusetts General Hospital. This undertaking bears the stamp of failure. She became Superintendent of a maternity hospital where she stayed several years. Later, she became for a time a housekeeper for a family living near Boston. In the end, she revived her artistic talents, and for more than twenty years she designed and executed embroideries. During most of that time she lived in Boston. She died while visiting in Lexington, on April 12, 1902.

Soldier

BELLE REYNOLDS

1840-19??.   Arabella L. Macomber was born in Shelburne Falls, Massachusetts, on October 20th. Her schooling was good, and the Macomber family included among their friends such well-known people as Wendell Phillips, William Lloyd Garrison, Harriet Beecher Stowe, and the Hungarian patriot, Kossuth. Shelburne Falls was a station on the Underground Railroad, and Belle's sympathies were strongly with the Abolitionists.

When Belle was fourteen years old, the family moved to Iowa where, a few years later, Belle taught in the first school to be established in Cass County.

On April 19, 1860, Belle married William S. Reynolds and they moved to Peoria, Illinois. On the first anniversary of their marriage, while they were in church, a messenger brought the delayed news of the attack on Fort Sumter. William Reynolds immediately enlisted in the 17th Illinois Regiment with the rank of Lieutenant, and Belle determined not to be separated from him. In August of 1861, she joined him at Bird's Point, Missouri, where his regiment was in camp.

She remained with him until her husband's enlistment period expired in the spring of 1864, caring for the wounded from the many battles in which her husband's regiment took part. Upon their return to their home in Peoria, Belle took up the study of medicine, going to Chicago to study under Dr. Ludlam, and she became a successful practitioner. For some years Belle was resident physician at the Home for the Friendless in Chicago, and in 1893, she represented Clara Barton at Pomeroy, Iowa, when that town was struck by a cyclone.

Later Belle moved to California and settled in Santa Barbara. When trouble arose in the Philippines, necessitating the use of troops, Belle closed her Santa Barbara house and, as a member of the National Red Cross, sailed for Manila expecting to serve with the soldiers as a medical officer. But the jungle campaign which ensued was impossible for a woman, and Belle started a school for young Filipinos. Subsequently, she returned to Santa Barbara to resume her medical practice. In her later years, she traveled extensively, spending some months in Europe in 1925, and in 1928, visited Honolulu, returning to Santa Barbara in 1929.[1]

[1] Much of the information about Belle Reynolds was supplied by the Illinois State Historical Library.

MARY LIVERMORE

1821-1905. Mary Ashton Rice was born in Boston on December 19th. Her father, Timothy Rice, of Welsh descent, served in the United States Navy in the War of 1812. Her mother was Zebiah Vose Glover of Boston. Mary was educated at the Hancock School in Boston and at the Charleston, Massachusetts, Female Seminary. In the latter place she taught Latin, French and Italian. She spent two years as a teacher-governess on a remote plantation in southern Virginia, an experience which confirmed her in strong anti-slavery views. She wrote about her plantation days in a book entitled, *The Story of my Life*.

Mary married the Reverend Daniel Parker Livermore in 1845. At this time Mary was an earnest worker in the temperance movement. In 1857, she and her husband moved to Chicago, where he edited, with her assistance, a religious weekly publication called *The New Covenant*, which continued to appear from that year until 1869.

After her war services with the Northwestern Sanitary Commission, Mary interested herself in the Woman's Rights movement, and continued her temperance work. She lectured in this country and in Scotland, and she continued to write. In 1869, she founded *The Agitator*, a magazine which merged, in 1870, with *The Woman's Journal*, of which she was associate editor until 1872. Her book, *My Story of the War*, was published in 1888 when she was living in Melrose, Massachusetts, where she died on May 23, 1905.

MARY PHINNEY OLNHAUSEN

1818-1902. Mary Phinney was born in Lexington, Massachusetts, on February 3rd. Her early schooling was at Franklin (Kite End) and later at the Lexington Academy and Smith's Academy at Waltham. Her parents were farmers, and Mary designed a bloomer costume in which to work on the farm, some years before Mrs. Bloomer's dress-reform crusade. After her father's death in 1849, she supported herself by designing patterns for printed fabrics, first in Dover, New Hampshire, and later in Manchester, New Hampshire.

In Manchester, there were a number of refugees from the political revolution in Germany, and among them she met Baron Gustave A. Olnhausen. They were married in May of 1858, and he died on September 7th, 1860.

After Mary's war service as a Dix nurse was over, she went West to live, remaining until 1870. In October of that year, she sailed for Liverpool, made her way to Berlin, and eventually to Orleans in occupied France. During the Franco-Prussian War, she served with ambulance units for brief periods and nursed at Vendôme, where she remained until March 30, 1871. In April, she went to Tharant, in Saxony, to stay with her husband's sisters.

Mary returned to Lexington in 1873, and in the fall of that year, she

MRS. FANNY RICKETTS

Fanny Ricketts was born in Elizabeth, New Jersey, but no record of the date of her birth has been found. She was the daughter of a British army officer, Captain J. Sharpe Lawrence. Her mother's name was Ricketts. Fanny was the third daughter, and she was educated by her mother.

In January, 1856, Fanny married a distant relative, Captain James B. Ricketts, an officer of artillery. She went with him to the Rio Grande, where his company was stationed on the Southwestern frontier. Here the Ricketts stayed for three years.

In the spring of 1861, Fanny traveled with her husband to Fortress Monroe, Virginia. They were together until the eve of the advance on Centerville in July of 1861. Subsequently, Fanny's husband was wounded three times and Fanny nursed him. After the war they returned to Washington and faded into obscurity.

MARY J. SAFFORD

18??-1891. Mary Safford was born in Boston. She came of a well-to-do family, received a good education, and, at the outbreak of war, she was living with a brother in Cairo, Illinois.

During her war services as a volunteer nurse, Mary's health gave way and her brother, feeling that she would benefit from a sea voyage, sent her to Europe. Upon her return to New York, she studied medicine, receiving her degree in 1867. She went to Vienna and studied for a year. She also studied and practiced surgery in Germany and she has been credited with performing the first ovariotomy ever done by a woman.[1]

Mary returned to Boston in 1874 where she practiced and taught. In that year, she raised several hundred dollars for the relief work Mother Bickerdyke was doing among the settlers in Iowa who suffered in a grasshopper plague.

Mary continued to practice in Boston and to teach at the University School of Medicine. She lectured on dress reform and other reform movements. In time, her health failed and she went to Florida where she spent the last years of her life.

ADELAIDE W. SMITH

1831-19??. Adelaide Smith was born in Brooklyn, but little has been recorded about her early years. She began to work for the sick and disabled soldiers early in 1862, serving in the Long Island Hospital, and the hospitals at Devil's Island, Fort Schuyler, Willet's Point and Bedloe's Island. She worked for the New York Sanitary Commission Fair in April of 1864.

Adelaide was anxious to serve at the front, but she was unable to get a

---

[1] The first ovariotomy was performed by Ephraim McDowell in 1809.

gh the Masonic Mission, she procured one from General
l for City Point, Virginia, on July 24, 1864, on the govern-
Patapsco. As representative of the Masonic Mission, Ade-
ating for Clara Barton. Her first duty was with General
Point of Rocks, near City Point.

the war Adelaide returned to Brooklyn, going daily to
New York to help in the disposal of Sanitary Commission surplus funds.
She remained active in work of one form or another, arising from the war,
through 1866. In 1911, she published a spritely little book about her war
experiences, called *Reminiscences of an Army Nurse during the Civil War.*

✦ HARRIET ROSS TUBMAN

c. 1821-1913. The date of Harriet's birth is unknown. She was born in
Maryland, the daughter of the slaves, Benjamin Ross and Harriet Green.
She had no education and remained illiterate to the end of her days, but
she seems to have acquired a considerable quoting knowledge of the Bible.

From her early teens, Harriet worked as a fieldhand on her master's
plantation. In 1844, her master forced her to marry John Tubman, and
there was a later marriage to a Nelson Davis, but she kept the name of
Tubman all her life.

In 1849, Harriet escaped from slavery, guiding herself to the North by
the light of the North Star. No sooner was she safely in the North than
she decided to return to rescue other slaves. In 1857, she found her father
about to be tried for aiding a fellow slave to escape and, as Harriet put it,
she "removed his trial to a higher court," by taking both him and her
mother to safety.

Harriet became known to many workers in the Underground Railroad.
She made nineteen journeys into the South, rescued, it is said, three hundred slaves, and inspired many more to escape. She met Captain John
Brown who enlisted her aid in his own campaign against slavery. After the
outbreak of war, she was sent to General David Hunter in South Carolina
with a letter from Governor Andrew of Massachusetts. She was attached
to the Union Army as a cook, laundress and nurse, frequently being called
away from these duties to act as guide on scouting parties, and raids into
enemy country. As a spy behind the lines she accumulated much useful
information.

After the war ended, Harriet continued to work for the Negroes, helping
to establish schools in the South, and an old peoples' home in Auburn, New
York. She lived in a small house of her own in Auburn until her old age,
when she moved to the old peoples' home she had founded, where she died
in 1913.

MADAME NADINE TURCHIN

1826-1904. Nadine Turchin was born in Russia on November 26th. She
came of a wealthy Russian family as did also her husband, John Basil
Turchin, who was a Don Cossack, his Russian name being Ivan Vasilievitch
Turginoff.

From that time until her resignation on January 13, 1864, Annie received and distributed goods valued at $115,876.93, or a startling total of $136,-440.93—money raised, and materials provided largely through the efforts of the women of Iowa.

Mrs. Wittenmyer's most important contribution to the war was the creation of a system of special diet kitchens for the sick and wounded in hospitals. After her years of war work, she served as National President of the W.C.T.U. from 1874 to 1879. In 1889, she established the Woman's Relief Corps, and inaugurated the movement for a National Woman's Relief Corps Home in Madison, Ohio. She is credited with having secured the passage of a law by the 52nd Congress, to pension army nurses, and she was instrumental in founding the Kentucky Soldiers Home.

Mrs. Wittenmyer wrote numerous books, articles and hymns, and for eleven years she was editor of the *Christian Woman*. One of her books, *Under the Guns*, tells of her war experiences; another deals with the temperance movement; a third is entitled *Woman's Work for Jesus*, and another, *Women of the Reformation*, is considered a standard work today.

Annie Wittenmyer died on February 2, 1900, at Sanatoga, Pennsylvania.

THE WOOLSEY FAMILY

The Woolsey family, of New York City, consisted of the mother, Jane Newton Woolsey, seven daughters and a son, and all served at one time or another during the war. The Woolseys were well-to-do, the women better educated than most of their day, and they were strongly abolitionist in sentiment. The family home was at Eight Brevoort Place.

Jane Newton Woolsey was widowed shortly before her son, Charles William, was born in Boston, on April 18, 1840. Abby Howland Woolsey, born in 1828 in Alexandria, Virginia, served largely on the home front during the war.

Jane Stuart Woolsey, born in 1830, probably in Alexandria, nursed at the Portsmouth Grove Hospital, six miles from Newport, Rhode Island, in company with her sister, Georgeanna. The sisters remained there for five months. Jane served as Superintendent of the Fairfax Seminary Hospital in Alexandria from November, 1862, until the end of the war, except for a period of service in Washington after the Battle of Chancellorsville. After the war, she worked among the Freedmen of Virginia, and also worked for the establishment of a training school for nurses at the Presbyterian Hospital in New York, where she was Resident Directress, and her sister, Abby, an associate. Jane wrote about her war experiences in a book called *Hospital Days* which is a thoughtful commentary on the successes and failures of wartime nursing.

Mary Elizabeth Watts Woolsey was born on January 1, 1832, near London, and married the Reverend Robert Shaw Howland. She became well-known for her wartime poems, and her early death, on May 31, 1864, was thought to have been brought about by over-exertion in behalf of the New York hospitals and the Metropolitan Sanitary Commission Fair.

Georgeanna Muirson Woolsey was born in 1833. She was among the first women trained under the program of the Woman's Central Relief Association, under the direction of Dr. Elizabeth Blackwell, finishing her training in June, 1861. She became Assistant Superintendent of the Portsmouth Grove General Hospital where she remained until the spring of 1863. She nursed the wounded at Falmouth after the Battle of Chancellorsville and on the battlefield at Gettysburg. She wrote a book about her work at Gettysburg for the Sanitary Commission. In the winter of 1863-64, she was at Hammond Hospital, Point Lookout, Virginia. During Grant's campaign of 1864, she served at Belle Plain, Fredericksburg, White House and City Point. In August of 1864, she was asked to help set up the Beverly Hospital in Philadelphia. After the war, she married Dr. Francis Bacon, and collaborated with her sister, Eliza Howland, in compiling a history of the family activities during the war, published privately in 1899 under the title of *Letters of a Family during the War for the Union.*

Eliza Newton Woolsey was born in Boston, but the date of her birth has proved elusive. She married Joseph Howland. Eliza trained for nursing in the early days of the war, with her sister, Georgeanna. On July 8, 1861, she became a nurse at the Patent Office Hospital in Washington. She served in the Transport Service with Georgeanna during the Peninsula Campaign. She and all the women of the Woolsey family attended the final meeting of the Woman's Central Relief Association in New York City.

Harriet Roosevelt Woolsey was born in Boston, and married Dr. Hugh Lenox Hodge. She worked mainly in New York, organizing hospital supplies.

Caroline Carson Woolsey was born in Boston, and married Edward Mitchell. She worked for the war in New York, and in August of 1864, she went with Georgeanna to Philadelphia to help in the organizing of the Beverly Hospital.

Sarah Chauncey Woolsey, the eighth Woolsey girl to serve in the war, was a cousin. She also nursed at the Portsmouth Grove Hospital and after the war, became a well-known writer, under the name of Susan Coolidge.

KATHARINE PRESCOTT WORMELEY

1830-1908. Katharine Prescott Wormeley was born in Ipswich, England, on January 4th. She was the second daughter of American-born Rear Admiral Ralph Randolph Wormeley and Caroline Preble of Boston. When Katharine was eighteen, the family settled in Boston and Newport, where they knew the literary people of the day.

After the outbreak of war in 1861, Katharine organized volunteers to make army shirts for the Quartermaster's Department. During the winter of 1861-62, about fifty-thousand shirts were finished, and the money received for them (about six-thousand dollars), was distributed to needy families of soldiers. Katharine was head of the Newport Woman's Union Aid Society and associate manager of the New England Branch of the Sanitary Commission.

In April, 1862, she joined the Sanitary Commission Hospital Transport Service as a volunteer nurse. Later, she became Superintendent of nurses at the Portsmouth Grove Hospital in Rhode Island, resigning in 1863 for reasons of health. The following December she wrote, in eleven days, a book to be sold at the Boston Sanitary Fair called *The United States Sanitary Commission. A Sketch of its Purposes and Work.* In another book, *The Other Side of the War with the Army of the Potomac,* she wrote about her experiences with the Transport Service. She became well known for her translations of Paul Bourget, Alexandre Dumas, Alphonse Daudet, Balzac and others.

After the war, Katharine continued to interest herself in charitable work, in sanitation, and in the education of women. She spent the last years of her life in Jackson, New Hampshire, where she died in 1908.

INDEX

Abolitionist movement, the, 3, 15
Adams, John, 214
Alcott, Bronson, 5, 28, 43, 231, 300
Alcott, Louisa May, 17, 28, 34-35, 38,
    45, 67-68, 228-32, 300, 308, 311
Anderson, Major, 40-41
Andrew, Governor, 47, 54, 191-92
Angela, Mother, 155
Anthony, Susan B., 8
Appleton, Fanny; see Longfellow, Mrs.
    Henry
Army Nursing Corps, 98-99, 193, 228,
    286

Bache, A. D., 80
Badeau, Adam, 332-34
Bagley, Sarah, 15
Baltimore *Sun,* 31
Banks, General Nathaniel, 192
Barbara Frietchie, 209
Barlow, Arabella, 276-78, 327
Barlow, Francis C., 276-78
Barringer, General, 335-38
Barton, Clara, 45, 51, 54, 60, 62, 88,
    99, 109-10, 135, 191-93, 201-202,
    211-13, 219, 221, 264, 308, 321
Beauregard, General Pierre G., 108,
    111, 132-33, 136, 303
Beecher, Dr. Edward, 91
Beecher, Henry Ward, 61, 91
Bellows, Dr. Henry W., 5, 67, *13,* 75-
    80, 108-109, 351
Benton, 257-58

Bickerdyke, Mary Ann (Mother), 91-
    94, 99, 145, 149-51, 155, 159, 166,
    168-69, 254, 265-66, 308, 312-13,
    319-20, 323, 330, 345-46
Blackstone, Sir William, 21
Blackwell, Dr. Elizabeth, 9, 20, 72-76
Blackwell, Dr. Emily, 72
Blackwell, Henry B., 20
Blair, Francis P., 51
Blatchford, E. W., 152
Bonham, General M. L., 108
Booth, John Wilkes, 345
Botume, Elizabeth, 305
Bragg, General Braxton, 234-35, 237-
    39, 243, 312
Breckinridge, John C., 36
Bremer, Fredrika, 7, 9-10, 13
Brown, John, 27-28, 31, 35, 38, 68,
    300-302
Brown, Mrs. John, 8, 28
Brown, Mrs. Simon, 67
Brownell, Kady, 95, 111, 114-15, 118-
    25, 308
Brownell, Robert, 115, 308
Brusen, Mary Blackmar, 331
Bryan, Thomas B., 311
Buchanan, James, 29, 32, 36-37
Buckingham, General, 216-17
Bucklin, Sophronia, 102
Buckner, General Simon, 149
Buell, General Don Carlos, 158-61,
    164-65
Buford, General John, 273, 275

Bull Run (Manassas), first battle of, 119-25
Bull Run, second battle of, 197-98
Burnside, General Ambrose, 50, 95, 125, 192, 210, 216-19, 234, 246, 308
Bussey, General Cyrus, 249-50
Bussey, Mrs. Cyrus, 249
Butler, General Benjamin, 47, 85, 108

Cameron, Simon, 63, 79, 115
Carroll, Anna Ella, 143-47
Casey, General, 187-88
Cass, General, 32
Cavell, Edith, 243
Century Club, 73
Chapin, Hermon, 300-301, 346-48
Chapin, Mrs. Hermon, 300-301
Chase, Kate, 113, 125, 308
Cheatham, General, 243
Chestnut, Mary, 41
Chestnut, Senator, 41
Child, Dr. Henry, 287
Christian Commission, the, 19, 225, 249, 264, 286, 319, 326
City of Memphis, 149-51, 170, 257
Clay, Mrs. Clement C., 29
Cobb, Howell, 37
Collis, General, 335
Collis, Septima, 335, 345
Commentaries on Equity Jurisprudence, 22
Commentaries on the Laws of England, 21
Cullen, G. W., 80
Cushman, Pauline, 95, 235-44

Dana, Charles A., 319
Daniel Webster, 176-77, 187
Davis, Jefferson, 236-37, 303, 342-43
Davis, Mrs. Jefferson, 342
Delmonico's, 62
Dickens, Charles, 13, 262
Dickinson, Anna, 310
Dickinson, Charles, 236
Divers, Bridget, 94-95, 327-28, 345
Dix, Dorothea, 55-57, 59-60, 62-63, 69, 73, 75-76, 96, 98-104, 134, 168, 178, 193-96, 209, 228, 231, 252, 287-91, 308-309, 328
Doherty, E. P., 132-33
"Domestic" novel, the, 10
Doubleday, Abner, 41

Douglas, Henry Kyd, 208-10
Douglas, Stephen A., 36
Dunn, Dr. James L., 193, 213
Duvall, Betty, 108

Early, General Jubal A., 341
Eliot, George, 10
Ellsworth, Col. Elmer E., 86-87, 110
Elm City, 178, 183, 187
Emancipation Proclamation, the, 34, 205, 215-16, 298, 310
Emerald, 163-66, 171
Emerson, Ralph Waldo, 27-29, 34, 300, 310
Emerson, Mrs. Ralph Waldo, 68
Esterhazy, Countess; see Griffin, Mrs. Charles
Etheridge, Anna, 113, 125, 136, 200-201, 322, 344
Eustace Diamonds, The, 23
Evans, Augusta, 10
Everett, Edward, 293-94, 312
Ewell, General Richard S., 273

Fair Oaks (Seven Pines), battle of, 183-86
Fales, Almira, 37, 201-202
Farnham, Amanda C., 186, 213
Female Labor Reform Association, 14
Field, Dr. D. D., 76
Finley, Dr. Clement A., 79
Floyd, General, 148-49
Floyd, John B., 37
Foote, Flag Officer, 147
Forrest, General Nathan Bedford, 149, 242-43, 247, 273
Fort Sumter, 4, 37, 40-41
Foster, Augusta, 125
Fowle, Elida Rumsey, 86, 203-204
Fowle, John, 203-204
Franklin, Dr. E. S., 155
Fremont, General, 104

Garrison, William Lloyd, 8
Gibbs, Dr. Wolcott, 80
Gilson, Helen, 99, 179, 182, 213, 300
Godey's, 15, 19
Gordon, General John B., 277-78
Grant, Fred, 266
Grant, General Ulysses S., 44, 92, 144-45, 147-49, 151, 158-61, 163-64, 169, 171-72, 234, 236-37, 239,

247-48, 250, 255-58, 260-61, 263-69, 309, 312-13, 318-22, 325-27, 333, 338, 342-46

Grant, Mrs. Ulysses S., 94, 257-58, 332-34, 345

Greeley, Horace, 197

Greenhow, Rose O'Neal, 29, 51, 108, 110-11

Griffin, General Charles, 332

Griffin, Mrs. Charles, 332-33

Griffin, Mrs. William P., 176-78, 182, 184

Hall, Mrs. M. M. C., 214

Halleck, General Henry W., 50, 147, 158, 160, 170, 234, 237, 247, 272, 318

Haller, Major G. O., 200

Hancock, Cornelia, 99, 287-89, 300, 307-308, 322, 327, 329, 344

Hardie, General, 272-73

Harkin, Mrs. M. V., 167

Harlan, Mrs. James, 170

Harper's Ferry, 29-30, 208-10, 271, 300

Harris, Dr. Elisha, 73, 77, 80, 86

Harris, Mrs. John, 185-86, 213

Harrison's Landing, battle of, 188

Harsen, Dr. Jacob, 77

Harvard Club, 73

Haskell, Lydia F., 201-202

Haupt, Colonel Herman, 198-200, 204-205

Havelock, General, 70

Hawthorne, Nathaniel, 11

Hay, John, 49, 312

Henry Clay, 258

Hoge, Mrs. A. H., 21, 152-53, 155, 225, 264, 309, 311

Holland, Mary, 214

Holmes, Mary Jane, 10

Holmes, Oliver Wendell, 33

Holstein, Anna, 210, 214, 308

Hood, General John, 342

Hooker, General Joseph, 212, 220, 234, 272-73

Howe, Julia Ward, 46, 54, 80, 177, 300, 311

Howe, Dr. Samuel Gridley, 61, 80, 300

Howland, Mrs. Joseph, 179

Husband, Mrs. M. M., 214, 328

International Red Cross, 5, 351

Jackson, "Stonewall," 192, 197, 208-10

Jefferson, Thomas, 21

Johnson, General A. S., 111, 160

Johnston, General, 265-66, 318, 342, 347

Kaiser, Lucy L., 168-70

Kearney, General Phil, 201-202

Keitt, Lawrence, 31, 37

King, Dr. W. S., 128-30, 135

Knickerbocker, 178, 184

Lamon, Ward Hill, 338

Lawson, Dr. Thomas, 50, 56, 79

Lee, Mary, 214, 322

Lee, General Robert E., 50-51, 141, 181, 192, 197-98, 207-208, 210-11, 215-17, 219, 271-74, 292, 309, 318, 321, 342, 344-45

Letterman, Dr. Jonathan, 186, 188, 214-15, 220-21, 252, 272

Lexington, 165

Lincoln, Abraham, 34-38, 41, 46, 50, 55, 64, 79-80, 142-44, 146, 158, 175, 188, 196-7, 199, 205, 207, 215-17, 248, 255-56, 272, 293-94, 310-13, 318, 321, 330-38, 342-45

Lincoln, Mrs. Abraham (Mary), 51, 87, 144, 331-35, 338

Lincoln, Robert, 332

Lincoln, Tad, 343

Lincoln, Willie, 332

Livermore, Mary, 21, 42, 44, 46, 70, 79, 97, 152-55, 225, 253-57, 264, 309-11

Logan, Colonel John A., 149-50

London Times, The, 106

Longfellow, Henry W., 16, 27

Longfellow, Mrs. Henry W., 16

Lozier, Clemence, 17

Magruder, D. L., 128, 130-31

Manley, Ann, 53

Mann, Mrs. Horace, 68

McClellan, General George, 50, 141-42, 174-75, 180-81, 186, 188, 192, 195, 197-98, 205, 207-208, 211, 215-17, 218, 234

McClellan, Mrs. George, 217

McClernand, General, 257

McDowell, General Irvin, 107-109, 111, 113, 115, 117-19, 128, 141, 205, 234

McKay, Charlotte, 327, 345-46
McLean, Wilmer, 344-45
McMahon, Anna, 167
McPherson, General James B., 256, 269
Meade, General George G., 272-74, 276, 278-80, 292, 318
Mitchell, Private B. W., 208
Montgomery, Colonel James, 302-304
Morgan, General John Hunt, 241-42
Morrell, Mrs. Ada, 201-202
Mott, Lucretia, 8
Mulock, Dinah Maria, 10

Nelson, General, 160
New York *Times,* the, 61, 72
New York *Tribune,* the, 197
Nightingale, Florence, 4, 9, 18-19, 61, 102-103, 160, 179, 193
Notes on Nursing, 19

Olmsted, Frederick Law, 80, 126, 176-77, 182-84, 290
Olnhausen, Mary Phinney, 193-96
Ord, General, 333
Ord, Mrs., 333-34
Owens, Mary, 95

Painter, Dr. Hettie K., 329-30
Pemberton, General John, 247, 267
Peterman, Georgianne, 95
Phillips, Wendell, 300, 310
Pierce, Tillie, 278-83
Pillow, General, 148-49
Pitzinger, Eliza, 150
Pomroy, Rebecca, 226
Pope, General John, 192, 195, 197-98, 205, 234
Porter, Admiral, 251, 257-58, 260, 343-44
Porter, Mrs., 313
Porter, General Horace, 333
Pryor, Roger, 31, 40-41, 330-31
Pryor, Mrs. Roger, 29, 31-32, 37, 40-41, 330-31

Quantrell, Mrs. Mary, 210

Raymond, Henry J., 61, 72
Reading, Mrs., 179, 184
Reynolds, Belle, 94-95, 159-67, 171, 257, 307
Reynolds, W. S., 159-62, 307
Richardson, "Fighting Dick," 113

Richmond *Examiner,* 37
Richmond *Whig,* 137
Ricketts, Fanny, 135-36
Ricketts, Capt. James B., 135-36
Rosecrans, General William S., 234-38, 243, 246, 312
Rosenberg, Ethel, 243
Ross, General, 162
Ruffin, Edmund, 40
Rumsey, Elida; see Fowle, Elida Rumsey
Russell, William, 85, 106-109, 112, 114-15, 120-21, 125, 130

Safford, Mary, 93-94, 99, 145, 151, 155, 168
Sanborn, Frank, 28, 300
Sanborn, Mrs. Frank, 68
Sanitary Commission, the, 4, 19, 63, 68, 77-81, 90-91, 103-104, 106, 108, 130, 134, 137-38, 149-52, 155, 166-67, 170, 176, 178, 182, 188, 191-92, 198, 221, 225, 249, 252-53, 264, 286-90, 309, 311, 319, 321, 326
Saturday Evening Courier, 53
Scott, Thomas A., 146
Scott, General Winfield, 37, 49-51, 78, 106, 112, 115, 135, 142
Seward, William H., 107, 344
Sheads, Carrie, 274-76
Shelton, Mary, 308
Sheridan, General P. H., 97, 341
Sherman, General William T., 46, 50, 71, 92, 110, 125, 158, 161, 164, 247-48, 251, 260, 266, 310, 318-23, 330, 341, 346-48
Sherman, Mrs. William T. (Ellen), 155, 308, 310
Shiloh (Pittsburg Landing), battle of, 162-71
Shiras, A. E., 80
Sisters of Charity, The, 186, 286-87
Sisters of the Holy Cross, 154-55
Skinner, Mark, 152
Small, Mrs. Jerusha, 167
Smith, Adelaide, 329-30, 345
Smith, Alice, 214
Smith, General C. F., 147
Souder, Mrs. Edmund, 287, 289, 293-94
Southworth, Mrs. E. D. E. N., 6, 10, 17, 68, 209

Spaulding, 178, 183

Sprague, Governor, 112, 118, 125, 308

Stanton, Edwin M., 103, 199, 213, 222, 272, 287, 337, 347-48

Star of the West, 251

Stewart, Colonel Isaac, 256

Stillé, Charles J., 73, 189

Stone, General, 269

Stone, Lucy, 19-24

Story, Joseph, 22-23

Stowe, Harriet Beecher, 10

Strong, George Templeton, 103, 106, 108

Stuart, J. E. B., 136, 271-73

Thomas, General George, 312

Thompson, Alice, 235

Trollope, Anthony, 13, 23, 65

Truesdail, Colonel, 238-39

Tubman, Harriet, 300-304

Turchin, Mrs. Colonel, 94, 321

Tyler, 165

Tyler, General, 113, 118

Tyler, Sister Adeline, 53-54

Uncle Tom's Cabin, 10

Underground Railroad, the, 34

Union League, 73

Van Buren, Dr. W. H., 77, 80

Van Dorn, General, 247

Vanderbilt, 184-85, 187

Vicksburg, battle of, 260-67; the H. L.'s of, 261-68

Victoria, Queen, 18

Wade, Jennie, 285-86

Walker, Dr. Mary, 319-20

Washington, Martha C., 181

Weed, General, 282

Wells, Mrs. Secretary, 226

Weston, Modenia, 167

Wheelock, General John, 275

Whitman, Walt, 171, 228, 255

Whittier, John Greenleaf, 209-10

Willets, Georgy, 322

Wilson Small, 178-80, 184, 187

Wittenmyer, Annie, 165-66, 225, 249-50, 253, 257-58, 265-69, 313, 323, 328

Wood, Dr. R. C., 56-57, 62-63, 78-80

Woodward, Dr. Benjamin, 91-92

Wool, General, 50

Woolsey, Abby, 291

Woolsey, Carolina, 291

Woolsey, Charles, 290

Woolsey, Georgeanna, 179, 184-85, 289-91, 307

Woolsey, Hatty, 291

Woolsey, Jane, 291

Woolsey, Jane Newton, 290-91

Wormeley, Katharine, 177-78, 180-84, 187-88. 290, 308, 311, 322

Wyman, Dr. Jeffries, 80

Yeatman, Mr., 268, 308

ABOUT THE AUTHOR

Agatha Young has written several books, both fiction and nonfiction, some of the latter under the name of Agnes Brooks Young. She was a designer for the theatre for many years, and taught at the Yale School of the Drama. During the Second World War, she was a dollar-a-year consultant to the War Department and to the War Manpower Commission. She lives in New York City and is now working on another novel.

The revolutionary role of the northern women in the Civil War has been one of Mrs. Young's continuing interests, and she began reading for this book fifteen years ago. Her research took her to libraries and historical museums in all parts of the country, and some of the most valuable material came to light in little known places. Records and privately printed books buried in small historical societies were a gold mine as were the journals kept by members of her own family. The tremendous capability of these women, who knew no precedent or guide, struck Mrs. Young from the start and continued to hold her interest and admiration.

Myvanwy

About the Author

Agatha Young has written several books, both fiction and nonfiction, some of the latter under the name of Agnes Brooks Young. She was a designer for the theatre for many years, and taught at the Yale School of the Drama. During the Second World War, she was a dollar-a-year consultant to the War Department and to the War Manpower Commission. She lives in New York City and is now working on another novel.

The revolutionary role of the northern women in the Civil War has been one of Mrs. Young's continuing interests, and she began reading for this book fifteen years ago. Her research took her to libraries and historical museums in all parts of the country, and some of the most valuable material came to light in little known places. Records and privately printed books buried in small historical societies were a gold mine as were the journals kept by members of her own family. The tremendous capability of these women, who knew no precedent or guide, struck Mrs. Young from the start and continued to hold her interest and admiration.